Makers of America

Volume 1   The Firstcomers

Volume 2   Builders of a New Nation

Volume 3   Seekers After Freedom

Volume 4   Seekers After Wealth

Volume 5   Natives and Aliens

Volume 6   The New Immigrants

Volume 7   Hyphenated Americans

Volume 8   Children of the Melting Pot

Volume 9   Refugees and Victims

Volume 10   Emergent Minorities

Encyclopaedia Britannica Educational Corporation

Editor: Wayne Moquin

General Editors: Mortimer J. Adler and Charles Van Doren
Assistant Editor: Dorothy Anderson
Consultants: Theodore C. Blegen (1891–1969), University of Minnesota; Nathan Glazer, Harvard University; Feliciano Rivera, San Jose State College

Makers of America
–The New Immigrants
1904–1913

Encyclopaedia Britannica Educational Corporation
William Benton, Publisher

The editors wish to express their gratitude for permission to reprint material from the following sources:

The Association for the Study of Negro Life and History, Inc., for "Francis J. Grimke to Woodrow Wilson, September 5, 1913," from *The Works of Francis J. Grimke*, ed. by Carter G. Woodson, Vol. 4, Copyright 1942 by Carter G. Woodson.

Houghton Mifflin Company and Clara Antin for portions for Chapter IX, from *The Promised Land*, Copyright 1940 by Mary Antin.

The Macmillan Company for portions of Chapter XI, from *Twenty Years at Hull-House*, by Jane Addams, Copyright 1910 by The Macmillan Company.

The Norwegian-American Historical Association for "The Cruise of the 'Anna Olga'," by Clarence Teien, from *Norwegian-American Studies*, Vol. XXI, Copyright 1962 by the Norwegian-American Historical Association.

Charles Scribner's Sons for "Italy in California," (Copyright 1910 Charles Scribner's Sons; renewal copyright 1938), from *Romantic California* by Ernest Peixotto.

Contents

I The Social Perspective 1904–1913 1

  1 The Slovaks in America 2

  2 The Lithuanians in America 6

  3 The Poles in Baltimore 12

  4 The Dukhobors 16

  5 Housing and Social Conditions in a Slavic Neighborhood 19

  6 The Ruthenians in America 23

  7 Bohemian-Americans in Urban and Rural Settings 25

  8 The Magyars in New York 34

  9 The Coming of the Italian 36

 10 Chinese Refugees in Chicago 41

 11 Racial Traits in American Beauty 42

 12 Race War in the North 48

 13 Anti-Greek Rioting in Omaha 52

 14 Boston's Italians 55

 15 Italy in California 57

 16 Syrians in the United States 62

 17 European Immigrants to Hawaii 68

 18 Fur Trader Among the Eskimos 74

 19 The Serbo-Croats of Manhattan 78

 20 A Bohemian Settlement in North Dakota 82

 21 The Negro and the Immigrant in the Two Americas 86

II The Economic Outlook 1904–1912 91

 22 The Influence of Trade Unions Upon Immigrants 92

 23 Slavs in the Anthracite Coal Regions 100

 24 Slavs in the Bituminous Mines of Illinois 103

 25 Italians in the Cotton Fields 108

 26 The Ruinous Cost of Chinese Exclusion 111

 27 Italian Farm Colonies in New Jersey 115

 28 A Lithuanian Farm Colony 119

29 The New Pittsburghers 123
30 The Bulgarians of Chicago 127
31 Pericles of Smyrna and New York 130
32 Industrial and Agricultural Communities 133
33 Immigrant Banks in the United States 142
34 Piedmontese on the Mississippi 147
35 Mexican Immigrants in the United States 149
36 Father Bandini's Tontitown 153
37 East Indians on the West Coast 157
38 The Multiethnic Composition of Minnesota's Iron Ranges 162

III Political Involvement 1904–1913 167

39 Rights of the Black Man 168
40 Order of the Sons of Italy 173
41 Anticlerical Italians at Hull House 174
42 Denouncing the Prohibitionists 178
43 Some Irish Advice for Greek Immigrants 180
44 Another Defeat for Restrictive Legislation 182
45 California's Alien Land Law of 1913 184
46 Nagging the Japanese 187
47 Letter of Protest to President Wilson 190
48 What I Am Trying to Do 191

IV Education and Assimilation 1904–1913 199

49 How It Feels to Be a Problem 200
50 Public Versus Parochial Schools 206
51 Americans of Irish Origin 207
52 Federal Report on the Japanese in San Francisco 209
53 The Sons of Old Scotland in America 214
54 The Future of Lithuanians in America 219
55 Finns As American Citizens 220
56 The Ordeal of Naturalization 224
57 The Dangers of Neglecting the Younger Generation 241
58 Generation Conflicts Among the Immigrants 243
59 Americanizing the Poles of Buffalo 246
60 A Mixing Bowl for Nations 250

61 The Case for Trade Schools 261
62 The Importance of Citizenship 263
63 The Promise of Free Education 264
64 Instructions on Naturalization 268
65 The Bookworms of New York 271
66 The Future of Bohemian-American Literature 275
67 The Difficulties of Becoming American 277
68 The German Language in the Public Schools 278

The Social Perspective

1904–1913

Every ethnic settlement, whether urban ghetto or rural farm community, was a colorful and curious blend of Old and New Worlds. In all immigrant neighborhoods contrary forces were at work; the clannishness of being with one's own people was offset by the unwillingness to be looked upon as a "greenhorn," a recent arrival. The Old World heritage endured side by side with an earnest desire to make an accommodation with "the American Way of life," however ill-defined it was.

The average native American, looking over the tumult of New York's Lower East Side, might have written it all off as hopelessly unassimilated, but he would have been wrong. Even in those badges of their nationality, their foreign-language newspapers, the immigrants were making the transition that was called Americanization. In the four decades prior to 1920 more than 3,500 such journals came into existence. Most of them were short-lived ventures, but they provided a literary bridge to citizenship for all the ethnic groups. Essentially they were American papers printed in a foreign language. True, they emphasized matters of ethnic pride and interest, but they did so in an American context. Some nationalities, the Lithuanians, for example, had never before possessed a newspaper in their own language until they came to the United States.

Besides their newspapers, the new immigrants devised institutions in much the same way as had the foreign-born of previous generations. They set up their own parish churches (mostly Roman Catholic, since the greater proportion were from Italy, Poland, Bohemia, the Austro-Hungarian Empire, and other Catholic countries); they started schools, and they founded fraternal and benevolent self-help societies. Many of these societies were at first entirely local affairs, but in time some of them affiliated on a national basis: the Sons of Italy, the Pan Hellenic Union, and the Polish National Alliance are examples.

Basic to the organizing of the immigrant associations were the mutual aid societies that provided sickness, death, and burial benefits. In Chicago alone the Italian community had 110 mutual aid societies by the end of World War I. Such a large number can be understood when one realizes that immigrants from each Italian province, or even separate villages, would insist on their own association. Out of these small, protective organizations grew the many lodges, fraternal clubs, and orders. In San Francisco, the Japanese Benevolent Association was so successful in working among its own people that no Japanese immigrant ever became a public charge. The well-known Chinese Six Companies were an example of the more highly developed mutual aid societies. In addition to the financial benefits afforded members, the Six Companies were also deliberative bodies that dealt with all important matters arising in the Chinese-American community, such as lawbreaking and personal disputes. The Jewish fraternal orders were also significant factors in Americanization of the immigrants. The members learned much of their English at meetings, and were kept in touch with the activities in the Jewish community. Many of the ethnic societies became catalysts for nationalistic consciousness, especially among groups such as the Poles or Lithuanians, whose homelands had been subject to foreign rule for so long.

The immigrant community was thus a microcosm of the larger American society, although distinguished by its ethnic peculiarities. It had its own economy, religious institutions, schools, theaters, newspapers, and politics. But they were not yet American communities, and the pace of assimilation for some of them has been slow. A few groups have wished more than others to remain in solitary, self-contained communities, while others have Americanized rapidly. The reasons for this vary with the nationality, but in general it is true that those nationalities which faced the least hostility were also the least defensive about associating with the native Americans.

(On facing page) Two Syrian women chat in front of a tenement on New York City's Lower East Side in 1914. Illustration Library of Congress.

1

The Slovaks in America

1

The main emigration of Slovaks from the old Austro-Hungarian Empire took place during the fifty years between 1873 and 1924. In the first decade of the 20th century nearly 350,000 Slovaks, mostly from an agricultural background, came to America. They settled in all parts of the country, but the largest colony was in Pittsburgh. In this article, P. V. Rovnianek, editor of the *Slovak Daily* in Pittsburgh, describes the Americanization of his fellow countrymen. [*Charities,* December 3, 1904.]

Of the additions in recent years to the great cosmopolitan population of the United States, that which is constituted of the Slovaks emigrating from northern Hungary is easily one of the first in importance. As yet, few Americans have an adequate conception of the influence which leaders of the people know that they are destined, and that in a very short time, to exert upon the national life and character of this country. During the period of their removal from the old homes to the new—the past two decades—they have made a progress which, considering their condition in Europe, must be admitted, when understood, to be little short of marvelous.

In the conditions under which the Slovaks lived at home are to be found the chief explanation for their settlement in America in large numbers and also assurance that they are a permanent as well as a large and increasing part of the future American citizenship. A Slovak, once settled in this country, in ninety-nine cases out of a hundred, is here to stay. . . .

The immigration to this country may be said to have come exclusively from the agricultural class, a class which includes a very large part of the Slovak population of Hungary. Previous to 1882 the immigration had been sporadic, but in that year the people began to come in companies of considerable size and settled in the mining regions of Pennsylvania. At first there was a disposition among them to return to their native country, but in a little

while some decided to stay. Then it was that they began to look around them for opportunities to settle on farms and return to the manner of life which they had led at home. There are now hundreds of Slovak farmers in Pennsylvania, Connecticut, and Ohio; and in Minnesota, Arkansas, Virginia, and Wisconsin there are colonies of them, where for many miles on every side the land is entirely in their possession. It would scarcely be possible to name a state in the Union where a few Slovaks have not settled and obtained farms which they own, having bought them with money earned previously during the time of their employment in the industrial centers.

Owing to the political persecutions from which they suffered at home, the Slovaks had little opportunity for acquiring education and knowledge of the ways of civilization. Since they began coming to this country in large numbers their advancement in these respects has been no less remarkable than the improvement in their material condition. This is due largely to the intense religious spirit which prevails among the Slavic people, and to the fact that here they have been able to combine schools with their churches. In every community in which they have settled in considerable numbers, they have started their church congregation and founded their church school where their children are being educated in the English and Slovak languages. In Pennsylvania there are now

Brown Brothers

A peasant woman gets her passport ready as she waits with other Slovak immigrants on Ellis Island, about 1910.

from 120 to 130 Slovak congregations, some of them very large and of considerable wealth. The people are divided in religious affiliation among four principal denominations: the Roman Catholic, the Greek Catholic (by which is meant that portion of the Greek Catholic Church which is united with the Roman Catholic Church, but preserves its own liturgy and customs), the Russian Orthodox, and the Lutheran. About one-half of the total number of congregations, and perhaps somewhat more than this proportion of the total number of communicants, are Roman Catholics. The Russian and the Lutheran churches have each about ten congregations and the others are Greek Catholics. The missionaries of the Russian church have been very active and considerable numbers have left the Greek to join the Orthodox church. Of late years, too, the Presbyterian and Congregational denominations have been working among the people with churches and missions.

Scarcely second to the influence of the churches has been the influence of the newspapers in the elevation of the condition of the Slovaks in their new home. It required considerable audacity to begin the publication of the first newspaper for circulation among these people in this country. In Hungary they had never read newspapers. They were taught by the Magyar government that newspapers were for the official class only; that the peasants had no business with them. And the government has had means of enforcing its opinion on the subject. So well is it enforced and so well on the other hand do the Slovaks appreciate the privilege they have in America which is not accorded them at home, that after less than twenty years of the experiment there are nearly as many newspapers in the Slovak language published in the United States as in Hungary, while the combined circulation of those published there nowhere nearly approaches the total circulation of those in this country.

The first Slovak newspaper published in America, the *Amerikansko Slovenske Noviny* (*American Slavonic Gazette*) was founded in Pittsburgh in 1886 by Jan Slovensky, a teacher in his native country—here a clerk in the office of the Austro-Hungarian consul. Associated with him was Julius J. Wolf, also a teacher. Mr. Slovensky retired in 1892 and the writer became associated with Mr. Wolf in the publishing business. We still conduct the paper founded by Mr. Slovensky and also the only Slovak daily paper published in the world. *The Slovak Daily* is well sustained and is making rapid progress, good evidence that the Slovaks are rapidly attaining a high standard of American citizenship.

There are a dozen or more other Slovak weekly and monthly newspapers thriving in various parts of the country. They have been instrumental to no small extent in causing the establishment of a variety of industrial and business enterprises in the Slovak communities through capital stored up by Slovaks while in the employ of various industrial concerns. The small mercantile establishments among them are almost numberless. They have their butchers and grocers, their clothing stores, their drug stores, and in fact are equipped throughout for supplying their needs from establishments which they can call their own.

In several of the large cities, especially in Philadelphia, New York, and Chicago, wire and tinware factories which have been established with Slovak capital and are conducted with Slovak labor are in a fair way to secure the cream of the trade of this kind in the whole country. A peculiar advantage is derived from the fact that for centuries the tinware of Europe was made largely by the Slovaks. In this country, also, electrical designs and other skilled work turned out by Slovak plants have attained a very high position in the markets.

Organization among Slovaks has played an important role, despite the fact that at home the government had not permitted any form of Slovak organization whatever. Here, again, the results of efforts in this direction were most gratifying. In 1890, the writer instituted the National Slavonic Society, the first organization among them, with a membership of 250. It has now over 20,000 active members and 512 lodges. It is primarily a beneficial organization, but it has besides done a work in the education of its members and in inducing them and those who come under their influence to become American citizens. As previously stated, the Slovaks who come to America do not as a rule return to their native country. The society requires its members to obtain naturalization papers after a reasonable time, and through the influence of the membership thousands of others, not members, have become citizens. Other societies have made this a feature of their work, so that directly and indirectly the work of the National Slavonic Society in making American citizens has been a notable one. Since its organization, the society has paid out nearly $1 million in benefits on account of the death or injury of members, or the death of members' wives. Besides this the local associations have paid out a total of much more than $1 million in sick benefits.

Further, the society has kept the Slav spirit alive among the immigrants. It is always the first to contribute to Slovak national purposes. It has helped hundreds of Slovak students, both here and in Hungary, giving them allowances sufficient to support them while they were obtaining their education, and has given, also, liberally to the support of national literary and patriotic workers. It has come to the rescue of Slavs in Hungary, who are persecuted by the government on account of their national sentiments, providing the money for the defense at their trials and in cases where they are convicted and imprisoned supporting their families until [they are] released.

With this National Slavonic Society as a root, there have originated many other societies, among them the First Catholic Union, the Greek Catholic Union, the Evangelical Union, the Pennsylvania Roman and Greek Catholic Union, the Zivena (Ladies' Association), the Presbyterian Calvinistic Union, the Catholic Slovak Ladies' Association, the Sokol (Gymnastic Association), and hundreds of literary, benevolent, and political clubs, so that there are now between 100,000 and 125,000 organized Slovaks in the United States.

Finally, these societies have sources of moral benefits, almost incalculable. They have given courage and spread the ideas of American liberty many years in advance of the time when they could have been obtained by other means. When a Slovak now returns to his native country he does not go to cringe to the official classes; usually he becomes a center of in-

Courtesy Chicago Historical Society

A Slovak bride in the stockyard district of Chicago in 1921. At the time of this article Slovak celebrations were reputed to be disorderly.

dependent spirit from whom ideas of liberty reach the minds of many of his downtrodden countrymen. Sometimes he gets into trouble by reason of his independence, but even the persecutions with which the government officials visit him serve to scatter the seeds of liberty which are bound sooner or later to work a great improvement in the condition of the entire Slav population of Hungary. It is in this respect that the influence of the Slavs in this country upon those at home has been most important. They have even financed the industries of their country in some degree, compensating it in a material sense for the withdrawal of their own labor from its agriculture.

Counterparts of the organizations among the Slovaks have been formed among the Slavs of almost every nationality that has representatives in this country—the Poles, Russians, Bohemians, Slovenians (Wends), Croatians, Serbians, and others. Relations of the utmost cordiality exist among them and they are frequently found working together for their mutual improvement and advantage.

The Slovaks in this country have been to some extent hindered in their progress by misunderstandings in the minds of Americans which are gradually being replaced by feelings of friendly interest. They still have sufficient force to be the occasion of considerable mischief. A belief spread by the daily press that Slovak weddings and christenings are usually occasions for disorder and riot is one of the most troublesome of them—one which will possibly not be thoroughly overcome until all the people understand American customs well enough to see to it, whenever they are accused of indulging in a riot, that their side of the matter is properly presented to the American public and the real disturbers exposed.

It has been the custom among the Slavic people for hundreds of years to celebrate events such as weddings or christenings with the greatest of festivity. If left

alone, this merrymaking would be harmless, but it usually happens that when the celebration is at its height, some emmisary of a constable or alderman, with fees and costs in sight, appears among them and starts a disturbance.

But although the public has been misled, it is gradually coming to know that so far from being peace disturbers and criminally disposed people, none of the immigrants coming to these shores are more law-abiding. The writer has examined reports from over fifty penal institutions, including the eastern and western penitentiaries of Pennsylvania, and found few among their inmates.

The army of the United States contains hundreds of young Slovaks. So also do the higher educational institutions of the country. The immigration is as yet too young to have produced an educated class of professional men in this country, but that condition of things is coming fast. It will be here in a few years and will have arrived much sooner than it did in the case of the Irish or of the Germans, or of any other class of immigrants. Then, the part which the Slovaks are playing, and are to play, in the making of this country will be made to appear in its true light; and their fellow citizens will be ashamed that they have believed them the savages the sensational press has often pictured them.

The Lithuanians in America

2

The Lithuanians are a Baltic people whose small, poor country was long incorporated in the czarist Russian Empire. Many Lithuanians came to the United States, the largest group settling in Chicago. Large numbers also went to the mine fields of Pennsylvania and West Virginia. The story of their coming to America was told by a Lithuanian immigrant, A. Kaupas, of Scranton, Pennsylvania. [*Charities,* December 3, 1904.]

The first group of Lithuanians came to New York in 1868—Kapses and Zana-

vyks driven out from their native country by a famine then raging in Lithuania. At first they worked on farms around New York but soon were lured by the agents of the railroad companies into Pennsylvania. At that time the Delaware, Lackawanna, and Western was laying its Bloomsburg division and the Philadelphia and Reading was extending its line from Shamokin to Sunbury. The Lithuanians came to work on those railroad branches and found themselves near the coal mines. The transition from Danville and Sunbury to Shamokin, Mt. Carmel, and other mining towns was easy. Possibly coal operators induced them to take the place of strikers in their mines, for it was a period of frequent strikes in the coal industry. At all events the pioneers of the Lithuanian emigration to America still remember atrocities of the Molly Maguires and these early reminiscences of a desperate struggle between labor and capital perhaps account for the firm support of the present Mine Workers' Union by the Lithuanians.

It is not improbable that mine owners used their first Lithuanian employees as a means of bringing to the anthracite coal fields more men of the same nationality, for the number of Lithuanian mine workers has steadily, though not rapidly, increased since that time. Another stimulus came with the introduction of compulsory military service in Russia in the early 1870s, and about 1875 the ranks of the Lithuanian emigrants to America were greatly augmented by deserters from the army. But still the movement was comparatively small.

In the beginning of the ninth decade, American agricultural products came into sharp competition with those of Russia, causing a large and permanent drop in the prices of Lithuanian rye and wheat. Soon after, Lithuanian flax, heretofore in great demand in Holland and a source of the comparative prosperity of the Lithuanian peasants, ceased to be marketable. The country began to feel hard times and it was then that young unmarried men started an exodus to the larger cities, chiefly to Riga, Libau, and St. Petersburg. These cities are still places of transit, where money for transportation to America is earned by many lowlanders. About 1885, the emigration was directed—by the way, by the Jews—to America. Southern Lithuanians began to emigrate in great masses to their old friends in the anthracite coal region, and those from Kovna to the cities mentioned. In 1896 commenced the real craze for emigration to America, and it is rather increasing than slackening. At present, many come in order to escape military service, a few—the number is exaggerated—as political refugees, but the majority to avoid poverty in the Old Country. In the mind of an average inhabitant of Lithuania, America means a veritable Eldorado, in which everybody can be rich, if he is able to work hard; so everybody who thinks himself strong enough to do "hard work" dreams about free and rich America. The poorer classes sell their small estates; some even borrow money from the Jews; still others—and there are many of them—receive the tickets from their American friends and relatives. Many well-to-do peasants come, also, to the New World, some to earn money enough to pay off debts, to build a new house or to buy more land. These generally, when back in Lithuania, find conditions so unattractive that they come back to America never to return to the Fatherland. At present the number of the Lithuanians in America probably has reached the 200,000 mark.

Although nearly all Lithuanians are raised on farms, they strangely enough do

These pictures document the progress of a Lithuanian immigrant, Stanley Balzekas, who settled in Chicago in 1913. In his first year in this country, Balzekas opened a grocery store and soon owned and operated three separate stores. (Left) Balzekas, at right, and a helper pose in one of the stores in 1913. (Below) Another of Balzekas' markets, 1916. In 1918 Balzekas sold his businesses to go away to college. Upon his return he opened this hardware and auto supply store (on facing page, top). (Bottom) In 1923 Balzekas established a car dealership for Hupmobile and is here shown, in a straw hat, with friends in his first showroom.

Illustrations on this and facing page, Courtesy Balzekas Museum of Lithuanian Culture, Chicago

not take to tilling of the soil in America. Some Polish colonies in Texas, Illinois, Michigan, Wisconsin, and Nebraska have been successful, but all attempts to found similar colonies for the Lithuanians have proved utter failures. . . .

The Lithuanians, generally speaking, do not like open-air work, preferring employment in mines, foundries, and closed shops. In the anthracite coal mines, they are miners and nothing else but miners. In Baltimore, Philadelphia, Brooklyn, and Boston a great many are tailors and excellent tailors they are; in fact, there is no Lithuanian settlement in which there is not a Lithuanian of that trade. In the West (Chicago, Kansas City, and Omaha) they are employed in packinghouses. They make up a large percent of the employees of the steel plants in and around Pittsburgh and also in South Chicago. In Newark they are hat makers, in Binghamton and Brockton they are in the shoe factories; in New England in the mills, and in the vicinity of Greater New York they are in the sugar and oil refineries. Others work on the railroads in Chicago and on the docks in Cleveland. . . .

The Lithuanians are not shrewd enough to be successful merchants. Still, in the majority of their settlements are to be found small clothing and notion stores, groceries, and butcher shops conducted by them, and the most secret desire of the average Lithuanian is to earn enough money to open a saloon. This explains why one sees so many Lithuanian beer-selling places in Chicago, Shenandoah, Pittston, and practically in all other settlements. . . .

Fortunately there are welcome indications that the reign of beer in all jollifications is approaching its end. "Socials" with high admission prices and scarcity of drinks are gradually taking the place of "balls" with their plenitude of beer; only limited numbers of the invited guests are in some instances admitted to the weddings in contrast to the old free-to-all system. So the undesirable element is excluded from amusements; and the fairs without beverage proved successful. Another temperance movement is not yet in sight, but a new spirit is visibly pervading all classes of the Lithuanian population in America, which can be expressed in one short sentence: "Too much beer! Too much!"

The Lithuanian emigration to America began before the awakening, in 1883, of the national spirit in Lithuania. Naturally at the beginning the Lithuanians lived in intimate relations with the Poles, their coreligionists and nearest neighbors, with whom they had been tied for 500 years by political union. They built churches in common, and entered the same benevolent societies and otherwise. But now the name of "Polander," instead of "Litwish," occasionally given Lithuanians by some obscure Yankee, is the only reminder of early friendly relations between two nationalities.

The separation began in 1884 with the advent of some Lithuanian nationalists to America, was widened by the subsequent unfriendly attitude of the Lithuanian clergy toward the Poles, and finally, about 1895, became an undeniable fact. At present, the two nationalities have nothing in common. . . .

As in all nationalities in which religious sentiment plays a larger part in the social life than any other factor, the factions among Lithuanians are based rather on religious notions than on economic, class, or intellectual tendencies. There are three great parties among the Lithuanians in America. The Catholic party, represented by congregations, so-called church societies, and the Lithuanian Roman Catholic Alliance (membership 2,000) are mostly under the leadership of the clergy. In extreme opposition stand the radicals, atheists, and Socialists, who are represented by the Lithuanian Freethinkers' Alliance. The third, the so-called national party, stands midway, its main tendency apparently being devoid of all religious color with slight leanings toward anticlericalism and radicalism. This party is represented by the Lithuanian National Alliance (membership 5,000). None of the factions has a clear program of action, unless in the negative sense, i.e., it is more in opposition to the others than in pursuit of any object.

There are no secret societies among Lithuanians (except the before-mentioned freethinkers' association) and few military organizations, formed during the period of closer relations with the Poles. The Lithuanians dislike unnecessary pomp and display, and are now even discarding showy caps, scarves, and badges. About 40 percent of the Lithuanians belong to one or another benevolent society. A majority—the "church societies"—require from their members the fulfillment of religious duties; others—the "national societies"—do not pay great attention to the religion of their members. There are two greater organizations with a total membership of 7,000, the already mentioned alliances, which pay a small benefit to the families of their deceased members. Of purely beneficial societies there are three in America. One prints cheap popular literature, which is distributed among poor Lithuanians gratis. Two are educational, one supported by the clergy and the Catholics, another by the "nationalists," their purpose being to help poor university students, both in America and in Europe. Of strictly charitable societies

the Lithuanians have none. Occasionally they make some contribution, chiefly through the papers, for their fellow countrymen who may be suffering imprisonment and banishment for the Lithuanian cause at the hands of the Russian government. Often they take up among themselves collections for the decent burial of those who have died in poverty, or for the support of unfortunate and destitute families. There is no immigration house for the Lithuanians in New York, the agitation for such an establishment, instituted in 1896, being dead long ago.

Each faction has its organs. The nationalists control three weeklies, which are pronouncedly anticlerical and at least two of them are used by Socialists and freethinkers for the propagation of socialistic and atheistic ideas. In opposition to them, the Catholics have also three papers, of which only one is controlled and edited by the clergy. In addition to this periodical literature, the freethinkers from time to time publish occasional antireligious and radical pamphlets, and the "Society of the Love of Fatherland," a series of popular booklets intended to be distributed among the poor in Lithuania. There is also one quarterly, published in the form of a magazine; its tendency is conservative. . . .

The standard of living of the newly come Lithuanians is lower than that of the American workingmen, but certainly is much higher than that of certain of the other recent immigrants. It is an undeniable fact that they are the best dressed people among all immigrants from central Europe, it being due perhaps to the abundance of tailors among them. Not covetousness or unwise thriftiness, but only poverty prevents the Lithuanians from buying better clothes and daintier dishes and from renting more comfortable houses. Those who come to America to stay here forever, and their children, try in all respects to be equal to their American neighbors.

In American politics they are stalwart Republicans, except when in some locality their countryman is put on another ticket. Their Republicanism is not due to the cognizance of the principles of the party, but solely to their opposition to the Democrats, whom they invariably identify with Irishmen, and the Irish are sincerely disliked by them. There are some Socialists among them, probably some 200 or 300, affiliated with the Socialist Labor Party.

The Poles in Baltimore

3

Most of the immigrants from Poland after 1890 gravitated to the larger urban centers. In 1900 there were more than 8,000 Poles in Baltimore, of whom 2,800 were foreign-born. They lived in the southeastern portion of the city, which had at one time been a fashionable neighborhood, and worked mostly in the various packinghouses nearby. The following appraisal of the Baltimore Poles was written by Laura B. Garrett of the city's Charity Organization Society. [*Charities,* December 3, 1904.]

The Polish people of Baltimore live chiefly in the southeastern parts of the city along the waterfront, where are the great packinghouses. There there are many large, old-fashioned dwellings, which were once lived in by well-to-do citizens, but are now occupied each by six or eight families. A family rents one to three rooms and mercenary landlords have covered many of the former yard spaces with rear buildings, leaving for each house but a narrow court with hydrant and closet, which are used in common by the tenants of the whole property. Four-room rear dwellings are frequently occupied by two families.

The more thrifty of the Polish people own much of the property in their neighborhoods. As landlords they are ignorant and grasping. They rent out apartments of one to three rooms for from $3.00 to $5.00 a month and are indifferent as to the sanitary condition of their property. During the packing seasons, many of these landlords leave the city and it is impossible to trace them, even when closets are overflowing and surrounding courts become saturated with filth.

Many of the people, besides these more ambitious landlords, have bought and are buying their own homes. They make payments by installment and often do without sufficient nourishment in order to meet payments. One of the large Polish Catholic churches is conducting a building association and the priests are the custodians, not only of this special form of saving, but of money laid by for other purposes. Many of the houses are empty during the seasons of the year when entire families are taken into the adjacent counties to the large truck farms and south to oyster-packing houses. At these seasons whole blocks in some parts of the district are deserted. Many of the people pay rent for their rooms while they are thus away, but sometimes several families combine and rent one or two rooms in which to store their small stock of furniture.

The houses are cleaner than those occupied by any other group of foreigners among us. The walls are whitewashed once or twice a year, the floors are scrubbed (the tenants in turn doing the

A Polish farmer and his wife at Ellis Island, about 1900.

general work), and the rooms are kept wonderfully neat. Even such as can afford to buy more generously get only the necessary pieces of furniture—a few chairs or boxes, a table, a stove, a bed or two, with often no other accommodation furnished for the children to sleep on than the floor. The mattresses are stuffed with straw and once or twice a year the ticks are emptied, washed, and then refilled with fresh straw. Those who leave the city for country packinghouses carry their clothing in these ticks. One old woman, whose husband is chronically ill, propped him in a rickety rocker while she emptied the mattress, washed the tick, and filled it with fresh straw. By night she had him back in bed, clean and comfortable. Neighbors,

businessmen, doctors, teachers, all lay stress on the extreme neatness and cleanliness of the Polish people.

To hang a few cheap prints of religious subjects in elaborate gilt frames on the walls and to arrange some pretty dishes on a shelf are the only attempts at decoration. The Polish people in Baltimore, coming as they do from the peasant class, are very fond of redbirds and many of them have two or three of these brightly colored songsters hanging by their windows. One of the saddest sounds of the district is the whistle and call of these birds. Every spring they seem to be pleading for fresh air and sunlight and freedom for themselves and their friends.

As it is difficult for Americans to learn the Polish names, the Poles often assume indiscriminately English names which at different times are varyingly given. One instance of this carelessness came strikingly to our notice. A Polish woman died suddenly and the neighbors rushed to our office to find her husband. They knew he was working at City Hall, but as they did not know what name he had given to the boss they could not find him. After ineffectual efforts to determine his assumed name, it was realized that the news must wait to be told until he should come home in the evening.

The men, women, and children are hard workers. The men work as stevedores, on the docks, and on the streets or in the packinghouses. A few are tailors or shoemakers, but hardly any rise to the rank of superintendent or boss. The great field for labor for the women and children is the packinghouse. They are eager for the seasons to begin and in crowds rush to the great canning houses from the time the first fruit and vegetables come in the spring until the last are received in the fall. The length of the season varies in different years. In 1904 the season began early in May and continued to the middle of November, with an off-season of three or four weeks in July.

In the packinghouse the work is done by family groups: the men, women, and older children paring or peeling, the younger children running to bring fresh supplies, to empty the baskets of prepared fruit, and to receive the pay. In most of the houses the packers are paid by the hour, in others by the quantity of fruit prepared. Five to ten or twelve cents is paid for a bowl or bushel basket. A child can earn from fifty to eighty-five cents a day; a woman, if expert, $2.00. The hours of work are long and the conditions unsanitary. The peelers start at four or five in the morning and keep at work until the supply of fruit or vegetables is exhaust-ed—often until six in the evening. The packers begin at seven in the morning and work, during rush seasons, until ten or eleven at night. Several of the managers of the packinghouses say that the Polish people are the best workers that they have ever had. "Even if the whistle is blown at two in the morning they will come and work with no fooling until five or six at night."

During the summer hundreds of these families leave Baltimore for the canning houses in the country. As spring fruits and vegetables ripen, there are great preparations in the district. Large wagonloads of Poles may be seen on their way to the country. In some are women and children; in others, men; and in still others, loads of provisions—great bags of flour, hams, bacon, etc. The women wear clean calico dresses, great aprons, and stiff sunbonnets. The children are bright and clean and eager to be off. Soon after the return, the hard-earned money is spent, as each year there are to be paid the standing bills of the winter past. Landlord, baker, and grocer each claim a share.

During the fall and winter many families go south as oyster shuckers. The traveling expenses are paid, but the work furnished is uncertain and irregular and many drift back before the season is over.

Mr. P——, a shrewd old carpenter of the district, says the Poles are "a great people for work; they work, work, work and then don't know anything to do with the money but hoard it up. They are a clean lot but are great for gambling and the children lie and cheat and steal anything worth having. The boys are great gamblers and play craps at every corner, and the parents take the money won. One woman recently bought a ton of pea coal. It was dumped on the pavement and as

Members of an American Bible society distribute Bibles among newly arrived Polish immigrants at Ellis Island, about 1900.

she carried it up the alley, bucket by bucket, the children crowded round and sneaked it off by the single piece, by the handful, by the boxful (little strawberry boxes); even little, toddling babies helped to steal it. Every time the woman appeared, the children retreated to sit on a neighbor's step. The children are immoral, dishonest, and lazy." But Mr. P—— adds, "Not worse than others brought up the same way."

Nearly all the Polish people in Baltimore are either Hebrew or Catholic. There are four Roman Catholic churches in the city, all in the southeastern district. When the writer has been present at high mass in any of these churches, the aisles and the halls have been crowded with men, women, and children. The congregations are quiet and orderly and neatly dressed; the older women in simple cloth-

ing, the younger women and girls in gaudy hats, cheap laces, and jewelry.

Most of the people have dull, heavy faces; the men's show stolid coarseness, the women's resigned indifference. They lack confidence in those with whom they are thrown; even their priests find it difficult to win their confidence. Teachers in the district say the Polish Hebrews are bright and dirty, the Polish Catholics stupid and clean. The parents are careless about sending the children to school. They are entered late in the fall, in October or November, and are removed in May when the packinghouses open for the spring season. Even during the winter months the attendance is irregular. The children in their play are not alert. Their chief amusement seems to be had in hanging around cellar steps and doors, sitting on the curb, dangling their feet in the dirty gutter water, or standing in crowds to watch a funeral or fight. The true spirit of play seems to have been crushed out of even the little ones by the hard conditions under which they live.

These people are independent and a Polish priest who is their wise friend believes that their standard of life is gradu-ally being raised. He holds that his pa-rishioners are not in need of material re-lief and has been unwilling to have estab-lished, in connection with his church, any relief-giving society.

The Dukhobors

4

This religious sect originated in Russia during the 18th century. Because of its egalitarianism and anti-authoritarian teachings, the society was frequently the object of persecution in Russia. In 1899, partly through the intervention of Leo Tolstoi, the members of the communal sect were allowed to emigrate. Several thousand went to western Canada where they continue to dwell, although some of the original cohesiveness of the society has been lost. This article by Joseph Elkinton traces the history of the Dukhobors and examines their economic principles. [*Charities*, December 3, 1904.]

The exodus of some 7,300 Russian peas-ants from the Caucasus six years ago at-tracted considerable attention because of the circumstances accompanying their coming to America. To understand this immigration to British Columbia, one must go back a century and a half to the time when there arose in southern Russia another of the many dissenting sects, composed of peasants.

According to the tradition of their el-ders, certain cossacks of the Don, begin-ning with three brothers, became con-vinced that Christ forbade fighting and that the ceremonies of the Greek church were not necessary to the worship of the Almighty. These views found a warm re-sponse in the hearts of the Russian mu-jiks, and within a score of years several thousands were refusing to bear arms or recognize the authority of the Greek church.

Persecution was inevitable and freely bestowed by the government under Paul the Mad. From 1785 to 1800, hundreds were banished to Siberia and others cruel-ly tortured. A ukase of 1800 reads, "Ev-erybody who shall be convicted of belong-ing to the sect of the Dukhobortsi shall be condemned to life-long hard labor." Ear-ly in the 19th century, Alexander I insti-tuted another policy toward them and provided a place for them to enjoy their convictions undisturbed. This was known as the Milky Waters Colony, just north of the Crimea reservation. Here they fairly prospered, until Nicholas I, coming to the throne, broke up the colony and drove these peace-loving farmers to the Cau-casus Mountains. The governor of the district testified, "They were active, inde-fatigable in labor and industrious in agri-culture, and being sober and well-living men, they were more independent than others."

The deportation of the 10,000 Dukho-bors from the Crimean settlement to Trans-Caucasia occurred between 1841 and 1845 and was a heartrending experi-ence. The mother of Peter Verigin, their chosen leader, was then about twenty-six years of age and she told us how she was driven with her little children, at the point of the bayonet, for a thousand miles; of the great perils to which they were subjected while crossing the Cauca-sus Mountains, and of the Kurds and oth-er hillsmen who threw stones upon them

Culver Pictures

An immigrant family of Dukhobors in Canada, 1908.

from the heights above. After some forty years residence in the Wet Mountains, of Georgia, at an altitude where cereals could scarcely be raised, but where, nevertheless, they accumulated considerable property as herdsmen, they were scattered by Alexander III among the Georgian villages of the lowlands.

It was in 1886 that Peter Verigin was banished to Archangel, on account of a dispute that arose about the distribution of money and ownership of an Orphan House, between the "Large Party" and the "Small Party" of 3,000 or 4,000, which had no objection to bearing arms or to bribing the government officials to rob their brethren by an unjust decision. In the face of this dissension, a widespread awakening took place among a large portion of them; they ceased to smoke, drink wine, and eat flesh; they also practised communism and resolved no longer to bear arms even in self-defense. It was almost ten years later that

Peter Verigin, who was being transported from Archangel to a remote corner of Siberia, in 1894–1895, met some of his brethren in Moscow and decided with them to propose to the "Larger Party" to abstain from oath-taking and military duty in any form and to burn their firearms. It was this last act which enraged the "Small Party," which forthwith brought upon the other faction the cruel whips of the Cossacks by sending a report to the officials that the "Larger Party" was in rebellion against the government. Two thousand people were present at one of these burnings, when the Cossacks were ordered to disperse them with whips and thereafter were "quartered" upon them in their villages.

This "execution," with many other details of the persecution, was brought before the English-speaking public by Count Leo Tolstoi, in a letter published in *The London Times,* October 23, 1895, and also published by the writer in his book on *The Dukhobors.*

In 1898 a petition was presented to the empress dowager as she passed through the Caucasus, asking that she intercede for these sorely persecuted peasants so that the emperor would allow them to emigrate or to settle all together in some remote part of his empire where they might escape the hand of the oppressor. Leave to emigrate was granted, if they would leave Russia before the next annual conscription took place. The marvel is how, without means for transportation, most of them escaped to America. Their sufferings were reported by Prince Hilkov and his appeals met with a prompt response on the part of the Society of Friends. Four steamships were chartered to bring them away from Batoum during the winter of 1898 and the spring of 1899, and their transference to unsettled tracts

Lacking horses, these Dukhobor women pull a plow, in Canada, about 1900.

of British Columbia was a humanitarian act on a large scale. At least $200,000 was raised by Friends in England and America.

The character, history, and customs of these exiled sons and daughters of Russia have subsequently afforded a most interesting, if sometimes perplexing, study— whether from a psychological or religious standpoint. Children in mental understanding, they are often innocently ignorant of what they reverently retain from the Greek church and the age-long customs of their Fatherland. They religiously observe "holy days," while refusing to bow before the images of "saints" and rejecting the sign of the cross. They continue to recite unwittingly some of the best hymns of the Greek Orthodox Church, although the greater part of their worship consists in singing collectively the Psalms of David and some of their own composition.

They have been associated in the popular mind with the Quakers, whereas they really have little in common except their testimony for peace and nonresistance, which the Society of Friends has continuously maintained for 250 years. It was rather a desire to relieve suffering humanity that prompted the Friends of Philadelphia to send them several carloads of food and clothing after they had settled in Canada, where they would have starved the first winter had they not received this succor. Further, their protest against the formalities of the Greek church made them interesting to the Friends, whose spiritual ideas about worship and formal religious observances generally have led them to dispense with much that is prevalent in the "services" of other denominations and so, sitting down in silent, reverential waiting upon Almighty God, they commune with Him in spirit and welcome only those utterances which proceed from that spirit in their assemblies for worship. Yet the contrast between one of these quiet Quaker meetings and the Dukhobor "Sunrise Service" is rather striking. In the latter there is a continual chanting of some Russian (Dukhobor) hymns and much bowing and kissing, with formal recitations from the Scriptures. Another possible likeness is the Dukhobor protest against the use of intoxicating drinks and tobacco.

In one particular, however, there is a most striking difference between these two peace-loving sects, and that is in the matter of education and governmental support. The Quakers have ever been foremost in all educational development and in fidelity to the governments under which they have lived as law-abiding citizens.

At the time the four ships, bearing over 7,000 souls, landed at Halifax and Quebec, it was supposed the refugees would at once assimilate with the settlers of the Northwest Territory, but all their traditions are much opposed to such a course and it will take the passing of a generation to bring them into line with the free institutions of this land in which they have so providentially found an asylum.

A majority refused to take up any land in their own names for three or four years after coming to Canada, for fear the Dominion government would somehow bring them into trouble. Most of them farmed their land as squatters. They had suffered so much from the Russian government that they are suspicious of any government. . . .

The indisposition to settle upon individual homesteads is their most serious hindrance to becoming Americanized, for they are completely under the direction of "the elders" in each village; thus little mental progress can be made by the adults and the present management enriches the commune at the expense of the individual. The whole situation is one of serious difficulty, requiring the continuance of tact and patience (which the Dominion government has shown from the first) before any advance can be made in an educational way.

Housing and Social Conditions in a Slavic Neighborhood 5

When Jacob Riis published *How the Other Half Lives*, his famous report on tenement housing among the immigrants in New York, in 1890, he intended the book to provide an impetus for the reform of the conditions he described. It was true that some of the worst of these were improved, but his book was also put to other uses. The opponents of immigration hailed it as a documentary of the social evils caused by letting so many "paupers and criminals" into the country every year. Those who favored the immigrant and worked to ameliorate his condition thus unwittingly provided ammunition for nativists who sought restrictive legislation. This selection by Mary Buell Sayles of the New York Tenement House Department describes the Slavic community in Jersey City, New Jersey, where several thousand Poles and Russians had settled. [*Charities*, December 3, 1904.]

In Jersey City there are two distinctively Slavic sections—one almost exclusively Polish, with a few Lithuanians sprinkled through it, the other made up of Russians and Poles in the proportion of about two to five, with again an admixture of Lithuanians and a few scattered Hungarian families. Both communities are situated close to the waterfront, edged about by

railroads, docks, and factories. As the housing conditions in the two sections are of the same general character, and the occupations and mode of living of the people practically identical, I shall confine myself in the main to a description of the larger and more interesting district, though many of my social statistics in regard to the Poles and Russians relate to all families of these nationalities found in the three districts which I investigated during the winter of 1901–1902. . . .

At the southeasterly corner of lower Jersey City, skirting the waterfront and the long sheet of water known as the "Gap," which extends inland at right angles to the Hudson River, lies a small and somewhat isolated tenement district. Although cut off on three sides by water and on the fourth separated by business streets from the other residence sections, it contains within the limits of some dozen city blocks a wide range of social and housing conditions. Along the northerly edge, on Sussex Street, are long rows of substantial and frequently elegant old brick residences, now generally let out by floors to German, Irish, and American families, in the main well-to-do working people. To the south along Morris and Essex streets, nearer the waterfront, are also many old brick and frame private houses. But we find here an almost equal number of four- and five-story brick buildings designed expressly as tenements to accommodate sometimes two, sometimes four families on a floor, with tiny triangular and octagonal airshafts, or none, and dark interior rooms. Here, too, are rear tenements in considerable numbers, in one case as many as ten in a single block. Often these are old frame houses, now neglected and dilapidated; often four-story tenements of wood or brick occupied by from four to eight families. In several places two rows of rear tenements stand back to back with an intervening space of but two or three feet.

It is to this part of the district that the various Slavic people have flocked, drawn by the presence of the great American sugar refinery and numerous other factories, and the nearby railroad docks. Along these streets I visited, three years ago, 254 Polish families, 101 Russian families, 22 Lithuanian families, and a smaller number of families from Austria-Hungary. Altogether it is safe to say that the entire Slavic community resident in this section comprised at that time from 400 to 450 families, or upwards of 2,000 individuals.

So strong was the impression of the predominance of the Slavic element in some of the blocks investigated, that it was a surprise to find, on tabulating the records, that not more than 60 percent in any one block were Slavs. Yet very generally in the rear houses, and throughout many front houses, a non-Slavic family was a notable exception.

Even where Russians and Poles are most solidly packed, however, the streets present no such panorama of foreign life as one is sure to see in a district where Italians are equally predominant. Anyone who has worked among Italians will have been impressed by the extent to which their family life overflows into halls and yards and over sidewalks. Those who have visited among the Slavs must have been impressed by contrast with the intensity of their home life and its definite confinement within each family's own four walls.

The typical Slavic home in Jersey City is located in a house occupied by from three to eight families and consisting of three rooms—one, a fair-sized kitchen and living room with two windows on the street or yard; the others, small bedrooms, one or both of them interior rooms ventilated only by tiny windows opening on the kitchen, the hall, or an airshaft perhaps five to ten square feet in area. The floors are generally clean, often, especially among the Poles, scrubbed to an amazing whiteness. The walls are hung with gorgeous prints of many-hued saints, their gilt frames often hanging edge to edge so that they form a continuous frieze around the walls. The mantel is covered with lace paper and decorated with bright-colored plates and cups, and gorgeous bouquets of homemade paper flowers are massed wherever bureaus or shelves give space for vases. Gaily figured cotton curtains at the windows and in doorways complete a bright and pleasing picture and numerous canaries in cages—I have found as many as ten in a single kitchen—lend vivacity to the scene. . . .

Perhaps the most interesting of the social statistics available in regard to the Slavs in Jersey City relate to their occupation. The scheme of classification adopted grouped the various occupations under the headings of "unskilled," "skilled," "mercantile," and "miscellaneous," or "special." It was applied to all members of the seven leading national or race groups found in the three districts investigated, among them, to 515 Polish and 101 Russian heads of families. Among both of these people the unskilled laborer predominates to a greater extent than among Italians, Irish, Americans, or Germans. Over 81 percent of Polish and over 90 percent of Russian heads of families are unskilled, in both cases the factories and workshops claiming more than one-half of this percentage, and the railroads and docks furnishing occupation to the greater part of the remainder. In the immediate neighborhood of the sugar refinery a question as to occupation is answered almost invariably by "Tsoogarhaus." Many other curious answers are forthcoming, as "Leawally," meaning Lehigh Valley Railroad. Among the Lithuanians, 95 percent of whom are unskilled, the railroads and docks are the commonest places of employment.

When we consider skilled workers, we find but one, a carpenter, among the Russians, while but five of all the storekeepers and saloonkeepers of the various districts are Russians. Thirty-one Poles are engaged in skilled trades, metal workers, carpenters, and cabinetmakers being most numerous; and there were found nineteen Polish storekeepers and eight saloonkeepers and bartenders. But two Poles had to be classified under the catchall heading of miscellaneous, and but one Russian—the priest of the Greek Catholic Church. In this connection it may be noted that nine Polish houseowners were found.

A custom which accounts for much of the characteristic overcrowding of the Slavic immigrants is that of taking so-called boarders, really, in most cases, lodgers who either get their meals outside the home, in restaurants or saloons, or prepare them independently on the family cookstove. It is among the Russians that this practice is most common. Over 60 percent of the Russian families I visited acknowledged that they kept boarders ranging in number from one to six. About the same percentage of Lithuanians eked out their incomes in this way. Of the Poles visited in the sugarhouse district, a considerably smaller proportion, but 28 percent, admitted that they took boarders. It is undoubtedly true, however, that all these percentages represent understatements of the truth. I recall one case where a Polish couple who had at first insisted that only they and their two children occupied their two-room apartment acknowledged, after unusual insistence on my part, that two women boarders used one of the rooms; and finally, when further pressed, threw open the door of a little closet under the stairs—a cubbyhole scarcely three feet wide and sloping to the floor—and showed me a cot on which a male boarder slept. This is not an extreme example of overcrowding. Of the sixty-four Russian families who took boarders, nineteen kept one, nineteen two, fourteen three, nine four, and three five boarders. Forty-nine Polish families kept from two to four boarders.

It is a common thing to find both men and women boarders in the same two- or three-room apartment, with a family including babies and half-grown children of both sexes. A case recorded, where eleven people lived in two rooms, two little girls of eleven and fourteen sleeping in a corner curtained off from the room occupied by the male boarders, is perhaps somewhat worse than the average, but it cannot be called an exception. I have at hand a large number of examples where overcrowding, with boarders, reaches the point of three persons or more per room with an allowance of less than 400 cubic feet of air space per individual.

It is important, however, that we look beyond these deplorable conditions to the underlying causes, among which is irregularity of employment, a conspicuous feature of longshore work and of some factory work. In many cases I was assured that the fathers of families where boarders were kept were on half-time work in the sugarhouse. In one case a Lithuanian woman whose husband had been ill and unable to work for two months, explained to me that four male boarders formed their chief source of income. Each of these men paid $4.00 a month into the family treasury for sleeping accommodations and washing. This family included three children, two of them under five, and their apartment consisted of three rooms for which they paid a monthly rent of $8.00.

From my point of view, as a student of housing conditions, and with my ignorance at the time of making my investigation of the Slavic people and their languages, I am naturally not in a position to attempt an extended interpretation of the facts presented. Certain conclusions would indeed seem inevitable in view of these facts. But as we are chiefly concerned, not with the racial traits or past history of the various Slavic people, but with the problem of making intelligent citizens of them, it will perhaps be well to fix our attention on immediate practical means to that end. Except for the problem of education, there is no more important problem affecting the immigrant population than that of providing them with decent and healthful homes. In Jersey City there are three serious housing evils: dark and unventilated bedrooms, of which nearly 2,000 were noted in the course of my investigation, and which are most common in the poorest quarters; the foul yard vaults, almost the only sanitary accommodation in the Slavic districts; and the fearful danger from fire in a district where less than one tenement house in twenty-five is provided with any sort of fire escape.

While such evils are permitted to surround the home of the immigrant, we American citizens must hold ourselves accountable for many of the evils for which we blame him. The education which the schools give needs to be supplemented by the practical education which goes with close supervision and inspection of both old and new tenements. Every possible leverage of law and educational effort is needed to assist the Slavic immigrant peoples in reaching a plane of living where they will be an aid, not a hindrance in our national development.

The Ruthenians in America

6

Many nationality groups emigrated from Russia to the United States, but statistics did not always bother to differentiate between "real" Russians, such as the Ruthenians, and Poles, Lithuanians, Jews, or Latvians, who did not consider themselves Russian. The number of "real" Russian immigrants was not very large; it totaled less than half a million by 1920. This immigration would probably have been much larger had it not been for the many obstacles to departure devised by the czarist regime to keep its people at home. This article by Ivan Ardan, editor of the newspaper *Svoboda*, describes the Ruthenian segment of the Russian arrivals. [*Charities*, December 3, 1904.]

The Ruthenians or Ukrainians, who come to America, called also the "Little Russians" or "Russians," are a branch of the second largest Slavic group, occupying at present the southern part of Russia, the eastern and southwestern part of the province of Galicia, and part of the province of Bukovina, in Austria, and northern Hungary. . . . The main reasons for this emigration have been economic ruin, political and national oppression, and religious persecution. . . .

About nine-tenths of the Ruthenians in this country are laborers and workmen. They are chiefly employed in mining and affiliated industries. They make good workingmen and good union men. Farmers constitute about one-tenth of their number; business and professional men are comparatively few in number. The Ruthenian girls and young women work, also, in different shops and factories, but prefer domestic service, at which they are efficient.

Their standard of life here is much higher than in Europe, but it does not come up to the American standard. They eat substantial food and plenty of it, but do not live in such good houses, or wear such clothes, or buy such expensive furniture as the American workingmen. They consider as luxuries a good many of the things, such as going to theaters and different social functions, which the American workingman takes as a matter

of course. They are, as a rule, saving, and hardly a Ruthenian but has from $50 to $200 at least saved and put away either in some hidden corner or with a private or public bank. In exceptional cases, their savings reach $2,000, $3,000, and $4,000. This saving habit gives them an advantage over the American workmen, especially in case of distress, sickness, death in the family, lack of work, or a strike. During the first years of immigration the Ruthenians sent the greater part of their savings to Europe to pay off debts or to improve their farms, and after a few years' stay would go back there. Within the last ten years, however, there has been a noteworthy change. A great many either renounce all claims to their Old Country possessions in favor of relatives, or sell them, and out of their savings buy lots and build houses in America, or take up farming. This is due partly to practical sense of their own and partly to the agitation of their wives and children, whose lot is far better here than in Europe.

Further, Ruthenians have organized societies which for a small monthly amount give to their members $5.00 or $6.00 a week in case of sickness or injury while at work. Some, also, pay death benefits of from $50 to $200 and these societies have been combined of late and aim to pay death benefits ranging from $500 to $600 on the death of the father of a family, and an additional $200 or $300 on the death of his wife. Of such Ruthenian organizations there are four, the largest with a membership of 13,000.

Ruthenian men and women drink, the farmers and Ruthenian Protestants being exceptions. Habitual drunkards, however, are few among them and are being looked down upon. This general drinking habit is due partly to the custom brought here from abroad, partly because they have more money and drinks are cheap, and partly to such causes as the instability of the immigrant's life and its tragedy, especially if he is married and the wife has not yet come. A marked improvement, however, is indicated by the complaints of saloonkeepers, and local movements are on foot to discourage drinking, especially among the young people and women.

The Ruthenians cling with some tenacity to their old customs despite the fact that the life in this country makes them discard a great many. They are superstitious, especially those coming from the Carpathian Mountains. They are devout, attached to their churches, and feel very badly if they do not find one in the place where they live. Religion, however, with a vast majority of them, is more a matter of custom and formality than a force regulating their daily conduct.

The majority of Ruthenians in the United States are members of the Greek Catholic Church. Greek Orthodox Ruthenians (almost all converts from the Greek Catholic religion) are less numerous and the number of Ruthenian Protestants, recruited chiefly from Russian Ukraine, is still smaller. There are 83 priests and ministers, and 108 Ruthenian churches, 80 Greek Catholic, 26 Greek Orthodox, and 2 Protestant, besides several Protestant missions where services and prayer meetings are held. The rallying to the church has been to a certain degree an obstacle to progress among Ruthenians, chiefly for two reasons, first, because of proselyting on the part of the Greek Orthodox Church of this country which is supported by the Russian government for political rather than religious motives, and is trying to lead the Ruthenians back into the atmosphere of the Dark Ages when religious fanaticism, superstition, and adoration of autocrats were supreme virtues; second, because of the attitude of the Roman Catholic Church, which is trying to dominate and control the Ruthenian church properties and their church affairs in general. The resentment resulting, religious disputes, dissensions, and lawsuits among members of the same colony and often of the same church, have absorbed energies much needed elsewhere.

Judging from what has been said of European conditions, the conclusion is natural that the intellectual life of American Ukrainians cannot be of a very high plane. Yet, coming to America, the Ruthenians are anxious and do learn their native and the English language. It is not a rare occurrence that a man of from thirty to fifty years learns to read from a prayer book and to write from a letter received from the Old Country. The "method" is this: at first the man tries to read out a prayer which he knows by heart, usually the Lord's Prayer, and from this he begins to distinguish the different characters. The letters are first learned by heart, afterwards copied, and in this way the man begins to write—a way of learning very primitive, of course, and laborious, and one which requires a great deal of patience on the part of one who learns. But it leads to the end.

In towns and camps where Ruthenians are more or less numerous and organized they have their schools in which the adults are taught to read and write their own and sometimes, also, the English language. And the children, who invariably go to public schools in the daytime, learn to read and write in Ruthenian. These schools average from thirty-five to 100 pupils. This fall, also, a Ruthenian boarding school on a small scale has been established in Yonkers, N.Y. Also, a fund has been started out of private collections for the support of Ruthenians in higher schools. It has already done some good and there is much more to be desired in this direction.

There are four Ruthenian weeklies (one with a circulation of 15,000) and one monthly published in the United States. The latter discusses such scientific subjects as *The Interior of the Earth, The Beliefs of Ancient People, The Races of Mankind,* and the like—a periodical unique among Slav publications in America. Some Ruthenian books are published in this country, but the majority—steadily on the increase—are imported from Europe. Periodicals and books published in

other languages, especially Slovak and Polish, are read, and the younger generation read, also, English books and newspapers.

Education among Ruthenians in this country is promoted, moreover, by reading circles, lectures, and societies for self-improvement, dramatics, and singing, which are found in places where a priest, or any person more educated than the rest, gives the thing a start. . . .

In America, and especially in the United States, the Ruthenians wake up to a new life. If they succeed within a generation or so to regain their former excellences, avail themselves of what is good in American civilization and avoid what is bad in it, they will surely make a worthy addition to the citizenship of the United States. To help them to attain this end, the educated people of their own race and patriotic Americans as well should take a livelier interest in the "contemptible Hun," to educate him, to lift him up, to make him a better man.

Bohemian-Americans in Urban and Rural Settings

7

The Bohemian or Czech immigrants went to all parts of the United States, but there were a few large concentrations. Among cities, Chicago received the largest number: by 1910 there were well over 100,000 there. Rural areas of Wisconsin and Iowa also attracted a considerable number, with nearly 80,000 in the two states by the same year. The first of the two following articles is by Alice G. Masaryk, daughter of Czech patriot Tomas Masaryk. The second is by Nan Mashek, a resident of the Czech community at Kewaunee, Wisconsin. [*Charities,* December 3, 1904.]

THE BOHEMIANS IN CHICAGO
Half a century has passed since Bohemians first crossed the ocean, and after a long and dreaded journey and much uncertainty, settled down in Chicago, which was then scarcely more than a large village on the lake shore in the endless prairie.

Today, Chicago is the third largest Bohemian city in the world, having about 100,000 Bohemians, grouped in several colonies of which "Pilsen" is the largest. Originally, the Bohemians lived on Van Buren and Canal Streets where now rushing business life is focused. But these settlers were accustomed to villages and small rustic towns, where they cultivated their fields and lived by their handicraft. Therefore, they soon moved from their first seats near the lake and, when the influx of Jews and Italians into their new quarters began to change the character of the settlement, they moved again. The growth of Pilsen thus began after 1870, and after thirty years shows a certain crystallization of what is typical and characteristic of Bohemian-American life. The other quarters are of more recent date and in many respects bear to Pilsen the relation of colonies to a motherland.

A marked though slight dialect, very common in Chicago, shows that a great number of the people came from the southern part of the kingdom, a district which is poorer than the central and northern parts. Nor is the education in this part as good, for poverty does not send out rays of education, though it absorbs them with craving rapidity.

The reasons for the Bohemian emigration are various. The stormy year, 1848, sent a few pioneers for the Bohemian colony; so did the wars with Italy and Prussia and the depressions that followed. Bad harvests, hailstorms, and droughts have been of influence, and the disproportionate land taxes, compulsory military service, and the lack of liberty in the bureaucratic system are certainly of moment.

The reasons for emigration must ever be strong, for the Bohemians cling to the inherited strip of land, to the cottage they were born in, to the little church on the hill, and the rattling mill on the brook. But when they decide to leave the village or town they were born in, the pain of parting gives life to a new, strong love for the new country, the unknown yet longed-for home. And they come with the intention of becoming American citizens.

Even by a conservative element, the Bohemians are considered desirable immigrants. The number of illiterates is small; in the country districts they make good farmers; they are clever handworkers in the towns. The last is of special interest for Chicago, and is borne out by the fact that of 9,591 Bohemians who came to the United States in 1902–1903, 2,609 were skilled workmen. The United States census of 1900 shows that 75.8 percent of the Bohemians live in the Northwest, which is prevailingly agricultural. Of the Bohemians who came over in 1903 only 1.2 percent were illiterate—and a proportion exceeded only by the Finnish and Scandinavian immigrants of this year.

The change the Bohemians undergo in crossing the ocean and settling down in Chicago is a radical one. From the Austrian monarchy under which the Catholic Church has been indirectly forced upon them, they come into a republic where freedom of religion is acknowledged. From villages and little, old towns, they come into the rushing city of Chicago. Their inward, often unconscious, store of principles and thoughts, superstitions and prejudices, has to be revised because it has been revolutionized. Sometimes the revision is swept away by the revolution.

What intense mental work it requires to distinguish the wisdom of ages crystallized into tradition from an organic prejudice—faith from superstition. Very, very few can do so much and therefore the hardship, the unevenness of the first generation of Bohemians.

The simple, gentle manners of a Bohemian peasant and artisan have to undergo a period of change through the distrust accorded all strangers and the imitation of those *beati possidentes* that inherited their traditions and manners from other ancestors. This queer mixture in the period of changing does not raise sympathy in those who, because they see only the surface, cannot understand and therefore cannot love.

The Bohemians at home have a strong family life. A married son or daughter remains under the same roof with the aged parents, who retire into a quiet nook, where they enjoy their flaxen-haired, brown-eyed grandchildren. This trait, though modified, continues in Chicago. On a Sunday afternoon, the Eighteenth Street car is filled with families, scrubbed, brushed and starched-up, bound for some festival hall to have a good time.

The Bohemian housekeepers know how to get great results from small means, which is most valuable for the poorer class and shown in the red and glossy cheeks of the children. On the other hand, the heavy food (pork with dumplings, for instance, is very common, and with it the usual glass of beer) produces those of full forms without corresponding strength, so general among the well-to-do citizens.

The Bohemians are capable of being amalgamated quickly. They learn the language easily, they give work for which even under competition, they can demand decent wages; they take an interest in politics.

What then is the reason for that vigorous Bohemian-American life, which forms a world of its own in the midst of the city of Chicago? A hundred years ago, after a long and dead slumber into which the Catholic anti-Reformation (one form of Christianity) put the country, the Bohemian national spirit began to breathe. Like an underground current that tries to find an opening for its waters and is untiring in the tiresome task of seeking and seeking, so tried the hidden, downtrodden Bohemian nation to find a way to live, and it slowly succeeded.

After the 1850s, one streamlet, diverted from the general current, found its way to the United States and to the city of Chicago. The obstacles, the bounds that held in this streamlet were removed. So sudden was the change that the waters which expected obstacles burst out into a jet instead of flowing slowly, running mills and factories. Liberty, longed for by generations of Bohemians, was given to the people here, and the energies of thought and longings pent up in the breast for generations without being examined and modified in the fire of deeds, have compelled a disproportionate display. In the meantime, the mother stream in the Old Country found its way more naturally because the movement was slower, the obstacles greater, because those who took part in it possessed the discriminating and radical conservatism of thorough education. The same longings that make the Bohemians in Chicago form endless clubs, which make them freethinkers, distrusting all denominational churches, took a more organic growth in the Old Country, in development in music, arts, and sciences, as well as in economic life. . . .

The emigration consists almost entirely of working people of whom it has been shown a large percentage is skilled handworkers. It must be borne in mind that while within the last fifty years, centralization of capital and subdivision of labor have reached an unparalleled height in America, in Bohemia, the old guild system which prevailed for centuries is slowly dying off through the same process. The old settlers, who came forty years ago and filled their stores with homemade goods (in those times one tailor flourished alongside of another on Nineteenth Street) look amazed on the newcomers and shake their heads: "The idea of an eight-hour day." "The idea of strikes."

The once independent handworkers become foremen in great establishments, cutters in tailor shops, butchers in stockyards, workers in the lumberyards, and a great many become shopkeepers. The middle class naturally dreads the great industrial revolution and hates with equal zest trusts and trade unions. But in the trade union movement the Bohemian workman, like all other intelligent working people, takes a part. And in Chicago, the unions with a Bohemian administration (over twenty in number) have a Bohemian central body.

A large factor in the industrial life is the fact that the Bohemians in Chicago practically have a third generation on this soil, though the first generation is still coming in. Therefore, it is natural that with the great thriftiness of the people and their desire to give their children a good education, Bohemians should be found in different branches of business as well as in all professions. In the home country brewing and the making of beet sugar are two of the oldest industries, and three breweries, founded by Bohemian capital, operate in Chicago, influencing the number of saloons not exactly to the benefit of the population.

The Bohemians have a tendency to own houses and so to have permanent homes. This tendency has been very much helped by the Subsidiary Loan Association. The first was started in 1870, and by 1902 there were over thirty Bohemian loan associations of this kind. Six percent is the highest rate of interest. Of the officers, only the secretary is paid and the books are revised once a year by a state officer. The system of mutual benefit societies has also taken on large dimensions. *Svornost* gives the name of sixteen orders, which in Chicago have 259 lodges. *Denni Hlasatel* gives about thirty

Catholic associations and this is far from being a full list. These orders pay sick and death benefits, the business basis of the lodges being combined with a social element.

In politics, the majority of Bohemians are Democratic; the oldest Republican settlers forming an exception. I have often heard the change from the Republican to the Democratic sentiment explained by the readiness of the Democrats to grant offices to the Bohemians. Another and more satisfactory explanation was given to me by a staunch old Republican. The first Bohemians, who left the bureaucratic Austrian monarchy, joined the Republican Party with enthusiasm. During all the years that Bohemians were coming in such numbers, the government was Republican. The government in Bohemia was far from popular and the very fact that the existing administration was Republican made the Bohemians willing to listen to the complaints of Democrats and even to join in these complaints. Cleveland's first administration did not change this point of view as the Democrats did not have a majority in Congress. The number of Social Democrats is growing as among other immigrant nationalities.

The Bohemians in Chicago have three daily papers. The freethinkers have *Svornost,* the Catholics *Narod,* and *Denni Hlasatel* claims to be independent in questions of faith.

The social life among the Bohemians is very much alive. There are dances, concerts, theatrical performances. Since the Columbian Exposition a company of professional actors has resided in Pilsen, who on Sunday evenings play before a full house in the large hall, Thalia.

Besides the tendency to avail themselves of the unaccustomed freedom, other factors enter into the social life, such as

Cover of the magazine of the Czechoslovak Benevolent Fraternal Society (C.S.P.S.) of Milwaukee, 1905.

the rivalry between the Catholics and freethinkers, the rivalry of individuals, and the indirect economic interest. A new settler finds customers in the club or lodge he joins. This can be reduced *ad absurdum,* when, for instance, all the grocers from the district meet in the same club with the same intention. The educational element is of great importance. I was struck by the cleverness and efficiency with which the Bohemian women conduct their meetings. The men gain here a training for political life.

Other than these mutual benefit organizations, you will find all kinds of societies especially among the freethinkers, such as turner (gymnastic) clubs (35), singing clubs (18), printing clubs (7), bicycle clubs (5), dramatic clubs (4), and many others.

The Bohemians are born musicians. "Where is the Bohemian who does not love music?" is a cadence in Smetana's music which says everything. You will find on the West Side many music schools, many violinists and pianists, amateurs besides the professional musicians who have three unions.

BOHEMIAN FARMERS OF WISCONSIN

Our first Bohemian settlers were of the most intelligent and more prosperous classes. Those who came West established themselves in two settlements, one in St. Louis and the other in Caledonia, Wis. (near Racine). In the next few years settlements spread to Milwaukee and Manitowoc counties. These first Bohemian farmers came almost without exception with money enough to buy their lands, at least in part. The country which they selected was heavily wooded so that their first great labor was to clear their farms. This they did by cutting and burning the logs, making no attempt to sell them as

timber, as did their countrymen who came later. With farms wholly or in part paid for, they could direct all their energies toward clearing and cultivating the land, finding an immediate means of subsistance in small crops raised among the stumps. From this small beginning, the way to prosperity was clear. Their farms in Milwaukee County, directly north of Manitowoc, are among the finest in the state.

These were the centers toward which the subsequent immigration naturally drifted. By 1870 the greater part of the later comers had arrived. These were mostly ambitious farm laborers and mechanics who hoped to find here an independent and more profitable livelihood. As they came with little or no money, their first need was for cheap farms upon which they could make a humble living from the very beginning. Such farms they found in the timber lands of Kewaunee County, directly north of Manitowoc. Here they settled in such large numbers that they still make up over one-third of the total population—6,000 of the 17,000 inhabitants of the county.

The early settler bought from forty to sixty acres of land, making only a small cash payment, and giving a mortgage for the rest. The price ranged from $5.00 to $10 an acre. With the help of his neighbors, who blazed trails as they came lest they should not be able to find the way back, he built a log cabin and felled a few trees to give space for a vegetable patch. Then came the serious work of clearing the land, and at the same time earning enough outside money to live and pay part of the debt. This was accomplished in various ways. Sometimes the head of the family and the eldest son worked part of the year in the nearest sawmill or in the logging camps of northern Michigan.

Sometimes they went to the large farms to the south of Michigan to help during the harvest. Very often they made hand-shaved pine shingles of the trees on their land, and exchanged them at the nearest market for what they most needed.

These were, indeed, hard years for our pioneers, but better times came after 1861. The war broke out and the forest products of which they had such an abundance increased in price. Tanbark, cedar posts for fencing, cordwood, railroad ties—all found a market so good that the village shippers bought them as fast as they could be made and brought to the shipping piers. Many of these merchant lumbermen advanced money to the farmers with which to buy oxen and sleighs. They also took timber products in exchange for flour, cloth, and other necessities; and in other ways the struggle for existence became less severe, the clearing of the lands went on more rapidly, and the farmers were able to meet more easily their living expenses and debts, notwithstanding war prices on food products and clothes, which put flour at $12 a barrel, coffee at sixty cents a pound, and ordinary sheeting at eighty-five cents.

But the war, even with its attendant prosperity, was not an unmixed blessing. Enthusiasm and patriotism, everywhere rife, were further encouraged among the Bohemians by their newspaper *The Slavie,* then published in Racine, Wis. Many entered the volunteer army, and when later a draft was ordered, large numbers of farms were left without men. There remained usually a large family with only a mother, and perhaps a fourteen-year-old son, to carry on the work of the place, an outlook calculated to overwhelm the most courageous of women. Yet our Bohemian wives were not disheartened and it is remarkable that in all that wartime

not one mortgage was foreclosed in Kewaunee County, and not one of these brave women forfeited the homestead that was given into her care.

After the war, the material progress of the farmers was steady. Today, were you to travel through their settlements, you would find large, well-ordered farms, with only here and there a stump or disused log house to remind you of pioneer days. In Kewaunee County, farm land is now worth from $25 to $50 an acre, five times its original value.

Very little was done during the early years toward education. Schools were widely scattered, hard to reach, and there was work for the children at home. The Catholic church, in the few places where it was established, had in connection with it no parochial school. Only a very few children learned even the beginnings of English. Some, however, were taught at home in the mother tongue, which enabled them to read the Bohemian newspaper.

When, later, more roads were opened, and pioneers had overcome their first difficulties, schoolhouses sprang up and children were given from seven to ten months' tuition each year. It would seem that once the "little red schoolhouse" was built, the way toward American citizenship would have been clear. But even here there were difficulties. The small Slavs insisted on talking Bohemian out of school hours, and the distracted schoolmaster could do nothing to stop them. As a consequence, they learned English slowly; other branches of knowledge, still more so. In communities where there were a few Irish and American children, conditions were somewhat better, but even here "recess language" was Bohemian. The minority of little Americans were overcome. It was a common complaint among their parents that even at home they spoke to each other in Bohemian and a strange, unnatural language it must have seemed to these English-speaking parents.

These beginnings belong to the past. It would be hard in our day to find a Bohemian of the second generation in Wisconsin who cannot read and speak English. The older people do not learn English so readily. Their children and neighbors can speak with them in the mother tongue, the village merchant provides Bohemian clerks of whom they can buy, and for reading they have the Bohemian newspapers. Those who can speak German adapt themselves somewhat more readily; for having a knowledge of one foreign language, they find it less difficult to master a second which is allied to it.

In the matter of higher education, the Bohemians of Kewaunee County have a remarkably good record. Within the last twenty-five years the local high school has sent to college fifty-nine young men and women and of these thirty were Bohemians. It is plain, then, that there is no lack of ambition in the children of our pioneers, and this ambition is upheld and fostered by progressive Bohemians of the West. Two years ago a council of higher education was organized at Cedar Rapids, Iowa, which, in the words of its constitution, is "to encourage the Bohemian youth to acquire higher education, to inform our people concerning the manner in which they may secure such education for their children, and the advantages which various educational institutions afford, and to aid promising students, who lack the material means necessary to higher education, by honor loans, without interest."

The society was organized mainly through the efforts of W. F. Severa, a prominent Bohemian of Cedar Rapids, and Professor Simek of Iowa University. To put the project in motion, Mr. Severa subscribed $2,500, a sum which has been so liberally contributed to by Bohemian societies and individuals that in the two years the society has been able to loan much more. Though in 1903–1904 there were seven students at various Western universities and this year the number has been increased to twelve, it is hoped that as the fund increases, both by contributions and repaid loans, the society will be able to broaden its scope.

The movement is further supported by another, the aim of which is to establish Bohemian libraries in the larger Bohemian communities. The public library of Milwaukee is to install 100 books on history, literature, biography, fiction, and science, and the Free Library Commission of Wisconsin is considering the purchase of two sets of books, seventy-five in each, to be used as traveling libraries in the thickly populated districts of the state. In addition to these libraries, there is to be another of about a hundred books at the University of Nebraska, and a second traveling library under the management of the council of higher education. Mr. Severa voices the ambition of progressive Bohemian-Americans when he says: "We want our young men and women to enter American colleges and to work hand in hand with Americans on the path of progress, but we want them at the same time to respect the land of their fathers, to know their language, and to be informed concerning their history and literature."

In the country the assimilation of Bohemians is not a problem which offers difficulties. The public school is everywhere so potent an Americanizer that it alone is adequate. There is, however, one other influence which if brought to bear,

Members of Chicago's Bohemian social club, photographed at their summer clubhouse at Fox Lake, Wisconsin, in 1914.

especially in the large communities, would be helpful. I refer to the Protestant faith. For the most part Bohemians conversant with their history as a people are naturally hostile to the Catholic Church, and when the restraints which held them in their own country are removed by emigration, many of the most enlightened quietly drop their allegiance and, through lack of desire or opportunity, fail to ally themselves with any other. So strong is this nonreligious tendency among Bohemians (especially in the cities) that it has resulted in active unbelief and hostility to church influence. This spiritual isolation, with its resultant social separation, is doing great harm in retarding assimilation. The benefits to be derived from social intercourse within a church would be especially marked as assimilative and educational factors.

Aside from this matter of religion, the Bohemian falls into American customs with surprising readiness. This is the more remarkable when we consider the great difference between American and Bohemian country life. Nowhere in the Old Country are there isolated farms as here—the cultivated lands radiate. To a Bohemian immigrant then, American farm life must at first seem extremely dull and void of social pleasure.

A general impression that Bohemians are like the Germans is not true. They are, to begin with, a very emotional people. In this they resemble more closely the Latin races, except that where the Latins are more or less consistently lighthearted, the Bohemians have an unconquerable tendency toward melancholy. They are excitable and have an unusual capacity for entering heartily into their pleasures; but, on the other hand, they are easily depressed and have not the cool-natured endurance of the northern German. Generally liberal money-spenders, hardworking and thrifty, they still have a fondness for good living, good clothes, and an occasional glass of beer, which makes it difficult for them to bear poverty.

But, perhaps, their most striking characteristic is their love of music and dancing. In the country, almost every village has a band of self-taught musicians, and the country dance is a time-honored institution. Their national music is peculiarly Slavonic and has in it the same undercurrent of strangeness and melancholy which one finds in their personal traits and again in their folklore.

The Magyars in New York

8

The Magyars are a non-Slavic people from eastern Europe many of whom emigrated to America in the late 19th and early 20th centuries. The census of 1910 reported slightly more than 225,000 of them in the United States, and twenty years later that number had nearly tripled. The following article by Louis H. Pink describes the largest Magyar settlement, in New York City. [*Charities*, December 3, 1904.]

The Hungarian colony in New York is comparatively small, but its interest is in inverse ratio to its size. Eighty percent of the Magyars arriving in New York go at once to the farms and mines. Those who remain in the city are found on the East Side in three distinct quarters. Only the largest of these is important enough to be called a colony. The two smaller quarters are on the Upper East Side, one on 117th and 118th streets settled almost entirely by recent arrivals, the other lying between 75th and 85th streets. The colony proper is bounded by Stanton and Seventh streets, First Avenue, and the East River. It contains from 50,000 to 60,000 Magyars and Hungarian Jews, besides large numbers of Germans, a colony of Polish Catholics, the shattered remnant of a once vigorous Bohemian quarter, a determined line of Irish who are making their last stand along the waterfront, and many Russian Jews.

It is almost impossible to distinguish between the Hungarian Jew and the Hungarian gentile in New York. They mingle indiscriminately, they both glory in the traditional freedom and patriotism of the Magyar, for in Hungary the Jew has never been persecuted. When driven from western Europe in the 14th and 15th centuries, he found refuge, security, and, to a greater extent than he had before known it, freedom, in the Alföld towns and villages. The Hungarian Jew still clings tenaciously to the belief of his fathers, but unlike the Russian, he regards Judaism as a religion, not as the mark of a distinct nationality. In all but creed he is a Magyar.

There are more Hungarian Jews than gentiles in New York. Marcus Braun, recently appointed special commissioner of immigration by President Roosevelt, is authority for the statement that while on the Upper East Side the gentiles are in the majority, 75 percent of the Hungarian colony are Jewish.

But few Hungarians of the higher classes come to the United States. The great mass of Hungarian immigrants are laborers. They come, not to escape oppression, but in search of enlarged opportunity. In some regions of Hungary it is as much "the thing" for the young men to go to America as it is for the sons of American farmers to seek the cities.

East Houston Street is the Broadway of the Hungarian colony; Second Avenue is its Riverside Drive; Avenues A, B, and C are important centers of social and business activity. The life of the quarter is one continuous whirl of excitement. Pleasure seems the chief end and dancing, music, cards, and lounging at the café are the means of attaining it. Intensely social, extremely fond of conviviality and gaiety, polished, graceful, bright—the Magyar soon learns the English language. The Russian Jew requires years of patient struggle to rid him of his guttural, and learns English pronunciation only because of his indomitable perseverance. The Italian takes equally long to discipline his vowel sounds and temper their use with mercy. The Magyar speaks English, and with the true accent, almost at once. The Hungarian Jew learns English more readily than the uneducated Christian because he has been brought up to use German as well as the Magyar language, while the uneducated Christian has been taught to eschew all languages but his own as a matter of patriotism. Quick as the Magyar is to learn and to adapt himself to strange circumstances, he likes to live and let live. He lacks perseverance. He prefers to live comfortably on a moderate income rather than submit to the hardships incident to the accumulation of a fortune. He prefers to spend the heat of the afternoon at the café rather than be the slave of high position and an impaired digestion. He has no taste for the "strenuous life."

Institutions have but slight hold upon the Magyar. The wild blood of his roving forefathers is strong within him. The same passion for untrammeled personal liberty which led them over the steppes of Asia and finally, under Attila, to cross into Europe, now inspires the Magyar peasant with scorn for improved machinery and for the slavery of the modern industrial system.

There are only three institutions which are extensively supported by the Magyar in New York—the newspaper, the literary society, and the charitable organization. There is but one Hungarian daily paper in the United States, *Hirmondo,* published at Cleveland, Ohio, but having a large circulation in New York. Besides this there are published in New York, several weeklies, semi-weeklies and semi-monthlies, and the *Austro-Hungarian Gazette,* printed in German, but having an interest to all the peoples of the dual monarchy. The literary societies are numerous, though their function is social, rather than literary, while the purpose of some is to arouse and to keep aroused the Magyar patriotism. There are two charitable organizations, the Hungarian Association of the City of New York and the Hungarian Relief Society. The former dispenses charity without regard to race or creed, the latter was until recently affiliated with the Austrian Society and confines its work to immigrants. As a rule only Christians apply for its assistance. The Jewish applicants are taken care of by the United Hebrew Charities. While the Magyar is easy-going and pleasure-loving above all the peoples who seek our shores in large numbers, in pride, in independence, in fertility of resource, he is inferior to none. He will starve rather than beg and will apply for charity only as a last resort and sometimes not then.

Magyar patriotism is kept alive in the new soil by societies organized for that purpose, by the agitation of several of the newspapers, and by emissaries from the Fatherland. There is a rapidly growing rift and not a little feeling between those who wish to retain their allegiance to Hungary and those who have chosen to cast in their lot with the adopted land. The immediate cause of the breach was the presentation of the Hungarian flag to the New York societies some two years ago. The recent visit of the Hungarian deputies has again aroused an ebullition of patriotic spirit.

Tailoring is the chief occupation in the colony and it is practically monopolized by Jews. Many Hungarians are furriers, others work in hotels and restaurants. Shopkeepers and merchants are numerous. On the Upper East Side the Magyars are to be found in cigar factories, wire factories, brass factories, shoe factories, gas works. The brighter young men enter the professions.

The Magyar women are unusually pleasing and graceful. Those who work prefer to sew at home for they consider it a disgrace to work in a factory. They are bright, have a passion for social functions, and are accomplished musicians and dancers.

The most important influence on the Lower East Side, the institution, if it may be called an institution, to which the Magyar is most deeply and passionately attached, is the café. It is the expression of his social life. It takes the place of the club and to a certain extent of the home. Almost every block in the Hungarian quarter has its café and some blocks have four or five. Each café has its special clientele. One is patronized by artists and musicians, another by shopkeepers, another by professional men. Here sociability and good fellowship reign. Here may be heard the clink of glasses, the hubbub of conversation, the fiery music of the gypsy orchestra. In the absence of restraint there is fascination. The most practical man has a streak of roving blood coursing through his arteries, and to this relic of the free life of our ancestors the café appeals. "Business be damned" archly whispers the spirit of the café into the ears of the lawyer, the banker, the financier, who out of curiosity visits the Hungarian café, and if there is a single strain of sentiment within he becomes a veritable Donatello for a night.

The Coming of the Italian
John Foster Carr

9

In the decades after the Civil War, Italy replaced Germany as the number one source of immigration to America. Perhaps because their numbers were so large and because they went to virtually every part of the nation, they were the most victimized by anti-alien sentiment of all the nationality groups arriving between 1885 and 1924. The following sympathetic article presented the case for the Italian-Americans, while acknowledging the problems they faced in adjusting to their new surroundings. The author, John F. Carr, was an educator who specialized in the Americanization of immigrants. [*Outlook,* February 24, 1906.]

To understand our Italians we need to get close enough to them to see that they are of the same human *pasta*—to use their word—as the rest of us. They need no defense but the truth. In spite of the diverse character that all the provinces

An Italian family landing at Ellis Island, about 1905.

stamp upon their children, our southern Italian immigrants still have many qualities in common. Their peculiar defects and vices have been exaggerated until the popular notion of the Italian represents the truth in about the same way that the London stage Yankee hits off the average American. Besides, as the Italian Poor Richard says, "It's a bad wool that can't be dyed," and our Italians have their virtues, too, which should be better known. Many of them are, it is true, ignorant, and clannish, and conservative. Their humility and lack of self-reliance are often discouraging. Many think that a smooth and diplomatic falsehood is better than an uncivil truth, and, by a paradox, a liar is not necessarily either a physical or a moral coward. No force can make them give evidence against one another. Generally they have little orderliness, small civic sense, and no instinctive faith in the law. Some of them are hot-blooded and quick to avenge an injury, but the very large majority are gentle, kindly, and as mild-tempered as oxen. They are docile, patient, faithful. They have great physical vigor, and are the hardest and best laborers we have ever had, if we are to believe the universal testimony of their employers. Many are well-mannered and quick-witted; all are severely logical. As a class they are emotional, imaginative, fond of music and art. They are honest, saving, industrious, temperate, and so exceptionally moral that two years ago the secretary of the Italian Chamber of Commerce in San Francisco was able to boast that the police of that city had never yet found an Italian woman of evil character. Even in New York (and I have my information from Mr. Forbes, of the Charity Organization Society) Italian prostitution was entirely unknown until by our corrupt police it was colonized as scientifically as a culture of bacteria made by a biologist; and today it is less proportionately than that of any other nationality within the limits of the greater city. More than 750,000 Italian immigrants have come to us within the last four years, and during that entire time only a single woman of them has been ordered deported charged with prostitution.

So far from being a scum of Italy's paupers and criminals, our Italian immigrants are the very flower of her peasantry. They bring healthy bodies and a prodigious will to work. They have an intense love for their Fatherland, and a fondness for old customs; and both are deepened by the hostility they meet and the gloom of the tenements that they are forced to inhabit. The sunshine, the simplicity, the happiness of the old outdoor ways are gone, and often you will hear the words, *"Non c'é piacere nella vita"* — there is no pleasure in life here. But yet they come, driven from a land of starvation to a land of plenty. Each year about one-third of the great host of industrial recruits from Italy, breaking up as it lands into little groups of twos and threes, and invading the tenements almost unnoticed, settles in the different colonies of New York. This is a mighty, silent influence for the preservation of the Italian spirit and tradition.

But there are limits to the building of an Italian city on American soil. New York tenement houses are not adapted to life as it is organized in the hill villages of Italy, and a change has come over every relation of life. The crowded living is strange and depressing; instead of work accompanied by song in orangeries and vineyards, there is silent toil in the canyons of a city street; instead of the splendid and expostulating *carabiniere* there is the rough force of the New York policeman to represent authority. There is the diminished importance of the church, and, in spite of their set ways, there is different eating and drinking, sleeping and waking. A different life breeds different habits, and different habits with American surroundings effect a radical change in the man. It is difficult for the American to realize this. He sees that the signs and posters of the colony are all in Italian; he hears the newsboys cry *"Progresso," "Araldo," "Bolletino";* he hears peddlers shout out in their various dialects the names of strange-looking vegetables and fish. The whole district seems so Italianized and cut off from the general American life that it might as well be one of the ancient walled towns of the Apennines. He thinks that he is transported to Italy, and moralizes over the "unchanging colony." But the greenhorn from Fiumefreddo is in another world. Everything is strange to him; and I have repeatedly heard Italians say that for a long time after landing they could not distinguish between an Italian who had been here four or five years and a native American.

Refractory though the grown-up immigrant may often be to the spirit of our republic, the children almost immediately become Americans. The boy takes no interest in *"Mora,"* a guessing match played with the fingers, or *"Boccie,"* a kind of bowls—his father's favorite games. Like any other American boy, he plays marbles, "I spy the wolf," and,

An Italian organ-grinder poses with his family in Chicago, about 1900.

when there is no policeman about, baseball. Little girls skip the rope to the calling of "Pepper, salt, mustard, vinegar." The *"Lunga Tela"* is forgotten, and our equivalent, "London bridge is falling down," and "All around the mulberry bush," sound through the streets of the colony on summer evenings. You are struck with the deep significance of such a sight if you walk on Mott Street, where certainly more than half of the men and women who crowd every block can speak no English at all, and see, as I have seen, a full dozen of small girls, not more than five or six years old, marching along, hand in hand, singing their kindergarten song, "My little sister lost her shoe." Through these children the common school is leavening the whole mass, and an old story is being retold.

Like the Italians, the Irish and the Germans had to meet distrust and abuse when they came to do the work of the rough day-laborer. The terrors and excesses of Native Americanism and Know-

Nothingism came and went, but the prejudice remained. Yet the Irish and Germans furnished good raw material for citizenship, and quickly responded to American influences. They dug cellars and carried bricks and mortar; they sewered, graded, and paved the streets and built the railroads. Then slowly the number of skilled mechanics among them increased. Many acquired a competence and took a position of some dignity in the community, and Irish and Germans moved up a little in the social scale. They were held in greater respect when, in the dark days of the Civil War, we saw that they yielded to none in self-sacrificing devotion to the country. Thousands of Germans fought for the Union besides those who served under Sigel. Thousands of Irishmen died for the cause besides those of the "Old Sixty-ninth." "Dutch" and "Mick" began to go out of fashion as nicknames, and the 1870s had not passed before it was often said among the common people that mixed marriages between Germans or Irish and natives were usually happy marriages.

From the very bottom, Italians are climbing up the same rungs of the same social and industrial ladder. But it is still a secret that they are being gradually turned into Americans; and, for all its evils, the city colony is a wonderful help in the process. The close contact of American surroundings eventually destroys the foreign life and spirit, and of this New York gives proof. Only two poor fragments remain of the numerous important German and Irish colonies that were flourishing in the city twenty-five or thirty years ago; while the ancient settled Pennsylvania Dutch, thanks to their isolation, are not yet fully merged in the great citizen body. And so, in the city colony, Italians are becoming Americans.

Legions of them, who never intended to remain here when they landed, have cast in their lot definitely with us; and those who have already become Americanized, but no others, are beginning to intermarry with our people. The mass of them are still laborers, toiling like ants in adding to the wealth of the country; but thousands are succeeding in many branches of trade and manufacture. The names of Italians engaged in business in the United States fill a special directory of over 500 pages. Their real estate holdings and bank deposits aggregate enormous totals. Their second generation is already crowding into all the professions, and we have Italian teachers, dentists, architects, engineers, doctors, lawyers, and judges.

But more important than any material success is their loyalty to the nation of their adoption. Yet with this goes an undying love for their native land. There are many types of these new citizens. I have in mind an Italian banker who will serve for one. His Americanism is enthusiastic and breezily Western. He has paid many visits to the land of his birth, and delights in its music, art, and literature. He finds an almost sacred inspiration in the glories of its history. Beginning in extreme poverty, by his own unaided efforts he has secured education and wealth; by his services to the city and state in which he lives he has won public esteem. Perhaps no other Italian has achieved so brilliant a success. But as a citizen he is no more typical or hopeful an example of the Italian who becomes an American than Giovanni Aloi, a street sweeper of my acquaintance.

This honest *spazzino* of the white uniform sent a son to Cuba in the Spanish War; boasts that he has not missed a vote in fifteen years; in his humble way did valiant service in his political club against the "boss" of New York during the last campaign. And yet he declares that we have no meats or vegetables with "the flavor or substance" of those in the Old Country; reproaches us severely for having "no place which is such a pleasure to see as Naples," and swears by "Torquaato Ta-ass" as the greatest of poets, though he only knows four lines of the *Gerusalemme*. Side by side over the fireplace in his living room are two unframed pictures tacked to the wall. Little paper flags of the two countries are crossed over each. One is a chromo of Garibaldi in his red shirt. The other is a newspaper supplement portrait of Lincoln.

A man like Giovanni Aloi, yearning for the home of his youth, sometimes goes back to Italy, but he soon returns. Unconsciously, in his very inmost being, he has become an American, and the prophecy of Bayard Taylor's great ode is fulfilled. Their tongue melts in ours. Their race unites to the strength of ours. For many thousands of them their Italy now lies by the Western brine.

Chinese Refugees in Chicago

10

On April 18, 1906, three-fourths of San Francisco was destroyed by earthquake and fire. Many of the residents of Chinatown lost everything they had, both homes and businesses. Most of them chose to remain and rebuild; some moved across the bay. Others dispersed to different parts of the United States to begin again, leaving not only the rubble behind them, but the traditional antipathy toward the Oriental as well. This news report from the Chicago *Journal* of May 23, 1906, tells of the arrival of numerous Chinese refugees in the city. [Chicago Foreign Language Press Survey, WPA Project, 1942.]

As a result of the San Francisco earthquake and fire many scores of Chinese who were driven from their ruined homes in the stricken California city have sought and found refuge in Chicago. The influx of the Celestials has been very steady, but the number who have come to this city has not been realized either by the authorities or the Chinese themselves until within a few days.

Being in most cases almost penniless after their railway fare had been paid, these immigrants were forced at first to depend for subsistence on the charity of their friends and countrymen, but now the majority of them have again become independent. These refugees are scattered far and wide over the city, their presence not being confined to Chinatown, although at first almost all of them drifted there.

So steady was the coming of the Chinese that their arrival was hardly realized at first even in the districts where they made their temporary homes. Coming by twos and threes from the stricken city, they immediately made their way to the South Clark Street district, where they soon were given help until they were able to take care of themselves.

A great many of the refugees were well enough provided with money to carry them over the period until they could find work. Those who were destitute, however, were immediately taken care of by individuals.

There was little organized work of relief among Chinamen, either for those of their countrymen left in San Francisco or those who came to Chicago. Chinamen sent individual donations to their suffering kinsmen and friends in the California towns, but they did little for the men of their own race by organized effort. The same was true of the aid which they rendered in Chicago. They were very liberal, but all of the giving was personal.

Until the living quarters in the Chinese section became filled with the refugees they remained in the downtown district, at least until they secured work. Then they scattered throughout the city and suburbs, many of them finding employment in towns as far away as Elgin, Aurora, and Joliet. When the South Clark Street houses could hold no more the Chinese began drifting through the city. Laundries, restaurants, and every other sort of an establishment run by a Chinaman became a refuge. From merely giving shelter in case of need these same establishments soon offered regular work, and so, instead of working for nothing but their board and lodging, many of the refugees became regular employees.

The fact that Chinamen are skilled in the preparation of dishes other than those characteristic of their race is just beginning to dawn on the owners of many "American" restaurants throughout the city, and even upon private families.

A few of the sophisticated, and those addicted to chop suey and similar incongruities, have long employed Celestials, but before scores of unemployed China-

men were turned loose in the city their general adaptability was unknown to but few.

In good restaurants very good cooks with very good wages have been employed from the ranks of the "Frisco" sufferers, but other places of less pretense have secured less expensive cooks, and so down the line, until many a place, which has nothing to say about chop suey, which advertises a "full meal for fifteen cents" has a Chinaman presiding at the range. And in the point of cleanliness and skill the change has generally been one for the better.

As a natural consequence of this the Chinamen so employed have secured places for their relatives and friends as dishwashers and porters until now there are certain sections of the city which, as far as the restaurants are concerned, are overrun with Celestials.

A particular example of this is in the neighborhood of 63rd Street, from Woodlawn to Chicago Lawn.

None of the refugees has as yet become a public charge, and it is very unlikely that any ever will. The majority of them have quietly settled down here to amass the fortune which will make them and their relatives happy when they return to the land of their ancestors.

Racial Traits in American Beauty

11

Ever since Crèvecoeur's famous question, "What is an American?", was posed in 1782, dabblers in sociology have sought to describe or predict the composite American. Such guesswork rested on the assumption that there would eventually develop an undifferentiated national type, a product of the "melting pot." The following article by Broughton Brandenburg, titled here as in the original, traced the various strains that supposedly would one day blend into the American woman. [*Cosmopolitan Magazine*, May 1906.]

The laurels of loveliness belong indisputably to the American woman even more

today than half a century ago, and I hope to show that there is every reason to believe that the world of the next century, perhaps even the second one, shall marvel still at a race of incomparable beauty reared on our soil.

If the reverse were to be expected the problem would be grave indeed, because, inasmuch as the phenomenon results from a combination of our life and climate with the mingling of the old racial strains of Europe, the consequences are inevitable.

Migrations of whole families of Irish, Scotch, and Devonshire stock occurred late in the 18th century to Newfoundland, the Gaspé Peninsula, the coast of Maine, the maritime provinces of Canada in general, and to western Pennsylvania. There were many other places in the United States to which groups came but they were amalgamated with other races and cannot be so readily traced. Their prevailing type of generous mouth, teeth not too closely set, hair with a bit of curl in it, and their exquisite color is one very familiar indeed. What has been the effect of climatic change? Those in Newfoundland, the Gaspé Peninsula, and Nova Scotia, though they have kept their blood so pure that Gaelic is still common among them as ordinary speech, are shorter in stature, smaller of mouth, higher of cheekbone, and the soft color has become a flaming red that is almost unchanging. I have seen little tots in the interior of the peninsula whose faces seemed to be painted with vermilion, the color was so bright. In Maine their features have shrunken, the general eye is smaller, and the blue eye has become grey. In Pennsylvania, however, they have grown taller, their bony framework is more symmetrical, their teeth have no outward slant, meeting squarely. A large percentage of the women are exceedingly beautiful, their skins being creamy white with a del-

icate tinting of color such as is usually seen with red hair, though it is only in the last two generations that that darker tint called auburn has appeared. The reason is that the climate is milder, and the chemical constituency of the food they eat, the water they drink, and the air they breathe is different.

Lay the picture of any Virginia beauty of pure Anglo-Saxon beside the miniature of her great-grandmother, who was born in Kent or Surrey, and the modification of all that was good in the grandmother's face into the perfect beauty of the young Virginian's features will be convincing. How tall a race has grown in the mountains of Pennsylvania, West Virginia, Tennessee, Kentucky, and the Carolinas! The exception there is the man under six feet. What strapping men are the third generation Iowans and Kansans!

It is a well-known fact, considered to be very amusing in California, that a shriveled father and mother from some rocky farm in a bleak spot of New England can migrate to California and raise a family of the most beautiful children. One can easily recall a great number of California beauties whose gifts have been so rich as to bring them before the public for beauty alone. The counterpart of this quality in the other sex is the athletic ability which young Californians have shown. It is a rare year when that state does not produce some "wonder."

A well-known lecturer on biology made a study of these phenomena and decided that the same influences of sun, air, wind, and moisture that made a plant which is ordinarily small and not over fruitful grow tall, bloom, and bear luxuriantly, would be expected to act in like fashion on human organisms. . . .

Inspiration is nearly imperative in tracing out the complex influences of mingled

These pictures and the pseudo-scientific racial
classifications given below were used to accompany
Brandenburg's article when it was originally published
in 1906. They illustrate several composite types of
American women. (Above) Composite American with
dominant Anglo-Saxon strain. (Right) Celtic-Teutonic
and composite American. (On facing page, top left and
right, and bottom left and right) Scandinavian-Teutonic,
with slight Semitic strain; Celtic-Anglo-Iberic, with
Celtic strain dominant; Anglo-Saxon-Celtic type, with
Saxon strain dominant; Teutonic type, with recurrent
Iberic strain.

Illustrations on this and facing page, Newberry Library

strains in any one type that is really American, for the reason that through the majority of the genealogies runs what I have chosen to call the composite American type. It is not the real American type; it is to be that when fully developed. For instance, an extremely beautiful Indiana girl, who came to notice in some recent studies of the racial effect of immigration on the great mass of people already in the United States, was found to have a German father who was a Schwabischer and very dark and compactly built. Her mother, however, was of the composite type I have named. Her maternal grandfather was a Scotch sailor, her maternal grandmother a French seamstress, her paternal grandfather was the son of a Dutch burgher and a Spanish refugee on Staten Island, and her paternal grandmother the daughter of a Polish revolutionary soldier. In the Scotch, we have the Celtic; in the French, the Iberic; in the Dutch, the Teutonic; in this instance, in the Spanish, the Iberic-Semitic; and in the Polish, the Slavic, resulting in equally balanced Celtic, Iberic, Teutonic, and Slavic strains, with a trace of Semitic on her mother's side, while her father augmented the Teutonic and Iberic. More than half our population in the United States is just as mixed racially and that great mass forms what I mean by the composite American.

When a person of such a composite type, already modified by climate and life in America, marries a newcomer or the child of newcomers of pure racial type, then we find the most extraordinary beauty as a frequent result. There seems to be an elimination of anything that has become objectionable by inbreeding in the unmixed blood, and an intensifying of the very best qualities. That is the secret of our American beauties.

The marked varieties which are such a delight to our foreign visitors, and to foreign society when our girls go abroad, are the result of some strain predominating or perhaps recurring strongly in one or two facial features. That is very markedly set forth in the Anglo-Saxon-Celtic type and the Teutonic type with recurrent Iberic strain. In the first the Scotch blood is predominant and signifies itself in the gentle, earnest eyes, the delicate, idealistic mouth, the tilted nose, and the hair. In the other it comes out in the long, thin, and delicate Iberic ear and the color of the hair, while never Teuton had such a mouth.

It is a not uncommon thing in America for people who have a strain of high lineage to ignore their noble ancestry. Many families which are predominantly Irish or Welsh prefer to trace back their origin to some English ancestor. From my studies of racial developments in this country I am convinced anyone should be proud to acknowledge Irish and Slavic blood. Many Jews call themselves Germans and many Germans by extraction wish to be thought English by blood. . . .

In the composite American type, with the predominating Anglo-Saxon strain, the deathless character of race is attested. From Chicago, born of many generations of Americans and of such typically American features as never to be mistaken for anything other than an American girl, her face need only be compared with those of the Anglo-Saxon type with recurrent Angle strain and previously mentioned Anglo-Saxon-Celtic, to see the convincing similarity. In connection with this type it seems interesting to remark that of the many judges, dilettanti, and connoisseurs who have examined the larger collection, nearly all picked her out for some especial notice and often confessed that her face, though not analyzing as satisfactorily as some of the others, was far more attractive. Never was she mistaken for a type not thoroughly composite American.

In the Celtic-Teutonic type the softening, blending, and reinforcing effect of the addition of the composite American is well portrayed. No one would expect to find such perfection of head, neck, and shoulder lines in a Celt nor would one believe such mouth and eyes could be Teuton. It is the effect of one on the other and then of the composite American blood putting all in proportion. American life and climate will effect this reproportioning alone sometimes.

Referring again to the Anglo-Saxon-Celtic type with the notable Celtic indications, a bit is learned from a comparison of the lovely Anglo-Saxon-Celtic type with the predominant Saxon strain. Though unknown to each other, with no family connections whatever and merely the same racial origin and the same American influences, the two girls, on the analysis of their features, would be taken for sisters. Many persons have been morally certain they were twins and some who have been hasty have even thought they were the same girl. The only real noticeable difference is in the quality of the hair and the slight variation in the jaw. They are two ideal faces.

American life has contributed vastly to the molding and blending of widely divergent strains in the Saxon-Iberic type where the heavy Iberic jaw has been rounded, the Saxon nose relaxed, and the eye orbits enlarged and rendered symmetrical with the modified jaw, thus producing a face not only beautiful but sweet, interesting, and mobile, and of a physical structure to resist time.

What a Celtic dominancy can do with Anglo-Iberic blood is shown in the Celtic-Anglo-Iberic type. It has proved generous to the Iberic nose, it has softened the Angle mouth, it has put mirth and humor into the Iberic temperament, and made less tractable the Iberic hair. The jaw is left unchanged. The inferior maxillary formation is hard to alter, and reformation for unusual beauty is rare.

When the enormous influx of Scandinavians, Germans, etc., into the country is considered, it is pertinent to inquire what effects such combinations with the composite American blood in its present constituency will have. It would seem that the Teutonic nose, with its slightly bulbous end, is made straight, the eye is enlarged, and the tendency to meagerness, so often seen in composite American faces, is beautifully offset by a rounding out of the neck, chin, throat, and cheeks.

A word as to the future in conclusion. The greater portion of the new racial admixture which we are accepting is Iberic, Slavic, and Semitic in its divisions. In the southern Italian's blood is some Norman, some Moorish. The blood of the Jews, racially the purest of the old strains, has not yet begun to tell its story, because with them the lines of race and religion are so nearly parallel, and few intermarriages have resulted as yet. The Slavs, however, are intermarrying freely with composite Americans, and in two more generations, when someone else makes a little study of the blood of the American beauty, he will have the Iberic, Slavic, and Semitic strains to untangle, while the Teutonic, Anglo-Saxon, and Celtic will have been almost completely merged into what *then* will be the composite American.

It is too soon yet to hazard any statement as to definite features, but that type, however built up, is certain to be beautiful in the extreme.

Race War in the North
William E. Walling

12

Violence against black Americans reached epidemic proportions between 1885 and 1920. From 1885 until 1900 there were more than 2,500 lynchings, a number well in excess of the legal executions of convicted criminals. Early in this century there were a series of race riots throughout the country, in the North as well as in the South. The worst of the Northern eruptions occurred at Springfield, Illinois, in August 1908. The occasion was simple enough: a crime committed by a white man was blamed on a black man, and the white mob took over from there. Journalist William English Walling described the aftermath of the riot in this article published a few weeks later. [*Independent*, September 3, 1908.]

"Lincoln freed you, we'll show you where you belong," was one of the cries with which the Springfield mob set about to drive the Negroes from town. The mob was composed of several thousand of Springfield's white citizens, while other thousands, including many women and children, and even prosperous businessmen in automobiles, calmly looked on, and the rioters proceeded hour after hour and on two days in succession to make deadly assaults on every Negro they could lay their hands on, to sack and plunder their houses and stores, and to burn and murder on favorable occasion.

The American people have been fairly well informed by their newspapers of the action of that mob; they have also been told of certain alleged political and criminal conditions in Springfield and of the two crimes in particular which are offered by the mob itself as sufficient explanation why 6,000 peaceful and innocent Negroes should be driven by the fear of their lives from a town where some of them have lived honorably for half a hundred years. We have been assured by more cautious and indirect defenders of Springfield's populace that there *was* an exceptionally criminal element among the Negroes encouraged by the bosses of both political parties. And now, after a few days of discussion, we are satisfied with these explanations, and demand only the punishment of those who took the most active part in the destruction of life and property. Assuming that there were exceptionally provocative causes for complaint against the Negroes, we have closed our eyes to the whole awful and menacing truth—that a large part of the white population of Lincoln's home, supported largely by the farmers and miners of the neighboring towns, have initiated a permanent warfare with the Negro race.

We do not need to be informed at great length of the character of this warfare. It is in all respects like that of the South, on which it is modeled. Its significance is threefold. First, that it has occurred in an important and historical Northern town; then, that the Negroes, constituting scarcely more than a tenth of the population, in this case could not possibly endanger the "supremacy" of the whites; and, finally, that the public opinion of the North, notwithstanding the fanatical, blind, and almost insane hatred of the Negro so clearly shown by the mob, is satisfied that there were "mitigating circumstances," not for the mob violence, which, it is agreed, should be punished to the full extent of the law, but for the race hatred, which is really the cause of it all. . . . For the underlying motive of the mob and of that large portion of Springfield's population that has long said that "something was bound to happen," and now approves of the riot and proposes to complete its purpose by using other means to drive as many as possible of the remaining two-thirds of the Negroes out of town, was confessedly to teach the Negroes their place and to warn them that too many could not obtain shelter under the favorable traditions of Lincoln's home town. I talked to many of them the day after the massacre and found no difference of opinion on the question. "Why, the niggers came to think they were as good as we are!" was the final justification offered, not once, but a dozen times. . . .

Springfield had no shame. She stood for the action of the mob. She hoped the rest of the Negroes might flee. She threatened that the movement to drive them out would continue. I do not speak of the leading citizens, but of the masses of the people, of workingmen in the shops, the storekeepers in the stores, the drivers, the men on the street, the wounded in the hospitals, and even the notorious "Joan of Arc" of the mob, Kate Howard, who had

just been released from arrest on $4,000 bail. (She has since committed suicide.—Editor.) The *Illinois State Journal* of Springfield expressed the prevailing feeling even on its editorial page:

While all good citizens deplore the consequences of this outburst of the mob spirit, many even of these consider the outburst was inevitable, at some time, from existing conditions, needing only an overt act, such as that of Thursday night, to bring it from latent existence into active operation. The implication is clear that conditions, not the populace, were to blame and that many good citizens could find no other remedy than that applied by the mob. It was not the fact of the whites' hatred toward the Negroes, but of the Negroes' own misconduct, general inferiority, or unfitness for free institutions that were at fault.

On Sunday, August 16th, the day after the second lynching, a leading white minister recommended the Southern disfranchisement scheme as a remedy for *Negro* (!) lawlessness, while all four ministers who were quoted in the press proposed swift "justice" for *the Negroes,* rather than recommending true Christianity, democracy and brotherhood to the whites.

Whites gather near the burned-out houses of Negroes during the Springfield, Illinois, race riots, August 14, 1908.

... Besides suggestions in high places of the Negro's brutality, criminality, and unfitness for the ballot we heard in lower ranks all the opinions that pervade the South—that the Negro does not need much education, that his present education even has been a mistake, that whites cannot live in the same community with Negroes except where the latter have been taught their inferiority, that lynching is the only way to teach them, etc. In fact, this went so far that we were led to suspect the existence of a Southern element in the town, and this is indeed the case. . . .

It was, in fact, only three days after the first disturbance when they fully realized that the lenient public opinion of Springfield was not the public opinion of Illinois or the North, that the rioters began to tremble. Still this did not prevent them later from insulting the militia, repeatedly firing at their outposts, and almost openly organizing a political and business boycott to drive the remaining Negroes out. Negro employers continue to receive threatening letters and are dismissing employees every day, while the stores, even the groceries, so fear to sell the Negroes goods that the state has been compelled to intervene and purchase $10,000 worth in their behalf.

The menace is that if this thing continues it will offer *automatic rewards* to the riotous elements and Negro haters in Springfield, make the reign of terror permanent there, and offer every temptation to similar white elements in other towns to imitate Springfield's example.

If the Political League succeeds in permanently driving every Negro from office, if the white laborers get the Negro laborers' jobs, if masters of Negro servants are able to keep them under the discipline of terror as I saw them doing at Springfield, if white shopkeepers and saloonkeepers get their colored rivals' trade, if the farmers of neighboring towns establish permanently their right to drive poor people out of their community, instead of offering them reasonable alms, if white miners can force their Negro fellow workers out and get their positions by closing the mines, then every community indulging in an outburst of race hatred will be assured of a great and certain financial reward, and all the lies, ignorance, and brutality on which race hatred is based will spread over the land. For the action of these dozen farming and four coal-mining communities near Springfield shows how rapidly the thing can spread. In the little town of Buffalo, fifteen miles away, for instance, they have just posted this sign in front of the interurban station:

All niggers are warned out of town by Monday, 12 A.M. sharp.

Buffalo Sharp Shooters

Part of the Springfield press, far from discouraging this new effort to drive the Negroes out, a far more serious attack on our colored brothers than the mob violence, either fails to condemn it in the only possible way, a complete denial of the whole hypocritical case against the Negro, or indirectly approves it. An evening paper printed this on the third day after the outbreak:

Negro Family Leaves City When Ordered

The first Negro family routed from Springfield by a mob was the Harvey family, residing at 1144 North Seventh Street, who were told Sunday morning to "hike," and carried out the orders yesterday afternoon. The family proved themselves obnoxious in many ways. They were the one Negro family in the block and their presence was distasteful to all other citizens in that vicinity.

The tone of this notice is that of a jubi-

A wrecked Negro-owned store in Springfield, 1908.

lant threat. As the family left town only the day after, not on account of the mob, but the standing menace, the use of the word "first" is significant.

We have not mentioned the Negro crimes which are alleged to have caused the disorders, as we are of the opinion that they could scarcely in any case have had much real connection either with the mob violence or the far more important race conflict that is still spreading geographically and growing in intensity from day to day. . . .

As we do not lay much emphasis on these or the previous crimes of Springfield Negroes, which were in no way in excess of those of the corresponding social elements of the white population, so we do not lay much stress on the frenzied, morbid violence of the mob. Mob psychology is the same everywhere. It can begin on a little thing. But Springfield had many mobs; they lasted two days and they initiated a state of affairs far worse than any of the immediate effects of their violence.

Either the spirit of the Abolitionists, of Lincoln, and of Lovejoy must be revived and we must come to treat the Negro on a plane of absolute political and social equality, or Vardaman and Tillman will soon have transferred the race war to the North.

Already Vardaman boasts "that such sad experiences as Springfield is undergoing will doubtless cause the people of the North to look with more toleration upon the methods employed by the Southern people."

The day these methods become general in the North every hope of political democracy will be dead, other weaker races and classes will be persecuted in the North as in the South, public education will undergo an eclipse, and American civilization will await either a rapid degeneration or another profounder and more revolutionary civil war, which shall obliterate not only the remains of slavery but all the other obstacles to a free democratic evolution that have grown up in its wake. Yet who realizes the seriousness of the situation, and what large and powerful body of citizens is ready to come to their aid?

Anti-Greek Rioting in Omaha

13

Black Americans were not the only victims of violence perpetrated by "native" whites. Chinese in the West had been maltreated on numerous occasions. In 1891, eleven Italians were lynched in New Orleans, and in 1899 five more met the same fate in Tallulah, Louisiana. This article from the Chicago newspaper *The Greek Star* of February 26, 1909, tells of another anti-alien outburst. [Chicago Foreign Language Press Survey, WPA Project, 1942.]

The recent bloody scenes and persecutions against the Greeks of Omaha, Nebraska, constitute an unfortunate reflection not only against our countrymen in Omaha, but also against the Greeks throughout America.

It is really disastrous to see the innocent masses of the Greek people being persecuted and violently attacked while their stores are burned to the ground.

These most unfortunate happenings began when a Greek in Omaha, by the name of John Masouridis, killed a policeman. Because of this, a huge demonstration was organized by lawyers, congressmen, city officials, and other prominent citizens, in front of the city hall. They discussed the murder under great tension; then, advised and encouraged, the enraged mob of Omaha proceeded to avenge the blood of the slain policeman by attacking and driving out all Greeks indiscriminately.

Naturally, no intelligent and coolheaded American would approve of such action, nor would he praise the barbarous acts of mob violence which were perpetrated against quiet and law-abiding Greeks. However, no sympathetic voice was raised among the Americans, with but a very few exceptions, to defend the mistreated and beaten Greeks. We doubt very much if the power of the law will be able to protect the interests of the sufferers, provide for the treatment of those who have been injured, and compensate the businessmen whose stores were ransacked and destroyed.

Whatever we Greeks say or do at this time will be in vain, because what has been done cannot be undone; nor can the voice of the weak prevail over the "rights" of the strong.

Only a few years ago, the Greeks of Chicago were looked down upon whenever some Greek violated the law, especially when some crime was committed. We ask: Were all the Greeks to blame for the acts of one or a few lawbreakers? Much intolerance, prejudice, and contempt have been directed against the Greeks of Chicago on the part of the native, older Americans, or other immigrant groups. By and large, this spirit of hatred and intolerance was not justified.

Not only the Greeks of Chicago, but those in every part of the country have protested the indiscriminate persecution of the Greeks of Omaha; first, because these attacks were unjust and brutal; and second, because this practice might spread further by arousing the American public against all the Greek immigrants in every part of the country.

Dr. Chris Petroulas, the president of the Greek community, sent a lengthy telegram to President Roosevelt in Washington, D.C., protesting the violence against the Greeks of Omaha. The following answer was received promptly:

Dr. Chris Petroulas,
President Greek Community of Chicago,
266 South Halsted Street,
Chicago, Illinois

The President has referred to me your telegram of February 22, which was addressed to him regarding the question of the ill treatment of the Greeks in South Omaha. The Greek ambassador in Omaha has taken charge of the case. Proper investigations are being made. The governor of Nebraska has given assurance that order has been restored and that the proper authorities are now in a position to enforce laws.

Robert Bacon
Secretary of State

We do not say that the guilty party, slayer Masouridis, should not be punished for this crime; but, should the American officials of Omaha permit the mob to beat innocent fellow countrymen of the murderer? Of course not. This would be in direct violation of the principles of a civilized society.

But, evidently, on this occasion as on other similar occasions, the American public has lost all respect for the Greek immigrant; so, they hate us as a people unworthy of its mission and of the glory of its ancestors. Has the American public classified us as undesirable aliens and unworthy citizens?

Our relations with the native Americans have come to a very delicate and serious pass, not only in Omaha, but in Chicago also. Therefore, we must realize that we are facing great perils. We very much fear that very soon we shall be facing more serious perils. Danger threatens us; we have noticed that, according to newspaper reports, even congressmen have begun to declare a war of extermination against us.

This phenomenon is truly discouraging because the future of our people in America is menaced.

We think it is about time that we consider our position more seriously. There is still time to save and redeem ourselves from the many dangers which are surrounding us, if we are willing to recognize our obligations to the American people which received us with gladness. We must not forget that we must prove ourselves worthy of the hospitality which the American people have extended to us. We have come here not to destroy but to build.

America, which feeds us and protects our rights and liberties, is fully justified in expecting us to repay her for her hospitality. This can be accomplished by obedience to the laws of the land and by good work, exemplary behavior, honorable relationships, and mutual esteem. In other words, the Americans demand of us that which the emigrating and colonizing Greeks of ancient times contributed to the foreign peoples with whom they traded.

Such was the nature of the repayments made to America by nearly all the other foreign nationalities in this country and that is exactly the reason why they have attained an equal political and social status with the native element.

This is how the marvelous feat of quickly adopting the American way of

Greeks outside a restaurant in New York City, about 1910.

life has been accomplished by these easily assimilated alien groups. . . .

We are proud to proclaim that there are thousands upon thousands of virtuous and honorable Greeks who are law-abiding and civilized citizens. They do honor to the Greek name, but they have not fulfilled all their obligations, because they have not cooperated for the obliteration of lawlessness and crime.

What good are our churches and drives to build up our Fatherland's naval forces when we as a people are being humiliated and discredited? It would be much better if we would turn our attention to the deplorable state of affairs here in America.

We, here in America, are the representatives of Greece, so when we are dishonored, our country too is dishonored.

So, it is about time that we mend our ways. The Greek embassy, the Greek consulates, clergy, professional men, press, and the leaders of our organizations, as well as the best elements in our communities, must band together and educate the Greeks of America from the Atlantic to the Pacific to the fact that we are in a civilized society, in a highly advanced country which is playing host to us. Our people must know that they are free to work, trade, and make great fortunes; but first of all, they must respond to the American spirit of hospitality, they must respect the law, and must lead a life which is in accord with the progress and principles of the 20th century.

Most of our fellow countrymen have learned how to conduct themselves and how to live like respectable citizens. All the useless and criminal characters in our community must be destroyed. Only then will we win the respect of the American people and only then will the persecutions among us cease.

Boston's Italians

14

No sooner had New England's native stock recovered from the Irish inundation of the 19th century than they found themselves confronted with a new set of newcomers: the southern Italians. This influx only reinforced the strong nativist sentiments of the region and infused new life into the work of the Immigration Restriction League. But not everyone in Boston spoke with foreboding. The author of this selection, Vida D. Scudder, had worked in Denison House, a settlement project in the Italian district of the city. Her experiences led her to the more optimistic conclusions stated in the article. [*Survey*, April 3, 1909: "Experiments in Fellowship: Work With Italians in Boston."]

Probably no late arrivals on our shores will play a larger part in the America of the future than the Italians. Anyone watching them must recognize their instinct for initiative, their keen curiosity about us, their eagerness to play an active part in our politics and in our social life. They are a people mentally alert, capable of enthusiasm for an abstract idea, and also bewilderingly swift in transition to cynicism and irony. For the present, they form in the cities large "self-contained" colonies, where Old World issues still seem of supreme importance, and where the only American ideas that really penetrate, apart from the valiant but inadequate work of the schools, are of the lower type. Journalism, art, music, religion, social life, are all furnished from within. But one feels that this condition is likely to be temporary. By what means and to what results the Italians are to enter our larger civic and national life, depends chiefly on us.

Our Boston Italian colony numbers 65,000 souls. With this colony, Denison House, the college settlement, has for some years known interesting relations through its Italian department. We have, to begin with, a sound organization of neighborhood work among the poorer people, mostly of the peasant class. They need all the connection with charitable agencies, all the helpful cheer of clubs, industrial classes, and social functions, which a settlement is so well qualified to give. Far more than we can offer would be necessary to meet the situation and to bring even the people of this small section adequately within reach of what welcome the city has to offer.

But suppose this done: the task of assimilation would in the deeper sense hardly have been approached. For we might not have come in contact at all with the real psychical forces that are swaying the Latin peoples among us. How many Americans do come in contact with them, one wonders? These forces work most evidently among people of a higher grade than those of whom we have been talking. We realize at Denison House the truth of the printed statements that over education of the middle classes in Italy is creating what may be called an "intellectual proletariat," driving numbers on unemployment, and sending them across the sea. We have formed relations with many persons of this type—men and women belonging to the higher trades or to the lower ranks of the professions. They have a hard time of it here, harder than those brought up to manual labor, though a surprising number of them do become absorbed into the economic structure. One longs, as in the case of their simpler countrymen, to get them away from the cities, on the fruitful land with which every Italian has an instinctive intimacy. Meantime, one perceives that they are here and that many of them will stay. Can we afford to wait for the second generation, and to leave these to find their way alone? Hardly. These great numbers of men and women, mostly young, with the best part of their lives before them, are to prove an important factor in our civic life. . . .

We find it significant to notice what these courteous, vehement people are really thinking about us. The general attitude toward American life was fairly represented by a lecture last season. The speaker, a distinguished Italian physician, chose as his theme, "The Reaction of American Life on the Italian Immigrant." What was the effect of America? Economically good, morally bad. More money, yes: better housing—though with a hit at our city tenements; the removal of many restraints; the gain, in particular, of religious liberty; training in business capacity, and practical power. On the other hand, the generation of new diseases, especially tubercular and nervous; the development of cheap social ambition, showing itself in "Americanization" of voice and dress; a lapse in courtesy; and, briefly, a general hardening and coarsening, and the supplanting of idealism by a purely materialistic attitude. Was it possible for Italians to feel any patriotic attachment toward the United States? The idea was scouted: "While their love for their own country grows lukewarm they gain no profound attachment for the new. For the love of country ceases to exist if instead of a basis in sentiment it is derived solely from material utility. Patriotism can never be felt by people driven here by the desire of greater well-being who are bound to the American people by no community of historic memories. In a country like this, where habits and traditions of so many nationalities blend, genuine patriotic sentiment yields to an opportunist and utilitarian travesty of patriotism. . . ." Was it a good plan for an Italian to be naturalized? Economically, yes, since except in some special instances it increased his practical advantages. Morally, no, since the possession of a vote meant entrance into the degrading corruption of our American politics. And so on and so on.

Surely we cannot allow this impression to endure if we can help it. We cannot accept the opinion of the lecturer that love for the United States is a ridiculous impossibility, nor can we acquiesce in the conviction that American life must always either coarsen or disappoint. How, insensibly to alter this attitude? This is the problem before us. . . .

Candidly, it is not easy to quicken loyalty to America among an immigrant people. Perhaps the best way to reach our end is to make them look forward. Let us cease sentimentalizing to them over a past that seems to them petty, or boasting over a present in which they experience at best a dubious good; let us enlist their cooperation in the achievement of the future which we all desire. If we can but flash on the eyes of the Italians that vision of the America to be which is the inspiration of the great fellowship of social workers, we shall steady and uplift them, and we may gain strong allies in our struggle for social righteousness. One longs to introduce a sacred passion to counteract the pettiness, the languid cynicism, that corrode these colonies. The dream may be utopian, yet we are dealing with the heirs of the risorgimento, with hearts that still leap at the name of Garibaldi. The Latins, call history to witness, need an ideal or they perish. High sacrifice is easier to them than tame respectability. I believe that if we can make them catch the light of that social ideal for which we strive, if we can bring them into touch with the great healthy movements of social reform in progress among us, with the campaigns against tuberculosis and child labor, with the struggle for the cleanliness and beauty of cities and for a living wage, we shall bring them effective help. This great mass of intelligent youth that so easily is slipping into captious apathy may at a touch become a menace to peace and productivity. At another touch, it might, it may, become enlisted on the side of good. The powers of salvation are positive, and faith, ardor, and purpose are the only means of routing corruption and despair.

Italy in California

15

California became a mecca for many immigrant groups after 1849. But none descended on the state in such numbers as the Italians. By 1920 they made up more than 10 percent of the population—the single largest ethnic concentration in the state. They became farmers, vine growers, fishermen, and merchants. Part of the attraction for the Italians was the similarity of California to their homeland, a theme that occupied the writer of this selection, Ernest Peixotto. [*Scribner's,* July 1910.]

Who that knows the Mediterranean country could fail to note the tie that binds the Latin lands to the hill slopes facing the channel of Santa Barbara?

The soft breeze, fanning the face like a caress, the limpid air—the *cielo sereno* dear to every Italian heart—the scent of the orange blossoms wafted from the terraces, the shimmering olives backed by dark oaks, the suave lines of the coast reaching from the headlands of Miramar and Montecito down toward the bluffs of Ventura, the lazy blue sea sending its subdued rumble to the ear, the islands floating like mirages upon its bosom evoke the noble panoramas of Camaldoli, of Positano, of Nervi, of Bordighera. Even the laborers plowing between the lemon trees chatter the liquid note of Italy's language, and toward evening when nature is still in the hush which comes with twilight, from the cottage behind our house come the soft notes of the romanzas of Posilippo sung by the gardeners and their families.

Such for a general impression. And even when you look more closely, the comparison holds. In the gardens the gorgeous hybiscus blooms along beside the agapanthus, the heliotrope, and hedges of strawberry guava; the bougainvillea transforms prosaic cottages into Sicilian villas, and row upon row of pink amaryllis balance their shapely heads along the pathways, their lilylike flowers undefiled by any leaf.

The finely drawn mountains, with infinitely broken surfaces, fold on fold along the sea, ashen in the white light of midday, rosy in the flush of evening, clothe their lower slopes with pungent thickets of southernwood and wild lilac, where canaries nest and, bluebirds, whose azure wings flash in the sunlight, and the canyon wren whose song at daybreak awakens one with a thrill of pleasure.

The choicer homes, too, affect the Latin type, and, when not frankly Spanish, are built to recall the villas of Capri or Sorrento. Such a one, for instance, is the large mansion that caps a rounded hill beyond Miramar, a veritable *castello a mare* —low, turreted, towered, blank and square facing the sea, and so well planned in ensemble that I hesitated to approach it for fear of dispelling the agreeable impression. Such another is a certain home in Montecito, a snow-white villa with grilled windows and pottery roofs, set in dark, cypress-grown gardens laid out on steep terraces, whose staircases and gleaming walls are reflected in long basins of silent water, and decorated with cacti in earthenware pots.

But southern California has often enough been called "Our Italy," and it is not so much my purpose to follow these reconstructions of Italy in California as to seek out the veritable bits of the Motherland that are to be found within its borders. For there *are* real bits of Italy in California—colonies that retain their traditions intact, living the picturesque life of the Old Country, cultivating their patches of *basilico* for the *minestra,* drying their strings of garlic on the rooftops, or mending their brown nets in the sunlight by the sea.

And besides these simple folk, one may chance to meet all sorts of interesting people in the colony (at the present writing the grandsons of two of Italy's most distinguished patriots), for California has always been a lure, a synonym for wealth, a land of gold for the Italian—a bit of his own Latin land, and an adventurer's land

too—so much so, in fact, that an unruly son who threatened to disgrace his family would often be told to "go to California" much as we would mention a rather warmer place.

The grapes were just ripening, and I had heard that up in the Napa Valley there was to be a vintage festival. Knowing how many foreigners dwell in the three valleys that form the last dimples of the northern coast range, I dreamed of some such sort of Bacchic revel as I had seen in Dalmatia, or in the Piedmontese hills.

So late one afternoon found me at St. Helena under the shadow of the mountain of the same name—known to all lovers of Stevenson as the home of the Silverado Squatters. Here a big auto was waiting and sped off in the gloaming up toward the mountains. Evening closed in, and the great eyes of the car, stronger far than the orbs of Jupiter, lit up, at each turn of the road, weird pictures succeeding each other with the bewildering rapidity of some phantasmagoria—reversing the truths of nature, as in imaginative scenery, making light objects dark and dark objects light; flattening everything in their shadeless light; disclosing now a farmhouse leaping from the darkness, now trembling aspens hung with heavy festoons of wild grapevine, bordering a Styx-like rivulet; now solitary oaks of giant size, blocking the whole horizon, their great branches soaring aloft only to fall low again in pendant boughs—then, in a moment, darkness, the stars overhead, and the white winding road.

The festival, from my point of view, was not a great success. There were, to be sure, some pretty grapepickers' costumes, and a country dance followed by a big dinner, with the first wine press of the valley used as the pièce de résistance in the decoration. Speeches were made deprecating the use of fiery liquors, but extolling the juice of the grape—and the temperate drinking of healthy wines that stimulate, but seldom inebriate.

From another point of view, however, the festival was a great success, for at it I chanced to meet one of the two men who have done more, perhaps, than any others for the cultivation of the vine in California.

A day or two later I was visiting his vineyards just over the mountain, named for the township in Piedmont that produces the most renowned of Italian sparkling wine—the Asti spumante.

Situated on one of the upper reaches of the Russian River, in a wide and comely valley, surrounded by partially wooded hills, with the tall shafts of redwoods, last remains of the northern woods, punctuating their crests from time to time, Asti recalls the foothills of the Bergamesque Alps, or the lower slopes of the Apennines.

While visiting there, I veritably passed my time in Italy, for everyone I met and everything I saw was Italian.

My host, with the true Latin courtesy, spent all his time in driving me about through miles of vineyards, each named for some township in the Motherland, and producing the various well-known Italian wines: the barolo and barbera and the chiantis, white and red.

We topped a rounded hillock, at one point in our drive, dominating the whole valley, and from it, as a general commands his field of operation, surveyed these acres upon acres of vineyards spread out in the sunshine, drawn up in regiments and brigades, climbing the hummocks and descending the other side; clothing the valleys with their battalions in close array, their vanguards even attacking the surrounding hills and, foot by foot, forcing back the natural growth of madrones and oaks to their fastness upon the hilltops.

And the vicissitudes of this twenty-eight-year campaign have been many and varying. Started with an acre of mission grapes (and a bad start too, for the strong Spanish stock has never produced fine wines), many a setback has been encountered. The dreaded phylloxera has been fought and conquered; the inroads of sheep in a night have destroyed armies of tender shoots, while clouds of locusts have accomplished similar destruction. But here, as a reward to the general for his years of effort, now lie these acres of well-grown vines, bearing their tons of grapes, here live his countrymen and their families, thriving and content. . . .

The Italian population of San Francisco has always affected the district under the shelter of Telegraph Hill. I remember when I was a boy the fascinations of Dupont Street, as it was then called, and its succession of wonder-shops where bologna sausages encased in tinfoil hung in dazzling clusters from the ceiling; where tinned eels from Commacchio and confetti in brilliant wrappers lay side by side in the showcases; where ponderous millstones rolled the dough in macaroni factories, while presses ground out yards of tortellini, lasagne, and reginnini. Today conditions are quite the same, for on this same street, now Grant Avenue, China-Bisleri and Fernet-Branca and Floria's Marsala tempt from the windows; big crescents and the hard nubs of bread that every traveler in Italy has sighed over are sold in the bakeshops; gay calicos flaunt in the doorways, and at the back of the wineshops they still press out with the feet that execrable *vin d'uva* so dear to the fisherman's heart—his own wine that he

EB Inc.

Italian fishermen bargain with Chinese fish peddlers on Fisherman's Wharf in San Francisco in the 1890s.

offers with such pride to his honored guest.

Montgomery Avenue, one of the few streets in San Francisco that consents to run at any other angle than a rectangle (how happy I should be if there were more like it), acts as a gateway to the quarter. It houses the larger industries: the steamship offices, La Veloce and the Florio Rubattino—how familiar they do sound—the Banca Populare and *La Voce del Populo,* the mouthpiece of the colony. It houses too, the most important bookstore, whose long windows are always stocked with the latest illustrated books and papers—the caustic *Asino* and *Mulo,* beside the more commonplace *Corriera della Sera,* the songs and bacaroles that one hears in Venice and Naples, beside pretty picture postcards of the Motherland; the paperbound *Storia dei Paladini*

di Francia, beside the *Cavalier di Malta* and other lurid melodramatic tales, among them *Il Processo Thaw.*

At the intersection of Broadway, the only other wide street of the quarter, you will find the principal restaurants, bona fide *trattore* like the Trovatore and the Fior d'Italia, where white-aproned waiters serve *minestra* and *fritto misto,* breaded cutlets and *zabaglione,* while a piccolo brings bottles of wine from a counter tucked under the stairs.

Near them the marionettes used to hold forth, and there I have often heard Orlando recount his fiery love, and seen the paladins of Charlemagne slay Turk and Saracen in true Sicilian fashion. Now, alas, the blatant nickelodeons and moving picture shows have drawn away the patrons, and the last expounder of the doughty deeds of Orlando Furioso is driven to make his final stand in a small Sicilian colony in the Mission.

A few blocks further up the avenue, as

it is familiarly called, and you come to Washington Square, whose rows of venerable cedars have sheltered generations of Italian children just as the elms of Washington in New York have long sheltered the Italian denizens of the Bleecker Street quarter.

Here the Italian theater thrives—a large structure, clean and up-to-date. Except upon festival nights, it is a ten-cent show, but, I assure you, a good one. If you watch the program you can have anything you like, from *Fedora* and *Camille* to *Giosue'il Guardacoste,* "an emotional drama," as the poster tells you, with its acts labeled "one who sells his honor," "twenty years after," "the portfolio and reward," and so forth; or, on other nights, if you prefer as I do, the *zarzuella* or vaudeville, combined with one-act farces. These latter are my special favorites. Modeled after the manner of Goldoni's comedies, simple, childlike in their naïveté, they are full of Italian character, and appeal strongly to the simple emotions of the fisherfolk and tradespeople in front of the footlights. To give an example: A young modiste is discovered trimming her bonnets; to her in turn appear three suitors: a decrepit but proud marquis, with monocle and rheumatic legs; then an overdressed but handsome young city chap; and finally Stentorello, the country clown, dressed after the old tradition in a sort of Watteauesque motley, with spiked wig, long velvet waistcoat, small clothes, and beribboned knees. He is fond of cracking vulgar jokes, but with all this has a certain peasant craftiness, getting the best of everybody, and finally, of course, outwitting his rivals and winning the pretty milliner.

The Italian quarter was practically wiped out by the great fire three years ago, so little of its outward picturesqueness remains. It was, however, one of the first districts to be rebuilt—thereby showing the thrift of its population, but its new buildings evince but little Italian influence, excepting in the back yards where tomatoes lie drying, or fishermen sit mending their nets, and on the rooftops, where a vast space is always reserved for lines of clothes flapping in rows like scarecrows against the clear blue sky. Its double character, half American, half Italian, may best be summed up, I think, in a sign I saw advertising apartments to rent, and concluding with the mixed information *"la chiave al* janitor in rear!"

Fisherman's Wharf still remains, however, to delight the lover of the picturesque.

In a rectangular basin, with but a single exit to the bay, lie the lateen-sailed fishing smacks, blue, green, or striped with red and yellow, with their warm brown sails shading groups of fishermen gathered round the demijohns of wine. Long lines of tawny nets hang drying along the wharves, while men in gumboots mend their broken strands, or readjust their corks and leaden weights, working, on rainy days, in a big shed nearby, whose somber interior presents great possibilities for the painter, with its Rembrandtesque effects of light disclosing the heavy nets suspended from the rafters, while dark figures in picturesque garb move about, or work in the scant patches of light. Adjoining this shed is the boatbuilder's house, full of flying chips, of bent timbers, and bits of spars and rigging. Most of the fisherfolk are Ligurians, and still count in soldi, awaiting the day when, with a tidy sum, they may return to the Old Country to settle themselves in some tiny villa in the olive groves above the sea. Many such a one have I encountered, passing his old age in the safe harbors of Sestri or Chiavari—men who have fished for years the far waters of San Francisco Bay.

But from the gaily painted house above the Ligurian Gulf they command no fairer prospect than the view surrounding Fisherman's Wharf. To the westward the dark mass of Fort Mason shades the narrow orifice of the Golden Gate shut between the bluffs of Fort Point and the Point Lobos Hills, which terminate in the volcanic silhouette of Tamalpais with Sausalito's safe haven, and its tall-masted ships lying beneath. To the eastward the pink hills of Contra Costa—the Opposite Coast—reflect the setting sun, while between spread the broad waters of the bay, flecked by the western trades, and dotted with shipping and with islands, Alcatraz, low, buttressed, grimly fortified, sailing like some grim dreadnought in the nearer distance.

Syrians in the United States

16

Oppression and persecution in the Moslem Ottoman Empire led to the partial emigration of several of its subject Christian minorities: Greeks, Armenians, and Syrians, among others. Most of the Syrians went to North Africa, India, or South America. But beginning in the 1890s several thousand came to the United States as a result of the foreign missionary efforts of the American churches. Author Louise Seymour Houghton, a former editor of *Evangelist Magazine,* investigated the Syrian immigration and reported her findings in a series of articles published in 1911. A portion of the first article is reprinted here. [*Survey,* July 1, 1911.]

The exact estimate of the Syrian population of this country must await the reports of the census of 1910. During the years 1899–1907, in which Syrians have been differentiated from other Turkish subjects, 41,404 Syrians have been admitted to the United States. Although 100,000 is the usual estimate, 70,000 is that of the best-informed Syrians.

Excluding those born in the country, the majority have come direct from Syria. Only twenty-five among the 3,708 Syrians who came in 1899 entered by the way of other countries.

Of the Syrians who entered the United States during the nine years from 1899 to 1907 (41,404), nearly one-half, or 48 percent (19,923), gave one of the six central Atlantic states as their destination, 21.3 percent (8,835), one of the six New England states, 12.15 percent (5,034), one of the six Middle states, a little less than 5 percent (2,010), one of the four Gulf states. The remaining 14 percent were divided between the five South Atlantic states (967), the four North Central states (2,055), the eight Central Western states (1,344), the six Northwestern states (348), the three Pacific states (364), and the four territories, including Puerto Rico (524). A full third of the whole number (about 33.5 percent) gave their destination as New York, many of them, doubtless, in transit.

These figures are to some extent misleading. Readjustments inevitably take place as newcomers become acquainted with the business opportunities of the country. Only one Syrian declared Alaska as his destination, but a score or more were known to be there in 1908. A much larger proportion than these figures indicate must have reached California, since its Syrian population, after careful inquiry, is estimated at about 8,000. Sixty are credited to Montana, but in the city of Butte alone, with its dependent mines, is a much larger Syrian population than this. Only one gave Nevada as his destination, but the Syrian population of that state is estimated at 700. Eleven gave South Dakota, but at least 200 are known to be in that state.

The more recent attempts at self-distribution are no doubt to be attributed to business instinct. Few instances of destructive competition are to be found among Syrian immigrants. Notwithstanding that disposition to herd in "colonies," which is natural to all immigrants, it is certain that the business success of any Syrian is by no means sure to attract others to the same place. In Ottawa, Ill., for example, a Syrian woman carries on a high-class candy kitchen. She has been there for fifteen years and has been very successful, yet without drawing another Syrian to that city. A single Syrian had been in Holyoke fifteen years, had won a respectable place in that community and married an American wife, before another Syrian settled there.

When once fully settled, Syrians appear to be stationary. Very few, for example, have left Springfield, Mass., or (with exceptions to be later noted) Troy. This might simply mean lack of means to go further, but the facts show the contrary. Nearly all the Syrians in Troy went directly there on landing. All began in bitter poverty, having borrowed money to come, and all have achieved at least so much success as is seen by the general possession of a bank account. Some who have been eminently successful have changed their state through the requirements of business. A prosperous owner of mines in Montana and Colorado, a large employer of Syrian and American labor,

A Syrian woman at Ellis Island, New York, about 1905.

has been in this country since 1882, but in Montana only about ten years. He had previously lived in Missouri and Colorado. . . .

In New York there are three Syrian colonies, and it is unfortunate that the least prepossessing of these is the most obvious—situated as it is along the waterfront near the principal ferries and steamboat landings—since it naturally fixes the general estimate in which Syrians are held by Americans. Within the limits of this colony have occurred these feuds and frays which have given the Syrians a bad name, and concerning which something will later be said. Yet the colony shows much which is creditable to the people as a whole; a number of prosperous factories, several importing houses, the one Syrian banking house, and a fine business block owned by Syrian bankers. These who own and conduct these enterprises do not, however, reside in the colony. Only those live here who must be near their place of employment, and those newly arrived; and the excessively high rents and generally wretched buildings of this district force them to live under unusually crowded and squalid conditions.

The other two New York colonies, both in the borough of Brooklyn, are superior to most immigrant colonies, of whatever people, in any part of the United States. That near Brooklyn Heights is both a residence and an industrial colony, though the embroidery and kimono factories, which are the principal business, are fast being removed to Jersey City, Hoboken, and elsewhere. The third, or South Brooklyn colony, is purely a residence district of well-to-do Syrians doing business in New York, and is eminently respectable. A small number of wealthy Syrians are scattered through Manhattan.

In Chicago there are also three colonies, resembling those of New York in gradation of living though not in size. The poorest is housed in an uncomfortable region near the railroad tracks, evidently chosen from considerations of rent. This was formerly one of the most disreputable quarters of the city, and it still has that reputation among those who are ignorant that the entrance of Syrians, killing off the saloon trade, has driven away the disreputable inhabitants. The other colonies, like those of New York, are of better standing in proportion as they are farther from the center.

In Philadelphia, a number of excellent Syrian families live in the best American neighborhoods, but there is a colony which is relatively ill-housed and too crowded. Its conditions are much better than those of the Manhattan colony in New York, but by no means equal to those of the lake and Northwestern cities. In certain respects they resemble the comparatively inferior colonies of Albany and St. Louis.

There is no Syrian colony in Baltimore, and though it is a port of entry, few Syrians could be found there. In Washington there are a few highly respectable Syrians, but nothing in the nature of a colony.

In Boston, the comparatively large Syrian population, 3,000, the second largest group in this country, is found to be "more clannish than any other immigrants, except Jews," living almost exclusively in colonies scattered in various parts of the city. It is an interesting question how far this excessive clannishness may be a natural reaction from New England reserve, and how far it may be due to the unquestionable fact that even the best Boston people, with a few notable exceptions, appear to be unable to appreciate certain characteristics of the Syrian nature and temperament which differ from their own standards.

In Lawrence, Mass., where the proportion of Syrians is greatest, the majority of them are gathered in two colonies. Several, however, own and carry on farms in the suburbs. In Providence the majority live in a colony, though there are a number of prosperous Syrians living among and much after the manner of Americans.

The Syrians of Worcester live in one colony, those of Springfield also; the latter keep so entirely to themselves that their existence is hardly known. There is in Holyoke a colony of some twenty single men, who go every morning to Springfield to work.

The majority of the 2,000 Syrians in Connecticut live in Danbury, Waterbury, New Haven, Norwich, and New London. In these five cities there are colonies, but a considerable number are scattered through the population, living rather among the Americans than among other foreigners.

With the exception of the Manhattan colony in New York, the Albany colony is the poorest and least Americanized until we reach St. Louis. Yet even the poorest Syrian home in Albany is cleaner and better than those of the Italians among whom they live, and some, even here, are fairly prosperous. Three rooms appears to be the smallest apartment, though some take boarders. And the rooms are large, in some cases even spacious, for these Syrians and Italians have taken possession of a once fashionable quarter along the riverside, whose former inhabitants, removing from the district, left their spacious homes behind.

Syrians in the lake cities are comparatively prosperous and generally respected. In Buffalo most of them live in a colony occupying two blocks pretty near the outskirts, and with a sufficient amount of room. Their places of business are scattered throughout the city, and some few, notably the family of a wealthy rug importer, educated and of polished manners, live in the best part of the city, and in a style which differs from that of their American neighbors only by greater simplicity and more luxury. From the point of view of the Cleveland Charities its two Syrian colonies are badly housed, though the worst Syrian home in that city compares favorably with the tenement homes of many Americans in New York. One Cleveland colony inhabits pretty poor tenements on a wide, clean street, with no such crowding as prevails in all New York tenement districts. The other seemed particularly interesting though affording ample room for improvements. It consists for the most part of a row of detached, two-room cottages in a marvelously ill-kept street, badly paved, and with sidewalks which are mere foot paths. The tiny dooryards with their ragged greenery are still breathing places and places to sit on a summer evening. A number of families of this colony live in a group of two-story buildings, which in a Parisian suburb might almost be called a villa, or in the north of France a *courelle*, built around and opening upon an irregular central court, paved, and reached from the street by a narrow alley. The grouping nearly resembles what one constantly sees in Syrian villages, the haphazard shape of the court lending itself to the illusion.

To Toledo, where Syrians are exceptionally prosperous and respected, no poor have come in late years. Nearly all the newcomers were brought by friends who had prospered here; they sold their home property, brought the proceeds with them, and began well from the start. To a certain degree this is the case in other lake cities, and in various Syrian communities in the Northwest. No Syrians in Toledo live in tenement houses; a few occupy four- or five-family houses, but nearly all are separately housed.

The Cincinnati and Pittsburgh colonies are inferior economically to any in the lake cities, although the Organized Charities report "no poor Syrians in Cincinnati." In both these cities rents are high, in Pittsburgh inordinately so, with the inevitable result of bad housing. Instances were found in Pittsburgh (and only there) of a newly arrived family hiring a single room, hanging a curtain across the middle, and keeping store in the front half. It is only just to say that in these cases the family was small, and the children, if any, were infants. A few years or even months will find their condition bettered, with a corresponding improvement in housing. There is an interesting though quite shocking "House of all Nations" in Pittsburgh, a huge tenement inhabited mainly, but not exclusively, by Armenians and Syrians. The men (not the women) go out peddling all the week, sleeping out in the bush, as traveling Syrians often do at home, and returning on Saturday night.

St. Louis is an exception to the almost invariable rule that living conditions improve as we go westward. The Syrians of St. Louis seem to be poorer than most of their race in this country. They live among other immigrants in two colonies, Protestants in one, Maronites in the other, the separation having taken place only a few years ago as a result of religious jealousies. Contrary to the usual experience, the Protestant is the poorer and less aggressive community; the anomaly is all the more striking because the Protestant church nearest this community has shown far greater and more sympathetic interest in its Syrian neighbors than is usual anywhere in this country.

The colonies of the Northwestern cities are young, as is shown by the paucity of school children. In the seventy-five Syrian homes in Minneapolis there are only twelve young children, with a few old enough to work; the other households are for the most part newly formed. There is no true Syrian colony; they live in small groups, mainly but not entirely in one section, and scattered among Americans. Nearly all have separate houses and cultivate flowers in their yards. Nor is there a colony in Duluth. The Syrians of that city are few, but superior, all young except one—the father of several sons, young heads of families—and all give good promise. On the whole this little group of Syrians gives perhaps the best example of

the contribution which American civilization may hope for from Syrian immigration.

In St. Paul there are two colonies; one in an undesirable region near railroad tracks and freight yards, and subject to inundation, where the standard of living is low; the other not far distant, but on high land where picturesque rocks towering above are, no doubt, a grateful reminder of the homeland. These have ample room, their houses are very clean, some of them with good gardens, and the style of living is good, though with Syrian peculiarities. The Syrians west of Duluth have not been personally studied, but correspondence shows little, if any, colony life—Syrians living among Americans rather than among other immigrants, though also among the latter to some extent.

As one goes southward one finds, with some exceptions, the proportion of those living in colonies diminishing, until in New Orleans and in California we find no Syrian colonies. The fact that in New Orleans there are only 200 Syrians after twenty years of residence, this being also a port of entry, seems to show that this immigration is discouraged there. It may possibly show that, as in Shreveport as is mentioned below, the earlier Syrian immigrants have become entirely assimilated. This seems to be the more possible since there appear to be no Syrian school children, but only grown persons. The excessively high rents, two or three times as high as in New York, in part accounts for these conditions. Only the well-to-do remain in the city, the newcomers and unsuccessful ones push out to more favorable regions. In Shreveport, La., there is a considerable number of Syrians, respected, and an integral part of the community.

Troy and Pittsburgh are examples of an interesting development of colony life. They are centers of congeries of Syrians which are breaking off in little branches, like swarming bees, to establish themselves in neighboring or more distant towns. This is in part due to their instinctive recognition of "what the traffic will bear," and in part to the fact that Syrians are beginning to see the social, as well as the financial, value of scattering. Such groups are now found in Cohoes and other villages surrounding Troy, and in a very large number of small towns in western Pennsylvania. When they reach the limit of profit they "swarm" again, thus being acted upon by their surroundings, as cannot be the case in colony life.

Without doubt the most interesting and hopeful Syrian colonies in this country are the farm colonies of the Northwest. They are found in Iowa, Kansas, Oklahoma, North and South Dakota, Montana, Wyoming, and Washington, but the greatest number is in North Dakota. In the neighborhood of Williston, N.D., there are about 100 Syrian farmers, all homesteaders. Though with some exceptions, the majority of Syrian farmers are successful. Some of these farmers are educated men, a few are graduates of the excellent American college in Beirut, the Syrian Protestant College. At least one farmer's wife was a school teacher in Syria, and a number of the women have had school privileges. Some of these farmers started with a fair capital (by which they appear to mean $600 or thereabouts), either the proceeds of the sale of property in Syria, or more commonly, money earned in this country by some other employment, peddling or farm labor. Others had little or no capital, and these secured loans upon their homesteads. The majority, by hard work and rigid economy, have

managed to pay off these loans, but some have been unable to meet their obligations, and their homesteads have gone into the hands of the loan companies and have been sold, the buyers frequently being Syrian businessmen of the Northwestern cities. One prosperous Syrian merchant of St. Paul has thus come into the possession of more than 800 acres in scattered quarter sections not far from Rugby, N.D., a part of which he rents on shares to a Syrian, and the other parts to Russians and a Norwegian.

The history of the Rugby colony needs to be cleared up. In 1907, correspondence showed it to be one of the most flourishing farm colonies of Syrians in the state. As this study is completed, a letter from an American clergyman of the neighborhood says that the Syrians there have all sold their farms and moved farther west. The reason of the exodus is unknown to this informant, who expresses a highly favorable opinion of Syrians as he has known them.

An intelligent Syrian of North Dakota is of the opinion that there are 2,000 Syrian farmers in the state, but this is surely an overestimate. Eight hundred would perhaps be nearer the mark; and fewer than half their farms are now mortgaged. The length of time before a homestead becomes self-supporting is variously estimated from two years, with ample capital, to four or five, when the capital is small.

Not all Syrian farmers, however, are in the Northwest. Seven farms in the environs of Lawrence, Mass., most of them comparatively prosperous, are operated by Syrians. The products are chiefly dairy products and cattle. One of these farmers has a reputation for his Syrian cheeses. Elsewhere in New England Syrian farmers are scattered. In the neighborhood of

Detroit and other parts of Michigan a number of Syrian farmers raise vegetables and sell dairy products. Syrians are oper- ating truck farms in various parts of New Jersey, raising vegetables for the Syrian restaurants in New York.

European Immigrants to Hawaii

17

The crossroads of the Pacific, the Hawaiian Islands, were strategically located to attract immigrants from North America as well as all parts of the Far East. But the source of immigrants extended beyond even this vast area, as the report reprinted here shows. Hawaii was a favorite destination of Portuguese immigrants. Although most Portuguese did go to the mainland, either to New England or California, several thousand settled in the islands. The policy of the territory at the time was to attract newcomers from other than Oriental countries, as is suggested by the report. [*First Report of the Board of Immigration, Labor and Statistics to the Governor of the Territory of Hawaii.* Honolulu, 1912. Pages 7–11.]

The earlier work in connection with European immigration, conducted by what was known as the Board of Immigration, is fully dealt with in the three reports made by that body, the last of which covered the operations of the board up to December 31, 1910. At that time Mr. A. J. Campbell, the then European agent of the board, was engaged in negotiations looking to the charter of a suitable vessel to bring a shipment of Spanish and Portuguese immigrants to Hawaii. On January 12, 1911, that gentleman advised the board that he had chartered the steamship *Orteric,* and this vessel arrived at Honolulu on April 13, 1911, landing some 1,451 people, comprised of 547 men, 373 women, and 531 children. These people appeared to be of a good class and were distributed generally throughout the territory, most of them engaging in agricultural work in connection with the various plantations.

The prospects for being able to obtain another shipment of people at an early date not being considered favorable by Mr. Campbell, he returned to Hawaii early in the month of June. There being, however, a steady demand for people suitable for agricultural work, and the general sentiment being in favor of the continued introduction of persons eligible and likely to become citizens, the board continued negotiations in London, through reliable agents, for the chartering of another vessel to bring a further supply of people to the territory, and on the 18th of July the steamship *Willesden* was obtained for this purpose. Mr. Campbell left Honolulu to resume the work in Europe on the 19th of July, and as a result of his activities the *Willesden* arrived at Honolulu on December 3, landing 1,797 persons, comprised of 639 men, 400 women, and 758 children.

A third shipment of Spanish and Portuguese arrived in Hawaii by the steamship *Harpalion,* also a specially chartered vessel, which in the month of April 1912, landed some 1,450 people, comprised of 496 men, 328 women, and 626 children.

The cost of immigrants brought by the *Orteric* was $112,341.59, an average cost per male of $205.37, and a per capita of $77.42. The cost of immigrants brought by the *Willesden* was $109,307.97, an average cost of $171.06 per male and a per capita of $60.82. The cost of the immigrants brought by the *Harpalion* was $117,926.13, an average cost per male of

Like the North American Indians, the Polynesian people who inhabited the Hawaiian Islands before the coming of the white man had a rich and colorful culture of their own. The islands were discovered in 1778 by an English sea captain, James Cook, who named them the Sandwich Islands after his patron, the earl of Sandwich. The following period of contact with pre missionary whites was one of political consolidation and religious disintegration. These two watercolors were done by a Russian visitor, Louis Choris, about 1817, when the island culture was feeling the influence of the West more and more. (Above) "The Port of Honolulu" shows native huts lining the ship-filled harbor. (Below) "The Interior of a Chief's House, Sandwich Islands."

(Left) King Kamehameha I, often called Hawaii's greatest king. In 1810 he brought all the islands under his rule and organized a system of government. He stopped a Russian plan to take over his kingdom in 1815–1816 and eliminated Spanish pirates in 1818. (Below) "Sandwich Island Hula Dancers" by Choris, about 1817. In 1819 a royal decree ordered the Hawaiians to give up their native religion, and in 1820 the arrival of Congregationalist missionaries from New England began a new era. By the beginning of the 20th century traditional Hawaiian culture was mainly a tourist attraction. (On facing page, top) Tourists near Waikiki in 1903. (Bottom) A hula dancer in 1919.

$237.75 and a per capita of $81.32. The total cost of the immigrants brought by these three vessels was $339,575.69, an average expense of $72.28 per individual, or $201.88 per adult male. These three vessels brought to Hawaii 1,682 men, 1,101 women, and 1,915 children, a total addition to the population of 4,698 persons, from which number, however, must be deducted twenty immigrants who were returned to their homes by the board for various reasons.

The people arriving by the *Orteric, Willesden,* and *Harpalion* unfortunately had to undergo a period of quarantine lasting from three to six weeks, notwithstanding the fact that all of them were subjected to a close physical examination before their embarkation, with a view of minimizing the risk of contagious diseases among them. The care taken in this respect, however, did not prevent sickness from developing among them during the voyage, which resulted in considerable additional expense to the board on their account upon arrival in Hawaii.

The *Harpalion* was also unfortunate in not obtaining a full complement of people. Advice at the time of the chartering of this vessel led the board, as well as its agents in Europe, to suppose that a full load would be procured, but at the time of the vessel's readiness to embark her passengers it was found that a considerable number less than those anticipated would be available. This shortage was caused chiefly by floods in the country districts and resulting difficulties of transportation, as well as other causes, attributable to the work of agitators in the villages from which they were expected to come.

From personal observation by the commissioner, and judging by reports received by the department from the various districts throughout the territory where they are engaged, these immigrants seem to be satisfactory and appear generally contented with conditions as they find them in Hawaii.

After some preliminary correspondence touching upon Russian immigration to Hawaii generally, the board during the month of July 1911, entered into an agreement with the International Immigration and Colonization Association for the introduction of small parties of Russian immigrants to Hawaii, and this agreement, with some subsequent modifications, was in existence, and people were brought to the territory under its terms and provisions, up to and until the 19th of April of the present year, when the association was notified of the unwillingness of the board to continue its work in Manchuria through the means of the agreement with it, but that it would assume responsibility for the then remaining people at Dalny and Kobe, as the case might be, who had arrived at those places with the intention of migrating to Hawaii through the representations made to them by agents of the association at Dalny, Manchuria. Under these circumstances the work of the board in connection with the introduction of Russians to Hawaii has been, for a time, suspended.

Shortly after the decision of the board that it would no longer operate in this quarter through the medium of the International Immigration and Colonization Association, the commissioner was dispatched to Manchuria for the purpose, primarily, of settling any outstanding matters in connection with the agreement in question for which the board might be liable, and also to make an investigation of that field with a view of ascertaining what the prospects were for a continuance of Russian immigration under the direct auspices of the department. After the departure of Mr. Clark on this mission, it was represented to the board that considerable dissatisfaction with the Russians as agricultural laborers existed in certain quarters, and that as long as people of Spanish and Portuguese nationality, of the same class as those hitherto introduced to Hawaii, could be procured, it might not be expedient to continue at this time the work of Russian immigration. The board had several meetings in regard to this question, at which lengthy and careful discussion of the subject from all points was had. A circular letter to managers of all plantations in the territory, as well as to other employers of this class of labor, was issued by the department, at the direction of the board, and while in some cases the replies received indicated a sentiment adverse to Russians as agricultural workers, there were a number of answers sufficiently favorable, in the estimation of the board, to warrant further efforts being made to introduce from Russia small parties of people accustomed to agricultural pursuits. With this feeling in the minds of the members of the board the commissioner was instructed to proceed to Russia for the purpose of making an exhaustive investigation of conditions existing in that country among people reared to farm work, with a view of, if possible, making arrangements for bringing a small party of such persons to Hawaii. The instructions of the board to Mr. Clark were explicit as to the class of people desired, and it is sincerely hoped that as a result of his mission a source of supply may be found from which people suited to conditions in the territory may be obtained.

It is expected that considerable time will be required for the proper prosecution of the work with which Mr. Clark has been entrusted, as it is the desire of the board to be fully and reliably informed of the people residing in the country districts of Russia proper before any further steps are taken for the continued regular introduction of Russian immigrants to Hawaii.

The number of Russians brought to the territory under this last operation of the board, i.e., since July 1911, is 266, and the cost to the government has been $16,055.10, representing an average cost per male of $140.83 and a per capita of $60.35. The total number of Russians introduced, since the commencement of this work in the year 1909 to date, is 2,056, comprised of 1,038 men, 457 women, and 561 children, and the cost of this immigration is $177,963.16, an average cost per male of $171.44 and a per capita of $86.55. It is estimated that of this total of 2,056 there now remain in the territory some 1,085, most of whom, however, are engaged upon general work throughout the country other than that supplied or offered by the plantations; and in many instances the reports of these people are gratifying. There are among their number skilled mechanics, carpenters, and laborers, nearly all of whom are now engaged in steady employment of one kind and another, thus tending to bring about the much desired increase in number of those capable of becoming citizens of the United States.

Fur Trader Among the Eskimos
Clarence Teien

18

Clarence Teien, a second-generation Norwegian-American, was born at Robbin, Minnesota, in 1895. In 1906 his family moved to Poulsbo, Washington. At the age of seventeen he took a job as a cook on the ship *Anna-Olga,* on the trading expedition he described in the narrative reprinted here. He returned from his trip in July 1914. [*Norwegian-American Studies,* Vol. 21, 1962: "The Teien Narratives," edited by Sverre Arestad.]

On the 15th day of June, 1912, all members of the crew appeared before the U.S. Commissioner of Shipping in Seattle, and the ship's papers were signed with Mr. Steen as master, John Erland as mate, John Sundblad as engineer, a Mr. Wagoner as pilot, and I, Clarence Teien, as cook.

The following day we cast off for what was believed to be the Big Adventure. The first serious trouble developed in Sey-

mour Narrows, the entrance to the Inside Passage. That evening, Erland gave Sundblad and me alarming news: Erland had checked the courses Wagoner had charted and had discovered that he was a fraud. Wagoner had shipped on as an experienced pilot of the Inside Passage on the recommendation of Mr. Steen. When questioned, Wagoner admitted having no experience as a pilot. He also admitted he did not own the price of a passage to Nome and, while he and Steen had been drinking together, the latter had prom-

An Alaskan Eskimo woman sits before her hut made of sod covered with animal skins, 1899.

Library of Congress

ised the passage. Erland was then given the responsibility of navigating the vessel over the Gulf of Alaska from the northern tip of Vancouver Island to Unimak Pass and thence to the Mackenzie delta.

Everything went well on our trip north in spite of Steen and Wagoner. The weather was good and continued so until we reached the Nome roadstead, twenty-eight days out of Seattle. Everyone would have enjoyed going ashore in the dory that we had signaled to take Steen and our greasy and bleary-eyed Wagoner off the boat—but taking leave of Wagoner was without regret.

When Steen finally returned, he was in a drunken stupor. So as to favorably impress the two men who had rowed him out he commenced to give orders and commands to get the engine started and to haul in the anchor. He wanted to imply that he was a great captain and we were but the dumb crew, and that he knew how to make us jump through the rings, as it were. To humor him, Erland and I tugged away at the anchor, and Steen with a triumphant gleam in his eye said, "We will show them how it is done on a real ship"—and commenced to sing a sea chantey in rhythm with our work at the winch. Steen was befogged and unsteady and he almost fell overboard as the boat rolled, but I grabbed him and Erland and I were able to get him to his quarters. He then changed into dry clothing and retired to his bunk with his whisky, where he remained in a stupor until we reached Teller.

At Teller, we saw our first Eskimos and they were busy harvesting fish. Upon leaving, the weather had turned disagreeably chilly and squally. We sighted the first iceberg in the vicinity of Point Hope. We anchored there in hopes of getting some information about the ice pack at

Point Barrow. As we dropped anchor, a kayak came alongside. It was Little Joe, a white who had been mate on one of the whalers. I believe he was English, but I never did find out his name nor his origin. He had married an Eskimo and had gone "native." He must have been sixty-five years of age, but was spry as a sparrow and chattered constantly. He was happy and apparently had not a care in the world. He informed us that some natives had recently arrived from up the coast, and that we would not be able to get any farther until the ice pack began breaking up and had moved. He offered to pilot us into a small cove for better and safer anchorage. . . .

Vilhjalmur Stefansson was at Point Barrow when we arrived. He was the first white man to see and live with the Copper Eskimos, referred to as the blonde Eskimos, on Victoria Island. All were agreed it would be a remarkable opportunity to bring our entire cargo of trading goods into such virgin territory, as it was a mere 600 miles north and east of the Mackenzie delta where we intended to go. But when Stefansson explained a few of the risks, dangers, and problems that would be encountered, our enthusiasm waned. He traveled by dog team and lived under native conditions, but to bring in a boat through practically uncharted waters was not to be considered. If we were to get into the moving ice pack there was the chance of our being crushed like an eggshell, and even if that did not happen we risked being frozen in and getting a two-to-three-year free ride around the North Pole. . . .

I could not help thinking of the different circumstances under which the Eskimos lived. Twenty Eskimo families made their permanent homes here. They lived in one-room sod houses, and during the

Christian Eskimos at a wedding in 1906. Living in a remote region with an extreme climate, most Eskimos were not affected by white culture until the end of the 1800s.

summer were busily engaged getting seal for its blubber and setting gill nets for their daily requirements of fish. Any extra fish was split and hung up to dry, later to be used for dog food. Some stored fresh meat and fish in cellars, and as only a few inches of topsoil ever thaws, these were practically equal to modern cold-storage plants.

Steen's Eskimo wife and four youngsters had recently arrived with her brother, and we were invited to dinner consisting of boiled salmon trout, tea, and home-baked bread, which was really a treat. Steen's wife had for a season attended the Indian Training School at Fort McPherson, so she had something of white men's ways. We knew little of the Eskimo language or of the more common lingo, which is a corruption of Eskimo, Portuguese, English, gestures, and grimaces. Steen was interpreter. Whether or not he

was talking about us we never knew for she just remained squatted on the floor chuckling, grinning, and replying in monosyllables.

The following day, Steen's family and equipment, consisting of bedding, a Sibley stove, and a few pots and pans, were brought on deck, and we headed for Shingle Point where Steen was to maintain his headquarters. It was a bare, desolate-looking sandspit with a high bluff facing the Arctic Ocean, but there was an ample supply of driftwood as well as a neglected log cabin in need of caulking and sodding. In fact, this was a cabin constructed by Roald Amundsen, following his successful trip through the Northwest Passage. Within a few days we had the Steen family comfortably established with plenty of cut and stacked wood. We had also built a cache, which was a platform on poles about seven feet high on which the bulky trade goods were stored and covered with canvas.

Steen had hired a husky Eskimo to pilot us on our way up the Mackenzie River to our destination. The pilot's equipment was a whaleboat in which he put all his earthly possessions of dogs, tents, traps, clothing, squaw, two daughters aged eight and ten, and an old, gray-haired grandmother. At first, we did not know if we could trust him, but our suspicions proved groundless and we found him thoroughly honest and upright. The *Anna-Olga,* considerably lightened by unloading the stores for Steen's camp, followed confidently.

For seventy-five miles up the river there was no timber except for a mass of impenetrable willows. When finally the timber line was reached, we found it was really a beautiful country with a range of snow-covered mountains to our right. We had for the time no fixed destination—it was merely a matter of deciding and choosing where to make our headquarters. Soon a bluff loomed ahead with the advantage of high ground in the event of high flood waters. The main branch of the river divided here, at Halkat Island. This proved to be a first-class choice for our camp. . . .

All in all, our new house was very comfortable. After a few shelves were up on which to display our trade goods of flour, gum, tea, sugar, canvas, calico, traps, rifles, powder, lead, and shot for self-loading, tobacco, beans, and rice, our native pilot decided to make his winter headquarters next door to us. So, a lean-to was built alongside our cabin. Caribou skins, with the fur up, were put on the bare ground. The ceiling was too low to allow anyone to stand upright. It did not seem possible that anyone could get along in such restricted quarters. The only way to get around was to crawl. But there was a family of five literally packed in with odors of seal oil, cooking fish, and human bodies. Our social calls were usually of short duration.

The days were getting noticeably shorter and the north country was freezing up. Several hours a day, three days a week, John and I spent with a crosscut saw felling pine trees, and cutting these into heater lengths. For our cookstove we located dry logs that had drifted down the river. On a crudely made sled we hauled these to the cabin. These excursions helped keep us in good physical condition. Besides, John and I maintained separate trap lines. Mine were exclusively for mink whereas John's were for mink, lynx, and red fox. The round trip over my line was made three times a week on skis, and covered about ten miles. Our outdoor wearing apparel was a muskrat parka, a pair of caribou pants, a pair of caribou socks, and a pair of fur gloves—all with the fur turned inward. This might seem a heavy, cumbersome outfit. On the contrary, it was comfortable and permitted freedom in walking and running, and kept one warm no matter how cold it might get.

The business of trading with the natives entered its first phase by our visiting them and serving them strong tea. They would coach us in pronouncing certain words and phrases, or they would tell us about recent experiences, or of happenings long, long ago. The buying or trading was permitted to seem incidental. The denomination "one" referred to "one skin" and represented fifty cents; trading for one mink, eight skins were represented— or $4.00; one forty-nine-pound sack of flour cost twenty-five skins, or $12.50. The standard price on ordinary staples was more or less set by the Hudson's Bay Company. The Eskimos seemed to be able to calculate how much they had coming as fast as we could. We treated them honestly and took no unfair advantage of them. This they realized and appreciated. It was the policy of some traders to give them the short end of the deal.

About May 1, 1913, John and I began expeditions to bring into camp as many muskrats as we could trap, shoot, or run down on the open ice. The latter we accomplished by using a club with which to whack them before they could beat us to a hole in the ice. The days were getting longer, and the sun was really warming things up. As there was a chain of lakes with many muskrats, we were on the run most of the time. We headed for camp as soon as we had a load. John was the official skinner. On a good day we would bring in a hundred "rats." We continued to bring muskrats to camp for three weeks, when the ice commenced to get mushy and unsafe. The muskrat population was pretty well reduced by then. . . .

Our fur trading was now finished. We packed the furs in three canvas bags along with a few personal belongings and set out for Shingle Point to put the *Anna-Olga* in shape. The boat was painted and a few repairs made to the shaft and the propeller, which had been damaged. With these things accomplished, we were ready to leave.

The Serbo-Croats of Manhattan

19

The Balkans, home of the Serbo-Croatians, were long the powder keg of Europe, the fuse of which was lit in August 1914. These small states were mostly under the rule of Austria-Hungary or Turkey, with the exception of independent Serbia and Montenegro. Political turbulence and misrule were leading factors in bringing Balkan immigrants to America, but many of them returned to their homelands when war promised liberation. The following study of America's Serbo-Croatians was made by Marie Sabsovich Orenstein for the Bureau of Social Research of the New York School of Philanthropy. [*Survey,* December 7, 1912.]

This Serbo-Croatian colony in New York is situated along Eleventh Avenue from 34th to 48th streets and on the adjacent cross streets between Tenth and Eleventh avenues. It is largely concentrated on Eleventh Avenue, where from 40th to 46th Street every tenement house has one or more of these tenants. Most of the Serbo-Croatian business establishments are to be found here, and along the waterfront the men find work. As early as 1888, a small number of Serbo-Croats were living on the fringe of the district, West 59th, 60th, and 33rd streets. As the colony grew, it gravitated from both ends toward 42nd Street. From 1904 to 1906 it grew by leaps and bounds, fed by immigrants who crowded into the country in response to the opportunities offered by the era of prosperity. The colony had reached its largest dimensions when the crash of 1907 precipitated a large exodus.

Since our group of Serbo-Croats is one which is contributing its quota to the victorious armies [in the Balkan Wars of 1912–1913], current interest is lent to their relation to the life about them here in the New World, and to the struggle in the Old against Mohammedan misrule on the one hand, and on the other the lust for territory among the great powers.

Perhaps no chapter in the recent history of Austria-Hungary more clearly epitomizes her policy toward the Slavic-Balkan states than that which recites the events leading to the annexation of Bosnia-Herzegovina. Desiring to detach this province from Serbia, of which kingdom it had for centuries been a part, the empire sought to secure the aid of Croatia by promising to her the annexation of the coveted territory. Four years of struggle and bloodshed followed. The attitude of many Croats toward this dark period of civil strife is expressed in the words of an immigrant who said, "My reason for coming to America was the fight over Bosnia-Herzegovina. How could I, a Slav, shoot a Serbian? We are one people, though now our religions are different. At one time we were all of the *Stara Vera* (old faith, Greek Orthodox). To shoot a Schwab (a scornful nickname for Austrians) is another story. They are our enemies, strangers to our blood; how can we side with them!"...

Children or women were scarcely more than incidental factors in the community life studied. In the early days practically the whole population was composed of men. Not over ten families would have been found fifteen years ago. The entire settlement lived in household groups managed by hired male cooks. But with the increased immigration of 1904 women and children began to come. Yet even now the old residents who place the Serbo-Croatian population of the district at 2,500 or 3,000 put the number of families among them at from 150 to 200. Of the households studied 573 individuals, or 85 percent, were nonfamily men. Only 25 percent of the men were married; less than 10 percent were living with their families, the remainder having left their wives and children in Europe.

The early age at which single men arrive and the scarcity of their countrywomen, the fact that they have come primarily to save money, return to Europe, and there marry, economic stress, and the difficulty of supporting a family in this country are the reasons they do not marry here.

Of the entire group 473, or 82.5 percent, come here between the ages of seventeen and forty-five, when they are of greatest productive and economic value to us. And it was the economic motive which in the answers received from 560 of the 573 men was the predominant one in causing them to emigrate. One man out of ten, to be sure, said he wanted to escape military service, but in half of these cases the desire "to earn" was also given.

The complete absence of political oppression as a cause of emigration among this group of men is not to be inferred from the fact that (except for the cases in which avoidance of military service was mentioned) its rate was not explicitly stated. Exorbitant taxes everywhere play a special part in making the lot of the agriculturist hard, vying with natural difficulties, such as a sterile soil, fluctuation and instability of crops, and the ravages of phylloxera among the vineyards. Still it is of interest to note that in no case, so far as the writer can recall, was it said that actual hunger or political oppression had threatened the life of a man and driven him to our shores.

Stalwart, powerfully built without being heavy, these men mature early. I saw a boy of thirteen who was as full grown as the average American youth of eighteen years. Of exceptional height were those from Dalmatia, Bosnia, and Herzegovina. "They are among the tallest men of Europe, and not only tall but sturdy and markedly fine in carriage."

Endowed though they are with rugged strength, a few years in America brings unmistakable signs of exhausting, strenuous labor and unsanitary housing. Often did I see men with lined, tired faces, bankrupts in health. Especially true was it of those who worked at night, for they could not be thoroughly rested by sleeping during the day. "I am always tired when I go to bed and when I get up," complained one tall, wan man. They, as well as others of us, are deeply impressed with the American employer's indifference to the health of his employees.

These Serbo-Croats have native intelligence and shrewdness, though little education. Recruited mainly from the peasantry, they are solid rather than stolid. "The Serb, though tenacious of purpose, is not dogged. The surface of his resolutions appears to rise and subside, but the depths are changeless."

These people are liberal borrowers, and because honor has been deeply inbred in them a man feels it incumbent upon himself to make good not only his own, but his father's or brother's debt. It is quite a wonted occurrence for a "greenhorn" to be housed and helped with money by relatives or friends, for as soon as he gets a job he repays them.

Sharing the generic characteristic of all Slavs, credulity lurks somewhere in them, but their long subjection to other rulers than their own has taught them suspicion of outsiders. This distrustfulness they extend to Americans, at whose hands they have, for the most part, suffered exploitation and deceit. When once their confidence is gained, however, they unbend and their hospitality is most liberal and charming. It was in rare instances that in the course of my investigations I was not treated to some drink—the men often running down to get soda water for me— or invited to partake of a meal. "But you have not yet visited with us," said one delightful host. "Your glass is still half-full." . . .

Seventy percent of the men are employed in freight handling. This is common labor, requiring little experience but a great deal of brawn and strength. Articles weighing one to one and a half tons must at times be pulled and lifted; two men generally handle such cargo. At one time the Irish and Germans handled freight along this waterfront, but within recent years they have been largely displaced by Italians, by Serbo-Croats, and very lately by Bohemian laborers.

Work is organized in gangs of ten or twelve men, and a foreman is put in charge of each pier. Originally Serbo-Croatians worked in homogeneous gangs, but in the notion of their employers "they became too independent and made too many demands." To crush this spirit of rebellion, the gangs were broken up and mixed with men of other nationalities. There were also at one time a number of Croatian foremen, but they did not make good. Hence at present these positions are held almost exclusively by the Irish.

In railroad work one man obtained such a monopoly that through him alone could the Serbo-Croats of New York and vicinity get work as freight handlers with the New York Central and West Shore railroads. During the freight handlers' strike of 1907, he shrewdly saw his opportunity and made overtures to the railroads to furnish them with men. Thereafter he opened an employment office under the guise of conducting an institution of learning. He is an adroit handler of people and as a result of wide advertisement in foreign newspapers and among men of his own nationality, his name and fame have long since traveled across the seas. "When you come to New York, go to Kristic," writes a man in Butte, Mont., to his friend in Dalmatia, "he will find you a job." And so he often does, but the man

Three Serbo-Croatian immigrants in New York City in 1912.

pays him and pays exceeding well. In hearings before the Bureau of Licenses there were many complainants to testify that they had been asked from $5.00 to $75 for a job, and had paid fees every time they were discharged and reemployed—which was frequent. . . .

To be an independent businessman is a dizzy height toward which many strive. "When the Slav goes into trade it is generally a round higher up and marks on his part a great rise in the world." There are several Slavic masons and building contractors to be found here. An asbestos manufacturing company, carried on by a Dalmatian, is a very successful enterprise. A number of stationery and tobacco stores, steamship ticket offices, and a barber shop are in the hands of Serbo-Croats. Most of their commercial enterprises, however, are groceries and butcher shops—often a combination of the two—saloons and poolrooms. The inclination to emulate the successful saloon and poolroom keepers has been mentioned before. In the course of this inquiry, which occupied some three or four months, two new poolrooms and one new saloon were opened in the district. It takes about $400 to open a saloon and $1,200 for a license.

Most of the businessmen are Dalma-tians, though there is a tobacco firm, both members of which are Serbians. Here tobacco and cigarettes are manufactured as well as sold. One of the partners came to the United States four years ago, and his family followed last year. The wife and, after school hours, the three children work in this store as well as the two men. No outside help is employed. Their merchandise is sold not only in this community but throughout the United States among their compatriots. Another very prosperous Serbian has a steamship and railroad ticket office, which has been doing business here for many years. Most of his trade is outside of New York, for through wide advertising in Serbian and Croatian papers he receives ticket orders from as far west as Seattle and San Francisco. In addition he has a stationery store and, like a number of businessmen in the neighborhood, he has leased the entire tenement in which his business is located, using it as a lodging house for incoming and departing immigrants. These businessmen depend upon their countrymen for most of their trade. They frequently sustain large losses, for they have a poor system of bookkeeping and most of the transactions are on a credit basis.

As in all foreign communities, the businessmen are the brains of the group and lead the rest. A few of them are good, neighborly men, who aid their countrymen with advice and money, without charging interest. Two saloonkeepers were often mentioned as the kindest, most helpful, and best men in the colony. As Professor Balch has written: "The saloonkeeper of a Slavic group may be the best man in it; he is at least very likely to be the most influential." It is but logical to expect that the more these immigrants become acclimatized, acquainted with our ways and means of living and working, the better able they are to earn a higher wage. Yet if they do forge ahead it is almost in spite of us, for we meet them but halfway and that reluctantly or because of financial motives. . . .

A few men have become naturalized because they see an economic advantage in such a step. There are in this group ten citizens, and twelve who have their first papers, a total of twenty-two, or 19 percent of the 115 men who have been in this country five years or more and are eligible to take one or both steps in the process of naturalization. For many do not look upon America as a place of permanent residence; others find the ways and means of acquiring citizenship incomprehensible or onerous. It is difficult to get witnesses and take the time to appear before the judge. A number of the younger men, however, expressed their intention to become citizens. . . .

Again and again the cry is raised that these immigrants will not assimilate. Pray what have we done to inspire them with our civic ideals? What have we done to teach them? For this particular group there stand Tammany Hall and lesser preceptors in politics, who hold behind them an ever ready and open palm for tips; among their Americanized countrymen many either alienate themselves or defraud them; unscrupulous American employers exploit them, control their waking hours, living conditions, and chance of advancement. How can these foreigners become imbued with American civic and social ideals?

Neighborhood agencies have not gone halfway to meet them. They do not come into close contact with Americans in their work or homes, hence why should they be acquainted with American institutions or adopt American standards? Thus the fault lies quite as much with us as with them. They are isolated, cut off, and we have failed to do the minimum which the most elementary ethics of civilization demand of us.

A Bohemian Settlement in North Dakota

20

Large numbers of Bohemian immigrants went into agriculture. Many thousands of them found their way to the rural areas of Wisconsin, Iowa, Nebraska, the Dakotas, and Minnesota; in fact, no state was without its contingent. This selection is a portion of a brief history by William H. Elznic of the Czechs in Richland County, North Dakota, the extreme southeastern section of the state, with Wahpeton as county seat. [*Collections of the State Historical Society of North Dakota*, Vol. 4, 1913. Pages 62–73.]

The early Bohemian settlers in Richland County came chiefly from Veseli, Tabor, Pisek, and Budejovice. They came to the United States during the period between 1859 and 1872, years in which an exceptionally large number of Bohemian immigrants came to this country. These were all of the peasant stock, belonging to the class of small farmers. Their parents were self-supporting and owned a few acres of land.

There were several causes that led to their coming to America, but not all of them who wished to come were allowed to do so, for many were unable to obtain passports. The general causes were the severe military requirements, the overpopulation of the country, and the consequent scarcity of land for farms and homes. The land was owned mostly by nobles and by the churches, and the poorer classes were obliged to work this land for a small compensation. The wages in some cases were so low that children were often required to herd geese or cattle in the summer months for mere board and clothes, and rather meager quantities of each. Thus as they grew up, many of the young people were easily induced to leave their mother country, and come to America. Many had friends who had already crossed the ocean and were quite prosperous here. These friends wrote them letters in which they told of the high wages, scarcity of labor, and of the opportunities to secure free land from the United States government. But the newspapers of the country discouraged immigration in every way possible. Immigration agents had not invaded that part of Europe and newspapers could say anything without much danger of denial. However, the letters and promises of the friends were relied upon rather than the printed accounts. . . .

Many of the Old Country customs still exist among the settlers, though most of them will pass away with the old pioneers. Some, however, are planted so firmly in the minds of the coming generation that they will survive the old settlers for years to come. Of these survivals, the Bohemian language is the most impor-

tant. Though the young people use English in their conversation to a large extent, the mother tongue is usually used at home. Every child is first taught to express his ideas in this language. English is acquired before the first school years, as the children speak the language quite fluently at the age of five or six. A large percentage of the children are taught to read and write Bohemian. The numerous papers printed in that language, which are found in nearly every home, contribute much to this result. Some of these papers are the *Hospodar, Amerikan, Hlasatel, Svornost, Hlas,* and *Katolik.* Very few books written in the native tongue are read in the community. Another cause which tends to perpetuate the use of the mother tongue is the constant immigration from the Old Country. These newcomers hire out to the farmers, and, not being able to speak English, are compelled to use the native language.

In early days, spinning wheels were used by the settlers very commonly. The spinning was always done during the long winter evenings and practically all the hosiery and mittens used were homemade. However, all the spinning wheels have disappeared, and knitting is a thing of the past.

The first buildings were of sod, clay, and other material close at hand. The natural clay served for the first floor. The walls were made of sod, or homemade bricks, and were about two and a half feet thick. The houses were usually boarded and whitewashed on the inside. The roof was also of clay, the rafters were tree trunks. The windows were made of small panes, which admitted just enough light for the people to see. These houses were much warmer than a modern house, and the settlers were able to economize on their fuel. The other buildings on the farm were made of the same material as the dwelling houses. These sod buildings are now no longer in use and even their ruins have disappeared. The first frame buildings, erected by Chezik and Lorenz in 1872 and 1873, still stand as relics of the pioneer days.

The Catholic religion has remained the predominating faith among the Bohemians. At first the settlers were poor and few in number, and they were unable to build a place in which to worship. However, at the present time, circumstances have changed. Two of the largest churches in Richland County have been erected by them, St. John Nepomuck Church located at Lidgerwood with a membership of about 275 and St. Adalbert Church located at Wahpeton with a membership of about 300. Each church has a pastor; the present pastors are Rev. Father Alois Gaydousek at Lidgerwood, and Rev. Father Jos. Gaydousek at Wahpeton.

Very important factors which tend to perpetuate unity among the Bohemian people of Richland County are the present religious and nonreligious Bohemian fraternal organizations. The two important national religious organizations of this nature are the Catholic Workman (*Katolicky Delnik*) and the Western Bohemian Catholic Association (*Zapadni Ceska Katolicka Jednota*).

The order of the Catholic Workmen at Lidgerwood was organized in 1899 with a membership of seventeen; its present membership is eighteen. The first officers of this organization were: president, Joseph W. Novotny; vice president, Wenzl Fuka; secretary, Wenzl Kuzel; accountant, Frank Pokorney; treasurer, John Pasak.

The Western Bohemian Catholic Association order at Lidgerwood was started in 1899 with a membership of eight, and since has increased to seventeen. The first officers of this order were: president, Albert Heley; secretary, Joseph Hajney; treasurer, John Heley.

Besides the two above named, the young people's societies have been organized in 1911, one for young men, having a membership of thirty, and the other for young ladies, having a membership of twenty-five. These four organizations are affiliated with the St. John Nepomuck Catholic Church of Lidgerwood.

Similar organizations are in existence in connection with the St. Adalbert's Catholic Church at Wahpeton, each of which has been quite prosperous. The Western Bohemian Catholic Association order at Wahpeton was organized in 1888. Its present membership is thirty-four. The Catholic Workmen was organized in 1890, and at present has a membership of twenty-six. In 1908 the married ladies of the St. Adalbert Church organized the Altar Society. At present they have a membership of twenty-three. The same year the young ladies of that church organized the St. Cecilia Society and have a present membership of sixteen.

The nonreligious fraternal organization is the Western Bohemian Fraternal Association (*Zapadni Cesko-Bratrski Jednota*), also national in character. The Lidgerwood order, August Herman, No. 30, was organized by Joseph Gadrny in 1889 with a membership of fifteen. The first officers were as follows: president, Peter Polda; secretary, Karl Parizek; treasurer, Peter Wacha.

The first meeting of this order was held on the farm of Frank Novotny, as there was no other more convenient place. Meetings were held later at the city hall of Lidgerwood till the year 1908, when enough money was raised among the members to erect their own hall at the cost of $9,000. Its membership has increased from fifteen in 1889 to 121 in 1912, making it the largest order of its kind in the state, there being thirteen such orders in the state at present. The membership is composed of eighty men and forty-one women.

The Wahpeton order, Red River, No. 42, was organized on August 1, 1897. This was the reorganization of a previous order having the name Red River, No. 155, affiliated with the national organization, C.S.P.S., of which the entire Western Bohemian Fraternal Association is an outgrowth. The order began with a membership of ten, and has now increased to seventy-one, consisting of fifty-two men and nineteen women. The charter members were as follows: Thos. Sramota, Frank Dolejsi, Alois Lesovsky, Jos. Matuska, Emil Hrubes, John Chada, Chas. Benes, Jos. Brush, Thos. Chezik, and Wenzl Mikesh. The first officers were: president, Thos. Sramota; vice president, Jos. Brush; recording secretary, Wenzl Mikesh; financial secretary, Chas. Benes; treasurer, John Chada; escort, Thos. Chezik; guard, Emil Hrubes.

The order holds regular meetings in the I.O.O.F. Hall every second Sunday of each month. In 1903 the order purchased its own cemetery and its next aim is the construction of its own hall.

The settlers have always taken much interest in educating their children. All children receive at least a common school education, and a fair portion go to the high school. For the last five or six years, students of Bohemian parents have graduated with every graduating class in both the Lidgerwood and the Wahpeton high schools. Up to the present time ten have graduated from the Lidgerwood High

A Czech grandmother at Ellis Island in New York, photographed by Lewis Hine in 1926.

School, and about twenty from the Wahpeton High School. Some twenty students are attending college every winter. Besides these several have already received their degrees or diplomas from some higher institution.

The Bohemians are naturally fond of music. Hardly a home is without its musical instruments, and there are always one or more performers in each family. The violin is the favorite instrument. Many, however, prefer the guitar, accordian, piano, or the organ, but lately wind instruments have been much used. Some five years ago the Elznic and Pavek Band was organized and it has furnished music for celebrations, fairs, and various social events throughout this part of the state.

The industrial development of the settlers has been marked by steady growth. Land has greatly increased in value since the pioneer days, the average price now being $60 per acre. In 1882 John Zimmerman traded a quarter section of land for an old horse, now the same land would sell for $8,000.

In the matter of buildings the settlers have always kept pace with the rest of the state. Nearly all the farmers have a windmill to pump water for the stock, and some have gasoline engines for grinding feed. The average farm is about 300 acres though many farmers own as many as 1,000 acres. The Bohemians are good grain growers and great lovers of trees. Each farm is surrounded by a thriving grove and every corner of the land is utilized. They are hard workers, and have little faith in schemes to save work; they give the same amount of energy to the virgin soil of North Dakota as they did to the crowded, and much used soil of old Bohemia. On the other hand they believe in using farm machinery and their farms are fully equipped with all modern improvements. The first rural telephone was built in 1908. It is not owned by the farmers, but by the Lidgerwood Rural Telephone Company. This company has built some thirty lines which extend through different parts of the surrounding country. Nearly all the families have a telephone and during the last five years they have also secured daily rural mail service. Many of the settlers own one or more shares in the Lidgerwood Farmers State Bank. Farmers' stores, and farmers' elevators have been organized in the different towns in the county, within the last five years. In these corporations the capital stock is subscribed entirely by the farmers, who thus control them and receive all the returns.

The Bohemians have always taken an active interest in politics, although not many of their nationality have held office. The men who have held offices are Albert Chezik, elected the first sheriff and assessor of Richland County in 1873, and Frank Heley, elected in 1908 to the office of sheriff, which he held for two years. In the party divisions the Republicans and Democrats predominate and there are a few Socialists.

During the last few years some of the pioneers have rented their land and others have gone into business in the neighboring towns, though most of them are still living on their farms.

The Negro and the Immigrant in the Two Americas

21

In general, social distinctions in Latin America are drawn along class lines, while in the United States they are drawn along racial or ethnic lines. In both cases there results inequality of rights and opportunities. In the United States the situation has been complicated by the arrival of millions of immigrants who first took their place at the bottom of the economic ladder and then climbed up. Thus, for every immigrant group, especially after 1865, the black man was a source of economic competition. For unskilled immigrants who had only the labor of their hands to offer, whiteness became a badge of superiority. James B. Clarke examined the contrasting attitudes toward color in North and South America in the essay from which this section was taken. [*The Annals of the American Academy of Political and Social Science,* Vol. 49, September 1913.]

To the colored man of foreign birth, and especially of Latin American origin, who lands on American shores fifty years after the issuance of the Emancipation Proclamation, the keenness of racial antipathy and the persistence of statutory discrimination in various states against persons of African descent form a feature of American life as puzzling in its raison d'être as it is annoying and unpleasant in its operation. "Why is it," asked the distinctly Negroid officers and sailors of the Brazilian dreadnaught which recently visited this country, "that in the street cars at Norfolk we had to be separated from our white or white Indian fellows and friends? In New York the petty officers of our ship were invited to an entertainment by the men of similar rating on an American battleship and the waiters at the hotel refused to serve some of our men who were black. We cannot understand these things."

Small wonder that the foreign visitors should have evinced surprise at this disagreeable feature of an otherwise memorably pleasant reception in the United States of America. It is hardly twenty-five years since the last vestiges of slavery were removed from the then infant United States of Brazil, but that country knows no distinction of color or race. Law and custom guarantee equal opportunity to all citizens in every field of usefulness to the republic, and some of the most distinguished presidents, to say nothing of lesser officials, have been men of Negro blood. In this country, on the other hand, where people have better opportunities for education and ought to be and claim to be more enlightened and humane than the peoples to the south, fifty years after a most destructive war which is supposed to have abolished all distinctions in citizenship, racial prejudice pursues with a most relentless and intolerant hatred the faintest trace of African blood and even overrides the common demands of international courtesy and renders im-

possible the attainment of that Pan-American Union, based on genuine goodwill and mutual respect, which the republic of the north is now so anxious to form. . . .

Knowing these facts, it is not surprising that white men in Latin America, and there are more of them than Anglo-Saxon America is inclined to think, do not regard the possession, real or suspected, of Negro blood as a crime punishable with eternal and irrevocable exclusion from everything that savors of honorable service and due consideration in one's country. If these facts were also known or acknowledged by white men between the Gulf of Mexico and the Great Lakes, it is possible that the Brazilian visitors would have been spared the dread of terrors unseen and, for them, perhaps nonexistent; but nevertheless, well founded on their observation of the gulf that separates the native white from the nonwhite of North America. "If I went into one of these restaurants along Broadway," asked the son of a Portuguese from the Azores, whose ability has won him a position of trust and responsibility as an officer in the navy of his colored mother's country, "would they serve me as they would in Paris or Newcastle-on-Tyne or Rio de Janeiro?" The only way to secure an answer to such a question, would, of course, be to enter the restaurant and order food. The response would perhaps be in the negative, but in any case it would most likely be made by a man who was not himself a native of this country, who had not become thoroughly familiar with the language and had not thought it necessary to relinquish his allegiance to some European monarch in order to enjoy the benefits of residence in a country which is, to him, free. For a most important element in the maintenance of anti-Negro feeling in this country since the Civil War is the constant and ever increasing stream of immigration from Europe.

Fifty years ago, the waiter in New York and in many other Northern cities was usually a man of color, as was the barber, the coachman, the caterer, or the gardener. True enough, he had little opportunity to rise above such menial occupation, but with the growth of the humanitarian, if rather apologetic, attitude toward the Negro engendered by the great conflict which had brought about the verbal abolition of slavery in the states where it then existed, it is possible that the Negro's status in New York and the other free states would have been rapidly and permanently improved, industrially as well as in civic recognition, had not the current of immigration, which had been retarded for a decade or two during the Civil War and the preceding agitation, started with renewed force on the cessation of the conflict. The newcomer from Europe had to be provided for. Being more suited to the climate and conditions of life in the Northern states and

Black women strikebreakers are led to work during the Chicago stockyard strike of 1904. Employers used Negroes in need of work to destroy the effect of unions.

at the same time possessing greater skill and experience, not only in the menial employments which had engaged the Negroes, but also in the trades and industries in which the freedmen had acquired during slavery a rudimentary foundation, the European immigrant soon outstripped his Negro rival for the employment and the respect of the American in the Northern states. With his economic position thus secured, the new American, knowing little or nothing of the terrible struggle which had preceded his coming, looked and still looks upon the Negro with the contemptuous eye of an easy victor over a hopelessly outnumbered, weak, and incompetent foe. I do not pretend to say that the immigrant is not often to be found among those who keep alive the torch of liberty and justice in America, but I do believe that the continuance of racial hatred in the North is traceable to the Europeans whose lack of contact with the Negro has been exploited and played upon by native whites who have nothing to think and talk about but an exaggerated idea of the virtues and capacities of the Anglo-Saxon race.

In the Southern states where, although there is little direct immigration, the poor white population, particularly in the Southwest, has been largely increased by recruits from the Americanized immigrant population of the North, the Negro, by reason of his numbers, has been able to make a better showing in industry. This condition is in no small measure due to the fact that the ruling classes prefer the Negro to the immigrant. But, whatever the reason, the black people still hold their own and, despite efforts to check them, they are constantly securing a firmer footing in the industries of the South. . . .

Without the hindrance of artificial restrictions, the effect of which cannot be permanent, the position of the Negro in the agriculture of the Southern states seems to be assured. Present tendencies in other industries in these states, and it is only in these that the Negro is ever likely to be an important economic factor, seem to guarantee the black man "the right to life, liberty, and the pursuit of happiness" in equal security with the white man. In the mining regions of Alabama and Tennessee the proprietors of mines, with the aid of aspirants to political honors, have been in the habit of fomenting race prejudice as a means of nullifying the power of union labor by forcing the men to form racial unions and by using the one as a club to suppress the other group in case of a strike. In Alabama two years ago the governor, without a shade of legal authority, ordered the militia to raze a strike camp just as the miners were nearing success, because the promiscuous arrangement of the tents occupied by white and colored people did not meet with the approval of a public opinion which cared nothing about the color of the men while in the mines. The miners themselves had very different ideas and it is probable that experiences of this kind will force them to a fearless recognition of the unity and identity of the interests of labor. The Socialist Party and the IWW have done much for the admission of colored men to labor unions and the IWW has met with notable success in this respect in the lumber camps of Louisiana. In many other important industries as, for instance, ship-carpentry at Savannah and other ports, colored men are admitted into the unions with white men. Southern cotton mills are beginning to employ Negro labor. As a result of the recent anti-Japanese agitation, employers and workmen alike have come to regard the Negro as the lesser of two evils and, in railroad construction in several places in the West and Northwest, black men have been engaged to replace the Oriental laborers. During the past half century, the dominant, if unexpressed, idea in the mind of the average white man toward the colored man who sought the right to earn his bread anywhere in this country was that he ought to be crushed and eliminated if his labor in any way savored of competition with the white man. But with the growing recognition of the interdependence of the races and the increased tolerance of labor unions toward black men, competition between Negroes and immigrants tends to give way to cooperation between black men and white all over the country.

This is the condition that exists in Brazil, where the free people of color, both on account of their numbers and of their ability, had secured a footing from which they could not be shaken by an immigration which has not been so large or so different in origin and standards of life from the native worker as has been the case with the immigrant and the Negro in North America. When the center of American interests is transferred from considerations of race to the recognition of those surer standards of birth, education, and ideals, by which alone citizenship is to be adjudged, racial prejudice against the Negro and Negroid will become as insignificant in Anglo-Saxon America as it is rare in Latin America. Toward this end the Negro and the immigrant should strive by removing the barriers of color and of mutual fear or distrust which separate them, in order to make possible the realization of the new and really United States of North America, without which there can be no union of all America.

Brown Brothers

The Economic Outlook

1904–1912

During the first decade of the 20th century, the leading spokesman for 10,000,000 black Americans was Booker T. Washington. He achieved his position—which, however, was not accepted by all—through a combination of circumstances. He was enthusiastically accepted by many blacks, but others were troubled by the fact that some of his viewpoints coincided remarkably with those of whites. Washington's emphasis was on acquiring technical skills: "For years to come the education of the people of my race should be so directed that the greatest proportion of the mental strength of the masses will be brought to bear upon the everyday practical things of life." On another occasion he said: "I plead for industrial education and development for the Negro not because I want to cramp him, but because I want to free him. I want to see him enter the all-powerful business and commercial world."

But, as his critics pointed out, Washington's advice was obsolete. It was the age of large industrial combinations, trusts, and huge aggregates of capital, not the era of Horatio Alger craftsmen, artisans, and tradesmen. Washington's predilection for craft work and small farming, plus his animosity toward labor unions, ill suited the needs of the nation's blacks, although his advice played into the hands of whites, both in the North and South, who were determined to keep the blacks within certain economic and social confines. With the rise of industrial farming the advantages for blacks were to be in the cities, not the rural areas.

The paths of economic opportunity were usually more apparent to the approximately 10,000,000 immigrants who arrived in the decade and a half before World War I. It was a generally prosperous time, clouded only briefly by the financial panic of 1907. These many new arrivals followed in the tracks of those who had preceded them—to the cities, the mines, and the factories. The great industrial centers of the East and Midwest attracted most of them: New York, Pittsburgh, Cleveland, Toledo, Detroit, Chicago, and the mining regions of Pennsylvania, Ohio, Kentucky, and Illinois. A few tried to seek a livelihood in agriculture, but they were a decided minority. The only groups among the later immigrants who turned to farming in significant numbers were the Czechs and the Russians. Many of these went to North and South Dakota, Minnesota, Nebraska, Iowa, Kansas, and other Plains states. Some Poles, Italians, and Portuguese also went onto the land, but this was usually a specialized form of agriculture such as truck farming, tobacco growing, or cotton cultivation. Some of the foreign-born became migrant farm laborers, notably the Mexican-Americans and Mexican immigrants to the Southwest.

The years from 1901 to 1910 saw much successful unionization compared to the 19th century; membership in labor organizations doubled during these years. The period also saw the arrival of immigrants in the greatest numbers ever; in fact, the growth of unionism directly paralleled the increase in immigration from eastern and southern Europe. In the first decade of the new immigration, from 1880 to 1890, more unions were organized than in the whole previous history of the nation. Even greater gains were made between 1890 and 1900. Both the tide of immigration and the organizing of unions reflected a generally improving industrial prosperity.

The same holds true for labor strife and strikes. In the highly industrialized regions with large numbers of immigrants, there were more strikes, more strikebreakers, more riots, than, say, in the South or West, where most workers were native-born.

It should be noted that the great majority of the unions of the time were trade, or craft, unions. The unskilled laborers—that is, the majority of workers—were still unorganized. And most of the already existing unions were distinctly hostile to the notion of organizing the unskilled. Not until the Great Depression of the 1930s were unskilled workers successfully organized on a national basis.

(On facing page) A German butcher in New York City, about 1900.

The Influence of Trade Unions Upon Immigrants
Carroll D. Wright

22

Carroll D. Wright was the first commissioner of the Bureau of Labor, holding the position from 1885 to 1905. As an economist and statistician, he acquainted himself, by on-the-spot investigations, with all of the problems of the workingman, from living conditions to unionization. He wrote the following report to the President on September 8, 1904, on the occasion of some labor troubles in Chicago's stockyards. At the time, the rights of organized labor were still uncertain, and the power of unions was overmatched by the strength of the trusts. [*Bulletin of the Bureau of Labor,* No. 56, January 1905.]

The immigrant is, in the first instance, a wage reducer, either directly or indirectly, although the extent of his influence upon wages cannot be well stated; but as a prospective wage reducer he is met by the trade union in self-defense, just as the trade union meets female and child labor, except in this: the union seeks to organize the immigrants while it seeks by legislation to prohibit or limit the work of women and children—that is, the union seeks the aid of the state to prevent wage reduction by means of female and child labor, and it seeks by organizing the immigrants to prevent reduction of wages by immigration. It makes no claim of undertaking any charitable or primarily civic education among the immigrants, but the secondary effect of the union on the immigrant is distinctively civic in character. It is the first, and for a time the only, point at which he touches any influences outside his clan. Even the progressive forces inside the nationality lines consider the immigrant hopeless and seek only to reach his children—as, for instance, the officers of the Polish National Alliance direct their effort toward getting the Poles to send their children to American public schools and to have them mix up with and become a part of the whole people. The trade union, however, must deal with the immigrant himself, and the immigrant, when he learns that the union wants to raise his wages, decrease his

hours of labor, etc., begins to see the necessity of learning the English language, of understanding the institutions he hears talked about in the union meetings, and other matters which interest him.

At the risk of taking up too much of your time, let me state a bit of history. From 1880 to 1886 the nationalities employed in the stockyards, in the order of their numerical importance, were Irish, Americans, Germans, and a few Scotch. The great strike of 1886 disrupted the only organization of workmen in the yards—that of the Knights of Labor—and after the failure of the strike a notable exodus of Americans and the more active men among the Irish began. Whether this was entirely voluntary, or in part resulted from activity in the strike, is not germane to this subject. The Poles began to come into the yards in 1886, after the settlement of the strike, but not as strikebreakers. This appears to have been a voluntary immigration, increasing in volume until by 1890 the most of the unskilled occupations were filled by Poles, who by 1894 had practical control of the common labor.

The Bohemians began to affect noticeably the situation in 1894, going first into the inferior positions, which they shared with the Poles. There were two minor strikes between 1890 and 1894, which in a measure aided in bringing about this result. There was some movement upward among the Poles—that is, from lower to higher occupations, but not so marked as among the Bohemians. The Bohemians, coming in later, began under the Poles—that is, took the lower positions as the Poles went up, and divided the entire unskilled labor possibilities with the Poles. The Bohemians, however, soon outstripped the Poles in the movement upward from unskilled to skilled occupations.

The strike of 1894 unsettled these movements temporarily. Negro labor was employed to break the strike and has been an element in the situation ever since. In 1880 but one Negro was employed in the yards, and he worked in Armour's killing gang. While few of the strikebreakers of 1894 were retained, yet that event marks the real beginning of the employment of Negroes. At the beginning of the present strike some 500 Negroes worked in the yards, many of whom belonged to the union.

After the strike of 1894 was settled the Bohemians were introduced more rapidly, and this continued up to 1896. In 1895 the Lithuanians began coming in, followed by Slovaks in 1896, and this continued steadily until 1899, when the number began to increase rapidly. Two years ago an enormous influx of Lithuanians, Slovaks, and Russian Poles occurred, swamping the labor market in the yards. This was caused largely because of the threatening war between Russia and Japan, and the consequent rush of people to escape compulsory military duty. This has been appreciably checked within the last six or eight months.

The proportion of workmen of the various nationalities in the yards at the beginning of the present strike (July 12) was, approximately: Irish, 25 percent; Americans and Scotch, about 2 percent; Germans, 15 percent; Poles, 20 percent; Bohemians, 20 percent. The remainder were Lithuanians, Slovaks, a very few Krains, and, among the most recent arrivals, Finns and Greeks, the latter, however, not being appreciable in number. No attention has been paid in this investigation to immigrants having a representation fewer in number than the Lithuanians and Slavonians.

Of these nationalities, excluding the Irish and Germans, which are not here considered as immigrants, the Bohemians are the most progressive, and have the industrial advantage in this, that many of the foremen are Bohemians and give preference to their nationality when taking on new men. There is no apparent surplus of Irish, Germans, Americans, or Bohemians in the labor market of the district affected, the surplus being composed of Poles, Slovaks, and Lithuanians.

Among all the immigrants mentioned, except the Irish and Germans, the clan spirit is at first all-powerful. The Bohemians, while Catholics, are Bohemian Catholics, and the Poles are Polish Catholics. This is even more true of the Lithuanians and the Slavonians, who are the most clannish of all. No doubt difference in language has much to do with this, but it is by no means the most serious feature. Each nationality has not only its own church, but its own school system, the Lithuanian schools making no pretense of teaching English, some of the teachers not being able even to speak it. The Slavs and Galicians have not as yet opened schools of their own. While the religion of these different nationalities may be said to be one, the associations are along exclusive nationality lines. They settle or rent properties by districts, and in branching out to occupy more territory one side of the street will first become Lithuanian for a block or so, and then the other side of the street will be occupied by the same nationality. The single men invariably board only in families of their own clan. Language has something to do with this, but really less than might be apparent on first consideration, and less than might seem to be true. When organizing building and loan associations, it is done along strictly clan lines. The Bohemians have four of this class of associations, the Poles three, and the Lithuanians one. The Slavs as yet have none. There are other clannish distinctions, as Lithuanian Republican clubs, Lithuanian Democratic clubs, Bohemian Socialist clubs, Bohemian Democratic clubs, everywhere and always along the strictest lines of nationality.

It is currently reported that before the organization of the union this condition occasionally threatened riots along clan lines, owing to the fact that foremen showed such preference for men of their own clan. The union was organized by trades and departments, and the officials refused to permit nationality lines to be recognized. In the sheep butchers' union are to be found all the men connected with sheep killing, regardless of nationalities. So severe was the fight made upon this plan by the clan leaders—those who drew emoluments or secured social prestige as leaders of the various strictly clan societies—and so seemingly insurmountable was the objection raised by the Lithuanians to the union that in 1900, when the Lithuanians were first organized, it was permitted in one case to organize a Lithuanian union. The experiment, however, was a signal failure. No subsequent experiments have been permitted.

The unions in the stockyards are controlled by the Irish, ably assisted by the Germans. As a Bohemian or a Pole learns the language and develops, he is elected business agent or other official. In the pork butchers' union, for instance, there are about 1,800 members, 600 of whom are Irish, 600 Germans, 300 Poles, and 300 Lithuanians and Slavs. This union recently elected a Pole as president of the local. In their business meetings the motions made, resolutions read, and speeches delivered are usually interpreted in five languages, though in some locals in only three. All business, however, is transacted primarily in English, although any member may speak to any motion in the language he best understands, his words being rendered into English for the minutes of the meetings and into all the languages necessary for the information of members. It is here that the practical utility of learning English is first brought home forcibly to the immigrant. In all other of his associations not only does his own language suffice, but, for reasons that can be well understood, shrewd leaders minimize the importance of learning any other. (The only notable exception to this is the National Polish Alliance, and even here only the Polish language is used. There is no apparent influence exerted, however, to create the impression that the Polish is all-sufficient.)

In his trade union the Slav mixes with the Lithuanian, the German, and the Irish, and this is the only place they do mix until, by virtue of this intercourse and this mixing, clannishness is to a degree destroyed, and a social mixing along other lines comes naturally into play. Not only is the Amalgamated Meat Cutters' Union an Americanizing influence in the stockyards, but for the Poles, Lithuanians, and Slovaks it is the only Americanizing influence, so far as could be determined in this investigation. It is true this Americanizing is being done by the Irish and the Germans, but it is Americanizing nevertheless, and is being done as rapidly as the material to work on will permit, and very well indeed. Again, the reaction is good in its results. The feeling among the Irish against the Dutch and the Polack is rapidly dying out. As the Irish in Chicago express it, "Association together and industrial necessity have shown us that, however it may go against the grain, we must admit that common interests and brotherhood must include the Polack and the Sheeny." It is also admitted that when the speech of the Lithuanian is translated in the meeting of the trade union the Irish and the German see in it the workings of a fairly good mind. Some of the best suggestions come from Bohemians, and mutual respect takes the place of mutual hatred.

The investigation disclosed the influence of the union in teaching the immigrant the nature of the American form of government. The records of this office, independent of this investigation, show that during an investigation of building and loan associations a few years ago information from the Bohemian, Polish, and other clannish associations of that character could be obtained only through the services of an interpreter. It was found that as soon as a Bohemian or a Pole heard the word "government," or "government agent," he closed his mouth, and it was impossible to secure any information.

This has been true in other investigations, notably in collecting family budgets; but with an intelligent interpreter, using their own language, the nature of the work was explained, and no further difficulty experienced. The union is breaking down this trait of character in the foreigners of the nationalities mentioned. This it is doing not as a matter of philanthropy, but from a selfish necessity.

The immigrant must be taught that he must stand straight up on his own feet; that the ward politician is dependent on him—on his vote, etc.—and not he on the ward politician. In this way he first learns that he is a part of the government, and while this is done by indirection, in a large sense, there is no other force that is doing it at all. The Pole, the Bohemian, the Lithuanian, the Slovak, and to a much lesser degree the Galician, have inherited the feeling that somehow government is a thing inimical to their natural development—a power forcing itself upon them from afar; an intrusive power for repression, taxation, punishment only; a thing which they must stand in awe of, obey, pay tribute to, and wish that it had not come among their people, even if they did not secretly hate it—a thing, in short, which ought not to be. Being weaker than it they must be silent in its presence, and if forced to speak, lie, as for them to tell the truth would mean imprisonment or death.

It is not necessary for these things to be true in order that the illiterate peasants should have believed them for generations. Seventy-five percent of the stockyards immigrants are of the peasant and agricultural laborer class of Europe, and comparatively few of them can read or write in their own language. To make such a people feel that the government is their friend, that they are a part of it, that development and education, not repression, are its objects and its purposes with and for them, is an enormous task, and one which a trade union single-handed and alone can not be expected to accomplish by indirection in a few years, with the flood of new ignorance that has been brought in by the high tide of immigration into the stockyards.

In every trade union, however conserv-

EB Inc.

(On facing page, top) Michael Donnelly, president of the
Amalgamated Meat Cutters and Butchers' Workers of
America, addresses a strikers' meeting in the stockyards of
Chicago in 1904. (On facing page, bottom) The stockyards
strike was accompanied by considerable violence; here
police guard meat after a fight in which a meat wagon was
overturned. (Above) An immigrant strikebreaker loading
meat at a Chicago slaughterhouse. Most immigrant workers
stood with the union. Meat-packing plants all around the
country closed as part of the nationwide strike.

ative, there are members who will occasionally get the floor and advise their hearers to vote high wages and shorter hours at the ballot box. As the groups of Slovaks gather around after the business is over to have these things explained to them, many get their first real idea of what the ballot and election day mean, and the relation of these to the government itself. In their own home countries the two essential, if not only, elements of the peasant and agricultural laborer's mind is to believe and obey, or follow. Advantage is taken of this fact here by clan politicians, as well as the clan leader in every department. Once the leader can make these people believe in him, he thinks for the entire group, and insists that their duty consists in following his lead implicitly. Necessarily, the trade union, in order to get them to break away from the leader that opposed the union on industrial lines, would be compelled to urge them to consider their own personal and group interests as wageworkers; to think and act for themselves along lines where they knew the real conditions better than anyone else, and certainly better than their leader in a child insurance society, or something else as remote. Here, too, are the first germs of what may be called the departmental thinking implanted in their minds—that is, that while a leader may be worthy of their confidence in one thing, it does not necessarily follow that he is so in some other class of interests.

It is doubtful if any organization other than a trade union could accomplish these things, for only the bread and butter necessity would be potent enough as an influence to bring these people out of the fixed forms and crystallizations of life into which they have been compressed. Certain it is that no other organization is

attempting to do this work, at least not by amalgamation, which is the only way assimilation can be secured among these various foreign elements. The drawing of these people away from their petty clique leaders and getting them to think for themselves upon one line of topics, namely, the industrial conditions and the importance of trade organization, result in a mental uplift. The only way they can pull a Slovak away from his leader is to pull him up until he is gotten above his leader along the lines of thought they are working on. The very essence of the trade argument on the immigrant is—unconsciously again—an uplifting and an Americanizing influence. The unionist begins to talk better wages, better working conditions, better opportunities, better homes, better clothes. Now, one cannot eternally argue "better" in the ears of any man, no matter how restricted the particular "better" harped on, without producing something of a psychological atmosphere of "better" in all his thought and life activities. If better food, better wages, or even better beer, is the only kind of "better" one might get a Slovak or a Lithuanian to think about, then the only way to improve him is to inject the thought of "better" into the only crevice to be found in his stupidity.

Of course, many object to attempts to improve these people because the immigrants from Lithuania, Slavonia, and Russian Poland are better off here than they ever were or could be in their own countries; that, left to themselves, they would not only be perfectly satisfied, but delighted with their improved condition; that the union must first produce discontent and dissatisfaction with what would otherwise be entirely satisfactory before it can get these immigrants even to talk about joining the union. Again, it is urged that at home these people do not expect to eat as good food as other people, nor to dress as well, nor to live in as good houses; that, as peasants, they never compare themselves with other people or classes of people.

In opposition to all these things, the union begins by teaching the immigrant that his wages are not so good as another man's, doing practically the same kind of work, while it neglects to tell him he is not doing it so well, so intelligently, nor so much of it perhaps; but the union gets him to compare himself not with what he was in Lithuania, but with some German or Irish family, and then "stings him with the assertion that he has as much right to live that way as anybody." The union attempts to show the immigrant that he can live better only by getting more money, and that by joining the union he will get it. If left alone he would be entirely satisfied, perhaps, with what he was getting before. It is perfectly true, probably, that in most cases the union does not care for the Lithuanian in the first instance, the real purpose being to protect their own wages by getting the immigrants to demand high wages for their labor. So later on some degree of fellowship is engendered, but self-defense is the real motive.

The union point of view is that for a Lithuanian peasant to be contented, satisfied, and happy with the Lithuanian standard of living in America is a crime, a crime not only against himself but against America and everyone who wishes to make individual and social development possible in America, and that whatever the union's motives for creating discontent, the fact that it does create a discontent among the immigrants—which is the first step toward their improvement and ultimate Americanization—renders the union so far a public benefactor.

Many persons were interviewed in securing information along these lines—bankers, professional men, and all classes. One gentleman, in the banking business in the stockyards district for many years, stated that the Slavonians and Galicians have been buying homes within the last eighteen months to a most remarkable and unprecedented extent, and that this is in a measure true of the Lithuanians, but not to such a marked degree. He testifies that the union has given these people a sense of security in their positions. By mixing up the nationalities in the union meeting it has made them acquainted with each other and dispelled an undefined dread of pending race war or struggle between nationalities in the yards. Formerly most of the Slovak and Lithuanian immigrants were a floater class. About the only ones who return to their homes now are the Galicians, in whose country a more or less representative form of government prevails. Others testified in a similar way, although some thought the union had done little except to agitate for higher, higher, and higher wages, regardless of economic conditions.

On the police side of the problem, a sergeant of the Twentieth Precinct, that known as "back of the yards," which is crowded with the Bohemian and Polish elements, stated that there has been the greatest improvement since the union was formed, in 1900—less disorder, better living, more intelligence, and more understanding of American institutions and laws; that they employ fewer policemen in the district, and that less crime is committed than prior to 1900.

The studies of the various nationalities involved in the present meat strike brings out some valuable points relative to the restriction of immigration. Among them there seems to be an unalterable opposition to laws excluding those who cannot read and write in their own language, and their argument is that the peasant population of central and eastern Europe, from which they came, have more rugged morals, simpler lives, and fewer vices than the inhabitants of the cities and towns, who can read and write, as a rule. They consider themselves not responsible morally or politically for the fact that Russia has fewer schools than Illinois and spends less money on education in a year than does that state. They claim that their ignorance is not of the kind that is synonymous with vice or with crime; that they are as innocent as ignorant, whereas a far worse town and city population would be admitted without question under such laws. They have some peculiar ideas about prohibiting absolutely any immigration for a specific term of years and then allowing only a certain percentage to come in each year thereafter; but the main point they make is as to the illiteracy of the peasant class, the most desirable we can secure, and the literacy of the criminal class of the great cities, which would come in under such restrictive legislation. Such things are only a part of this study brought out by your two letters, and the study has seemed to me so interesting and, in a way, so novel, that I have taken courage to give you the results quite in extenso.

Slavs in the Anthracite Coal Regions

23

Until the last two decades of the 19th century, the mining industry in Pennsylvania was the province of English, Welsh, Irish, and German workers. But by 1890 the so-called new immigrants had moved into the region, which was the scene of what were probably the worst working conditions in the United States. By 1914 well over half the workers in the mines were Poles, Slovaks, Ruthenians, and other immigrants from eastern Europe. This article by Peter Roberts depicts the ethnic and social makeup of the mining region. [*Charities,* December 3, 1904.]

The racial elements in our communities are many. Men inaccurately speak of our late immigrants as "Huns." There are actually no Hungarians in the coalfields. The nearest approach to them are the Magyars, who are not Slavs. Of these, we have only a few hundred, who are chiefly located in the Wyoming and Lackawanna valleys. We also have some 6,000 Italians, less than half of whom are employed in and around the mines. These are found in the Wyoming and Lackawanna valleys and on the Hazleton mountains. We have also a few hundred Tyrolese who are sometimes spoken of as Italians and sometimes as Slavs. Another group is the Lithuanians and their kinsmen, the Letts, of whom only a few live in northeastern Pennsylvania. These are found in Shenandoah, Mahanoy City, Hazleton, Freeland, Wilkes-Barre, Plymouth, Kingston, Pittston, Duryea, Scranton, Priceburg, and Forest City. Their total number will be possibly about 30,000. None of the above four groups is of Slav origin. The remaining 90,000 are Slavs proper. They are made up of Poles, Ruthenians, Slovaks, a few Bohemians, Slovenians, Croatians, etc.

Of the Slavs proper, the Poles are the most numerous in our territory, and will possibly number some 35,000 souls. They come from the three empires into which their country was divided when they lost independence. The German Pole is better educated and trained than those from either Austria or Russia. His industrial efficiency is greater; he is more susceptible to the influence of a higher civilization, and more readily appreciates the advantages of education to his children and culture to himself. Hence we generally find the German Poles at the head of racial movements for the amelioration of this people. They have their societies such as the "Sons of Poland," "Polish Beneficiary Society," "Polish Literary Clubs," "Polish Political Clubs," etc., and with rare exceptions the German Pole is the leading spirit. He is not so far removed in his social status from his brother from Austria and Russia that he forgets the ties of kinship. All Poles, no matter from what country they come, stand together. Several Polish aspirants for political or social honors will conduct a vigorous campaign before a caucus decides which is to be the standard bearer, but once the candidate is chosen all Polish electors fall into line and stand by their compatriot.

The Ruthenians stand next to the Poles in numbers in the anthracite fields and would possibly number 27,000 souls. In many of our towns in the northern, middle, and southern districts, the presence of the Little Russians is attested by the churches which have above them the Greek cross, although they all profess allegiance to the Roman Catholic faith. Father Lorisias of Shenandoah mentions the fact that in this town wherein 60 percent of the population is Letto-Slav, his people were the first to erect a house of worship. The Ruthenians also pride themselves on the fact that their language stands nearest the fountain whence the Slavic dialects have sprung and that the scholar who studies the language in common use among the Little Russians will have,

Loading coal in the Livingston mine in the bituminous regions of southern Illinois, about 1900.

comparatively speaking, little difficulty in comprehending the languages spoken by the other members of the Slavic races.

The Slovaks in the hard coalfields are not as numerous as the above two branches and would possibly number about 25,000. These are the people generally designated "Huns" in the mining regions, for they all come from the Austro-Hungarian Empire. The *Slovak Daily*, published in Pittsburgh, has a standing refutation of this error on its editorial page, and educated Slovaks always insist on the fact that they are not "Huns" and do not wish to be called such. Their protest should be honored. The nomen "Hun" is a generic term and used by the average citizen in the coalfields in an opprobrious sense as synonymous with the lowest type of immigrants from southern Europe. The Slovaks do not occupy a

Miners' children in Pennsylvania, about 1905.

lower economic or social status than other immigrants of this race, and the opprobrious term "Hun" should not be applied to them any more than to other members of the Slavic race.

The Bohemians, Croatians, Slovenians, etc., found in our territory, are a drop in the bucket compared with these three great groups. The minor elements amalgamate with the greater in their religious and social life, and can be spoken of as one with the major elements.

This, then, is the racial composition of the Letto-Slavs and Italians in the hard coalfields.

All Slavs do not dwell in unity. Racial antipathies, national jealousies, and historical antecedents divide them. On new soil, they cannot forget their quarrels and prejudices; they cannot cast behind them animosities whose roots are buried in centuries of conflict and oppression. If they should forget these things, their lot here would be happier and their social progress swifter. Their jealousies and hatreds are met with on all sides, and their common religious faith is wholly inadequate as a solvent. Although followers of the same teacher, the Nazarene, the Poles and the Letts, Slovaks and Ruthernians are alienated in sympathy, antagonistic in social and political affairs, and quarrelsome when they meet over their cups. The Pole is an Ishmaelite in his own family. He hates the Russian, the Little Russian, the Slovak, and in turn is hated by them. In discussing the Pan-Slavic movement lately with an educated Slav, I asked, "Where does the Pole stand upon this question?" "Oh," was the reply, "he wants it, but asks us to make him king. The Pole always wants to be king, all the rest of us his serfs."

The Pole and the Lett can never agree. Their antagonism dates from the political allegiance effected in the 14th century. The Lithuanians tell of centuries of antagonism under Polish princes, which was as galling and obnoxious as any recorded in the annals of the world. The Pole will, on the other hand, assert his right to a higher social status than that of the Lett, because of his glorious record in European history for at least 500 years, when the kingdom of Lithuania was joined to Poland. The Little Russian tells how the Polish nobles fled from oppression and tyranny in Russia and settled in Galicia, but no sooner were they settled there than they began to oppress the peasants as

102

mercilessly as ever Slavs were oppressed. The Slovaks say the Poles are treacherous, unpatriotic, and unreliable; in Austria-Hungary they betray their Slavic brethren by siding with the Germans in political conflicts to defeat measures deemed beneficial to Slavic interests in the empire.

Thus there is constant antagonism between the Poles and the Letts and between these and the other Slavs. It has its effect upon the political, social, and industrial life of the people. In politics, the Letto-Slavs seldom combine their forces, and keen politicians aim to nullify the "foreigners'" votes by dividing the house against itself. When Poles and Letts meet in saloons or at social gatherings, they fight with the instinct of savages. Lithuanian laborers will not work with Poles, and a Pole will not labor for a Lithuanian. These antagonisms and prejudices injure none as they do the Slavs themselves. They interfere with their industrial efficiency, hinder their social advancement, and deprive them of the political influence they could exert if they were a unit in municipal or county elections. The interests of the Letto-Slavs in the coalfields are identical and if they manifested the same spirit of communistic activity here as is known to exist in Slav communities in the Fatherland, there is little they could not effect.

Slavs in the Bituminous Mines of Illinois
John R. Commons

24

The British, Welsh, Cornish, and Irish workers in the bituminous mines of the Midwest eventually gave way, as their fellows in the Pennsylvania anthracite fields had done, to the unskilled laborers arriving from eastern Europe. Many of the original miners moved into managerial positions or left mining altogether. This article on the Illinois miners is by John R. Commons of the University of Wisconsin, one of the leading authorities on the history of organized labor. Commons was also a nativist, a member of the Immigration Restriction League, and a proponent of Anglo-Saxon superiority. His views on Slavic miners were therefore as much influenced by these opinions as they were by his knowledge of the labor movement. [*Charities*, December 3, 1904.]

Practically all of the Slavs in Illinois, outside of Cook County, are at work in or about the mines, as very few of them are employed on railway and other kinds of construction which attract the Italians. Of the 37,000 mine workers in Illinois, about 60 percent are foreign-born, and of this 60 percent, about one-fourth are Slavs and Lithuanians. The four or five divisions of the Slavs exceed in number any other nationality of the foreign-born, the Italians coming next, to the number of 3,000. Among these, the Slavs predominate in the order Poles, Slovaks, and Bohemians, while the Lithuanians number less than a thousand. The great majority of them have entered this field since 1894, their introduction at that time being brought about through the general strike of the American and west European miners. The strike ended in a complete defeat of the improvised union of the time, and as a result, the Slavs and the Italians have become in certain districts the predominating elements.

The circumstances of their immigration cannot be understood without a word on the characteristics of the mining industry in the state of Illinois. The northern field was the first in development, but it had the disadvantage of exceedingly thin veins of coal, a seam of forty inches being a prevailing depth. The southern field, on the other hand, is characterized by veins of six to ten feet in thickness. Owing to the greater facility of mining in the southern field, the introduction of machinery, and the thickness of the seam, the competition of coal in the markets had become so serious that many mines in the northern field were reduced to two or three months' work in the year, and even at prices per ton for mining double the prices in the southern field, the miners were unable to earn similar wages. On this account the northern field has been the source of labor agitation, and the prominent leaders of the mine workers' union, both in state and national fields, have had their training in that section. It was consequently into this field that the majority of the Slav and Italian immigrants were brought by the operators, as is plainly shown by the statistics compiled by the Illinois Bureau of Labor Statistics, showing that in the first, second, and fourth mining districts of the state the percentages of foreign-born miners are respectively 89 percent, 72 percent and 62 percent; whereas in the other parts of the state, the highest proportion is 51 percent, and in the seventh, the most southerly district, only 20 percent are foreign-born.

This distribution of the Slavs, who, with the Italians, constitute the bulk of these large percentages of foreign-born, applies not only to districts throughout the state, but also to working places within the mines. For it is the Slav and the Italian who are willing to take the places where the difficulties of mining are greatest, and consequently the output and earnings of the miner are least. The American and west European stock tend to distribute themselves in the better districts of the state and to keep the better paying positions within each mine.

After the strike of 1894, notwithstanding a remarkable decrease in wages, there was practically no improvement in the mining business for three years. The conditions, not only of the English speaking miners, but even of the Slavs and Italians, became so oppressive that in 1897, when the strike was called by the remnant of the former union, practically every miner and mine worker in the state, including Slav and Italian, laid down his tools. The union entered the strike with no treasury and only a few hundred members, and at the end of four months won a complete victory and a general increase in wages, together with the eight-hour working day. The organization in Illinois is much stronger than in other parts of the bituminous field, mainly because the mine workers in this state held out at least a month longer than those of the other states of the competitive field, and thereby secured terms in the final settlement with the operators much more to their advantage than those secured in the other states. Since the success of the strike in 1897, the mine workers' union has made annual agreements with the operators, the terms regarding both wages and conditions of work being most minutely described.

The English-speaking miners universally show an inclination to keep Slavs and Italians from coming into the mines, and their immigration has been very slight since 1897. Practically the only way in which the Slav coming from the Old Country can now get employment as a miner is through the intervention of a relative or friend, who agrees to be responsible for him. The state law requires two

Czech miners relaxing, southern Illinois, early 1900s.

men to work together in a "room," and the miners' union requires them to share their earnings equally. Consequently, a new miner who wants work must find an old miner who will teach him and share with him. This naturally is not easy to do. Furthermore, he must serve a year's apprenticeship above ground as a laborer before going below. This applies to miners proper who are paid by the ton. A different restriction exists for "mine workers" who are paid by the day, to be mentioned below.

The union at first established an initiation fee of $50, which practically excluded all newcomers. Owing to the strenuous opposition of the operators in their annu-

al conferences, this initiation fee was reduced to $10, at which figure it now stands. At the same time, the agreements distinctly provide for the open shop, the employer being given the right to hire new men not members of the organization, provided he does not discriminate against union men. However, on account of the high minimum wage for day labor which the union secured and has been able most effectually to enforce, it is not to the interest of the operator to employ fresh and inexperienced men, provided older employees are on the ground. The significance of the minimum wage will be seen in the fact that whereas for common labor prior to the strike of 1897, the rate of pay for ten hours' work had been reduced as low as $1.40, the union gradually increased the minimum rate for all day labor employed above ground to $2.02 1/2 in 1903, although a reduction was accepted in 1904, bringing it to $1.91 for eight hours' work. For underground work, the minimum was increased until it stood at $2.56 in 1903, but was reduced in 1904 to $2.23 for eight hours' work. With such a high minimum, notwithstanding the open shop privilege, the employer has little inducement to take on new men.

The high minimum has also an important effect on the employment of boys, and the attitude of the Italian and Slav toward the public school system. At such rates of pay, the employer is not inclined to take boys into the mines; in fact, they secure their employment after they reach the age of sixteen mainly through the responsibility which their fathers and brothers assume on their part. Owing to the complete exclusion of boys from the mines in any capacity whatever, there has been a remarkable increase in school attendance of children of foreigners, who otherwise would be found at work in order to help out the family income. The Slavs are beginning to take an interest in the public school system, several instances being known where representatives of this race, as well as of the Italian, have been elected to the school boards. This fact, however, should not be made too much of, since Americans, businessmen and mine superintendents, invite and urge Slavs and Italians to accept such representation on these boards. The object, of course, is to interest foreigners in the school system, but the interest must be cultivated from without and does not spring voluntarily from the Slavs themselves. In many cases it is a difficult matter to secure a Slav or Italian who will accept such a position.

The Italian shows more intelligence and appreciation of his position in the union than does the Slav. The policy of the mine workers' union is to distribute the offices among the different nationalities in order to have interpreters at their meetings, and agents to keep the several nationalities in line. Undoubtedly, the greatest difficulty encountered in the mining region at the present time under the system of agreements with the operators is the presence in such large numbers of non-English speaking miners and mine workers. The enforcement of the interstate and state agreements is a matter of difficulty, sometimes on account of dishonesty of the interpreter, and often on account of his inefficiency, and this is especially serious in the northern fields where the unions are controlled by the Slavs and Italians. There have been several local strikes and violations of the agreement on account of this barrier of language, and there is no one object which appeals more to the operators of the state than that of instruction in English. This object, of course, did not appeal to them prior to the organization of the mine workers and the establishment of the agreement system, but now that they have for eight years been running their mines in cooperation with the union, they find it necessary to assist the latter in bringing forward its more conservative and intelligent members, and to raise the general level of intelligence of the mass. This accounts for the interest which they show in the public school system and there is no subject of which the operators speak with greater pride than of the high grade of schools in the mining districts. Frequently, a superintendent or other officer of a company will be found on the school board in company with a Slav, an Italian, and representatives of other nationalties. The parochial schools, which

Miners pose with the first bushel of coal removed from the O'Gara mine at Harrisburg, Illinois, early 1900s. Coal mining was one of Illinois' most important industries at the beginning of the 20th century.

are attended by a majority of the Slav children, are of an unusually high order, and not only is the English language taught in all of them, but English may be said to be the language of the parochial schools.

The fact which interests the observer most of all is the marvelous thrift of the Slavs. Notwithstanding the prevalence of the use of intoxicants among them, as well as other nationalities, large numbers have good bank accounts, and the movement towards purchasing homes has become, perhaps, the most noticeable feature of mining communities. In many cases, company houses have been sold to employees, and often it happens that a Slav miner is able to pay cash of $600 to

$1,000 for his house. These houses are of course not elaborate, but there are none so inferior as those which one sees in the southern anthracite fields. It is agreed on all sides that the stability of employment which has prevailed since 1897 has been the main incentive of this movement towards home proprietorship.

Compared with the situation of the Slavs in the cities, that of those living in the mining districts of Illinois is idyllic. Their houses, though small, are not over-crowded, as they are in Chicago, each has its garden plot, and the hills and woods are near. Notwithstanding their work is underground, ventilation is always good, temperature is even the year round, hours are short, and in addition the union has a way of taking holidays for all nationalities whenever a particular nationality has a saint's day.

Of course, the isolation of the mining

camp brings its special problems, a peculiar one being the absence of the wider and higher educational opportunities. The situation is ripe for a large movement of an educational kind, based on instruction in English with the addition thereto of manual training and household economics for the young people, and centers of amusement and civic education for all. The friendliness of the mining companies and their superintendents towards a movement of this kind would be insured from the start, while the strong organization of the mine workers, reaching every individual, would cooperate if the enterprise were properly launched. There could apparently be no more useful work established through great benefactions like those of Mr. Carnegie than the diffusion throughout the mining district of agencies for these higher activities of American life.

Italians in the Cotton Fields

25

Many of the Southern states that had begun to encourage immigration after the Civil War maintained their immigration bureaus through the end of the century and succeeded in drawing many new arrivals to their region. The Italians were the most numerous of these immigrants. Some cotton planters optimistically predicted that the Italians would eventually replace blacks in Southern agriculture. One temporarily successful colony was at Sunnyside, in Chicot County, Arkansas. The initial success of the Italians there led white supremacist Alfred Stone, a wealthy Delta cotton planter, to write the following article under the title: "The Italian Cotton Grower: The Negro's Problem." [*South Atlantic Quarterly,* January 1905.]

In respect of its influence upon trade balances, and as a factor in our general commercial supremacy, cotton is probably the most valuable American agricultural commodity. The association of the Negro with the production of this crop is so fixed in the public mind that it is as a cotton grower that his economic importance in this country is chiefly measured. Not unnaturally this association has resulted in fixing in the public mind the idea of the absolute dependence of the Southern crop upon Negro labor. This idea has been fostered to an unwholesome extent in both sections of the country, and its constant emphasis is largely responsible for the ignoring of a movement destined to threaten the conceded supremacy of the Negro in his oldest American field. This movement is the immigration of foreign whites to the Southern states, and to my mind it possesses more significance for the Negro's future than any other economic factor that touches his life today.

There is no other section of equal area in the United States in which the Negro has enjoyed so nearly an absolute monopoly of the field of manual labor as in the riparian lands of the Mississippi River and its tributaries in the states of Mississippi, Louisiana, and Arkansas. In the various counties and parishes of this large section the proportion of Negroes to whites runs from three or four to one to more than fifteen to one. Every consideration of climate, soil, and economic condition tended to render absolute the hold of the Negro agriculturist; yet right here the white man, in the person of the Italian immigrant, has proved his ability to more than meet the Negro upon his most favored ground. The experiment with Italians in this section is not a large one, but the number of these people engaged in cotton growing is constantly increasing. Indeed, the matter has long since passed the experimental stage. Measured by whatever standard may be applied the Italian has demonstrated his superiority over the Negro as an agriculturist. I am not now discussing the merits of the two as tenants, or weighing their respective advantages from the planter's point of view. I have reference merely to the ability of the Italian to produce more cotton on a given acreage than the Negro, and to gather a greater percentage of it without outside assistance.

The cause of this superiority is not far to seek. Given equal soil and equal climatic conditions for growing cotton, and the odds are with the man who cultivates his crop best and most carefully. The Italian works more constantly than the Negro, and, after one or two years' experience, cultivates more intelligently. In comparing the two it is scarcely necessary to go beyond the appearance of their respective premises and fields to gain an insight into the difference between them. The general condition of the plantation premises occupied by Negroes, under whatever system of cultivation, has been an eyesore in the cotton states for more than a generation. The spectacle of broken-down fences, patchwork outhouses, half-cultivated fields, and garden spots rank with weeds, is too familiar to the traveler through the Southern states to need description here. The destructive propensity of the Negro constitutes today a serious problem on many a well-ordered plantation. On the property in which the writer is interested the effort to maintain the premises of the Negro tenants in keeping with the general appearance of the plantation seems yearly to become a more hopeless undertaking. It seems difficult to escape the conclusion that back of all this lie the characteristics that apparently have always been a curse to the race—whether in Africa, the Southern states, or the West Indies—shiftlessness and improvidence.

On the other hand, the appearance of the Italian cotton grower's immediate surroundings, working on the same tenant system as the Negro, is alone sufficient to tell the story of the difference between the ultimate end and purpose of the labor of the two. The contrast is not alone in the things that appeal to the eye; it is much more emphasized in the respective uses made of the same material and opportunities. From the garden spot which the Negro allows to grow up in weeds, the Italian will supply his family from early spring until late fall, and also market enough largely to carry him through the winter. I have seen the ceilings of their houses literally covered with strings of dried butter beans, pepper, okra, and other garden products, while the walls would be hung with corn, sun-cured in the roasting ear stage. In the rear of a well-kept house would be erected a woodshed, and in it could be seen enough firewood, sawed and ready for use, to run the family through the winter months. These people did not wait till half-frozen feet compelled attention to the question of fuel, and then tear down the fence to supply their wants. Nor would they be found drifting about near the close of each season, in an aimless effort to satisfy an unreasoned desire to "move"—to make the next crop somewhere else.

It is always difficult to get a Negro to plant and properly cultivate the outer edges of his field—the extreme ends of his rows, his ditch banks, etc. The Italian is so jealous of the use of every foot for which he pays rent that he will cultivate with a hoe places too small to be worked with a plow, and derive a revenue from spots to which a Negro would not give a moment's thought. I have seen them cultivate right down to the water's edge the banks of bayous that had never before been touched by the plow. I have seen them walk through their fields and search out every skipped place in every row and carefully put in seed, to secure a perfect stand. I have seen them make more cotton per acre than the Negro on the adjoining cut, gather it from two to four weeks earlier, and then put in the extra time earning money by picking in the Negro's field.

It is not within the scope of this article to discuss the use of his opportunities by the Italian, as contrasted with the Negro's neglect of his. But the frugality and thrift of the former offer a contrast to the latter's careless, spendthrift ways no less striking than that between the methods of cultivation of the two. Given a soil as fertile as the alluvial land to which I have referred, and people who apply the methods of the Italian to its cultivation will soon own the fields they till. And this is what they are doing—buying land and paying for it. Handicapped as they are at first, by ignorance of the language and ignorance of the cultivation of the plant they raise, still they are becoming property owners, taxpayers, and citizens. . . .

I have referred here to a small portion of the cotton belt, one with which I am personally familiar. But the entire South is turning its attention to white immigration. It is being encouraged through the organized efforts of business associations and transportation companies, while there are well-defined movements in some

states toward the creation of state immigration bureaus. The climate is here, and the soil—and the need for labor; it is a mere question of time before the story of the immigration to the West will be repeated in the South.

What is the significance of all this to the Negro? To my mind here at last the white man has become the Negro's problem. His problem, because the wisest leaders among his own people agree with his most sensible white advisers upon two points vital to his future in this country; that the home of the mass of the race must remain in the Southern states, and that its destiny must be worked out upon the soil. The field of the Negro's activities thus becomes doubly circumscribed, and any invasion of that field by the white man must present for him a serious aspect. I would not be understood as attempting to set up a "scarehead" here. There is no danger of an inrush of foreigners buying up all the land in the South, and leaving none for the Negro. Not at all. But with every encroachment by the white man upon the Negro's ancient field, there follows a corresponding diminution of the latter's opportunities in that field. If the Negro this year produces 65 percent of our cotton, and twenty years hence is producing but 45 percent, then certainly the two decades would mark for him a distinct loss of ground.

How rapid this movement may become it is of course impossible to forecast. It may be many years before the Negro, as a race, will be in any wise visibly affected by it. But henceforth it can no more be ignored than can the progress of any other economic struggle between the black race and the Caucasian. The man who argues that the Negro agriculturist today fills a place that cannot be wrested from him by the white man—that because he is today essential to the production of the country's greatest crop, he is therefore essential for all time—displays as little wisdom as does he who contends that the Negro will someday altogether cease to be a factor of economic value in American industrial life.

The Ruinous Cost of Chinese Exclusion
Joaquin Miller

26

The Western states, with California in the lead, had agitated successfully for the exclusion of Chinese from the United States during the 1870s and 1880s. But the decrease in Chinese immigration was almost immediately made up for by the arrival of Japanese after 1885. Westerners then turned their attention to the Japanese and sought also to exclude them. But Japan's powerful position in the Far East made it impossible to deal with her nationals in America as arbitrarily as the Chinese had been treated. Nevertheless, in 1907, the federal government did reach what was called a "gentlemen's agreement," by which Japan would voluntarily restrict the number of emigrants bound for America. Although the anti-Oriental agitation had been basically racial, the argument that Chinese and Japanese took jobs from white workers was frequently heard. There was very little truth to the argument; in fact, proscription of the Orientals caused labor problems rather than solved them. Poet-adventurer Joaquin Miller, a longtime resident of California, explored the economics of Chinese exclusion on the eve of the "gentlemen's agreement." [*North American Review*, November 1907.]

The editor of a certain magazine has written me asking for an article on the exclusion of the Japanese. After careful consideration, I have decided to answer directly to the laboring men, in whose interest, no doubt, the article is asked.

In the first place, then, I must decline to urge, or even entertain, the impossible. There can be no Japanese Exclusion Act; but there must be, and there should be, very soon, a repeal of the Chinese Exclusion Act. I can remember, and so can some of my fellow laborers, when the most unpopular man in any community was an "Abolitionist." At the first political convention I ever attended, at Eugene, Oregon, the two leading Democrats, afterwards United States senators, in their heated rivalry violently and vociferously accused each other of "Abolitionism." The same sort of reproach, even extending to personal violence in some quarters of California, rests on the man who dares say the Chinese Exclusion Act must and should be repealed. The change of sentiment in this matter must come, and it will come as suddenly as the odium passed from the Abolitionist in the earlier time.

Let me quote a paragraph from a dispatch from Washington, on September 13th:

The labor question on the coast, the secretary said, was becoming more serious every day, and he instanced the fact that the navy yards at Mare Island and Bremerton were working far under their capacity by reason of the labor famine. He pointed out that in the West farmhands were being paid as high as $6.00 a day.

Six dollars a day for farmhands! I have only now returned from a three months' tour through Oregon, Washington, and Idaho. I saw in that tour fruit of all sorts, in their season, rotting on the ground, not only by tons, but by hundreds and hundreds of tons. I saw great machines in the harvest fields, all kinds of traction en-

Brown Brothers

Oriental farmer working in a field of bean sprouts. The Chinese Exclusion Act of 1882 produced a shortage of skilled inexpensive labor, causing food prices to rise.

gines, mighty reapers drawn by as many as thirty-six horses. Yet, despite this energy and industry of the brave producers, there lay thousands on thousands of acres all going to waste. And the feeling of the honest tillers of the soil at such loss, after all their care and their great outlay, was at fever heat. I promised them to appeal to the people.

The honest farmer is not the only sufferer. The world wants this bread. In some parts of the world it is needed, and needed badly. The Chinese people are starving for this bread, starving to death in multitudes. These people would be willing to work for fifty cents a day. This nation is going to say, "Let them come and work." They want the work, the farmer wants them to have it.

And is their work going to compete with you or me, my fellow laborers? Not

in the least. On the contrary, it is the very thing we need, as much as the farmer needs it. To illustrate. I paid, the last time I was down to my grocer's, eighty cents for a twenty-pound sack of flour. A few years ago, before the Exclusion Act, I paid only seventy-five cents for a fifty-pound sack of flour. You all did the same. You are paying just about a triple price now. Why? Because the farmer is paying more than a triple price for his labor. This sort of labor does not at all conflict with the labor of anyone in the industrial storm centers. No laborer in the city wants to get out to work on the farm, be he white or black. But the little yellow Cantonese laborer and the little brown Nipponese, growing close to the ground and able to get down to the work they so much need, want to get out into the fields by thousands and by thousands. They could, and gladly would, bring bread prices back and down to their old normal conditions. They could, and gladly would, not only reduce the cost of living at least one-half, but they would save many a good man, the real laborer, from bankruptcy; they could save many a beautiful farm of today from being turned back to chaparral tomorrow.

Last summer, the Japanese asked only $1.25 a day in the raisin fields. This season they demand double that wage. Last year we paid seventy-five cents a box for raisins; this year we will pay $1.50. And for what? Solely to suit a few uninformed and shortsighted labor leaders of the city, who have decided that they don't like "an Abolitionist."

California has survived in the interior, she has even prospered, not because of the Chinese Exclusion Act, but in spite of it. But with farm labor at $6.00 a day, or even one-half, one-quarter, or one-sixth

that figure, she is not going to prosper long, even if she survives.

Take my own little steep and stony ranch. The story of its unprofitable struggle will illustrate, in a small way, the whole situation. I wanted a home for my invalid mother in a mild climate, and bought about a hundred acres, and began to plant fruit trees and grow garden stuff. I first tried Portuguese, at forty cents a day. But these thrifty fishermen from the Azores soon got gardens of their own. Then I tried the nomadic, drunken tramp, tried to sober him up and set him to work. I need not recite the dismal struggle or the pitiful results. Then I got a Chinaman, whom I had known long ago in the mines, to get me five Chinese. This was when all things were at ebb tide. Denis Kearney was in command, so to speak, and Coxey's army was in embryo. This old Chinaman got five little Cantonese, to be housed and fed at my cost, for

Japanese laborers at work in an orange-packing house near Los Angeles, California, 1903.

Courtesy Los Angeles County Museum of Natural History

Japanese workers load oranges into a boxcar, 1903.

$25, $5.00 each—that was all they asked—he to have $10, per month.

Then came the Exclusion Act. The rich folk must and would have Chinese servants. There was not a sufficient number for both rich and poor people, and my little yellow farmers, who could now get five times what I was paying, left my "quarters" empty on their very first pay-day.

By help of my first farm laborers, I had set the place into fruit and berries. But after two years' struggle, toiling with my own hands day and night, I had to let my Nova Scotia apples, Georgia peaches, and all sorts of costly plants die where they stood, because, even when I could get white men to help me, they didn't know their work as Chinese do; besides, they were, sometimes, drunken and dirty, body and soul.

Leaving my orchards and gardens to die, as others are beginning to do for the same reason, I set most of the place in forest trees. I am now leaning on this grove of more than 50,000 trees, hoping that I may yet be able to make the place pay taxes!

Meantime, after the orchards and gardens had been allowed to go to waste, a few Japanese students came and, between lessons, took generous interest in teaching me how to trim and make trees grow, as if they had been masters of forestry. Of course, they were of the higher class; but I am bound to say that the dozen or more of these people whom I have had with me, more or less, for the past twenty years, have compelled me to regard this sort of fellow laborer with the greatest respect. The Japanese, at home or abroad, is entirely sober and temperate. Born and bred in the water, so to speak, he is as clean as the water can make him. He is industrious beyond belief. He rises with the birds, as we all should; but he burns the "midnight oil" to excess.

And now, my fellow toilers, a serious word about those vast millions of acres now being opened up by irrigation in Nevada, Oregon, Washington, and Idaho. If the lack of men to harvest fruit and grain this year has entailed the loss of millions on millions, what is going to happen next year, and the next year, and the next, with these millions of acres added to our present acreage. Think it out for yourselves. For you can think, and the time is at hand for you to think reasonably and humanely.

And now let me ask you of the San Francisco union laborers, who insist on the exclusion of Chinese labor, How do you compare, either in numbers or in strength, with the vast army of laborers in the interior who have neither time nor money to attach themselves to any sort of union? In the language of the Bible, you are, both in numbers and in strength, "as grasshoppers in their sight." Bear in mind that you and all your unions put together are only a very small part of San Francisco. Remember that all San Francisco put together is only a very small part of California, and that all California is only a small portion of the United States. And yet you, a small, contentious portion and faction of a single city, assume to say that California and all this vast interior of new homes shall let their crops rot to humor your blindness, which has already doubled, trebled the price of your own bread!

You remind me of a dear friend to whom I looked up with great respect when I was a lad in Oregon. He was a state senator, a kinsman of the great Sam Houston, of Texas, and his one hobby was to keep people out of Oregon. He would cry aloud in the Senate: "Too many people in Oregon already! Wall up the passes! Wall up the passes! Keep the people out! They will trample down the grass! They will ruin the grass, and we want the grass for our cattle. We want the cattle for California. Wall up the passes! Wall up the passes!"

Italian Farm Colonies in New Jersey   27

The most obvious solution to the congestion of the cities seemed (until World War II) the removal of urban immigrants to farms. No immigrant group escaped the pressure and the propaganda to take up agriculture. Unfortunately, the pressure came at a time when the trend was going the other way: America was rapidly becoming urbanized and thousands were leaving farms each year to seek the greater financial rewards of the city. The new immigrants, too, knew that the jobs in factories and mines, ill-paying though they were, met their needs better than farming. In any case, they had no money for the initial investment required to make farming successful. Agricultural colonies were nevertheless attempted in various parts of the country, and their occasional success stimulated others. Some experiments in New Jersey are described in the following article by Kellogg Durland. [*Chautauquan,* March 1908: "Immigrants on the Land."]

The two races amongst whom these colonization experiments have recently been made, are those giving us their greatest numbers—the Jews and the Italians. Nearly 150,000 Jews were admitted to the United States last year, and, approximately 300,000 Italians. If these two races could be attracted to the soil, to the cultivation of our vast farming lands, the importance of the movement would be beyond estimate.

I have had occasion to visit the oldest and most notable experiments in Jewish and Italian colonization, those in southern New Jersey, and this article ... is based on the results of my personal observations among the colonists of these two peoples. The Jew is temperamentally, characteristically, physically, traditionally, and historically different from the Italian. It could not be otherwise, therefore, than that their colonization efforts should be along different though parallel lines, and that their work should of necessity be viewed from different standpoints. Geographically these experiments in South Jersey are near together, but in no other respect. In this article I shall discuss the Italian colonies. . . .

The story of the first Italian land colony in southern New Jersey is soon told. It was founded by an Italian political refugee to this country, Signor Secchi de Casale. This man had established the first

Italian newspaper in New York, called *L'Eco d'Italia,* through which he had endeavored to keep alive the flame of Italian patriotism among the Italians who were then in the United States. He was a disciple of Mazzini and a companion of Garibaldi and other Italian patriots who were instrumental in the union of Italy and with whom he had fought for her independence.

In the year 1849, after the unsuccessful attempt to form a Roman republic, he and several of his companions in the cause migrated to New York. De Casale lived with Garibaldi in the village of Stapleton, Staten Island, in a house still standing. As the Italians in this country increased, De Casale found his interest in the welfare of his immigrant countrymen growing and their need was at that time so apparent to him that he felt called upon to suggest some legitimate and wise channel for the expression of their energies and for the development of their abilities.

As a reward for his services to the Italians in America, King Victor Emmanuel later knighted De Casale.

While his efforts were constant in many directions, the most important accomplishment of his life was the establishment of an agricultural colony near Vineland, New Jersey.

Mr. Charles Landis, the founder of the city of Vineland, cooperated with Chevalier de Casale in this colonization scheme. The first group of peasants brought here in a body were sent to the colony in 1878, although a few years previous to this time certain individual Italians had exploited the work of berry picking in the vicinity, notably at Hammonton. From these beginnings grew the somewhat extended Italian colonization that we find today.

On the whole, the district of South Jersey is drear and unlovely; it is flat and hill-less, covered with scrub oak, stunted pine, and in many places consists chiefly of large swamps. For years it lay in its primal state because few American farmers had the energy to apply themselves to its improvement and reclamation. Certain towns on the railway there were, small and not very prosperous, and with these as a basis, the work of the immigrant colonists has gone on. The surface soil for the most part is light and sandy, often white like the sand of seabeaches, but there is a subsoil which is fairly rich, and on the whole it has been proved adaptable for certain crops. Grapes, sweet potatoes, beans, and tomatoes all grow admirably throughout this belt, and peaches and other fruits have been satisfactorily grown in certain sections.

Italian peasants born and accustomed to intensely hard work took hold of the great task of reclaiming the difficult lands that surrounded their settlements, and by dint of patience and great labor they have learned what crops can be depended upon. With the berries, the beans, and the sweet potatoes, and later the grapes, for a beginning, the early colonists developed farms of remarkable prosperity. American settlers who had once occupied farms in the neighborhood grew discouraged and many of them left, allured by the call of the town, or the more fertile fields of the Middle West. These deserted plantations were quickly occupied by the olive-skinned newcomers, and today the farms once occupied by Americans are worked side by side with the farms of the brothers of the Italian pioneers who themselves cleared away the virgin tangles and made the sandy, barren dunes fertile.

Since the first settlers took up their living these Italian colonists have slowly increased until today they number some thousands. Not a large population, perhaps, when compared to our aggregate Italian population, but these colonies are only experiments, samples as it were, and in many other sections are similar experiments. Taken together the results are important. For convenience we are noting the story of South Jersey, but there are other colonies in California, in Louisiana, in Connecticut, in Massachusetts, Rhode Island, Pennsylvania, New York, in Tennessee, and Texas. These have each sprung up independently without special attention but the readiness shown by the colonists to adapt themselves to the soil is clear indication of what may be expected when the government undertakes in a systematic way the work of settling the Italians on the soil throughout the country in such places as their labor is most needed.

No people coming to America can live as economically as do the Italians. Their standard of living is by no means in conformity with that general condition of comfort that is called the "American standard of living." Ultimately, however, the Italians desire things which are foreign to them at home and gradually they raise their own standards. But at the outset the rigid economy they practise is a help.

The Italians start in life absolutely independent. Families come down from the cities, Philadelphia and New York, as berry pickers. They acquire a little money and a small, crude shack in which they live until they have paid off all indebtedness and get a little ahead, when they begin to build their own homes. The Jews, on the other hand, invariably start with a burden of debt to carry for their land and for their homes, and the cost of living to the Jew is always greater than to the Italian. He must have his wine at Passover and he must support his Talmud-Torah

and his lodge, and oftentimes he is sending money home to Russia to bring over the remainder of his family, and it is a number of years before he finds himself on a clear footing. The Italian, in the meantime, free of debt, forging ahead by small steps, succeeds in acquiring his house and land free from all debt.

The Italian, more than any other alien, comes to America with the idea of saving a sum of money sufficient to enable him to return to his native land for the remainder of his life. But the immigrants who have been a few years in this country acquire certain habits and customs which they are unable to take back with them to Italy, and rather than repudiate these, they prefer to bring their families to America. Each year more and more Italian families are thus brought to America by Italian immigrants who have established themselves in this country and who, contrary to their early expectations, have renounced their early ambition of returning to Italy, and are now only desirous of making a permanent home in this country. This is a phenomenon, however, which is only acquired unconsciously with their Americanization.

The comparative agricultural conditions in America and in Italy are tremendously in favor of America. At home the Italian peasant has lived for many generations in towns which are in many cases the outgrowths of burgs and feudal castles under whose protection they were originally built. The peasants go out in the early morning to the farms and gardens, the fields and vineyards, which sometimes are distant several miles, and return at evening. This regime carries with it certain discomforts and physical disadvantages resulting from lack of proper and comfortable houses, from excessive toil, and such heavy taxation as leaves a residue of profit so small that the comforts and many of the necessities of life are impossible. This toilsome regime has been the direct cause of the low standard of living which the Italians bring with them, but which in this country enables the Italian to more readily adjust himself to a difficult and stubborn environment and to reclaim land which ordinary American farmers have despaired of. Italian peasants who come to New York are, for the most part, entirely ignorant of the agricultural possibilities of this country. To them America is New York, but when offered a safe conduct to the soil in the agricultural districts, the Italian finds the advantages of American country life far in excess of any dreams he may have cherished. The comforts and independence afforded the American farmer, even the Americanized immigrant farmer, appeal to him, and he willingly undertakes the most difficult and disagreeable of work for a period of years in order that he may win the position of an American citizen. This ideal which is so easily placed before him is stimulating to good citizenship, to industrious labor, and to rapid, though not too rapid, Americanization.

One of the great difficulties in the establishment of agricultural colonies in any section of the country is in the matter of securing a ready market for the crops. The South Jersey colonists do not have this difficulty to contend with. The grape juice companies in and near Vineland use not only all the grapes which all of the colonists in that section can produce, but many more.

The most profitable crop of all, however, is probably that of sweet potatoes. The Vineland brand of sweet potatoes brings from twenty-five cents to $1.00 more in the market than any other brand. Some of the Italian farmers make as much as $800 a season from six acres of sweet potatoes. The Allivine Company, also near Vineland, has an enormous cannery. This cannery offers an adequate market for all the sweet potatoes, lima beans, and tomatoes that the colonists can raise. The canning of sweet potatoes is carried on on an enormous scale. Every inducement is made to encourage the colonists (Jewish and Italian alike) to raise more of these products each year, and yet the demand is entirely out of proportion to the supply. This cannery employs 200 hands and runs three months in the year, from the middle of August to the middle of November. Its output is sometimes as high as 30,000 cans of tomatoes a day. The machinery is most perfect and tomatoes are canned at the rate of forty-two cans a minute.

The labor employed is mostly Italian, men and women. Rough work of the cannery is generally undertaken by Italians. The skinning of tomatoes, for example, which is unskilled labor and fairly remunerative, will not be touched by Jewish girls—it hurts their hands; and while the work really is perfectly clean, it looks nasty; it also hurts their hands, owing to the fact that the tomatoes are acid and the water out of which they have to be taken is hot. The Italian women are paid at the rate of three cents a bucket for skinning these tomatoes and the average woman makes anywhere from seventy-five cents to $2.00 a day. Occasionally an expert worker will make $3.00 a day. Here as in many other cases the Italians come bringing their entire families and it is common to see a man and woman and several children at work filling buckets with the skinned tomatoes. The company pays farmers $8.00 a ton for the tomatoes which they bring in. To stimulate tomato raising the Allivine Company furnish the local farmers with manure and fertilizer at low rates, sometimes cost price, exacting in return promises from the farmers that they will put in so many acres of tomatoes for the following season. It is rare, however, to find a farmer who abides by his promise and puts in as many crops of tomatoes as the company prescribed. They utilize their fertilizers for other crops. Sometimes they take a chance on another crop being more successful, as, for example, sweet potatoes. One year several farmers made a good deal of money from their sweet potato crops, so the next year instead of putting in a reasonable number of sweet potatoes and a reasonable number of tomatoes and other crops, they, so to speak, put all of their eggs in one basket by devoting themselves very largely to sweet potatoes. If they do this for several years successively, there is danger of a sweet potato "slump," in which case they will lose heavily.

The canning of sweet potatoes is an industry which the Allivine Company has been developing extensively, and they are restricted in the matter of more extensive development only through the lack of supply of sweet potatoes. In the West and Middle West where sweet potatoes are not grown, there is a tremendous demand for canned sweet potatoes. For the so-called prime sweets, that is to say, the first size, largest sweet potatoes, the farmers receive $5.00 a barrel. They have had heretofore no market for their small potatoes but now the Allivine Company pays seventy-five cents a barrel for them.

Although the Allivine Farm is closer to Jewish colonies than to the Italian it is a boon to both peoples. It is sufficiently near to the Italians to offer a ready market for their produce and at the same time to give employment to pickers in season, and indoor work during the canning of the crops. The Allivine Farm, which is run in conjunction with the cannery and vice versa, not only serves as a model for the foreign farmers of the region but gives employment to a large number, who are frequently glad of such an opportunity for apprenticeship.

A Lithuanian Farm Colony

28

The following promotional article was written by J. J. Hertmanavicius, president of a Lithuanian land colonization society, Zinycia, and was published in the foreign language paper *Lietuva* on June 12, 1908. To make his point, the writer contrasts the worst industrial conditions of the day with an idealized picture of American agriculture. Success in such ventures as the one proposed was infrequent. The economic plight of the small farmer in America had steadily worsened since the 1870s, so even if the immigrant could get the money to go into farming, his prospects for making a success of it were gloomy. [Chicago Foreign Language Press Survey, WPA Project, 1942.]

Nearly all Lithuanians were either born or reared on a farm. After emigrating to America, they became factory workers, coal miners, mill hands, store employees, stockyards workers, etc. Therefore, a comparison between the lives of a workman and a farmer in America should be of immense interest to our people. In order to become thoroughly acquainted with the lives of a workman and a farmer, and learn which is more desirable, it is necessary to make a detailed review of the various social and economic aspects of these two classes of people, and then compare them with each other. The results of this comparison will speak for themselves.

A Lithuanian workman in the United States, if he is not the master of a trade, or is unable to speak the English language, can find only that kind of employment which requires a great deal of bodily health and physical endurance at very low wages. The average laborer receives from $1.00 to $2.00 per day. His job is very insecure. He is subject to frequent and sudden layoffs. During the years of national prosperity, many labor strikes spring up and the worker is compelled to go out on strike with his fellow workers. He receives no income during these periods. When a business and industrial depression occurs, the worker is laid off and again he has neither job nor income.

Even during those periods of national prosperity, when no labor strikes take place, the industrial worker often loses his job because of illness. After he recovers from an illness, he is again forced to go out and look for another job, which usually takes a very long time. If he is fortunate enough to locate a good job, and works for a comparatively long time, then he is able to save some of his earnings. However, when a period of forced unemployment occurs, then his savings become exhausted. When he is reemployed, he must start saving all over again.

We must bear in mind that the above is only the example of an industrial worker who is sincerely interested in his future welfare, and who does not squander his earnings in saloons or for other foolishness. This type represents a very small minority. The earnings of a greater majority of workers do not stretch from one payday to another. When these workers lose their jobs, they find themselves without even a bite to eat.

The living expenses of a workman are very high all over the United States. His earnings are so meager that he is unable to meet the expenses of all the necessary requirements of life, especially if he is married. He cannot afford to live in suitable living quarters, wear decent clothing, attend theaters, send his children through the higher institutions of learning, enjoy a vacation in the country during the summer months in order to get a breath of fresh air and build up his failing health, and he cannot afford to eat any of the more expensive foods, because his meager earnings cannot stand it. He is forced to lead a miserable life of poverty. Even his children have little hope of ever reaching a better, brighter, and happier life.

The only commodity which a worker has to sell is his health. As long as he enjoys good health, he is able to earn enough for a bare subsistence. However, when his health fails, he comes to the sad realization that with the labor of his entire lifetime he was unable to earn enough even for bread in his old age, nor for shelter, clothing, or other vital necessities of life.

Therefore, the life of a workman is full of grief and misery, and without hope for a better and brighter future. He is at all times dependent upon those who are more fortunate than himself. He must fear his superiors and be careful not to be late for work. Regardless of whether he is sick or healthy, he must perform a full day's work; otherwise he will be discharged and left without bread or shelter, and his friends will shy away from him. It is, therefore, not at all surprising that workmen complain so frightfully about their plight and engage in bitter struggles in order to ease the great burden of their lives.

However, the various struggles between the workers and their employers do not produce any satisfactory results. Whenever the employers shut down their factories, or other forms of enterprise, the workers either starve to death or move to other sections of the globe.

Therefore, the life of a workman appears to be highly undesirable. It seems that we should seek other lines of endeavor for our livelihood.

Now let us review the life of an American farmer.

A farmer owns a strip of fertile land; he owns a home, a herd of cattle, and enjoys healthy air, water, and food. He does not find it necessary to go out into the garden of nature on weekends, because he lives in a garden of nature all his life.

A farmer does not need to pay rent or water tax; he does not need to buy coal if he has kindling wood; it is not necessary for him to buy milk, cheese, or butter; it is unnecessary for him to buy potatoes or other vegetables; it is unnecessary for him to purchase eggs or even meat, because he can always slaughter some of his cattle and have plenty of fresh and healthy meat. A farmer does not need to pay streetcar fare to get to work; he can ride to work with his own horses. In other words, a farmer who owns a good farm does not need to buy anything as far as food is concerned, and for that reason he is independent; he does not know the meaning of a financial crisis. He works on his own farm for himself; he does not fear anyone and is not obliged to obey anybody; he has no fear of losing his job or coming late to work. He is a king on his own land and does not have to fear any bosses.

A farmer does not need to buy any necessities of life. On the contrary, he has many products to sell. He raises wheat and, after providing for his own needs, he can sell the surplus and receive money for it. When a farmer raises some cattle or poultry, he sells them and receives money. He keeps cows and receives money for their milk. The longer he lives on his farm, the more profits he derives from it. His wealth increases from day to day. It is very plain, therefore, that the life of a farmer is incomparably much more fortunate and happier than that of a workman. All this leads to the inevitable conclusion that there is but one salvation for us Lithuanian-Americans, and that is to take to the land in order to free ourselves from foreign bondage.

A farmer can send his children first to a country school and later through the higher institutions of learning, because it is not necessary for him to depend upon his children for support. He derives enough bread from his farm for a decent livelihood without the aid of his children. An intelligent and industrious farmer not only provides for the education of his children, from whom he derives great joy and assistance in his old age, but in doing so he also fulfills his obligation to raise the intellectual level of society. Therefore, it would be a very good thing for all Lithuanian-Americans, who are now suffering hopelessly in the service of foreign masters, to give very serious consideration to the idea of settling down on mother earth; we should leave the cities and towns, and shy away from them as from a plague.

Although the best farm lands are already occupied, nevertheless, there is plenty of good land for colonization purposes still available in the United States. Much of the land, however, is unsuitable for profitable farming, even if it can be procured at comparatively low prices. Therefore, such factors as fertility of the soil, transportation facilities, water supply, etc., must be thoroughly investigated. Climatic conditions, in order to suit the Lithuanian racial characteristics, also must be taken into consideration. Furthermore, we will be able to preserve our national traditions better and lead a more happier life if we group together, and not scatter ourselves in various sections of the country among farmers of other nationalities.

The question, then, is how can we realize all these wonderful ideals? The solution of this problem, has been assumed by the Lithuanian colonization society Zinycia (Fountain of Knowledge). During the past three years this society has been actively engaged in a thorough investigation of the various farming sections in the United States. When this society was first organized, and the colonization question was seriously discussed, the members advanced a great variety of suggestions. Some wished to colonize in a warm climate in the Southern states; others preferred the Western states; and a third group pulled for the Eastern states. The latter was soon eliminated from consideration after we learned of the high land prices and dense population of the territory.

In order to select the best location for the colonization of Lithuanian-Americans, the society decided to launch a very extensive and thorough investigation of all the available farm lands in the United States. The United States Public Land Office was contacted for information about available homesteads. A number of railroad representatives and other land agents were invited to attend meetings of the society to present information on the land situation in America. Contacts were made with individual farmers, both personally and through the mails. Justin F.

Jakavicius toured the states of Kansas, Oklahoma, Indiana, and the Indian Territory; his brothers, George and Julius Jakavicius, made a tour of the Southern states; Alex Bendris investigated the states of Tennessee and Missouri; Anton Mazeika went to Alabama and the neighboring states; Stanley Mikolaitis and Frank Domeika were sent into the states of Washington, Oregon, and Colorado; other members of the society conducted an investigation in the states of Wisconsin and Michigan. Information was also sought and received concerning prospective farm lands in the states of California, Utah, Idaho, Iowa, Nebraska, Wyoming, Ohio, South and North Dakota, Minnesota, and in Alaska and Canada.

After three years of extensive investigation and study, the members of the society finally came to the conclusion that the states of Wisconsin and Michigan offer the best opportunites and advantages for the establishment of a Lithuanian-American farm colony. The Southern states were eliminated because it had been learned that Lithuanians would experience some difficulty in adopting themselves to the hot and dry climate. About fourteen years ago Anthony Olis, an active member of the society, had formed a Lithuanian colony in the state of Arkansas. Although the soil was very fertile, nevertheless, the climate proved to be very unhealthy and the colony was forced to disband.

Minnesota and Dakota were eliminated because of the high cost of land. In the Western states too much irrigation is required for successful farming. Heavy and prolonged rainfalls interfere with the prosperity of the farmers in the states of Washington and Oregon. The prevalence of tornadoes, earthquakes, and violent storms in the Southern states was also taken into consideration.

Therefore, after carefully considering the colonization problem from all angles for three years, the Lithuanian colonization society Zinycia has decided to establish a Lithuanian agricultural colony in the state of Wisconsin. There the land is very fertile, the climate is very suitable and healthy for Lithuanians, and there is an abundant supply of healthy water. It has excellent railroad transportation, good roads, and many large cities and towns. Thousands of farmers in Wisconsin are already enjoying wonderful prosperity. It is, therefore, an established fact that any industrious farmer can make a very good living in Wisconsin.

The society has selected the northern part of Clark County in the state of Wisconsin as the most ideal location for the establishment of a Lithuanian-American agricultural colony. The society already has purchased a large tract of land in that section of Wisconsin and has named it Zinycia, after the name of the society. An extensive campaign is now under way to colonize the territory with Lithuanians. Most members of the Zinycia society are already established there and are making splendid progress.

All land in the northern part of Clark County is very fertile, without stones, mountains, sand, or large swamps. Transportation facilities are excellent. A beautiful river flows through the territory. There are many old towns nearby, offering a very good market for farm products.

After the colonization work of the territory is well under way, it is planned to set up a Lithuanian town in the vicinity, with factories, a Lithuanian church, school, etc.

Therefore, here is an excellent opportunity for all those Lithuanians who desire to free themselves from the misery of city life. It is advisable to purchase a piece of land as soon as possible, while the prices are still low. All Lithuanians are invited to visit the territory and make a personal investigation.

The New Pittsburghers

29

By the first years of the 20th century Pittsburgh had become one of the most ethnically variegated cities in the United States. The immigrants were drawn to this industrial center by the need for unskilled labor in the steel mills. This article by YMCA official Peter Roberts describes the new immigrants who had replaced the Germans, Irish, English, and others after 1880 [*Charities and the Commons,* January 2, 1909.]

The day laborer of a generation ago is gone—a change which has been swifter and more complete in Pittsburgh than in many other of our industrial centers. "Where are your Irish? your Welsh? your Germans? your Americans?" I asked an old mill hand. "Go to the city hall and the police station," he said. "Some of them are still in the better-paid jobs in the mills; but mostly you'll have to look for them among the doctors and lawyers and office holders; among clerks and accountants and salesmen. You'll find them there."

The day laborer in the mills today is a Slav. The foreign-born of the steel district comprise, it is true, every European nation, but I shall deal here only with the races from southeastern Europe, which for twenty years have been steadily displacing the Teutonic and Celtic peoples in the rough work of the industries. The be witnessed here. The most backward of these foreigners are superstitious and ignorant and are the victims of cunning knaves and unscrupulous parasites. On the other hand, the whole territory is thrown into a stern struggle for subsistence and wage standards by the displacements due to these resistless accretions to the ranks of the workers. The moral and religious life of the city is not less affected by this inflow of peoples. Their religious training differs widely from that of peoples of Protestant antecedents, and institutions that were dear to the founders of the city are fast undermined by the customs of immigrants from southeastern Europe. Yet as a whole, they bring with them physical and cultural resources which the English-speaking community fails to elicit or thoughtlessly wastes. . . .

Poles, Italians, and Jewish immigrants lead the list. Lithuanians, Croatians, Serbians, Slovaks, and Ruthenians are numbered by the thousands, and Magyars, Greeks, Bohemians, and Rumanians are here in lesser groups.

The representatives of these nations touch elbows in the streets so that the languages heard when the people are marketing in the foreign quarters on Saturday night are as numerous as those of a seaport town. Twenty dialects are spoken. Yet the polyglot mass that confuses the visitor and induces pessimistic impressions as to the future of the city, is each morning marshaled without tumult. The discipline of the industrial establishments converts this babel of tongues into one of the. chief forces of production. Therein lies an appraisal not only of the American entrepreneur, but also of these men coming from nations of low efficiency, who are able so quickly to fall into line and keep step in an industrial army of remarkable discipline and output. . . .

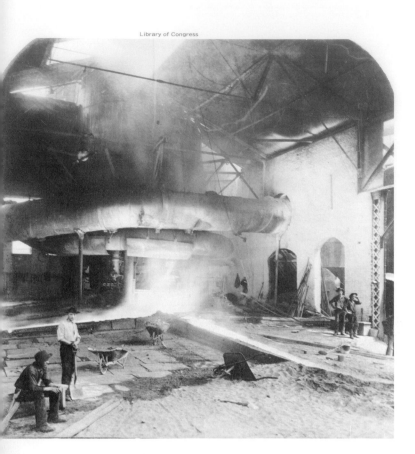

Workers drawing off iron in a Pittsburgh steel plant, 1905.

tendency of the Italians is to go into construction and railroad work, a few entering the mines, rather than into the plants and yards; and my group narrows itself down to the dominant Slav and Lithuanian. What I have to say of them in Pittsburgh and Allegheny City is in the main representative of the manufacturing towns of the whole district.

Roughly speaking, one-quarter of the population of Pittsburgh is foreign-born. The foreigner is nowhere more at home than here, and nowhere has he been more actively welcomed by employers. The conflict of customs and habits, varying standards of living, prejudices, antipathies, all due to the confluence of representatives of different races of men, may

Up to September 1907, the men in charge of furnaces, foundries, forges, and mills in the Pittsburgh district could not get the help they needed. The cry everywhere was, "Give us men." A foreman, therefore, could assure Pietro and Melukas that if their brothers or cousins, or friends were sent for, they would get work as soon as they arrived. More than that, the Slav and Italian are no longer dependent on the English boss in the matter of finding work for their countrymen. The inflow of immigration from south eastern Europe has assumed such proportions in the industries of the cities that superintendents have, in some instances, appointed Italian and Polish and Lithuanian foremen; and with these, as with German and Irish, blood is thicker than water. They employ their fellow country-

men. They know the condition of the labor market and can by suggestion stimulate or retard immigration.

The tonnage industries of Pittsburgh have expanded tremendously in the last two decades. Such industries need manual laborers as do no others. The Slavs have brawn for sale. Herein, at bottom, is the drawing force which accounts for such a moving in of peoples and the readiness with which they find their places in the specialized industries of the district. Pittsburgh has clamorous need for these men. Take the average Lithuanian, Croatian, Ruthenian, or Slovak, and his physique would compare favorably with that of any people. Most of the immigrants are from agricultural communities. Their food in the fatherland was coarse, their habits simple, their cares few. They had an abundance of vegetable diet, pure water, pure air, and sunshine, and they de-

Steelworkers making rails in a foundry, about 1908.

George Eastman House Collection

veloped strong physical organisms. Taking them as a whole, we get the best of the agricultural communities. The day has not yet come when the weak emigrate and the strong stay at home. No ship agents, however active, can reverse the natural order of the tide of immigration, and natural selection added to federal scrutiny gives us a body of men physically most fit for the development of our industries. Nowhere has this been better illustrated than in Pittsburgh.

These men come to be "the hewers of wood and carriers of water." There are representatives of each race far removed from the lowest industrial stratum, but taking these people as a whole, it is safe to say that the bulk of the unskilled labor in the city—the digging and carrying in the streets, the heavy labor in the mill, the loading and unloading of raw material on railroad and river, the rough work around forge and foundry, the coarse work around factories, and the lifting necessary in machine shops—all is performed by them. . . .

My belief is that certain employers of labor have reaped advantage from racial antipathies. The Pole and the Lithuanian have nothing in common and each of them despises the Slovak. Foremen know this and use their knowledge when foreigners are likely to reach a common understanding upon wages or conditions of labor. All these considerations have helped make it less difficult for factory operators to keep open or nonunion shop in Pittsburgh. The constant influx of raw material from backward nations into the industries of the city has had somewhat the same effect as the flow of water at an estuary when the tide is rising. All is commotion. It will continue to be so as long as the inflow of Slavs and Italians continues as it has in the last decade. But

when they have become permanently placed and their average intelligence and grasp of American conditions rise, racial prejudicies will give way to common interests. When this time comes, Pittsburgh will witness the rise of stronger labor organizations than were ever effected by Teuton and Celt. . . .

The influence of the industries reaches still further into the lives of the immigrants. Each people has a tendency to colonize in one section of the city and work in some one mill. The Bohemians are strong in Allegheny City, but few of them are found in Pittsburgh. The Slovaks predominate in McKees Rocks and Allegheny City, and many of them are found in the Soho district of Pittsburgh. The Poles are numerous in many parts of the greater city. The Lithuanians live in large numbers on the South Side, and near the National Tube Works and the American Steel and Wire Company. Many Ruthenians work in the Oliver Steel Works, while the Croatians and Serbians have worked for the most part in the Jones and Laughlin plants. My information is that foremen try to get one nationality in assigning work to a group of laborers, for they know that a homogeneous group will give best results. National pride also enters into selection. In talking to a Lithuanian of the serious loss of life which occurred when a furnace blew up, I asked, "Were any of your people killed in that accident?" He answered quickly, "No; catch our people do such work as that! There you find the Slovak." Of the grades of unskilled labor, the Slovak, Croatian, Serbian, and Russian (Greek Orthodox) may be said to perform the roughest and most risky, and the most injurious to health. There is, then, a more or less natural selection of peoples in the neighborhoods of the different great mills.

The Bulgarians of Chicago
Grace Abbott

30

*Of the small number of Bulgarian immigrants to America after 1900, several thousand settled in Illinois, many of these in Chicago. Sociologist Grace Abbott, who worked at job placement of immigrants in the city, wrote the following survey of the Bulgarians for the League for the Protection of Immigrants. [*Charity and the Commons,* January 9, 1909.]*

The Chicago newspapers of April 8, 1908, told the story of 600 unemployed and starving Bulgarians who had marched on the city hall and demanded work. The demonstration was as harmless as it was ineffective and so, viewed only from the standpoint of the industrial crisis and its accompanying social unrest, it was soon forgotten by the public as a closed incident; but viewed from its much larger social significance it raised inevitably certain questions—questions which made an investigation of these people who are so little known seem important for Chicago.

Bulgarian immigration to the United States is still in its infancy. The twelfth census showed that 10,040,085 of our population were foreign-born and enumerated twenty-eight European countries or parts of countries from which they had come, and then credited to "Europe not otherwise specified" 2,272. To this number Bulgaria contributed. Since 1900, immigration from that part of Europe has increased. From Bulgaria, Serbia, and Rumania 11,359 immigrants came in 1907 as compared with 657 in 1901.

Statistics of the distribution show that the majority of these immigrants are coming west. Of the 27,174 Bulgarians, Serbians, and Montenegrins who came during the fiscal year ending June 30, 1907, Pennsylvania received 5,461, Illinois 5,347, Ohio, 4,423, New York 2,643.

During the past winter there were probably about 8,000 Bulgarians in the tri-cities, Madison, Venice, and Granite City, Illinois; and about 1,000, who had come within the past six months, in Chicago. These figures are most significant. Although still in its pioneer stage, it is evident that immigration from the southeastern corner of Europe has been well started and the "endless chain of letters" sent home will increase it enormously in the future. At present the men are coming without their families, expecting to return; but if the history of the Irish, the Germans, the Scandinavians, and the Italians repeats itself in the case of the Bulgarians, America will become the permanent home of the great majority of them and the women and children will follow as soon as the necessary passage money can be saved and sent back home.

In view of the newness and the remarkable increase of Bulgarian immigration to the United States, and the fact that so large a proportion is coming to Illinois, it is believed that some definite knowledge of the characteristics of these people, their economic and political condition at home, their reasons for coming, and their experiences since their arrival in Chicago would be interesting and valuable. For this reason a concrete study of 100 of the men who marched on City Hall was undertaken. It was made possible through the assistance and cooperation of Ivan Doseff, their leader and organizer. . . .

Many of these Bulgarians are intelligent and capable workmen, but like most foreigners they must serve an apprenticeship in the ranks of the unskilled until

Courtesy Immigrant Service League

Bulgarian immigrant woman waiting outside the offices of the Immigrant Service League, Chicago, 1930.

temporary from its very nature and can be obtained only from a casual labor center such as Chicago. Unable to secure work of this sort from the free employment offices as maintained by the state of Illinois, the foreigner is compelled to rely on the private employment agencies. The Bulgarians had the same experience with these agencies that most immigrants as well as the hard pressed and the unskilled American workmen have. They suffered from overcharging, division of fees with contractors, and misrepresentations of the work offered, but they secured enough work to convince them that this was the only way to get jobs in America, and they paid whatever was demanded as a gambler stakes his last dollar on the chance of winning. . . .

The fees were high, and what was more serious, they brought little return. One man who came in October paid an agent $18.50 and secured twenty days' work, ten at $2.00 a day and ten at $1.50 a day. Another who left seven children in Bulgaria and had been here a year last May, paid $8.50 and had in all two months' work at $1.75 a day. And still another, a blacksmith by trade who had been here six months, had had five days' work at $1.00 a day and to secure this he paid $7.00 in fees. Fifty of the men paid one agent $6.00 each for a job on the railroad. They were sent to Abingdon, near Peoria, Illinois, found no work, were without money and so walked back to Chicago, eating raw corn on the way. An effort was made by Mr. Doseff to have the money refunded but he was unsuccessful. The agent had paid to the contractor half of the $300 he had collected from the men, supposedly for railroad fare although the company's books showed no such receipts. The agent claimed that the men refused to work without an interpreter. The

they learn the language and American methods of work. Most of them came in October just as the winter was coming on. Their chances of obtaining work at that season under favorable circumstances were small and during the financial depression of the past year it became impossible. . . .

Under a fellow countryman who has learned some English and can act as interpreter, immigrant men usually find employment on railroad construction work all over the country. The work is

Board of Commissioners attempted a compromise; the agent's license was revoked but the fees were not returned to the Bulgarians. Another group was sent by an agency to Leslie, Arkansas, to work on a railroad which was being built from that place to Searcy, Arkansas. About half of them got work and the others, having no money, were forced to walk back. These men recovered the $14 fee each of them had paid and were so delighted that they forgot how many days' work they had lost and how much they had suffered in that long walk from western Arkansas to northeastern Illinois, and fortunately did not think of asking for damages.

The agents were not the only ones who took advantage of the Bulgarians. Two men, older than most of those who came and who have wives and children on their mortgaged land at home, worked for a contractor in Michigan for forty-five days and were paid $25 apiece. A young man of nineteen worked with a construction gang for forty days and was paid $3.00.

These are some of the experiences the Bulgarians had during the past winter. That their misfortunes are typical not only of their own race but of others is unquestioned; indeed they were much better looked after than many other foreigners, for their leaders were especially active in their behalf. For example, thousands of foreigners in Granite City and Madison, Illinois, who formerly found employment in the rolling mills, foundries, and car shops of that neighborhood, were out of work last year, among them many Bulgarians. P. D. Vasileff, a Bulgarian Methodist minister, secured the help of influential Americans in Granite City. They appealed to Governor Deneen. He was sympathetic; called up the superintendent of the South Side Free Employment Office in Chicago and urged him to make a special effort to place the Bulgarians. The men hoped for much but were disappointed. Fifty were given from three to six days' work by the Chicago Traction Company and then discharged. A few days' work obtained in this way and a few more after each snowfall was the only work the men had during the winter and early spring. In the fall many of them had rented houses and lived together; others were in Bulgarian lodging houses, but the cooperative housekeeping soon had to be abandoned and the lodging-house keepers were poor and could not give the men credit. News began to come from home that the mortgage was due, the wife was sick, or the children needed food, and the despair of the men increased. It was then that Mr. Doscff planned an appeal to Mayor Busse and the little Bulgarian "army of unemployed" was started on its march to the city hall. The men did not see the mayor, they did not get work, but the demonstration was not without its effect. Temporary relief was given by the organized charities of the city and a special effort was made to get the men work. With the coming of warm weather work on the railroads and streetcar lines was begun and the Bulgarians had jobs at such work, paying them from $1.25 to $1.75 a day. But this is seasonal work which ended in the fall and the men have had to pay from $4.00 to $5.00 a month for board so they are returning to Chicago with insufficient money to live without work during the winter.

These Bulgarians are splendid material for skilled workmen—strong, quiet, sober, intelligent, and eager to work. There should be some way by which they could be turned more quickly and with much less suffering into the valuable citizens they are sure to become.

Pericles of Smyrna and New York
Walter Weyl

31

The Horatio Alger success story became a reality for very few Americans, but there were just enough examples for everyone to continue to dream that one day fortune would come his way. For most immigrants, of course, any success at all was an improvement on the poverty and deprivation they had known in Europe. Economist Walter Weyl told the story of a Greek immigrant for whom the right combination of circumstances led to great wealth. [*Outlook*, February 26, 1910.]

When, forty years ago, a son and heir was born to the Greek bazaarkeeper Michael Antonopulo, of Smyrna, Turkey, it seemed eminently fit and proper to name the child Pericles. Christian names had gone out of fashion. The Greeks are excellent Christians, of a Christianity so ancient that it almost antedates Christ. But forty years ago, as today, there was alive in Greece and among the Greeks in Turkey a strong, enthusiastic nationalist spirit, and the Hellenes went back in their dreams beyond the dreary centuries of decline under Rome and Christianity to a glorious antiquity when the world beyond Greece was barbarian. Thus it happened that thirty puling infants of Smyrna were endowed with the name of Pericles, and one of these, Pericles Antonopulo, was destined, after many adventures, to become one day a dishwasher in the New York Yale Club. . . .

At the end of fifteen months Pericles had saved $150 out of a total of $240 received. With this sum he was persuaded to open a little cigarette establishment in the cellar of a downtown tenement. "There isn't a good Turkish cigarette in all America," decided Alcibiades, and Alcibiades knew, for he smoked all day.

It was a humble counselor who had directed the attention of Pericles to the infinite possibilities of the cigarette and tobacco business. Alcibiades was an oyster vendor. He kept a very small stand, enclosed in glass, from which he sold clams and oysters on the half shell and a varied assortment of dubious sandwiches. Above his wares hung a card with the motto "In God We Trust," and to no one else did Alcibiades extend credit.

A native American stopping to chat with Alcibiades was always informed in a lapidated English that the oyster vendor was the first of all the Greeks to arrive in America. "I come here," he would say, "thirty years past as little baby child. I work in Lowell. I save thousand dollars. My do-nothing brothers come to New York. I go into restaurant business with them. I lose my money. I marry. That also bad. I like Lowell—the Athens of America. I like not New York, where no one speaks a swell English." But to Pericles the street merchant admitted that he had been in America only six years, and was going back as soon as the oyster business permitted him to retire. In scholastic Greek and Miltonian English Pericles praised this intended repatriation, while the oyster vendor urged the graduate of the Athenian University to embark upon the cigarette business.

No one ever knew how it happened, Pericles least of all. Yearly, hundreds of persons become tobacconists, only to emerge from the business poorer than they entered it. The stock of the American Tobacco Company did not fall when Pericles issued his little cards announcing in Greek that the best and cheapest cigarettes in America were for sale at his emporium. Nor did Goliath tremble when he saw David approach.

During the first few weeks Pericles sold fewer cigarettes than he smoked. The following month business was still worse. Then the stroke of fortune came. A member of the Yale Club stumbled miraculously onto the cellar shop, and Pericles, remembering the man but not his name, addressed him as Mr. Yale. In another week the Yale Club bought its cigarettes from Pericles Antonopulo, and by the end of the year Demetrius, the fruiterer, had invested $10,000 in the business and begun an active canvass for the "Pyramid," the best and cheapest Egyptian cigarette in the world. The "Pyramid" took, and in a short time the new firm was in the proud position of refusing an offer of purchase from the American Tobacco Company.

Today Demetrius is a very wealthy man, and even Pericles counts his dollars in the hundreds of thousands. His wife is the daughter of a retired Greek merchant of Alexandria, Egypt, and his six-year-old boy is a pupil in a private school on Central Park West. Pericles still has dreams of New Greece, though they are now "sicklied o'er by the pale cast of thought"; he still talks in Miltonian English of the glories of ancient Hellas, and he is always a generous contributor when money is sent to the home country to repair a church, construct a road, or purchase a ship of war. He is all that a son of Greece should be, and yet—he is an American citizen and an American voter, and he is beginning to devote less thought to the Greeks of the Old World and more to the Greeks of the New.

These Greeks of the New World are still but a small number, not over 150,000, but they may someday become more numerous than the Greeks of Greece. The Hellene has always loved his native country—and always left it. In the olden days Greeks were to be found in Italy, France, Spain, Northern Africa, Asia Minor, on all the shores washed by the waters of the Mediterranean. Even today there are Greeks in all the world, and more Hellenes in the sprawling, crumbling Ottoman Empire, with its shadowy dependencies in Europe and Asia, than in Greece itself. And every year from the 6,000,000 Greeks of Greece and Turkey a larger contingent sets sail for America.

At first the migration was insignificant. In 1868 only eight Greeks came; during the next five years those who arrived might have all been housed in one tenement; until 1900 no year brought as many as 3,000. But in the year 1907 no less than 46,000 Greeks came to America; in other words, far more than the total number who arrived during the four centuries from 1492 to 1892. The immigration, though it has been temporarily stayed by the commercial depression, is bound to grow in the future to even greater proportions. . . .

It is fortunate for the Greeks that their strongest come first. It is a hard fight that meets them. In their struggle for the control of the shoe-blacking trade they must compete with the indefatigable Italian. In the pushcart business they again meet the Italian, and a far more formidable competitor, the Jew. In whatever occupation, from running an elevator to keeping a candy stand, the Greek meets the competition of men as determined, as industrious, as vigorous as himself.

All immigrants are at a temporary disadvantage, but certain disabilities affect the Greek more fundamentally than his competitors. Above all, the language. The majority of our Greek immigrants are peasants and shepherds, unused to the ways of even the remote Greek towns, and a third are unable to read or write their own language. To even the literates the English language is likely to remain a closed book. The characters are different, and the words, which an ignorant Italian might interpret through the common Latin, are "Greek" to the Greek. The sign "Keep Off the Grass" means no more to an immigrant from Attica, Arcadia, or Zanthe than does a line from Homer to a district messenger boy. . . .

There are many Greeks who are peddling without a license, or are violating provisions of the corporation law or the sanitary law, who have never even heard of such laws and do not know that they exist. There is rarely an interpreter at hand to explain so insignificant a procedure as the imposition of a fine, and as for the law, though ignorance is no excuse, there is no attempt to inform aliens of its provisions. In the little towns of Hermopolis or Pyrgos you can throw things on the sidewalk; in the big cities of Chicago and Boston you cannot. Of all the Greeks summoned before the courts, five-sixths have been guilty of nothing beyond the violation of ordinances of which they have never had an opportunity to know.

You can't stop a nation's gaining its foothold by fining or throwing into jail, though you may halt its progress. And despite his ignorance of the law and his ignorance of the language the Greek gets along. Gradually he begins to learn something about the pitfalls in these great cities of ours. He congregates in the Greek quarters of New York, Chicago, Philadelphia, or St. Louis, in the Athenian grocery store, in the Hellene barber shop, in the Levantine restaurant, or in the little cafés where, through dense clouds of smoke, you can see Greeks of all conditions seated behind their black coffee and

Oriental pipes discussing the brigands of Bulgaria, the woes of Macedonia, and the latest news of the Greek colony. In their two New York dailies the Greco-Americans read not only of the doings of their Motherland, not only well-digested accounts of the progress of the age, but all the news, from the election of a President to the pettiest details of police court proceedings.

And gradually the Greek in America learns. When he learns, he is a formidable competitor. He goes out on the street with flowers or candies or fruit, knowing not even the name of the article he sells, but knowing the words nickel and dime and quarter, and the significance of each. Gradually he learns other words. You cannot help learning words if you stand twelve hours on a thronged street and have ears and mind. And gradually he learns to know the psychology of the free-handed American; he learns to distinguish the "sport" who will pay fifty cents for a fifteen-cent bunch of moribund violets from the cautious purchaser who wants his money's worth even from a Greek peddler. The Greek, who for thousands of years has haggled in all the lands upon which the sun sets, even learns in America when not to haggle.

It is difficult to meet this silent, insistent, overpowering competition of the hard-working, hard-saving, canny, subtle, pleasing Greek, anxious to gain his foothold. The Greeks entered the retail food business as the camel entered the Arab's tent, first nose, then head, then camel. Today, in all our big cities they are the manufacturers and venders of cheap candies, of which it might be said that glucose by any other name would taste as sweet. They have almost monopolized the retail fruit business and flower industry, and the Greek restaurant, once a novelty, has now become an established institution. There are already thousands of these little restaurants in our Northern American cities.

Not all the Greeks can go into retail trade, for which they are so preeminently fitted, but there are manual positions which may serve as stepping-stones for a petty commercial career. One may gain enough nickels at shoe shining or pennies at paper selling to permit one to dream of a pushcart or a fruit stand. One may go out with the laborers and earn a dollar and a half a day at digging ditches, or run an elevator for ten hours a day and go to night school for two, emerging after a few years as a candidate for any industrial position in America. You may open a barber shop and shave your flourishing fellow countrymen, or start another of the infinite number of little Greek grocery stores, where all goods are sold at all prices and one clerk knows not what the other clerk charges. Or, finally, you may become a steamship agent and notary public, and sell exchange and transmit money, and thrive so long as deposits come to you, and fail only when the money is asked for again. There are always ways and means in good times of earning what the Greek immigrant calls a living in America.

There are avenues to even higher success. The first Greeks who came were men of the soil; the new Greeks who are arriving are, in some cases, professional men. The Greek doctor leaves Athens or Patras for New York or Chicago, and, even without knowing English, gives advice to the Greeks. The Greek pharmacist settles in a foreign neighborhood, and, though he does not like the Italians— were not Greeks and Romans ever enemies?—he ministers to them with as glad a heart as to the sons of Hellas. Other professional men from Athens make a modest career in the great cities of the New World.

But a cultured Greek, like a cultured immigrant from any nationality, is at no advantage in the struggle for a foothold. If, like Pericles of Smyrna, he is willing to start as a dishwasher, he may by dint of work succeed, or by force of unusual fortune gain a glittering success. But, however cultivated he may be, however gifted in rhetoric, however exact is his use of the "written" Greek, he is doomed to disappointment and failure without the cruder virtues of the peasant. America asks of its immigrants not fineness but strength.

Industrial and Agricultural Communities

32

In 1907 Congress set up a United States Immigration Commission under the chairmanship of Senator William P. Dillingham. The commission investigated all phases of immigration and presented its findings to Congress in a huge forty-one volume report in January 1911. The two articles reprinted here in part were written by staff members of the commission. W. Jett Lauck, author of "Industrial Communities," was in charge of industrial investigations, and Alexander E. Cance prepared the report entitled "Immigrant Rural Communities." [*Survey,* January 7, 1911.]

INDUSTRIAL COMMUNITIES

The widespread existence of immigrant communities or colonies in the United States at the present time may be realized, when it is stated that in the territory east of the Mississippi and north of the Ohio and Potomac rivers there is no town or city of industrial importance, with the exception of the lead- and zinc-mining localities of Missouri, which does not have its immigrant colony or section composed of Slavs, Magyars, north and south Italians, or members of other races of recent immigration from southern and eastern Europe. In the South and Southwest, because of the large areas devoted almost exclusively to agriculture, the immigrant community is less frequently met than in the Middle West or East. In the bituminous coal-mining territory of West Virginia, Virginia, Alabama, Arkansas, and Oklahoma, immigrant colonies in large numbers have been developed in the same way as those in the coal-mining regions of Pennsylvania and the Middle West. Southern and eastern Europeans have also attached themselves to the iron- and steel-producing communities of the Birmingham district in Alabama; and a large Italian colony, as is well known, exists in New Orleans, a considerable number of whose members are employed in the cotton mills of the city and in the manufacture of cigars and cigarettes. South Italians, Cubans, and Spaniards have entered the cigar-manufacturing establishments of Tampa and Key West, Fla., and have built up colonies in these cities. Outside New Orleans, however, no recent immigrants in the South are cotton-mill operatives. Southern mill owners have frequently tried to introduce southern and eastern, as well as northern, European and British immigrants into their operating forces, but all attempts have resulted in failure because of the refusal of the present cotton-mill workers, recruited from isolated farm and mountain sections, to work alongside recent immigrants. This same intense race prejudice on the part of Southern wage earners of

native birth has rendered impossible the extensive employment of southern and eastern Europeans in other branches of manufacturing in the South, and has consequently prevented the development of immigrant industrial colonies, except in the instances already mentioned, and in the case of a number of agricultural communities, principally located in the Mississippi Valley. . . .

Whether located in the South or elsewhere, however, immigrant communities, which have come into existence because of the recent industrial expansion and the resultant influx of wage earners from southern and eastern Europe, are of two general types. The first is a community which has by a gradual process of social accretion affixed itself to the original population of an industrial town or city, which had already been established before the arrival of races of recent immigration. Foreign communities of this character are as numerous as the older industrial towns and centers of the country. The textile-manufacturing centers of New England and the Middle states, such as Fall River, Lowell, and New Bedford, Mass.; Manchester, N.H.; Providence, R.I., and Patterson, N.J.; cities in which other industries are located, such as paper manufacturing in Holyoke and boot and shoe factories in Haverhill and Lynn, Mass.; hardware, cutlery, and jewelry, localized in New Britain and Meriden, Conn.; or leather finishing and currying, as in Wilmington, Del.; clothing manufacturing, as in Rochester; collars and cuffs in Troy; hosiery and knit goods in Cohoes and Utica, N.Y.; oil refining in Bayonne, N.J.; or cities engaged in diversified manufacturing, as Passaic and Newark, N.J.—all these have colonies or sections populated by recent immigrants. The same condition of affairs is found in the iron and steel, glass, and other older manufacturing cities and towns of New York, Pennsylvania, and the Middle West. As representative types of this class in connection with the manufacture of glass, Tarentum, Pa.; Morgantown, W. Va.; Steubenville and Rossford, Ohio, may be mentioned; and as typical iron and steel localities, Steelton and Johnstown, Pa.; Youngstown, Ohio, and South Chicago and De Kalb, Ill. Pittsburgh, Pa., or the Pittsburgh district, may be said to be practically made up of industrial towns or cities engaged in the manufacture of iron and steel, glass, and allied products, each of which has an immigrant colony or section composed of households of wage earners of recent immigration. . . .

The second general type of immigrant community has developed within recent years because of the growth of some natural resource, such as coal, iron ore, or copper, or by reason of the extension of the principal manufacturing industries of the country. These communities usually cluster around mines or industrial plants, and their distinguishing feature is that a majority of their inhabitants are of foreign birth and recent immigration. This type of immigrant community is common in the bituminous and anthracite coal-mining regions of Pennsylvania and in the coal-producing areas of Virginia, West Virginia, Alabama, Ohio, Indiana, Illinois, Kansas, and Oklahoma. In the Mesabi and Vermilion iron-ore ranges of Minnesota, as well as the iron-ore and copper-mining districts of Michigan, many such communities are also found. The usual mining community of this character consists of a small town or urban center in the vicinity of which mining operations are conducted at a number of points. These outlying mining locations are generally connected with the urban center by steam or electric railroads. The town of Windber in western Pennsylvania, by way of illustration, has a population of about 8,000 persons, and is the center of twelve mining camps. It was founded in 1897 by the opening of bituminous coal mines, for which purpose 1,600 experienced Englishmen and 400 native Americans were brought into the locality. With the opening of new mines southern and eastern Europeans were attracted to the community, and at the present time eighteen races of recent immigration are numbered among its mine workers. The town of Windber proper has a section occupied by native Americans and three foreign colonies. The outlying mining villages consist of company houses in which recent immigrants live almost exclusively. The southern and eastern Europeans have their churches, banks, steamship agencies, and business establishments in the town of Windber itself, to which they go to transact their affairs and to seek amusement. Food and other articles are principally purchased in the company stores of the mining villages.

Although not so numerous, communities of this type are not infrequently established in connection with the leading industries, such as the manufacture of iron and steel, glass, cotton and woolen goods. Gary, Ind., is an industrial community largely made up of recent immigrants, which has been brought into existence because of the erection of a large steel plant within the past few years. Whiting, Ind., is likewise a small city, recently established in connection with the oil-refining industry, the population of which is composed principally of southern and eastern European immigrants. Charleroi, Kensington, Tarentum, and Arnold, in western Pennsylvania, and

Brown Brothers

A group of Russian immigrants upon arrival at a Kansas farm community, about 1910.

Crystal City near St. Louis, Mo., furnish examples of glass-manufacturing communities of this description. Charleroi has at present a population of about 10,500, composed chiefly of French and French-Belgians, with an admixture of Poles, Slovaks, north and south Italians, and other races from the south and east of Europe. This community was established about 1890 when its first glass factory was erected, and has grown in size and importance as the glass industry within its borders has been extended. Another illustration is the recently established iron- and steel-manufacturing community at Granite City and Madison, Ill., which under normal working conditions possesses the distinction of being the largest Bulgarian colony in the United States. These two cities immediately join each other, and for practical purposes are one industrial community, the distinction between them being more artificial than real. In 1892 its site was an unbroken stretch of cornfields. During the past seven years it has had an extraordinary expansion in business and population, due to the extension of its industrial activities. The original wage earners were English, Irish, Germans, Welsh, and Poles. By 1900 the demand for unskilled labor, because of the erection of new steel foundries and a car-building plant, could no longer be supplied by English-speaking people. Consequently, in that year, Slovaks from St. Louis were employed by the local industries. In 1902 came the Magyars followed by a few Croatians. Mixed groups of Rumanians, Greeks, and Serbians followed. In the years 1904 and 1905 began the swarming of the Bulgarians to the community, and by the autumn of the latter year fully 1,500 had arrived. Two years later Bulgarian immigration reached its high-water mark with 8,000 of this race.

In addition to the Bulgarians there were about 4,000 recent immigrants, Armenians, Serbians, Lithuanians, Slovaks, Magyars, and Poles being the principal races represented. The total population of the community is estimated under normal industrial conditions to be about 20,000. The Bulgarians and other foreign races have built up practically an exclusively immigrant town a short distance from the American section of the two cities, which has come in popular parlance to be called "Hungary Hollow." Here Bulgarians, Serbians, Rumanians, and a few Magyars and Armenians live together entirely apart from any American influences.

All immigrant communities possess one or more institutions of a class peculiar to, or resultant from, such a population, each of which has an important bearing upon the life of the community. The most important of these is what is commonly known as an immigrant bank. As a matter of fact the term immigrant bank is a misnomer, for the institution is practically a bureau of information and a clearinghouse of services necessary to an immigrant population. An immigrant community of alien speech has many needs which can be satisfied only by a person or company familiar with the language, customs, habits, and manner of thought of the people. To meet these requirements, the institution popularly known as the immigrant bank has come into existence. The immigrant banker exercises, in the majority of cases, no banking functions beyond receiving money for safekeeping, for transmission abroad, and for exchange. He combines with his banking business the sale of steamship tickets, merchandise, books, and other articles. He is often a political leader, or conducts a boardinghouse, bakery, labor agency, or saloon. In some of the more recent communities, however, as in the case of Granite City and Madison, Ill., one or more banking houses are sometimes found owning and operating large rooming houses, the occupants of which buy their provisions from the banker's stores and bakeries, drink in his saloon and coffeehouse, deposit their money in his bank, read the paper printed by his establishment, and follow, in a large measure blindly, the counsel of the banker himself.

Another interesting institution often met with is the immigrant coffeehouse, which is modeled after similar institutions in Europe. It is intended to meet the tastes and habits of the Greek, Macedonian, Bulgarian, and Turkish races who do not patronize the American saloon or drink intoxicants after the manner of the Germans, Croatians, Slovaks, Poles, Magyars, and the members of other races. The coffeehouses are usually large, well-lighted rooms, furnished with small tables and plain chairs. Tobacco in all its forms, including even the Turkish pipe, is to be had, as well as tea, coffee, cider, soft drinks, and ice cream.

In many communities immigrant newspapers, usually issued weekly, are published in a foreign language and appeal for support to a certain race or races. These papers are often owned and controlled by immigrant mercantile banking houses. The immigrant saloon also has certain features peculiar as compared with the ordinary American institution. Often an immigrant bank, steamship agency, labor agency, or boarding or rooming house is operated in connection with it. A large number of fraternal and beneficial organizations also flourish in immigrant communities. Moreover, in each foreign colony of any importance, churches have been erected by the different races. They are usually Roman or

Greek Catholic, and are often costly and imposing edifices. Usually parochial schools are conducted in connection with these churches, and offer religious and secular instruction. A foreign language is, as a rule, used in the schools, but in the greater number of instances instruction in English is given.

IMMIGRANT RURAL COMMUNITIES

Something like one-fourth of all male breadwinners of foreign parentage in the United States were engaged in agricultural pursuits in 1900. Although by far the greater part were of the older immigration, who came from northern Europe and settled in the Middle West years ago, among them are a not inconsiderable number of recent immigrants from southern and southeastern Europe who have established themselves on the land. The races under consideration by the Immigration Commission were chiefly Italians,

Hebrews, Poles, Bohemians, and Portuguese; and most of these were settled rather recently in more or less sharply defined rural communities.

The inhabitant of the upper Mississippi Valley is well acquainted with immigrant farmers, and a township of Scandinavians, Germans, or Bohemians excites no comment and invites no comparisons. There the foreigners, long settled in rural districts, have become so thoroughly American, have so completely lost themselves in the rural population, that they retain very few of their distinctive race characteristics. In the East and South, however, and in the instance of certain recent colonies elsewhere, the foreign rural group, composed of Italians, Poles, or Hebrews, is still an object of curiosity. Not only are the foreigners on the land infrequent, but they have yet to prove their fitness for agricultural pursuits—for country life. . . .

As a farmer or permanent farm laborer, the immigrant becomes a real element

Alsatian peasants in St. Paul, Minnesota, 1902.

Minnesota Historical Society

in such rural communities. There is a second way in which the incoming foreigner may come into contact with the soil, but without gaining other than a casual economic interest in rural pursuits, as a seasonal agricultural laborer who lives in the city and works for a few months yearly, usually in the fruit or vegetable districts.

This class of laborers is usually composed of foreign-born persons, who work in gangs and who are recruited outside the neighborhood in which they find employment. They are employed for short seasons only, frequently on piecework; ordinarily men, women, and children work together; often they follow a regular itinerary, leaving the cities in the spring and returning in the autumn. Thousands are employed every year in all parts of the United States where specialized crops, for whose culture a relatively large amount of hand labor is essential, are produced. Of the seven groups of "black" Portuguese, Poles, Belgians, Sicilians, Japanese, and Indians studied by the commission, only the south Italian berry pickers of New Jersey can be considered. . . .

Of the forty or more Italian communities visited in thirteen states, the oldest and largest groups are the berry and truck growers on the pine barrens of New Jersey, some of them the landowners for whom these picking gangs labor during the harvests. Both north and south Italians are landowners at Vineland, and Hammonton is one of the most promising south Italian settlements east of the Rocky Mountains. In origin and development both are typically unassisted colonies, whose progress has been continuous since the 1870s and whose numbers have been augmented chiefly from abroad. These groups number perhaps 1,200 families of Italian origin, and here veritably the "magic of property" has "turned sand into gold." The hundreds of little berry farms, vineyards, or sweet potato or pepper fields which make these Italian communities real oases in a waste of sand and lowland, bear unmistakable testimony to the ability of the much maligned south Italian to create wealth and to make progress materially, morally, and politically under rural conditions. . . .

Italian farming in the South covers a wide range of products, widely diversified soils and climatic conditions, several forms of land tenure, and various systems of culture. The north Italians among the mountains of western North Carolina practise a self-sufficing, diversified agriculture. In southeastern Louisiana and in the coastal plain belt of Alabama, the south Italian truckers and small fruit growers are doing exceptionally well on the light sandy soils, when they succeed in marketing their products in a satisfactory manner. In the Delta both north and south Italian cotton tenants are teaching the cotton growers how valuable careful cultivation, kitchen gardens, and small store accounts may be to the cotton "share hand." In the Ozarks Italians from the Sunnyside group have taken up new land, planted orchards, and become successful apple and peach growers. It is plain that the Italian farmer has been profoundly influenced by his environment. His farming has been directed and his agricultural methods taught him by his new neighbors. He has not been uniformly successful, but his economy stands out in contrast to the more or less shiftless, thriftless Southern methods, much more conspicuously than Italian agriculture in Wisconsin or New Jersey.

Italian immigration to the South has been in part stimulated by the cotton and sugarcane planters, who, dissatisfied with Negro labor, alarmed at the increasing scarcity of every sort of farm labor, and desirous of settling acceptable farmers on the immense tracts of unimproved land, have for years been striving to turn the tide of immigration southward. Instances are cited of plantation owners who advanced the passage money for the transportation of groups of Italian families and settled them on their cotton plantations. The total immigration induced in this way is not significant, except as it forms nuclei around which gather subsequent immigrants to the United States. Sunnyside colony, originating in the importation of 100 or more families from northern Italy in the Nineties, is the mother of several rural settlements.

A number of colonies, notably in Texas and Louisiana, seem to have originated in the purchase of a few acres of land by some Italian farm laborer who, arriving practically without money at a Southern port of entry, sought employment on some neighboring plantation.

One of the most notable examples of this method of settlement is the south Italian group of strawberry growers at Independence, La. Independence began to be known as a strawberry center about 1890, about the time the first Italian came with his family from New Orleans to pick berries and remained to purchase a few acres of land. A second family followed in the autumn; these two waxed enthusiastic over the possibilities of berry culture and urged their friends and relatives to join them; more Italian berry pickers came and many remained; now there are perhaps 250 Sicilian small farmers in the neighborhood.

Much of the purchased land was lowland, more or less swampy and covered with a heavy forest growth. A large number who were not able to pay $30 to $50 an acre for land operated a few acres on

shares; the owner furnishing the land, preparing it for cultivation, providing one-half of the fertilizer and berry boxes, and paying one-half the cost of picking; after picking, the berries were equally divided between landowner and grower. The Italians without capital found this form of tenure satisfactory, and many of them in two or three years saved enough to purchase five or ten acres.

The holdings are small, the homes, in consequence, have the appearance of a straggling rural village and the community spirit is strong. It is not a homelike village, and in the poorly constructed, rude frame, two- or three-room cabins are few evidences of prosperity or comfort. But their farms are well tilled, their berries are excellent and yield well, and thanks to their organized marketing the returns are fairly remunerative. School waits upon the berry field, but interest in education is increasing. There is little civic spirit, and of 350 adult males not twenty are voters. They have had no adequate Italian leadership, and their American neighbors have apparently given little or no attention to the development of a wholesome social or civic interest in the foreigners.

A very important economic feature is a cooperative marketing association with a membership of more than 200 Italian growers, organized two years ago. The Independence berries go to Chicago and neighboring cities; formerly they were shipped to commission merchants by individual growers. The results were unsatisfactory, sometimes ruinous. Prices were low, handling charges high, and complaints of unjust dealing innumerable. In the crisis the Italians got together, organized a selling association, hired an inspector and a selling agent, and notified the commission houses to come to Independence for their berries. At present all berries are sold to platform buyers f.o.b. Independence. The expenses of management in 1909 were about two cents per twenty-four-pint crate.

During the spring of 1910 the association sold $357,639 worth of berries for its members.

Ability to cooperate is characteristic of Italian farmers who are engaged in highly specialized forms of agriculture. They may not have a strong class consciousness, but they are racially homogeneous, and a community consciousness is readily developed. Moreover, some at least have some knowledge of cooperative organization in Italy. In ability to work together they are far in advance of the native Southern farmers. . . .

This brief characterization of Italian settlements sets forth the diverse conditions and circumstances incident to the settlement of immigrant rural communities.

In the large, the history of the founding of Polish settlements differs little from the Italian record. The goal of early Polish immigration was northern Illinois and Wisconsin. After 1885 the stream of Slavic immigration set in very strongly, and Polish rural colonies began to dot the prairies of Minnesota and the Dakotas as well as the lake states. Unlike the early peasants who came directly from Europe in search of cheap land and homes of their own, a large percentage of these men are day laborers who have been engaged in the mines, steel mills, quarries, or urban industrial pursuits, and who are attracted to farms by advertisements in Polish papers or the solicitation of Polish land agents. They settle in small groups, their location is directed, they bring more money than the arrivals directly from abroad, and when they are fairly dealt with they make more rapid progress than the earlier immigration.

Hebrew agricultural colonies are interesting from many points of view. Most of the Hebrew farmers are in New York, New Jersey, and southern New England, within easy reach of large commercial centers. Practically all of them were established on the land directly or indirectly by the aid or influence of a Jewish immigrant aid society of some sort. Practically all of the colonies have received artificial support by means of subsidized clothing or other factories, or by loans or virtual gifts from trust funds or philanthropists. A very large percentage of the 1,000 or more Hebrew farmers in New England and in Sullivan and Ulster counties, N.Y., practise what may be designated summer boarder agriculture—since the soil is sterile, the topography rough, hilly, or even mountainous, and the principal part of the farm income comes from boarding summer visitors.

Other Hebrew farmers in New England are landowners, who depend to a greater or less extent on some outside enterprise—peddling, cattle buying, junk dealing—for the greater part of their incomes, or who are speculators in real estate rather than permanent, simon pure farmers. Excepting the recent settlements near Ellington and Hartford, Conn., where agricultural conditions are favorable, comparatively few Jewish farmers in New England may be called successful.

The colony or group of colonies near Vineland, N.J., presents Hebrew agriculture in America at its best. Of the several colonies of Hebrews studied none shows greater apparent material prosperity, a more general dependence on agriculture for a livelihood, a more intelligent, resourceful husbandry, or a more wholesome community life, educationally, socially, or politically, in a large sense.

There is no doubt that a great deal of material encouragement has been given; that many of the social and educational enterprises were conceived, organized, and supported by leaders without the community, and that cooperative business associations and marketing facilities were promoted by leaders who do not live in the settlements; but once established the colonists have entered into all these enterprises with some degree of interest and are beginning to support them. To all appearances the colonies near Vineland, N.J., are permanently established on the basis of a commercial agriculture adapted to the soil, climate, and demands of the market.

The study of the several Jewish settlements emphasized these facts at least: that the Hebrew is not adapted by training or tradition to make a pioneer farmer; that to win success he should start with some capital on improved land; that settlement in groups of sufficient size to maintain a synagogue is almost essential; that those who are likely to succeed are either those who have been farmers abroad or who have had some successful experience in agriculture in the United States previous to permanent settlement.

Immigrant Banks in the United States

33

Every nationality group that migrated to the United States had its benevolent and protective associations, drawn strictly along ethnic lines. These societies were meant to help the newcomer adjust to America, to find a job and a place to live, and to protect him from being victimized by those who preyed upon unknowing aliens. The associations provided a variety of services, one of which was helping the immigrant with his finances, especially that all-important task of saving his money to bring other members of his family to America. The associations thus were quasi banks, and indeed some of them eventually developed into full-fledged banking corporations. The following article by W. H. Kniffin assesses the value of these savings institutions from the point of view of the established bankers. [*Bankers Magazine,* February 1911.]

One of the principal arguments, or "excuses," as some would have it, for the establishment of the postal savings bank in this country, is that the foreigner within our borders has inadequate banking facilities. Being unacquainted with the merits of the American banks and suspicious withal, and finding, as a rule, no one in the average bank able to speak his tongue, he turns either to the nearest representative of governmental banking, the post office, or to one of his fellow countrymen who poses as a banker, and, by alluring gold signs, and a tempting display of foreign money behind flimsily barred windows, holds himself out as a "friend indeed" who is worthy of his trust. How worthy this friend has proven himself to be is for the present paper to unfold.

The "immigrant banker" flourishes in every part of the United States, especially where the immigrants from southern Europe congregate. They have no capital, little or no legal responsibility, and, excepting in Massachusetts, New Jersey, and, since September 1 last, in New York, are without legal control. They generally operate in conjunction with agencies for steamship tickets, and are frequently located in groceries, saloons, and other gathering places for immigrants. Besides keeping their money (too often *keeping* it), the genial banker writes letters for them, receives their mail (as the letters usually displayed in their windows testify), and is their legal, social, and business advisor. The business consists in receiving money on deposit and transmitting funds abroad. Deposits are not subject to check and no interest is, as a rule, paid. No restrictions are placed on the deposits and frequently they are used in the banker's business. They are payable on demand, *if the banker is in funds.* Transmission of funds is usually by means of money orders furnished by large banking houses and express companies, and it is estimated that $275 million was sent abroad in 1907 by aliens, one-half of which went through these immigrant banks.

Out of 113 of the banks investigated by the Immigration Commission recently, located in large cities east of the Rocky Mountains, the nationalities were found to be as follows: Bohemian, 1; Bulgarian, 6; Croatian, 8; German, 7; Greek, 5; Hebrew, 15; Lithuanian, 2; Magyar, 9; Polish, 13; Portuguese, 1; Slovak, 4; Italian, 47. New York City, having been the subject of state investigations, was not covered by the government, but the results of such researches were supplemented and confirmed. The facts herein set forth, however, may be taken as representative of this class of bankers wherever they exist.

ORIGIN AND CHARACTER

There are at present at least 2,625 immigrant banks in this country, New York leading with over 1,000, followed by Pennsylvania with 410; Illinois with 275; Massachusetts with 175; Ohio, 150; New Jersey, 80; and the rest scattered. The records of the state comptroller in New York show that only 336 of these banks complied with the law and furnished the

legal bond. This does not include the multitude of saloonkeepers, who, in a quiet way, receive money for safekeeping or transmission abroad.

It will be noted that immigrants from the United Kingdom and northern and western Europe are not represented in the list of nationalities, as these people readily adapt themselves to our present banks and send money home through regular channels. These people do not send as large amounts home as those of southern Europe, but whether this is due to the influence of the immigrant banks is problematical.

It is but natural that the immigrant should look to the steamship agency as the connecting link between him and the Old Country. Representing the "big boat," the agent has a standing all his own, and it is but natural that the ignorant foreigner should send his money home through the same channel that brought him over. And having sent his money home successfully, what more natural than to leave his savings also? Carry this to its logical conclusion and the steamship agent soon becomes a "banker."

THE CHARACTER OF THE BANKERS

But all ticket agents do not become bankers, nor are all bankers steamship agents—"there are others." Wherever there is a foreign population there are foreign groceries, saloons, butchers, bakers, etc., and in the friendship engendered through trade, what more natural than, finding the grocer with a big safe, to trust him with the surplus on Saturday night? And in due course, Mrs. Grocer either adds a banking department or forsakes the sugar barrel and coffee mill for a rolltop desk and a more pretentious safe behind barred windows. Some of these are clever men—very, as financial history will prove. Racial ties are strong, and it matters not that the banker may have been a swindler, or that he may have been discharged for dishonesty, the fact that he is an Italian among Italians, or a Pole among Poles, he will flourish. The writer knows personally of one merchant who was about to fail, and subsequently did so, who was fitting up a "bank" in one part of his store while his creditors were pushing him hard for money. He hoped to get it for them.

Hundreds of saloonkeepers and small tradesmen act as bankers without the least fitness. Thirteen such had the boldness to apply for a charter for a savings bank in New York recently, only to find the gates closed against them.

THE PATRONS

The patron is usually the recent arrival—the man not yet Americanized, easily influenced by those who speak his native tongue. His gullibility is often pathetic. He believes all the banker tells him; he frequently loses his deposit receipt and must take whatever the banker chooses to give him. The question naturally arises, why does he prefer to trust an unknown "friend" to the American banks? The answer is: (1) suspicion and ignorance; (2) the established banks, as a rule, do not have facilities for this foreign business (savings banks in New York never make remittances), although some large savings banks in New York employ interpreters for their foreign patrons; (3) the "collateral" services rendered by the private banker; (4) suspicion often aroused by the lavish equipment of the average American bank; (5) having learned that the regular banks are not government insitutions, they prefer to trust their own countrymen; (6) the publicity given to

bank failures; (7) the short hours of the regular bank against the "all night and sometimes Sunday" banker.

In many places, however, the Americanized foreigner makes free use of the established banks, and in cities like St. Louis, Chicago, Pittsburgh, and Cleveland, foreign departments have been established in banks and trust companies with considerable success. Pittsburgh has twelve such institutions.

To return for a moment to equipment. Strange as it may seem, the presence of marble and bronze does not attract the foreign trade. A Slovak banker apologized for the appearance of his room and states it was ill-kept because the men would come in their working clothes, often covered with mud and soot, frequently intoxicated, which, with the customary smoking and spitting, kept the room in a constant state of disorder. The dirt was really an asset to him, for many of his people would hesitate to come into a clean, well-kept room.

Then, too, the short hours of the banks and post offices make banking inconvenient to the man who works, and the fact that in the former they must generally talk English and in the latter fill out a blank, negatives their usefulness as a transmitting agency or depository.

Not infrequently does the saloonkeeper act as employment agent for his bank patrons, and his place frequently becomes the headquarters for idle men, as well as the meeting place for the "sick and aid" and other friendly societies characteristic of our foreign population. The grocer-banker keeps his patrons supplied with provisions on credit when work is slack, and book credits of $5,000 or $6,000 are not unusual. All these services are, of course, eventually turned into a profit to the banker, as the cashing of a pay check

Depositors lining up to withdraw their savings during a run on an immigrant bank on the Lower East Side of New York City, 1912.

may mean trade at the bar, and the deposit of money with the grocer, "trading it out" later when dull times come upon him.

OWNERSHIP AND CAPITALIZATION

It is generally recognized that to start a bank no capital is required, and only six out of 116 were capitalized. The manager of a large bank in New York states that $1,000 will start a pretentious bank in that city of pretentious banks, but insisted that at least $1,000 more ought to be converted into foreign money and placed in the show window to "inspire confidence and attract business." The owner usually invests the funds in his own affairs, and the problem is to determine where the bank's affairs begin and his personal interests end. Legally and financially he is

usually irresponsible.

BOOKKEEPING METHODS

Nearly all banks give the customer some kind of acknowledgement, sometimes a passbook, sometimes an ordinary receipt. The money is not usually separated from the proprietor's funds, and one Italian banker deposited the bank money in his wife's name to "avoid confusion!" A Croatian saloonkeeper who did business for his boarders kept but one book of account, in which deposits were entered and scratched over as withdrawn, no receipt being given, the customer being satisfied by "seeing the entry made." Another, in St. Louis, merely kept a duplicate deposit slip; and another kept account on the stubs of the receipts issued; while others give no evidence of the deposit whatever.

METHODS OF SECURING BUSINESS

Between 3,000 and 5,000 "runners" are

engaged in selling steamship tickets, and also act as solicitors for the banker as opportunity affords, frequently on a commission basis. Aside from the gaudy window display of steamship posters, foreign money, and waiting-to-be-called-for letters, newspapers and circular advertising figure prominently in the campaign for business, the foreign newspaper being filled with alluring advertisements.

SUBTERFUGES
Aside from claiming in large gold letters that they are "banks" in such language as to lead the ignorant to believe that they have governmental backing, many clever subterfuges are devised to attract custom. For instance, where a postal substation is operated in the same room, as in one case in New York where the banker failed for $275,000, his private money order receipts were labeled "Offici di Postali e Telegraphos" (postal and telegraph office), which to the average Italian is likely to mean that the bank is under governmental control, since in Italy the postal banks are under the minister of posts and telegraphs. The bond requirement in New York (which met with poor success and was ineffectual if not inoperative) was also a cause of abuse, since these bankers frequently conspicuously advertised that they were secure in the sum of 75,000 lire ($15,000 bond to state), while permitted by the surety company to advertise that they were bonded by a $5 million surety company. The attention of the reader has doubtless been called to the frequent use of the term *notary public,* usually in connection with a seal, prominently displayed by these bankers ("immigrant lawyers" also) especially on their windows. This means much more to the foreigner than to Americans, to whom the notary is simply an attesting officer; but to the foreigner, the notary is a man of great dignity, learning, and authority, carefully trained for his duties. Most of the bankers are notaries, and find this a most useful adjunct, as their services are frequently required. . . .

THE UNSOUNDNESS OF THESE BANKS
The dangers arising from such a class of institutions are obvious. First, the proprietors are usually irresponsible; they are privately owned, loosely managed, and under no supervision or control (except in the states mentioned). Second, they deal with the ignorant. Third, the affairs of the bank and the proprietor's private business are not separated; he may use the funds as he sees fit, and they are often used in speculative enterprises. The temptation to make a display of wealth has often proved disastrous. Fourth, the owner is usually ignorant of his legal and unmindful of his moral responsibility. The methods are not businesslike, either for the owner's or the patron's protection.

Evidence of deposit is usually inadequate and sometimes entirely lacking. The purchaser of a money order receives no proper receipt and does not know the medium used in transmitting funds. There is no check against absconding, as the numerous instances of such happenings will prove.

The panic of 1907 found most of these men totally unprepared, and left many of them in dire straits, and even though they were honest in intention, the previous management was so lax as to make prompt payment impossible and suspension inevitable. Twenty-five failures and suspensions were recorded in New York City between Sept. 1, 1907 and Sept. 1, 1908, with assets of $295,331 and liabilities of $1,459,300, representing 12,379 depositors.

Piedmontese on the Mississippi

34

Despite the general reluctance of the more recent immigrants to go into agriculture, a few farming colonies did develop in some parts of the nation. For example, quite a number of Italians went into farming in California and in the South. This selection describes a group of immigrants from northern Italy who settled at Genoa, Wisconsin. The report was written by Alexander Cance, a member of the United States Immigration Commission. [*Survey,* September 2, 1911.]

Southward from St. Paul, the Mississippi winds its way between banks that frequently rise abruptly, almost perpendicularly, from the water's edge to a height of several hundred feet. The traveler over the Burlington Railroad, which closely hugs the east brink of the river, has noticed numerous coves or pockets, a few acres in extent, marking the place where some small tributary creek has cut its way down through the rocky barrier to reach the level of the great river. Through these narrow defiles or coulees, the woodsmen and farmers living back on the uplands were accustomed to bring their produce to the river for barter or shipment. In time little villages grew up in these narrow openings, huddled, disorderly hamlets, poorly laid out, depending for their existence on the traffic between the back-country farmers and the rivermen. One of these hamlets is Genoa. About 200 persons live in the village, 1,000 in the township—207 families, of whom forty-four are of Italian descent. . . .

The first arrivals came immediately from Galena, Ill., whither, fifty years ago, they had somehow come together from various parts of the globe—one from South America, another from the California mines, a third from a picturesque career in Africa. Genoa was selected for settlement because one of their number, who had gone on an exploring trip up the river, brought back news that he had found the duplicate of his Piedmont home. They chose the site because it looked like Switzerland, and renamed it Genoa. The colony grew slowly; there was no colonization and no considerable influx of immigrants at any one time. The settlers are all from Piedmont or Lombardy, Italy, and practically all the foreign-born arrived before 1890. . . .

Dairying is perhaps the most important present industry. The impetus came with the introduction of the creamery between 1885 and 1890. The dairy region of Vernon County is practically included in the tract of rough, hilly territory, some twelve miles wide, lying along the river and including Genoa township. This section is well adapted to grass, despite the insufficient supply of running water, and some cattle have been raised since the inception of the settlement. But dairying did not enter largely into the pioneer farming system; it was confined chiefly to the few pounds of butter which the farmer's wife had difficulty in exchanging for groceries at the village store. Cows were seldom milked in winter either by Italians or Americans, and in summer butter was frequently a drug on the market at eight to ten cents a pound.

The dairy industry was developed in the Italian settlement exactly as it developed elsewhere in Wisconsin. The creamery made the Wisconsin farmer a dairyman after the opening of the Minnesota wheat lands and the ravages of the chinch bug had wrought havoc with his wheat growing. The central feature is a farmer's cooperative creamery, really a joint stock company in which the patrons, Italian, German, and American dairymen are shareholders. The cream is separated from the milk by hand or power separators before it leaves the farm; a cream collector hauls it to the creamery, where a hired butter maker determines by test and weight the amount of butterfat in each farmer's cream, and churns it. Cream is paid for on a butterfat basis, the patron receiving his check every two weeks. The butter is sold by the cooperative company, and any surplus is returned as dividends to the stockholders in proportion to the shares held. Last year the dividends were 11 percent on the par value of the outstanding stock. Since the patrons hold shares roughly corresponding to the quantity of the cream delivered, the division of surplus is fairly equable.

The Italians have been fairly successful dairymen and stock raisers. Their dairy herds range from three to sixteen milk cows and about the same number of young cattle. In addition to an average of 200 pounds of butter made and consumed yearly at home, the income from dairy cows run from $50 to nearly $500 for each farm. Not a large average, surely, for there are no purebred or high-grade herds, but comparing well with the income of other patrons in the vicinity. While the principles of breeding are not well understood, the Italian farmer takes great pride in his herd. . . .

The farmsteads of the Piedmontese in Wisconsin present a better appearance and represent a larger outlay of capital than those of any group of Italians known to the writer. The houses, even on the small farms, are neat, well constructed, and comfortable. On the larger farms, many of them are of brick or of stone, some of them erected years ago. Most of them are surrounded with well-cared-for lawns, ornamented with shrubbery and native trees. The big basement barns, the granaries, the tobacco sheds, the corn-cribs, the tool sheds, and the milk houses on the greater number of farms give a picture of thrift and prosperity that one seldom associates with an Italian farmstead. The Italian has made sure, if slow, progress. The long granary or the hog house, he tells you, was his dwelling house for twenty years. He built his new barn out of stone which he and his son quarried, and every timber and rafter he hewed out of trees that grew in his woodlot; it was put up the year following a very profitable tobacco crop, and paid for as soon as the cupola was in place. Not one of the forty farmers brought any large amount of material wealth with him to the community. Every one endured many discomforts and inconveniences in order to become independent. And with the majority economic independence is a religion. An Italian rarely goes into debt for anything less than an economic necessity. For example, one rarely finds a top buggy or a bicycle that is not fully paid for. The American frequently contracts debt for luxuries, very often for comforts; the Italian, as a rule, never . . .

This Wisconsin settlement is one of the very few Italian communities where the Italian and the Italian-American are not regarded nor spoken of as Italians, but as fellow citizens. Most of them speak fluent English, the young people all do, and converse intelligently, frankly, and without suspicion, on agriculture, politics, or topics of current interest. They attend strictly to their farming, and display more intelligence and real knowledge of diversified agriculture than any group of Italians investigated. They remind one of the German and German-Swiss farmers who have proved so successful both as farmers and as citizens. They have confidence in themselves, and the community feels that they can and do take their places and assume the responsibilities of citizenship shoulder to shoulder with the non-Italians in the neighborhood,

It may be that the environing conditions—natural and social—have molded this community differently from others where the opportunity for race isolation was afforded and conformity to the traditional type of agriculture was the line of least resistance. At any rate, Genoa exemplifies the adaptability of the north Italian, and illustrates his capacity for diversified agriculture and for American rural life as it has developed in our Midwestern states. The community has not yet begun to live abundantly, or to enjoy fully its evident prosperity. On the other hand, who shall say that the great rank and file of American farmers has advanced farther or more rapidly in rural wealth, welfare, or well-rounded citizenship than this small group of Italian fellow citizens?

Mexican Immigrants in the United States 35

The restriction of Oriental immigration into the Southwest was intended to be an economic boon to the area because it would eliminate unfavorable competition in the job market and enable thousands of whites to find work. That, at least, was the theory. The reality was that the Chinese and Japanese very often worked at jobs that white men would not accept, especially as farm laborers. So restriction, rather than solving a problem, created one: a shortage of seasonal farm help. When the Orientals were no longer available, California agriculturalists turned to other sources of labor, one of which was the Mexican immigrant. [*Survey,* September 7, 1912. By Samuel Bryan.]

Previous to 1900 the influx of Mexicans was comparatively unimportant. It was confined almost exclusively to those portions of Texas, New Mexico, Arizona and California which are near the boundary line between Mexico and the United States. Since these states were formerly Mexican territory and have always possessed a considerable Mexican population, a limited migration back and forth across the border was a perfectly natural result of the existing blood relationship. During the period from 1880 to 1900 the Mexican-born population of these border states increased from 66,312 to 99,969—a gain of 33,657 in twenty years. This increase was not sufficient to keep pace with the growth of the total population of the states. Since 1900, however, there has been a rapid increase in the volume of Mexican immigration, and also some change in its geographical distribution, with the result that distinct social and economic problems have arisen.

Until 1908 the officials of the Bureau of Immigration who were stationed upon the Mexican border concerned themselves chiefly with the examination of Japanese and Syrians who sought to enter this country by the way of Mexico. Since that time some effort has been made to secure data with regard to immigrants of Mexican birth, but the results obtained are so obviously incomplete as to be of little value. In 1908, it was estimated that from 60,000 to 100,000 Mexicans entered the United States each year. This estimate, however, should be modified by the well-known fact that each year a considerable number of Mexicans return to

Culver Pictures

A Mexican immigrant and his family entering the United States at Nuevo Laredo, Texas, about 1905.

Mexico. Approximately 50 percent of those Mexicans who find employment as section hands upon the railroads claim the free transportation back to El Paso which is furnished by the railroad companies to those who have been in their employ six months or a year. Making allowance for this fact, it would be conservative to place the yearly accretion of population by Mexican immigration at from 35,000 to 70,000. It is probable, therefore, that the Mexican-born population of the United States has trebled since the census of 1900 was taken.

This rapid increase within the last decade has resulted from the expansion of industry both in Mexico and in the United States. In this country the industrial development of the Southwest has opened up wider fields of employment for unskilled laborers in transportation, agriculture, mining, and smelting. A similar expansion in northern Mexico has drawn many Mexican laborers from the farms of other sections of the country farther removed from the border, and it is an easy matter to go from the mines and section gangs of northern Mexico to the more remunerative employment to be had in similar industries of the southwestern United States. Thus the movement from the more remote districts of Mexico to the newly developed industries of the North has become largely a stage in a more general movement to the United States. Entrance into this country is not difficult, for employment agencies in normal times have stood ready to advance board, lodging, and transportation to a place where work was to be had, and the immigration officials have usually deemed no Mexican likely to become a public charge so long as this was the case. This was especially true before 1908. Thus many penniless Mexicans who would be rejected at an Eastern port have been admitted without question on the Mexican border. . . .

Most of the Mexican immigrants have at one time been employed as railroad laborers. At present they are used chiefly as section hands and as members of construction gangs, but a number are also to be found working as common laborers about the shops and powerhouses. Although a considerable number are employed as helpers, few have risen above unskilled labor in any branch of the railroad service. As section hands on the two more important systems they were paid a uniform wage of $1.00 per day from their first employment in 1902 until 1909, except for a period of about one year previous to the financial stringency of 1907, when they were paid $1.25 per day. In 1909 the wages of all Mexican section hands employed upon the Santa Fe lines were again raised to $1.25 per day. The significant feature is, however, that as a general rule they have earned less than the members of any other race similarly employed. For example, 2,455 Mexican section hands from whom data were secured by the Immigration Commission in 1908 and 1909, 2,111, or 85.9 percent, were earning less than $1.25 per day, while the majority of the Greeks, Italians, and Japanese earned more than $1.25 and a considerable number more than $1.50 per day.

In the arid regions of the border states where they have always been employed and where the majority of them still live, the Mexicans come into little direct competition with other races, and no problems of importance result from their presence. But within the last decade their area of employment has expanded greatly. They are now used as section hands as far east as Chicago and as far north as Wyoming. Moreover, they are now employed to a considerable extent in the coal mines of Colorado and New Mexico, in the ore mines of Colorado and Arizona, in the smelters of Arizona, in the cement factories of Colorado and California, in the beet sugar industry of the last mentioned states, and in fruit growing and canning in California. In these localities they have at many points come into direct competition with other races, and their low standards have acted as a check upon the progress of the more assertive of these.

Where they are employed in other industries, the same wage discrimination against them as was noted in the case of railroad employees is generally apparent where the work is done on an hour basis, but no discrimination exists in the matter of rates for piecework. As pieceworkers in the fruit canneries and in the sugar beet industry the proverbial sluggishness of the Mexicans prevents them from earning as much as the members of other races. In the citrus fruit industry their treatment varies with the locality. In some instances they are paid the same as the "whites"— in others the same as the Japanese, according to the class with which they share the field of employment. The data gathered by the Immigration Commission show that although the earnings of Mexicans employed in the other industries are somewhat higher than those of the Mexican section hands, they are with few exceptions noticeably lower than the earnings of Japanese, Italians, and members of the various Slavic races who are similarly employed. This is true in the case of smelting, ore mining, coal mining, and sugar refining. Specific instances of the use of Mexicans to curb the demands of other races are found in the sugar beet industry of central California, where they were introduced for the purpose of showing the Japanese laborers that they were not indispensable, and in the same industry in Colorado, where they were used in a similar way against the German-Russians. Moreover, Mexicans have been employed as strikebreakers in the coal mines of Colorado and New Mexico, and in one instance in the shops of one important railroad system.

Socially and politically the presence of large numbers of Mexicans in this country gives rise to serious problems. The reports of the Immigration Commission show that they lack ambition, are to a very large extent illiterate in their native language, are slow to learn English, and most cases show no political interest. In some instances, however, they have been organized to serve the purposes of political bosses, as for example in Phoenix, Arizona. Although more of them are married and have their families with them than is the case among the south European immigrants, they are unsettled as a class, move readily from place to place, and do not acquire or lease land to any extent. But their most unfavorable characteristic is their inclination to form colo-

Farm laborers in Ventura County, California, about 1900.

nies and live in a clannish manner. Wherever a considerable group of Mexicans are employed, they live together, if possible, and associate very little with members of other races. In the mining towns and other small industrial communities they live ordinarily in rude adobe huts outside of the town limits. As section hands they of course live as the members of the other races have done, in freight cars fitted with windows and bunks, or in rough shacks along the line of the railroad. In the cities their colonization has become a menace.

. . . .

In Los Angeles the housing problem centers largely in the cleaning up or demolition of the Mexican "house courts," which have become the breeding ground of disease and crime, and which have now attracted a considerable population of immigrants of other races. It is estimated that approximately 2,000 Mexicans are living in these "house courts." Some 15,000 persons of this race are residents of Los Angeles and vicinity. Conditions of life among the immigrants of the city, which are molded to a certain extent by Mexican standards, have been materially improved by the work of the Los Angeles Housing Commission, upon which Johanna Von Wagner has served as an expert social worker. However, the Mexican quarter continues to offer a serious social problem to the community.

As is to be expected under the circumstances, the proportion of criminals and paupers among the Mexicans is noticeably greater than among the other foreign-born or among the natives. In Los Angeles County, California, the Mexicans comprised 11.4 percent of the total number of persons bound over for felonies in 1907. In 1908 and 1909 the percentages were 12.6 and 13.4 respectively. During the year ending July 1, 1908, the chief of police of Los Angeles estimates that approximately 20,000 police cases were handled, in 2,357 or 11.8 percent of which Mexicans were the defendants. In Arizona, where the proportion of Mexicans to the total population is greater than in Los Angeles, a correspondingly large proportion of the inmates of the various penal institutions are of this race. In 1908, 24.2 percent of the prisoners in the jail at Tucson, Ariz., were Mexicans, while in the Pima County jail they comprised 62 percent of the inmates. The territorial prison reported in the same year 61 percent of those incarcerated were Mexicans. In both Arizona and California the offenses for which they were committed were in the large majority of cases traceable to gambling or excessive drinking. Most of the serious trouble with Mexicans, however, arises from quarrels among themselves which interfere very little with the white population.

In the matter of poor relief, Mexican families were concerned in 11.7 percent of the cases dealt with by the Associated Charities of Los Angeles in 1908. The proportion has increased since that time, and in 1910 it was estimated that Mexicans comprised fully one-third of those given relief from this source. The county authorities had charge of approximately 3,000 individuals in 1908, of whom about one-third were Mexicans. The proportion of Mexicans among those dependent upon the County Board of Charities has

continued about the same, for in the month of November 1910, which was said to be typical of that year, 30.1 percent of the applications for aid were made by members of that race.

In conclusion it should be recognized that although the Mexicans have proved to be efficient laborers in certain industries, and have afforded a cheap and elastic labor supply for the southwestern United States, the evils to the community at large which their presence in large numbers almost invariably brings may more than overbalance their desirable qualities. Their low standards of living and of morals, their illiteracy, their utter lack of proper political interest, the retarding effect of their employment upon the wage scale of the more progressive races, and finally their tendency to colonize in urban centers, with evil results, combine to stamp them as a rather undesirable class of residents.

Father Bandini's Tontitown

36

In 1895 an Italian agricultural colony had been started at Sunnyside, Arkansas, under the sponsorship of Austin Corbin, president of the Long Island Railroad. This initially successful enterprise began to fail when Corbin died, agricultural prices fell, and sickness hit the settlers. In the wake of this failure a young Italian priest, Pietro Bandini, came to Arkansas to help his fellow countrymen out of their troubles. In 1898 they purchased 900 acres in the northwest corner of the state and established a community named after Enrico Tonti, who had descended the Mississippi with La Salle in 1682. The article reprinted here summarizes Tontitown's history and successes. [*World's Work*, June 1912: Anita Moore, "A Safe Way to Get on the Soil."]

In the midst of a crowd of noisy, eager peasant immigrants that were disgorged upon the Battery Pier from an Italian steamer some twenty-one years ago, walked a man in the garb of a priest. His face was very thoughtful and earnest as he watched the bewilderment of these newcomers at their journey's end. Now and then he addressed one of them with a

low-spoken Italian phrase, or quieted the wails of some frightened, straying child. He stood on the pier until the last fantastically clad stranger with the last bit of preposterous luggage had vanished into the mystery of streets that stretched away from the other side of Battery Park, and then he too turned and left the waterfront. The priest was Father Bandini, and he had come to America on a mission—to investigate and to better the conditions of his countrymen who drift untutored to these shores.

A DOUBLE-EDGED SOLUTION

What Father Bandini found out is a familiar tale to us now—the helplessness of the alien in the hands of glib porters and hotelkeepers, the loss of his small store of savings to the pretended friend who offers to find him a job in return for a competence, the inevitable drifting toward slum life, and the daily round of hard street labor to ward off starvation—all this is a scandal too old to bear repeating. Father Bandini went to work at once to find a remedy. The fact that seemed to him important was that the large majority of his countrymen had come from small farms at home. For that reason the priest felt that the only hope for them was to get them on the land and let them earn their bread in their accustomed way. The big obstacle that confronted this theory, however, was the social, pleasure-loving nature of the Italians which would make the isolated life of the ordinary American farmer intolerable to them.

Father Bandini's solution was to put a whole colony of these Italians on the land in one place, thus restoring the community life and the hopefulness of their former homes. The success of his experiment puts before social workers a new solution of the whole immigration problem. It also offers "a way out" to the man of small means who wants to get back to the land—be he Italian, or German, or just plain American. Here are the facts of this interesting experiment.

THE STORY OF TONTITOWN

Father Bandini, once having decided on a plan of colonization, plunged immediate-

ly into a study of government bulletins about climatic and agricultural conditions in various parts of the United States and at last decided upon the region of the Ozark Mountains in Arkansas, where the 1,500-foot elevation insures a healthful climate and where the seasons are long and open. The land had no very encouraging crop record, but a test of the soil gave promise of fair productivity under the proper cultural conditions.

To this country in March, 1898, Father Bandini came with a band of twenty-six hardy and all but penniless families. They picked out a tract of 300 acres in Washington County, within six miles of the St. Louis and San Francisco Railroad, and they purchased the land at $15 an acre. The scheme was not cooperative. The land was divided into lots varying in size from five to twenty acres, and each man paid what he could for his share—$10, $15, $25—and gave his note and a mortgage on the land for the balance, Father Bandini personally endorsing each note. They called their settlement Tontitown in honor of an early Italian immigrant, Enrico Tonti, who had served as lieutenant to La Salle and had established a small military post near the Arkansas River. . . .

THE FAT YEARS

The colony is now fourteen years old. It numbers 700 inhabitants, and owns 4,760 acres of good productive land, all clear of encumbrance, the value of which has increased from the original $15 paid for it to $50, $100, and even $150 an acre. In the village there are a modern hotel, three stores, a post office, a land office, or town hall, and a school—St. Mary's Academy—which contains five large, well-equipped classrooms, several living rooms for the three Sisters of Mercy and the two young women teachers, and a gymnasium. Here 130 children are enrolled.

The good priest who caused all this prosperity has kept constantly before his people the secret of their success. "One of the great dangers which threaten the farmers in America," he says to them, "is that they may become land poor. Forty acres is all that one man can profitably till. With twenty acres he can support a large family in comfort and save a little money. With forty acres he can become a man of means if he is industrious."

The Tontitown colonists follow this teaching. They build up their land by rotation of crops and fertilization. With the long open seasons they grow two or three crops of the same vegetables in the same season. Thus, for instance, they plant early spring onions for the market between rows of young peach trees or grapevines. After the onions have been harvested for the market, stringbeans are planted on the same ground. When the stringbeans have been marketed, the same ground is planted with some nitrogen-producing crop—such as cowpeas. The cowpeas are used as fodder for the cattle, thus providing a fertilizer directly and indirectly—the productivity of the soil is increased, yet it has yielded three crops and nourished an orchard or vineyard.

The first year that the young apple orchards produced a full crop, fruit in the Ozark Mountain region was most abundant. Commission men bought apples in the orchards from the native farmers at sixty cents a barrel—twenty cents a bushel. The Tontitown people bought and installed two fairly large fruit evaporators and established canneries and cider and vinegar factories. They fancy-packed their choicest apples and sold them at good prices. The seconds they canned or evaporated; the culls and parings they

used for cider, then ran the pulp through the presses again with water and made vinegar; and at last the pulp was put back on the land for fertilizer. In all they received at the rate of $6.00 a barrel for their fruit as against the sixty cents received by the American farmers. They ship their choice peaches, and the seconds are canned or evaporated. Every farmer has a vineyard of from four to eight acres which yields him returns from $500 to $600 per acre. The grapes are made into wine. One man alone makes 1,500 gallons of wine every season. The Tontitown wine is a fine domestic vintage that finds a ready market at $1.00 a gallon.

By his energy and initiative Father Bandini has promoted the establishing of other industries besides agriculture. Tontitown now possesses brickyards and limekilns. Three creameries profitably handle the milk; one of these creameries is devoted to butter making and the other two to cheese manufacturing. There are also a broom factory, a brickyard, a blacksmith shop, and a cobbler's shop.

The best proof of the triumph of Father Bandini's theory, however, lies probably not so much in a record of material achievement as in evidence of the satisfaction of the inhabitants. One formal statement of this satisfaction, because of its quaint phraseology, is too good to omit:

Tontitown, Ark.
February 8, 1912.

I, the undersigned, a resident of Tontitown from its very beginning, about fourteen (14) years ago, was not formerly a farmer, neither am I an expert farmer at present; yet I am glad to state that I am very well satisfied and pleased of my position and pleased with the crops I get from my farm, on which I raised almost everything I tried to.

Last year we had an exceptional dry season for a few months; had not a drop of rain for four months; yet from my little vineyard of 70 vines I got 6,200 pounds of first-class grapes.

On a surface of three-fourth of an acre I had a ton and a half of hay, 12 bushels of beans.

On another acre I raised sweet potatoes, on an average of 488 bushels an acre, extremely large; 40 bushels of Irish potatoes; 500 pounds of beans and half a ton of hay.

In consequence of the drought, as said above, the crop of strawberries and oats was light, but corn we had in abundance.

(Signed) Adriano Morsani.

Perhaps the greatest asset of the community is in the development of its children. They are healthy physically, morally, and intellectually. Of the children of the original families who first settled in Tontitown, nine girls—now grown to young women—are established as school teachers, holding university, state, or second grade certificates. Three sisters, who lost their father during the first year of the colony, have just built and furnished a little cottage for their mother, besides which they have finished paying for the farm which their father had bought before his death. Two of the first boys—now quite grown up—purchased eighty acres of land in 1910 and that spring planted twenty acres in strawberries. From the berries in the spring of 1911 and their fall crops of potatoes, hay, and corn they realized enough to pay for their farm.

The best part of the story of Tontitown is that it is only an introduction to a great extension of the colonization plan. In 1911, Father Bandini went back to Italy and there he told his story to all who would listen. He enlisted the sympathies of the pope, the prime minister, and the Queen Mother, and of several societies and organizations, all of which are pledged to do what they can to direct the flux of emigration away from the old channels and into the safe and pleasant outlet of our Western country. As an evidence of their earnestness a new little colony has already sprung up in Arkansas which the good priest is now fostering with the same devotion that he lavished on Tontitown.

That is what Father Bandini has done for his countrymen. What he has done to help solve some of the most momentous problems that confront us can be stated almost as definitely.

He has again illustrated the value of intensive cultivation of the soil. His success also suggests that farm colonies may be the simplest means by which the poor man can get on the land, and that colonization on a large scale may yet empty the city slums by putting the agricultural immigrant at once in touch with the opportunity to practise the only kind of productive industry for which he is fitted.

East Indians on the West Coast

37

The periodic labor shortages that developed in the West, occasioned largely by the restriction of Chinese immigration, led industrialists and ranch owners alike to seek new sources of labor. Among those who were brought in to work in lumber camps and on railroad construction were a few thousand East Indians, mostly Hindus. The following report on the East Indian immigration was written by Harry A. Millis, who had been in charge of the investigations of the U.S. Immigration Commission in the Western states. [*Survey*, June 1, 1912: "East Indian Immigration to the Pacific Coast."]

Previous to 1907 there were very few East Indians in the United States, and most of these were nonlaborers and in the eastern cities. In that year, however, 1,072 were admitted, as against 271 in 1906. In 1908 the number admitted increased to 1,710. Late in that year, however, the immigration officers began to turn back many of those who applied for admission, lest these wandering laborers should become public charges. As a result of this policy and of the measures adopted restricting their admission to Canada, whence most of them had been coming, the number admitted in 1909 was but 337. During the year 1909–1910, however, the interpretation of the general immigration law at the port of San Francisco, to which most of the applicants then came, was less restrictive, and the number who gained entrance again increased to 1,782. This increase, together with the facts that many almost immediately secured employment in the construction of a railroad near San Francisco (this giving rise to a widespread belief that there was organized traffic in this labor) and that an unusually large number of those who came were in the summer of 1910 found to be afflicted with disease, gave rise to an agitation against the Hindus, a change in the administration at the port of San Francisco, and the rejection of the majority of those who arrived. The total number of East Indian immigrants rejected at our ports was 438 in 1907, 331 in 1908, 411 in 1909, and 391

in 1910. For the three years 1908 to 1910, 447, or about 39 percent of those denied admission, were rejected because afflicted with trachoma; 177, or about 16 percent, because of "surgeon's certificates of defect mentally or physically which may affect ability to earn living"; and 464, or about 41 percent, because they were "likely to become a public charge." These figures indicate that either a large percentage of those who applied for admission were unfit, or that the interpretation of the law was severe. Perhaps they indicate both. At any rate the numerous rejections wrought much hardship. In this connection it is to be said, however, that the problem of East Indian immigration has been solved and that the hardship incidental to rejection at our ports has been eliminated, for those who have come since the change of policy at the port of San Francisco has become known are few. . . .

The policy of restriction, which temporarily at least has resulted in practical exclusion, when leniency would in all probability have brought in large numbers because of the cumulative effects of migrations, meets with almost unanimous approval on the Pacific coast, where the Hindus are regarded as the least desirable, or, better, the most undesirable, of all the Eastern Asiatic races which have come to share our soil. Except for a comparative few of an idealistic turn of mind who do not reckon carefully with details,

Brown Brothers

Sikh immigrants from India at Ellis Island, 1910.

a few who look upon this country as a place of refuge for the Hindu, whom they believe to be oppressed in his native land, and a very few of the many whose chief interest and point of view are industrial, the West stands opposed to the immigration of East Indians as to that of no other race.

In 1909 the federal Immigration Commission made an investigation of the employment, earnings, salient characteristics, and mode of life of the East Indian laborers in the Pacific coast states. The details which follow are drawn almost entirely from this investigation, which was made under the writer's supervision, and the results of which are set forth in greater detail in a special report submitted to the commission.

In the Western states, with rare excep-

tions, the East Indian laborers, who up to July 1, 1910, were estimated to number about 5,000, have engaged in the roughest, most unskilled work outside of factory walls. Perhaps with a continued immigration and a longer residence they would advance to higher occupations, as they did in British Columbia in spite of their low efficiency, but as yet their employment in the three Pacific coast states and Nevada has been narrowly limited to "yard work" in lumber mills, as section hands—chiefly in Nevada, but also in other places—as construction laborers, as wandering agricultural laborers engaged in handwork in California, and as unskilled laborers in a pottery and in a few quarries. The only instance known where they have secured employment in manufacture was in a rope factory in Portland, Ore.

Since 1906 Hindus, immigrating for the greater part from British Columbia, have been employed as "yard laborers" in some of the lumber mills of the Northwest, and chiefly about Bellingham, Tacoma, Gray's Harbor, and Astoria. They have been paid higher wages than the Japanese but as a rule lower wages than "white men," the Hindus not being recognized as of the white race. Their wages have been fixed by the lumber companies at comparatively high rates, because of the strong hostility exhibited towards them by laborers of other races, who have feared that they would undermine wage rates. In a few instances they have been regarded as worth the wage paid them, but most employers have regarded them as dear labor at the price, because they are physically weak as compared to "white" men, very slow to understand instructions, and require close supervision. Because of these things and the widespread and at times violent opposition to them they are not so extensively employed in lumber mills as formerly. In fact, most of the members of the race have migrated from Washington and Oregon to California in search of a warmer climate and of work in the fields and orchards.

In several instances groups of Hindus have been employed in railway construction. In all of these cases where the details are known they were paid somewhat less than the members of the white races, but were found to be too weak because underfed and too slow to be worth the price when other laborers could be secured at somewhat higher wages, with the result that their employment was in but few cases of more than brief duration. Nor have they been more successful as section hands, as is evidenced by the fact that, though they have been employed by several railway companies, only seventy-three were reported in a total of 34,919 section hands employed on railroads in the western group of states in the spring

and summer of 1909. In this occupation they have sometimes been paid higher wages than other Asiatics, but with few exceptions they have been regarded as the least desirable of all races employed. Unless of the soldier class (and members of that class were found in the ratio of 1 to 30 by the agents of the Immigration Commission), they have proved to be physically weak, unintelligent, and slow to acquire a knowledge of the work to be done.

For various reasons most of the East Indians have drifted into agricultural work in California, where there has been the greatest dearth of cheap labor because of the extension of specialized farming and fruit growing, and because of the diminishing number of Chinese and Japanese available as wage laborers for seasonal work. In 1908 they made their appearance in the orchards, vineyards, sugar beet fields, and on the large farms devoted to the production of various kinds of vegetables in northern and central California. In 1909 three small groups made their appearance in southern California.

East Indian farm laborers at work in California spray crops for protection against insects, about 1905.

Brown Brothers

Their work has been of the most unskilled type and limited to hoeing and weeding in field and orchard, and to the harvesting of grapes, other fruit, and vegetables, certain branches of which have long been largely in the hands of Asiatics. In only a few instances have they been assigned to work with teams. In the Newcastle fruit district and along the Sacramento and San Joaquin rivers, where a large part of the land is cultivated by Asiatics, they have found employment without much difficulty, because of a widespread desire to break the monopoly control of the labor supply by the Japanese, or because of the higher wages than formerly commanded by other Asiatics. The ranchers of most communities, however, have been averse to hiring them, even at relatively low wages, because of their uncleanliness and outlandish looks, wearing as they do the Hindu turban. They usually wander in small groups from place to place in search of work, under the leadership of one of their number who acts as interpreter and business agent, and they do not remain long in one place. These groups are not permanent, but are built up as circumstances dictate. The leader is not in a position of authority and usually earns somewhat higher wages than his men, rather than a share of their earnings. In 1908 their wages varied from twenty-five to fifty cents per day less than was paid to Chinese and Japanese. In some instances when paid on a piece basis they worked at a lower rate than other races. This difference has tended to disappear, however, for the Hindus, when they have found employment in a community, have sometimes demanded as high wages as were being paid to other Asiatics. In 1909 the difference had been reduced to twenty-five cents per day, and in some cases to even less. Though they have commended

themselves to some ranchers, they have generally been regarded as distinctly inferior to laborers of other races and not cheap labor at the wages which they have been paid. In few cases have they displaced any other race; usually they have done the work not desired by other races, or have been employed when other laborers were not available at the customary or even a higher wage.

Thus it is evident that the East Indians are practically all unskilled laborers, and chiefly wandering farm hands; that their industrial position has been very insecure; and that in general they have been looked upon as a possible source when laborers of other races were not available on satisfactory terms. In extreme need, they have frequently offered to work for very low wages and in some instances have even demanded employment; yet their competitive ability, because of low efficiency and a general disinclination to hire them, has been comparatively small. With larger numbers, more experience and time, however, their position would doubtless become more secure and their competitive ability greater. With the number of Japanese and Chinese laborers diminishing as a result of the restrictions placed upon the immigration of these classes, the East Indians with freer immigration might fall heir to the kinds of work which have been done in part by these other Asiatics; for employers are inclined to follow the line of least resistance in finding a supply of labor, and competition between races engaged in unskilled work apparently depends more upon the rate of wages than upon efficiency. . . .

Practically all of the Hindus on coming to the United States expected to return to India within a few years. Like other immigrants, however, who first came under similar circumstances, some of them now

Under police protection, East Indians return to mills to draw their pay after having spent the night in the city hall as prisoners of a mob.

expect to remain in this country permanently. Thus, of seventy-nine interviewed in Washington and Oregon in 1909, thirty-six expressed an intention of returning to India, six intended to remain permanently in the United States, while thirty-seven were in doubt as to what they would eventually do. With an immigration of considerable size, the passing of time, and better adjustment to the industrial situation, no doubt a relatively large permanent element would be formed, with its political and social problems. Indeed, in spite of the efforts of the Bureau of Naturalization a few East Indians have secured their first naturalization papers, and before the change in the administration at the port of San Francisco it was stated that some expected to have their wives join them.

The assimilative qualities of the East Indians appear to be the lowest of those of any race in the West. The control exercised by caste and custom has been referred to. So has the relatively low efficiency, which would make assimilation economically very difficult. Moreover, between one-half and three-fifths of them are unable to read and write. Of more importance, assimilation involves a bringing together of different elements; and in the case of the Hindus the strong influence of custom, caste, and taboo, as well as their religion, dark skins, filthy appearance, and dress, stand in the way of association with other races. It is evident from the attitude of other races that they will be given no opportunity to assimilate.

For the present, at any rate, they could find no place in American life save in the exploitation of our resources, and those who are directly interested in that prefer others to serve that end.

The Multiethnic Composition of Minnesota's Iron Ranges

Minnesota is often regarded as almost a Scandinavian province. But work on the vast iron deposits in the northern portion of the state attracted immigrants from every corner of Europe, so much so that the range became as vivid a portrayal of the "melting pot" as existed anywhere in the United States. The report reprinted here in part was written by Leroy Hodges, who served as geographer for the United States Immigration Commission from 1908 to 1910. [*Survey,* September 7, 1912: "Immigrant Life in the Ore Region of Northern Minnesota."]

North of Duluth there is a region where the falling rains and melting snows on one hill drain northward to the ice wastes of the Arctic Ocean. The waters on a second hill pass down to the Great Lakes, plunge over Niagara, and rush through the St. Lawrence into the gray, storm-tossed Atlantic. Providence has also decreed that the more favored waters of this place shall fall on a third hill and flow southward into the majestic Mississippi, traverse the heart of the Southland, and empty into the blue, sparkling depths of the Gulf of Mexico.

Great wastes of land stretch for miles covered only with the charred, blackened stumps of a once magnificent pine forest. Yawning chasms, in all their ugly nakedness, mark the spots where man has discovered and removed or is now at work removing the treasures of the hills which nature so carefully stored away.

The babel of more than thirty different alien tongues mingles with the roar of mine blasts and the crash and clank of machinery. Here side by side work Finns, Swedes, Montenegrins, south Italians, English, Irish, Bohemians, Frenchmen, Hollanders, Syrians, Belgians, Croatians, Danes, Russians, Magyars, Bulgarians, Germans, Greeks, Scotchmen, Welshmen, Dalmatians, Norwegians, and Serbians.

More than 22,000,000 tons of iron ore are produced here annually, giving employment to about 15,000 men. Nearly 2,000,000 tons a year of the hard hematite ores are taken from steep shafts which reach 1,000 feet down into the bowels of the earth, while more than 20,000,000 tons of soft hematite and limonite ores are dug from the surface of the earth with as little difficulty as though they were the common sands of the sea.

Embedded in these rock-strewn hills lie the wealth and the power of the American steel industry. Here is the home of thirty great iron-mining companies. Man can lay back a few feet of topsoil and load, with steam-driven shovels, an almost pure ore into the cars of waiting trains. It is an Eldorado where iron takes the place of gold!

This region is divided geologically into two districts, or ranges as they are popularly called, known respectively as the Vermilion and the Mesabi.

The Vermilion, the oldest of the two ranges, was explored and recognized as an iron-bearing district as early as the late 1840s; but was not developed to any extent until about 1880 when the locating of large deposits of iron ore caused a stampede. The majority of the new settlers came from the iron ranges of Michigan to seek employment. In 1882 the town of Tower, the first permanent mining camp in Minnesota, was established. A mining company was soon organized which has since been merged into a controlling iron-mining and steel-manufacturing interest which now owns and operates all mining properties on the range.

The records of a Roman Catholic church built in 1884 show that in that year the congregation was composed of thirty families of Irish, Germans, Italians, and French-Canadians: 120 souls, forty-five of them single, most of them from the Michigan ranges.

Systematic mining operations in the Mesabi range were begun in 1890, thirty years after the ore was discovered. The most important find was that of an exploration party from Duluth which struck a rich deposit of iron at what is now the Mountain Iron Mine.

After the first discoveries of the vast ore wealth of the Mesabi were made, towns and railroads were built and a steady immigration from the Vermilion and the older ranges of Michigan set in. By the fall of 1892 the first shipments of ore went from the Mountain Iron Mine.

The production of ore on the whole range in 1892 amounted to only 4,245 tons. Today the Mesabi, with its annual production of more than 20,000,000 tons of high-grade ore, is the greatest iron-producing region in the world.

The same company which owns the Vermilion properties controls and operates about two-thirds of the mines on the Mesabi, employing three-fourths of the men working in the industry. More than thirty other important concerns also own properties on the range. The centers of production are the towns of Hibbing and Virginia, and after them Chisholm, Eveleth, Coleraine, Nashwauk, Bovey, and Biwabik.

About 1900, to the original inhabitants—Finns, Slovenians, Scandinavians, Irish, north Italians, Cornishmen, and native Americans—were added an influx direct from Europe of Bohemians, south Italians, Bulgarians, Serbians, Croatians,

Montenegrins, and other south and east Europeans who now make up the unskilled element required in the development of the mines. At present the Finns and Slovenians greatly outnumber all other races, and about 77 percent of the total population of the region is composed of aliens. . . .

During the seasons of the year when lake transportation is open the demand for labor greatly exceeds the supply, and the mining companies make sweeping concessions in order to keep their payrolls full. Unskilled labor from the south and east of Europe is imported and mine discipline has been made as lax as possible, in order to keep the men satisfied after they are secured. This practice, the absence of both state and federal laws compelling the companies to employ only trained and experienced miners in the responsible and dangerous occupations, the inability of the majority of the operatives to speak English and understand the rules of the mines and the orders given them, and the recklessness and rank carelessness of a number of them, no doubt account for the appalling annual accident rate.

As the lake transportation lines are tied up during the winter, this season is slack in the mines. On account of its open-pit system of mining the Mesabi is more seriously affected by winter weather than the Vermilion. The mines on the latter range, all being underground, can be operated even in the most severe weather, the ore being stockpiled at the surface and held for shipment during the summer. If the demand for ore is active, employment can be secured on the Vermilion range the whole year round, which is not the case on the Mesabi.

Under normal conditions, during the shipping season, ten-hour periods for

The iron-rich Mesabi range made Minnesota the nation's chief producer of iron ore after 1911. Mesabi range miners posed for this photograph in front of their equipment, about 1900.

both day and night shifts are worked on the two ranges. No regular Sunday work is carried on except that of repairing, cleaning, and track laying which is done in a day shift of six to eight hours.

Wages average from $12.50 per week to $20 and over. More than 90 percent of the Poles, Slovenians, and Finns earn under $15 per week, while only a very few of the native Americans, English, Irish, Germans, Scandinavians, and other races from northern Europe earn under this amount. Wage payments are made monthly in currency by all the more important companies. Gold and silver coins are principally used. There are no company stores, or other institutions, upon which scrip can be issued. . . .

Labor is unorganized on the ranges, and an "open shop" is maintained by all companies. There is an unimportant local union at Hibbing, on the Mesabi, but it

has never been recognized by the operators. The Western Federation of Miners has made several attempts to organize the miners, but all have failed on account of the militant opposition to organization on the part of the larger mining interests, who import immigrants as strikebreakers.

Drunkenness is common among all races, and the efficiency of the Finns and Slovenians especially is visibly impaired by excessive drinking; the Scandinavians, though heavier drinkers, carry their drink better.

Each town in the region has its full quota of saloons. The only community in which the number is not abnormally large is Coleraine—the "model ore town"— with an estimated population of 2,000 on the western Mesabi range. There are only two saloons in this town, while a mile away, Bovey, the sister town, with a population of about 1,200, has twenty-five saloons. Bovey conditions are typical of the ore region.

In the principal fifteen towns on the two ranges, with a combined population of about 50,000, there are more than 350 saloons, or one saloon for 140 individuals. About 110 of these places are run by Poles, 80 by native Americans, 60 by Finns, 50 by Slovenians, 45 by Scandinavians, 35 by Croatians, about 30 by south Italians, and the remainder by the several other races in the region. . . .

The Scandinavians are making the most noticeable progress. They entered the region as unskilled laborers, but are moving up in the scale of occupations and are found chiefly as skilled workmen in the ore mines, or as industrious law-abiding citizens who have established independent businesses.

The Irish, English, Scotch, and French-Canadians have worked up from unskilled labor to skilled occupations in the mines. The Russian Hebrews are mostly storekeepers, and are slowly progressing, as are the Finns and the Slovenians on the Vermilion range.

A few of the Finns have gone from the mine colonies into the northern wilderness and cleared small patches of land miles away from the centers of population where they remain practically the whole winter living on provisions hauled out during the fall. They seem to thrive where the hardships are most severe, but their progress in the mines is retarded by their surliness and radicalism.

There has been very little advancement in the scale of occupations on the part of the Bohemians, Bulgarians, Croatians, Greeks, Poles, Serbians, Montenegrins, Italians, and Syrians. The Poles are good workmen but not at all ambitious. The Croatians are lazy, indifferent workmen and are among the lowest in the industrial scale.

Political Involvement

1904–1913

Reformers and foreign-born met head on in this, the Progressive Era. It was an era of municipal corruption, muckrakers, political bossism, temperance movements—altogether a time of domestic problems and proposed solutions. But the Progressive movement was primarily an endeavor of white, Anglo-Saxon, Protestant, old stock Americans to reform the evils of industrialized society. One of the major obstacles in their path was the large number of immigrants, who benefited from some of the evils, though they were victimized by others.

The immigrant was not at heart a reformer. His European background had made him pessimistic and suspicious about what government could or would do. The government he had known had been arrogant, bureaucratic, often oppressive, a gatherer of taxes, and a conscripter for military service. In his view, even his new government was likely to be an instrument of the ruling class. This attitude contrasted starkly with the civic interest expressed by native Americans, especially those with a penchant for reform. They saw the United States, at every jurisdictional level, as a servant of the people. Politics was the business of everyone, for it was the arena in which the ills of society could be successfully attended to. The reformer lent his support to such political innovations as the initiative, referendum, and recall, which the immigrant did not usually understand. The reformer promoted women's rights, Sunday closing laws, and temperance, which to the foreign-born were either irrelevant or insulting.

The immigrant, indeed every ethnic bloc, wanted government that was attuned to his needs. He turned, therefore, to the local political machine, caretaker of the seemingly bottomless pork barrel of jobs and sinecures. He saw in the local government the possibility of fulfilling his personal needs, and he was not interested in listening to reformers talk about efficient and economical administration. As a result, reformers and immigrants found a great gulf between them; and it is perhaps not surprising that the Progressives gradually came to espouse the idea of immigration restriction.

The party loyalties of the foreign-born remained much as they had been after the Civil War, although party affiliation was frequently nothing more than the result of old ethnic rivalries. The Irish were still overwhelmingly in the Democratic column, while many of the Protestant groups lined up with the Republicans, partly out of antipathy to the Irish and to Catholicism. Many of the new immigrants also went Republican, until the New Deal wooed them away. The black vote, where there was any, was firmly Republican, a heritage of Reconstruction. It should be noted, however, that how a man voted locally, with the machine, was not necessarily the way he voted on national issues.

Early in the 20th century there was severe competition between the parties for the votes of ethnic blocs. Republicans sought the votes of southern and eastern Europeans as a counter to the Democratic hold on the Irish. One of the most successful gambits contrived by Republicans was the financing of the American Association of Foreign Language Newspapers, which distributed political editorials that were read in many languages by millions of naturalized citizens and voters.

One issue that brought the ethnic societies into active politics was the continued call for restriction of immigration sounded by many Progressives and by nativist organizations. The demands for a literacy test produced open opposition from a few of the older immigrant groups, but particularly from Italians, Slavs, and Russian Jews. Politicians currying favor with ethnic blocs were often hard pressed to explain their party's stand on restriction. Woodrow Wilson, running for President in 1912, found that his published unfavorable views on immigrants came back to haunt him when they were translated for the benefit of the foreign-language press.

(On facing page) Census taking in an Italian section of New York City, 1920. Illustration EB Inc.

Rights of the Black Man
Carl Schurz

39

During his long public career, Carl Schurz took up a number of controversial issues: civil service reform, Indian affairs, opposition to the war with Spain, and, as in the selection below, the status of black Americans. Like many who criticized the white treatment of the Negro, he saw the issue only as a sectional one, instead of the national one it had in fact become. True, the South had been very flagrant in its denial of rights to the Negro. But blacks were hardly first-class citizens in the North or West either, as the frequent riots of the decade from 1900 to 1910 were to prove. [*McClure's Magazine,* January 1904: "Can the South Solve the Negro Problem?"]

That the suppression of the Negro franchise by direct or indirect means is in contravention of the spirit and intent of the Fifteenth Amendment to the Constitution of the United States hardly admits of doubt. The evident intent of the Constitution is that the colored people shall have the right of suffrage on an equal footing with the white people. The intent of the provisions of the state constitutions in question, as avowed by many Southern men, is that the colored people shall not vote. However plausibly it may be demonstrated by ingenious argument that the provisions in the state constitutions are not in conflict with the national Constitution, or that, if they were, their purpose could not be effectively thwarted by judicial decisions—yet it remains true that by many, if not by all, of their authors they were expressly designed to defeat the universally known and recognized intent of a provision of the national Constitution.

Can it be said by way of moral justification that the colored people have deserved to be deprived of their rights as a punishment for something they have done? It is an undisputed matter of history that they came to this country not of their own volition, that they were not intruders, but that they were brought here by force to serve the selfishness of white men; that they did such service as slaves patiently and submissively for two and a half centuries; that even during a war which was waged, incidentally if not directly, for their deliverance, a large majority of them faithfully continued to serve their masters while these were fighting to keep them in slavery; that they were emancipated, not by any insurrectionary act of theirs, but by the act of the government; that when, after their emancipation, they confronted their old masters as free men, they did not, so far as known, commit a single act of vengeance for cruelties they may have suffered while in slavery; that the right of suffrage was given to them, not in obedience to any irresistible urgency on their part, but by the national power wielded by white men, to enable the emancipated colored people to protect their own rights; and that when their exercise of the suffrage brought forth in some states foolish extravagances and corrupt government it was again principally owing to the leadership of white men, who worked themselves into their confidence and, for their own profit, led them astray.

The only plausible reason given for that curtailment of their rights is that it is not in the interest of the Southern whites to permit the blacks to vote. I will not discuss here the moral aspect of the question, whether A may deprive B of his rights if A thinks it in his own interest to do so, and the further question, whether the general admission of such a principle would not banish justice from the earth and eventually carry human society back into barbarism. I will rather discuss the question whether under existing circumstances it would really be the true interest of the Southern whites generally to disfranchise the colored people. . . .

Negro suffrage is plausibly objected to on the ground that the great bulk of the colored population of the South are very ignorant. This is true. But the same is true of a large portion of the white population. If the suffrage is dangerous in the hands of certain voters on account of their ignorance, it is as dangerous in the hands of ignorant whites as in the hands of ignorant blacks. To remedy this, two things might be done: to establish an educational test for admission to the suffrage,

excluding illiterates; and second, to provide for systems of public instruction so as gradually to do away with illiteracy, subjecting whites and blacks alike to the same restrictions and opening to them the same opportunities. This would easily be assented to by the Southern whites if the real or the principal objection to Negro suffrage consisted in the ignorance of the black men. It is also said "that education unfits the Negro for work." This is insofar true as it makes many Negroes unwilling to devote themselves to the ordinary plantation labor, encouraging them to look for work more congenial to their abilities and tastes, and sometimes even seducing them to live upon their wits without work. But the same, then, is true in regard to white men. . . .

That the evil of ignorance as an active element on the political field presents a more serious and complicated problem in the South than in the North cannot be de-

Primary school for Negroes in Henderson County, Kentucky, 1916. Photograph by Lewis W. Hine.

This scene of white children laughing at a Negro was part of a series of pictures used to accompany a popular song called "Coon! Coon!" in movie theater sing-a-longs, about 1910. Racist humor was common in both North and South.

nied, for the mass of ignorance precipitated into the body politic by the enfranchisement of the blacks is so much greater there than here. But most significant and of evil augury is the fact that with many of the Southern whites a well-educated colored voter is as objectionable as an ignorant one, or even more objectionable, simply on account of his color. It is therefore not mere dread of ignorance in the voting body that arouses the Southern whites against the colored voters. It is race antagonism, and that race antago-

nism presents a problem more complicated and perplexing than most others, because it is apt to be unreasonable. . . .

The colored people, originally brought here by force, are here to stay. The scheme to transport them back to Africa is absolutely idle. If adopted, its execution would be found practically impossible. . . . It must, to start with, be taken as a certainty that the Negroes will stay here and that the Thirteenth, Fourteenth, and Fifteenth amendments will stand; and if they are to be made inoperative at all, it must be by means of a sort of tricky stratagem in flagrant violation of the spirit of the Constitution. . . .

And here is the critical point: There will be a movement either in the direction of reducing the Negroes to a permanent condition of serfdom—the condition of the mere plantation hand, "alongside of the mule," practically without any rights of citizenship—or a movement in the direction of recognizing him as a citizen in the true sense of the term. One or the other will prevail.

That there are in the South strenuous advocates of the establishment of some sort of semi-slavery cannot be denied. Governor Vardaman of Mississippi is their representative and most logical statesman. His extreme utterances are greeted by many as the bugle-blasts of a great leader. We constantly read articles in Southern newspapers and reports of public speeches made by Southern men which bear a striking resemblance to the pro-slavery arguments I remember to have heard before the Civil War, and they are brought forth with the same passionate heat and dogmatic assurance to which we were then accustomed—the same assertion of the Negro's predestination for serfdom; the same certainty that he will not work without "physical compulsion";

the same contemptuous rejection of Negro education as a thing that will only unfit him for work; the same prediction that the elevation of the Negro will be the degradation of the whites; the same angry demand that any advocacy of the Negro's rights should be put down in the South as an attack upon the safety of Southern society, and as treason to the Southern cause. I invite those who indulge in that sort of speech to consider what the success of their endeavors would lead to.

In the first place, they should not forget that to keep a race in slavery that had been in that condition for many generations, as was done before the Civil War, is one thing, comparatively easy; but to reduce that race again to slavery, or something like it, after it has been free for half a century, is quite another thing—nobody knows how difficult and dangerous.

In the second place, they should not forget that the slavery question of old was not merely one of morals and human rights, but that it had a most important bearing upon the character of democratic government as well as upon economic interests and general progress and prosperity. . . .

What the reactionist really wants is a Negro just fit for the task of a plantation hand and for little, if anything, beyond. Therefore, quite logically, the reactionist abhors the educated Negro. In fact the political or social recognition of the educated Negro is especially objectionable to him for the simple reason that it would be an encouragement of higher aspirations among the colored people generally. The reactionist wishes to keep the colored people, that is, the great mass of the laboring force in the South, as ignorant as possible, to the end of keeping it as submissive and obedient as possible. As formerly the people of the South were the

slaves of slavery, so they are now to be made the victims of their failure to abolish slavery altogether.

And now imagine the moral, intellectual, and economic condition of a community whose principal and most anxious—I might say hysteric—care is the solution of the paramount problem "how to keep the nigger down"—that is, to reduce a large part of its laboring population to stolid brutishness—and that community in competition with other communities all around which are energetically intent upon lifting up their laboring forces to the highest attainable degree of intelligence, ambition, and efficiency. . . .

A girl and her nurse in Charleston, South Carolina, 1899.

171

As to the outlook, there are signs pointing in different ways. The applause called forth by such virulent pronouncements as those by Governor Vardaman, and the growls with which some Southern newspapers and agitators receive the united efforts of high-minded Southern and Northern men to advance education in the Southern states among both races, as well as the political appeals made to a reckless race prejudice, are evidence that the reactionary spirit is a strong power with many Southern people. . . .

On the other hand, the fact that the united efforts for education in the South, which I mentioned, are heartily and effectively supported not only by a large number of Southern men of high standing in society, but by some in important political office in the Southern states, and by a large portion of the Southern press, and the further fact that the crimes committed in the peonage cases were disclosed by Southern officers of the law, that the indictments were found by Southern grand juries, that verdicts of guilty were pronounced by Southern petit juries, that sentence was passed by a Southern judge in language the dignity and moral feeling of which could hardly have been more elevated, and that the exposure of these crimes evoked among the people of the South many demonstrations of righteous wrath at such villainies—all these things and others of the same kind are symptoms of moral forces at work which, if well organized and directed will be strong enough effectually to curb the reactionary spirit, and gradually to establish in the South, with regard to the Negro problem, an order of things founded on right and justice, delivering Southern society of the constant irritations and alarms springing from wrongful and untenable conditions, giving it a much needed rest in the assur-

ances of righteousness, and animating it with a new spirit of progress.

No doubt the most essential work will have to be done in and by the South itself. And it can be. There are in the South a great many enlightened and high-minded men and women eminently fit for it. Let them get together and organize for the task of preparing the public mind in the South by a systematic campaign of education, for a solution of the problem in harmony with our free institutions. . . .

They would be able to banish the preposterous bugbear of "social equality" which frightens so many otherwise sensible persons, in spite of the evident truth of Abraham Lincoln's famous saying that if he respected and advocated the just rights of the black man it did not follow that he must therefore take a black woman for his wife.

They might at the same time puncture those curious exaggerations of that dread "social equality" which exhibit themselves in such childish follies as the attempt to make a heroine out of a silly hotel chambermaid who thought she did a proud thing in refusing to make Booker T. Washington's bed. . . .

They will appeal to Southern chivalry, a sentiment which does not consist merely in the impulse to rush with knightly ardor to the rescue of well-born ladies in distress, but rather in a constant readiness to embrace the cause of right and justice in behalf of the lowliest as well as the highest, in defense of the weak against the strong, and all this the more willingly as the lowliest stand most in need of knightly help; and as in the service of justice the spirit of chivalry will shine all the more brightly, the harder the task and the more unselfish the effort. . . .

Such a campaign for truth and justice, carried in by the high-minded and enlightened Southerners without any party spirit—rather favoring the view that whites as well as blacks should divide their votes according to their inclinations between different political parties—will promise the desired result in the same measure as it is carried on with gentle, patient, and persuasive dignity, but also with that unflinching courage which is, above all things, needed to assert that most important freedom: the freedom of inquiry and discussion against traditional and deep-rooted prejudice—a courage which can be daunted neither by the hootings of the mob nor by the supercilious jeers of fashionable society, but goes steadily on doing its work with indomitable tenacity of purpose.

Order of the Sons of Italy

40

Every substantial immigrant group had at least one social, cultural, and fraternal organization. The largest of the Italian societies was, and is, the Order of the Sons of Italy in America, founded in New York in 1905. The preamble and first article of the order's constitution are reprinted here. [*Congressional Record*, 91 Congress, 1 Session, March 25, 1969.]

We, the members of the Order Sons of Italy in America, a fraternal organization, being a part of the United States of America, which we serve at all times with undivided devotion, and to whose progress we dedicate ourselves; united in the belief in God; conscious of being a representative element of an old civilization which has contributed to the enlightenment of the human spirit, and which through our activities, institutions, and customs may enrich and broaden the pattern of the American way of life; realizing that through an intelligent and constant exercise of civic duties and rights, and obedience to the Constitution of the United States, we uphold and strengthen this republic; in order to make known our objectives and insure their attainment through the harmonious functioning of all parts of our organization, the said Order Sons of Italy in America do hereby ordain and establish the following as our constitution:

Article I. Purposes

The purposes of the order are:

(a) to enroll in its membership all persons of Italian birth or descent, regardless of religious faith or political affiliation, who believe in the fundamental concept that society is based upon principles of law and order, and who adhere to a form of government founded upon the belief in God and based upon the Constitution of the United States of America, which government rests upon the proposition that all men are created equal and functions through the consent of the governed;

(b) to promote civic education among its members;

(c) to uphold the concept of Americanism;

(d) to encourage the dissemination of Italian culture in the United States;

(e) to keep alive the spiritual attachment to the traditions of the land of our ancestors;

(f) to promote the moral, intellectual, and material well-being of our membership;

(g) to defend and uphold the prestige of the people of Italian birth or descent in America;

(h) to encourage the active participation of our membership in the political, social, and civic life of our communities;

(i) to organize and establish benevolent and social welfare institutions for the protection and assistance of our members, their dependents, and the needy in general, with such material aid as we are able to give;

(j) to initiate and organize movements for patriotic and humanitarian purposes, and to join in meritorious movements for such purposes which have been initiated by other organizations or groups.

Anticlerical Italians at Hull House
Jane Addams

41

Old World conflicts and animosities were frequently perpetuated by the various immigrant nationalities, especially in the first years after their arrival. One, characteristic of nearly all groups, was the division over loyalty to the church. Anticlericalism was a feature of the immigrant communities that included small, liberal, and educated minorities who equated ecclesiastical domination with political authoritarianism. Political and social clubs that dealt with controversial issues of church and state were often misunderstood by other Americans at a time when foreign radicalism in any form was coming under increasing attack. In an interview published in the *Chicago Record-Herald* on March 1, 1908, Jane Addams, founder of Hull House, defended the Italian immigrants against charges of anarchism. [Chicago Foreign Language Press Survey, WPA Project, 1942.]

"The Italian colony around Hull House is composed almost entirely of immigrants from southern Italy," said Miss Addams. "They are strong admirers of Garibaldi and adherents of the king. The centenary both of Garibaldi and of Mazzini were enthusiastically celebrated at Hull House.

"Two liberal clubs of young Italians organized at Hull House. The Mazzini Club, which still meets there, is composed of young Italians who are devoted to the study of modern Italian literature and history. This club, although viewing modern Italy from the monarchist point of view, has maintained a noncontroversial attitude. The Giordano Bruno Club is a much more recent organization and held its meetings at Hull House until last September. The most successful public meeting of this club was held September 20, for the benefit of the eight Garibaldian veterans still surviving in Chicago.

"Although the club is avowedly an anticlerical organization, it removed its meeting from Hull House solely on the ground that it was a partisan political organization and should have a meeting room of its own. In this it merely followed the custom of Hull House in regard to partisan meetings. It was not at all because Hull House considered it an anarchist organization!"

"Do not the anticlericals sometimes carry their partisan sentiments almost to the point of violence?" was asked.

"There seems to be an unfortunate confusion in Chicago as to the anticlerical party of Italy," Miss Addams replied. "The present party dates its activity from the beginning of the movement for political unification of Italy. It opposes the temporal power of the Vatican and the domination of the clergy in political affairs. Its platform distinctly affirms the authority of the church in spiritual matters. Doubtless it has many foes of the church in its ranks, but also devout Catholics and priests.

"Many of the leading citizens of the Italian colony in Chicago who are devout Catholics and yet belong to the anticlerical party say that it is hard to be at once a good Catholic and a good patriot. They contrast their position with that of the Irish whose loyalty to Home Rule does not conflict with their loyalty to the church.

"There were incidents in the Italian colony which were attended with much irritation between the clericals and the anticlericals. The first of these was the proposition to name the old Polk Street School after Garibaldi. This proposition was received with enthusiasm by a large proportion of the Italian colony, but met with serious opposition by the clergy. The name was finally abandoned, but the controversy over it lasted for almost two years.

"It was difficult for Americans to understand the bitterness of feeling shown by both sides. *La Tribuna Italiana* became the organ of the Italians wishing the school called Garibaldi and carried on the controversy with a zeal and invective of which the southern Italian is past master. The other side was taken up with equal zeal in the pages of the *New World*. I myself and several other residents of Hull House had conversations with both Father Dunne and Signor Valerio, in which we deplored the bitterness of feeling which it would certainly take years to allay.

"The perusal of both sets of articles left upon one's mind an impression of a hostility whose bitterness was based upon a struggle much older and sterner than the mere matter of the naming of a school, but neither of the journals contained even a veiled threat of personal injury to its opponent. Indeed the threat which has been quoted from the *Tribuna Italiana* as presumably the worst one was a quotation from Dante implying that the leader of the opposition must in the end 'weep tears of repentance more bitter than the salt mines of Cervia.' On the other hand the article in the *New World* most hotly resented by the Italians was one entitled 'Garibaldian's Nose Is Broken in Chicago.'

"The Italians look on Garibaldi as a national hero. Almost every Italian town has his statue and a street named after him. The Italians in Chicago point to the fact that the Poles are permitted to call a school after Kosciusko and the Hungarians one after Kossuth, and they cannot understand why they are not permitted to call one after Garibaldi.

"The second instance which again stirred antagonism between the two parties occurred at the burial of Count Rozwadowski, the Italian consul, when the effort was made to bar the Italian flag from the church."

In Italy itself, where the battle had been raging for more than fifty years, competent observers agree that the antagonism between the black or Vatican party and the white or anticlerical party is fast dying out, and it seems deplorable that it should be continued in Chicago, and most unjust to revive it in connection with the dastardly murder at Denver.

"The patriotic Italian dreads and fears the small body of desperate anarchists in Italy quite as much as does the patriotic American here. He recognizes them as entirely distinct from the anticlerical party and from that of the Socialists, who again form a separate political party, with their own members in parliament. The Christian Democrats constitute a large party of devout Catholic laymen and cler-

Illustrations on this and facing page, Wallace Kirkland

Jane Addams was the influential co-founder of Hull House in Chicago, one of the first social settlements in North America. Hull House was founded in 1889 to serve the educational, cultural, social, and personal needs of the city's poor. Among those who benefited most from Hull House were many immigrants who lived in the racially mixed neighborhood where the settlement was established. (Right) This portrait of Miss Addams hung for many years in the first Hull House building. (Below) Children in a nursery school class at Hull House. (On facing page, top) Members of the staff at dinner, about 1930. The staff was made up of many talented and well-known volunteers from diverse professions who gave their time to classes and activities at the center. (On facing page, bottom left and bottom right) An Italian woman demonstrates use of the spinning wheel in the Hull House Labor Museum and a gypsy boy plays caroms at the Hull House Boys' Club.

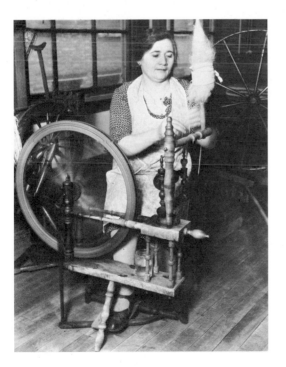

gy, but which also, like the anticlerical party, is opposed by the Vatican. . . . To confound the anticlerical party with the anarchists is almost as unjust as to so call the party in England which has long stood for the separation of church and state."

Denouncing the Prohibitionists

42

In the opening years of the century, the activities of the antiliquor forces in America reached a crescendo that culminated in the legal Prohibition of the 1920s. The movement for Prohibition was a feature of the Progressive program and was advocated by a majority of white Protestants; but it was opposed by virtually every immigrant group in the country. This newspaper article from the Czech paper *Denni Hlasatel* of February 28, 1910, typifies the reaction of immigrants to the efforts of the Prohibition Party. [Chicago Foreign Language Press Survey, WPA Project, 1942.]

Our people are not ignorant of the fact that the Prohibition Party does not attack the Chicago saloon only. They have long ago learned that the fanatical Prohibitionists' intentions are directed against personal liberty in general. There is hardly a single Bohemian in Chicago who does not know the Prohibitionists' trump card, and consequently all know that the drys play a crooked game. All know that they want first to annihilate the saloon, and after they succeed in that, they will turn to other issues and finally dictate to us not only what to drink but also what to do at all times. This of course we shall not and must not allow to happen, and it is therefore the duty of all liberal-thinking citizens to enlist in one mighty army to repel the attack against the first strong fortress of liberty, the saloon business. Bohemians will not be told by anyone in the world what to drink, what to eat, and how to live. There is one person, it is true, to whom we will listen—the physician whom we consult when we are ill.

In the meeting held last night in the Pilsen Sokol Hall under the auspices of the United Societies, the Prohibition movement was thoroughly discussed, so that not even one who may have lent a willing ear to the blandishments of the pharisaical Prohibitionists could hesitate any longer to rise against that riffraff and fight them on every front. The hall overflowed with enthusiastic liberals who filled it with peals of applause during every one of the speeches, which bristled with pointed remarks.

Mr. John A. Cervenka, first vice president of the United Societies, opened the meeting at 2 P.M. He was then elected chairman and explained to the assembly the purpose of the meeting. He then gave the floor to Mr. Michels, who immediately sailed into the Prohibition movement with these words:

"These people begrudge us the pleasure of having a glass of beer in an inn with agreeable conversation; they want us to drink in alleys and shanties, as people drink in those sections where Prohibition has succeeded."

Mr. Michels was followed by Mr. Michaelis, editor of the *Illinois Staats-Zeitung,* who expressed his joy at the tremendous response to the invitation to this mass meeting, and then continued:

"We are all immigrants or the children of immigrants, and it is immaterial how long we have been in America. Immigrants deserve great credit for the development of this country, and that is why we are proud to be known as immigrants. The Prohibitionists, on the contrary, are continually attempting to prove that as native Americans they are superior to the immigrant. Well, I am glad to admit that they are Americans and the offspring of Indians, and Indians, as is well known, must not be allowed to take a single swig of alcohol because this will result in an eruption of bestial ferocity dangerous to their environment. But it is impossible to get along with that paltry trash who have no red blood and no honor in them."

Alderman Anton Cermak, the next speaker, exposed by incontrovertible evidence and precise conclusions the hollowness and falseness of the arguments of Prohibitionists:

"It is not a question of whether we shall have saloons in Chicago but the question of personal liberty for every one of us. Prohibition cannot prohibit the use of liquor, but it can put upon us such burdens that we shall be sorry that we have allowed affairs to go so far. We still have the power to destroy the Prohibition movement, but unless we do so now, it will rise to attack us over the entire state. The struggle will then have fatal possibilities and may easily end in disaster. I wish to submit some figures which show that Prohibition cannot forbid liquor but will put a burden upon the liberal-minded taxpayer."

And then Mr. Cermak produced some very interesting statistical data. He compared towns where there is no Prohibition with such as are under the heel of the drys; invariably in the former towns there are fewer instances of punishment for drunkenness than in the latter. The reason for this, Mr. Cermak said, is that in the free towns beer is used to quench the thirst, whereas in towns which have Prohibition liquor is consumed only to aggra-

vate thirst. Internal revenue from the sale of liquor has increased 50 percent in states which have adopted Prohibition. In Chicago the Sixth, Seventh, and Twenty-fifth wards, dubbed "silk stocking wards," the very hotbeds of Prohibition, yield $375,590 in city taxes for general consumption. The Fifth, Eighth, Ninth, Twelfth, and Twenty-ninth, populated by the liberal element, pay $1,369,500. On the other hand, the general expenditure of the city for the upkeep of the Prohibition wards is $643,345.78, while the liberal wards receive $868,738.86; this shows that the taxpayers of the liberal wards have to pay for the Prohibition wards populated by the wealthy.

After these telling comparisons a certain Gilchrist Lawson, a Protestant preacher and a protagonist of Prohibition, appeared and asked for the floor. He demanded of Mr. Cermak whether it is not true that the inhabitants of the Prohibition wards, for the very reason that they are wealthier, are those who maintain the charitable institutions for the benefit of the poor. The arrogance of this half-crazy fanatic caused much indignation in the gathering, but Mr. Cermak promptly demonstrated by figures which he had ready that it is the poor who pay for the police in the rich wards, for the old peoples' homes, and for the hospitals as well. Mr. Cermak's explanation had the desired effect, and the preacher retired with dejected mien.

In a brief speech Mr. Cyril Jandus pointed out economic consequences of Prohibition.

"Seven thousand stores would have to close, and 20,000 men would have to look for other occupations; besides that, $7 million in taxes would have to be raised from other sources," he warned.

Congressman Sabath then took the

floor and said: "This multitude of intelligent men and women and their attitude convince me that our liberty will be preserved, and that no one will succeed in wresting it from us."

Mr. Sabath then charged the Prohibitionists with taking money from the poor without contributing any for their needs. He did not spare the heads of the railroad and streetcar companies, who almost without exception are Prohibitionists.

"How well they care for their property and foster its growth!" the congressman exclaimed. "And what do they do for their workingmen? When a car is damaged, they promptly have it repaired for further use. But when a man becomes incapacitated while working for them, he is abandoned, and another takes his place."

The speaker characterized such behavior as downright criminal and unworthy of citizens of the United States. He referred to the struggle against Prohibition in the city of Baltimore, where as a speaker he had put the question squarely before the leaders of the Prohibition Party:

"What are you going to give the people in return for the saloon? Do you think that workingmen can gather in clubs like yours and drink champagne? No, gentlemen, the workingman today needs the saloon for the discussion of public affairs and as a place for social gatherings."

Several other speakers appeared on the platform and spoke in various languages. The meeting was an unqualified success. However, we recommend that someone be engaged for the next meeting to speak in Bohemian for the benefit of those who do not understand English very well.

Some Irish Advice for Greek Immigrants

43

The following speech was delivered to the Achaian League of Chicago by George F. Mulligan on November 6, 1910. His audience consisted mostly of relatively recent arrivals in America, for the Greek emigration was largely a 20th-century affair. Many of the Greeks were locating in Chicago on the near Southwest Side, where the Italians had settled before them. The proposals made by the speaker had been standard procedure for every ethnic group, none more so than the highly organized and politically astute Irish-Americans. [Chicago Foreign Language Press Survey, WPA Project, 1942.]

There was a time when the Greek people were the wonder and the admiration of the world, when science, art, literature, and government yielded mastery to you. Today you have drifted away from the high ideals of your forefathers and hold no place of high repute among the people of this great country.

Today when the name of one of you appears in the public press of this country it is followed by the words, "a Greek," as though you were some strange and unknown factor in modern civilization. You have only yourselves to blame for the conditions that now exist, because your own disunion, your own lack of organization, lies at the bottom of the public's lack of respect for you.

Why does the public press say "George Dontopoulos, a Greek," was injured or arrested, as the case may be? You never see them say "Mike O'Brien, an Irishman," or "Herman Meyersberger, a German!" I will tell you why; it is because the Irish are organized and influential, and because the Germans are organized and influential, while you are without organization and therefore without influence.

Bettmann Archive

Newly arrived Greek immigrants at Ellis Island, about 1920.

I can remember some twenty or twenty-five years ago when advertisements for clerks, laborers, and other help would appear in newspapers and on signboards with the expression "No Irish Need Apply" at the end of the advertisement. You don't see such advertisements now. And why? Because the Irish began to organize. In the East they organized the "Sons of St. Patrick"; in the West, the "Ancient Order of the Hibernians." They got their people into these organizations, got them naturalized so that they could vote, and they voted! They became a power in the affairs of government and in the elections. Soon their members were on the police force, fire department, then in the town and city councils, then in the city offices, the state legislature, the state offices, in Congress, in the Senate—everywhere the Irishman began to force his way in public

affairs and always through organization. It was the same with the Germans. They formed their *Turnverein*s, their *Sängerbund*s, and their various other organizations, and today the German is found everywhere in our American public life, from the police force up to the halls of Congress.

You Greeks can do the same. You have behind you the sentiment and traditions of ages; all you lack for success is organization and united effort. You all know how easy it is to take one slender stick in the hands and break it with little effort; but take a hundred sticks bound together tightly and no man can break them.

It is the same with yourselves; singly and alone, it is easy to ignore you and defeat you, but if you were all united into one organization your power and influence would be so great, no man nor set of men would dare to ignore you or your rights.

There has been formed in Chicago an

organization called the Achaian League. Its purpose is to promote American citizenship among the people of Hellenic descent and to enforce and protect the rights of such citizens. Join this league, and get your friends to join! Its officers will see that you become naturalized, that your citizenship papers are issued to you, that you are registered as voters, and that you are kept informed on matters of public interest and of interest to you.

The Achaian League is nonpartisan; its purpose is not to favor any one particular party, but to enable the people of Hellenic descent to demand and secure representation in American government and in public affairs by means of organized and united effort on the part of the Greek people themselves.

By your being organized and being interested in public affairs, you will soon become familiar with the customs and the language of the country, and as the Irish and the Germans and the Poles, the Greeks will soon be found in the police department, the fire department, the city council, in city and county offices, in the state legislature, and in Congress. Then will you aid in making Chicago the Athens of America, and, in the upbuild-ing of yourselves, will secure for the Greek people in America a return of the glory they once had in Greece.

You gain recognition in no other way. Your voting strength alone will gauge the position that will be accorded you in the affairs and the life of America. You can win advancement just as the Irish and the others have done. There is much in common between the Irish and the Greeks. I don't know whether the Greeks came originally from Ireland or the Irish came from Greece, but somewhere, sometime, someplace in the fog and gloom of forgotten ages, they seem to have had a common origin. The pictures and statues of the ancient Greeks look like pictures or statues of Irish statesmen.

If you do not avail yourselves of the opportunities this country gives you, and of the traits of character you have inherited from the past, you will be false to your own history and a shame to your posterity. Organize, then join the Achaian League, see that all your people are naturalized and, with your united and organized voting strength, demand and secure your rightful place in public affairs and in the future history of American government.

Another Defeat for Restrictive Legislation

44

There was a great deal of concern in the United States during the period from 1901 to 1924 over keeping the country free of foreign ideologists: anarchists, Communists, and revolutionaries in general. Popular sentiment had equated the terms "foreign" and "radical," and most social protest was considered to be the work of "outside agitators" rather than the result of unsolved problems in an inequitable industrial system. Congress found one solution to the problem of foreign radicals in 1912: make the country of origin responsible for the character of individuals who emigrate. The fate of this proposed legislation was announced in the following article from the Czech newspaper *Denni Hlasatel* on January 22, 1913. [Chicago Foreign Language Press Survey, WPA Project, 1942.]

As a result of the efforts of Senators La Follette, O'Gorman, Stone, and others, the so-called conference bill, which is a compromise between the Senate and the

"In the height of the tourist season." A cartoon from *Judge,* 1907, contrasts the good effect of Americans going abroad with the alleged menace of increased immigration to the United States.

House of the Burnett-Dillingham Bill aimed at the restriction of immigration, was defeated in Washington last Monday. The bill has been returned to conference because of the Senate's protest against the article concerning the immigrant's good reputation.

The adoption of this article would have made it necessary for immigrants from countries where certificates of good repute are issued to emigrants to present their certificates upon arrival in America. Apparently, this article was directed against members of such societies as the Black Hand and Camorra but it would soon have become a welcome means to all European governments desirous to gain control over their emigrants. In Austria, for instance, where it is a crime to evade military service by emigrating from the country, all that would be necessary to prevent young men from emigrating to the United States would be to pass a law providing for the issuance of certificates of good repute. Obviously, because a certificate of good repute could not be issued to a political criminal, this bill would have provided the Austrian government with a powerful weapon, and made of the American government an efficient police force for Austria.

This inhuman, un-American bill, which would, in effect, completely stop emigration from Russia by giving the czar's government complete control thereof, has stirred all who have a sense of right and justice. The senators from states with a large population of immigrants have therefore received a great number of telegrams urging them to prevent the passing of the bill.

The *Česko-Americká Národní Rada* (Bohemian-American National Council) has sent to both Senator Cullom of Illi-

183

nois and Senator La Follette of Wisconsin the following telegram:

"The *Cesko-Americká Národní Rada* (Bohemian-American National Council) urgently requests you to do all that is in your power to prevent the passage of the vicious conference bill on immigration. The bill is un-American, it has no good purpose, and is aimed at aiding certain European countries in the suppression of their subjects.

E. St. Vraz, President"

Another telegram sent to both senators reads thus:

"*Cesko-Americká Tisková Rancelár* (the Bohemian-American Press Bureau) requests you to oppose vigorously conference bill article requiring the presentation of certificates of good repute. Its passage would endanger the liberty of the American people. We protest most emphatically against such laws and shall appreciate your intervention.

J. F. Stěpina, President"

As we said before, it was only because of the article on the certificates that the bill was defeated. Both organizations will express their thanks to those senators who voted against the bill.

California's Alien Land Law of 1913

45

By 1910 the Japanese had successfully established themselves in agriculture, largely through the development of California's marginal lands, which had previously been unproductive. As in the case of the Chinese, the California whites would not tolerate successful economic competition from those whom they considered outsiders, and who were, in any case, ineligible to become citizens. The Webb-Henry Bill, or Alien Land Law, was passed in 1913 to stamp out this competition. This state law was so drawn, however, that it failed to accomplish its purpose; and Japanese farming prospered during the boom years of World War I. After the war, anti-Japanese forces began pressing for an amendment to the 1913 law, charging that the Japanese owned all the best land in the state. The new law of 1920, by forbidding Japanese the right to lease land, did succeed in reducing the number of them engaged in farming. [*Consolidated Supplement to the Codes and General Laws of 1909 for the Years 1911–1913,* Act 128, pages 848–851.]

An act relating to the rights, powers, and disabilities of aliens and of certain companies, associations, and corporations with respect to property in this state, providing for escheats in certain cases, prescribing the procedure therein, and repealing all acts or parts of acts inconsistent or in conflict herewith.

OWNERSHIP OF LAND BY ALIENS
Section 1. All aliens eligible to citizenship under the laws of the United States may acquire, possess, enjoy, transmit, and inherit real property, or any interest therein, in this state, in the same manner and

to the same extent as citizens of the United States, except as otherwise provided by the laws of this state.

RIGHT TO ACQUIRE AND LEASE LANDS
Section 2. All aliens other than those mentioned in Section 1 of this act may acquire, possess, enjoy, and transfer real property, or any interest therein, in this state, in the manner and to the extent and for the purposes prescribed by any treaty now existing between the government of the United States and the nation or country of which such alien is a citizen or subject, and not otherwise, and may in addi-

A successful Japanese-American family.

tion thereto lease lands in this state for agricultural purposes for a term not exceeding three years.

CORPORATIONS, MAJORITY OF MEMBERS ALIENS, MAY ACQUIRE AND LEASE LANDS
Section 3. Any company, association, or corporation organized under the laws of this or any other state or nation, of which a majority of the members are aliens other than those specified in Section 1 of this act, or in which a majority of the issued capital stock is owned by such aliens, may acquire, possess, enjoy, and convey real property, or any interest therein, in this state, in the manner and to the extent and for the purposes prescribed by any treaty now existing between the government of the United States and the nation or country of which such members or stockholders are citizens or subjects, and

not otherwise, and may in addition thereto lease lands in this state for agricultural purposes for a term not exceeding three years.

PROBATE COURT MAY ORDER LANDS SOLD
Section 4. Whenever it appears to the court in any probate proceeding that by reason of the provisions of this act any heir or devisee cannot take real property in this state which, but for said provisions, said heir or devisee would take as such, the court, instead of ordering a distribution of such real property to such heir or devisee, shall order a sale of said real property to be made in the manner provided by law for probate sales of real property, and the proceeds of such sale shall be distributed to such heir or devisee in lieu of such real property.

LANDS ILLEGALLY ACQUIRED TO ESCHEAT TO STATE
Section 5. Any real property hereafter acquired in fee in violation of the provisions of this act by any alien mentioned in Section 2 of this act, or by any company, association, or corporation mentioned in Section 3 of this act, shall escheat to, and become and remain the property of the state of California. The attorney general shall institute proceedings to have the escheat of such real property adjudged and enforced in the manner provided by Section 474 of the Political Code and Title 8, Part 3 of the Code of Civil Procedure. Upon the entry of final judgment in such proceedings, the title to such real property shall pass to the state of California. The provisions of this section and of Sections 2 and 3 of this act shall not apply to any real property hereafter acquired in the enforcement or in satisfaction of any lien now existing upon, or interest in such property, so long as such real property so

Brown Brothers

A large chicken yard on a Japanese-owned farm in Los Angeles County, California, about 1910.

acquired shall remain the property of the alien company, association, or corporation acquiring the same in such manner.

LEASEHOLD ILLEGALLY ACQUIRED TO ESCHEAT TO STATE

Section 6. Any leasehold or other interest in real property less than the fee, hereafter acquired in violation of the provisions of this act by any alien mentioned in Section 2 of this act, or by any company, association, or corporation mentioned in Section 3 of this act, shall escheat to the state of California. The attorney general shall institute proceedings to have such escheat adjudged and enforced as provided in Section 5 of this act. In such proceedings the court shall determine and adjudge the value of such leasehold or other interest in such real property, and enter judgment for the state for the amount thereof together with costs. Thereupon the court shall order a sale of the real property covered by such leasehold, or other interest, in the manner provided by Section 1271 of the Code of Civil Procedure. Out of the proceeds arising from such sale, the amount of the judgment rendered for the state shall be paid into the state treasury and the balance shall be deposited with and distributed by the court in accordance with the interest of the parties therein.

ACT NOT LIMIT ON POWER OF STATE

Section 7. Nothing in this act shall be construed as a limitation upon the power of the state to enact laws with respect to the acquisition, holding, or disposal by aliens of real property in this state.

Section 8. All acts and parts of acts inconsistent, or in conflict with the provisions of this act, are hereby repealed.

Nagging the Japanese

46

The American attitudes and policies toward Japanese immigrants were not without their effect on foreign affairs. Japan was becoming the major power in the Far East, and her national pride was deeply offended by the treatment accorded Japanese nationals on the West Coast. New England theologian Francis G. Peabody explored the ramifications of the California Alien Land Law in relation to Japan's strength in the Pacific in this article, titled as in the original. [*North American Review*, September 1913.]

An American who has spent the spring months of this year in Japan and returns this summer through California encounters a sharp sea change of public opinion. In Japan, among responsible people, the anti-Japanese legislation of California created a general sense of bewilderment. The United States had been regarded as the most disinterested and trustworthy of Western nations. A monument to Commodore Perry had been recently unveiled. A "gentlemen's agreement" had checked the migration to America, so that the number of Japanese in California had decreased by 4,933 during the last three years. The holdings of land by Japanese in 1910 amounted to but 12,726 acres, or about 1 percent of the 12,000,000 acres of agricultural land. The purposes of the Japanese government were conspicuously directed to the promoting of emigration to Korea and Manchuria rather than to the West. Suddenly, and with no apparent provocation, California descended on this insignificant number of Japanese settlers with legislation which was practically confiscation. The prevailing public opinion in California, with many exceptions of individuals and neighborhoods, seemed to be made up in about equal parts of racial prejudice and economic fear. All Orientals, it was often maintained, were unclean and immoral, and their presence was a threat to our families and children. This was a white man's country. The Japanese, it was more particularly urged, were undesirable citizens

because they were so industrious and acquisitive. They make a living where a white man would starve. They lease a bit of unproductive land, and soon they own it, and the next piece, too. They crowd out white competition in the fisheries, the potato fields, and the market gardens. Thus a question of landholding which, after twenty years remained insignificant, and which showed no signs of immediate gravity, was magnified in the public press into "a horde of settlers," "a stranglehold on the state," "the grip the Japanese are securing." The consequence was a policy which may be described as nagging the Japanese. Precisely as in a home there may be no legitimate ground for divorce, but life may be made miserable by petty irritations and insults, so California, being precluded by treaty from direct discrimination, proceeded to make life as uncomfortable as possible for a handful of Japanese, and to treat a proud and friendly nation as though it were a nation of lepers. Some of the talk which one might hear in California was of the loosest and most reckless description. A wall, it was half-humorously said, ought to be built round the state, and its resources reserved for its own people.

Here, then, is a situation which takes on a wholly different look when seen from opposite sides of the ocean. What to California is a local irritation created by a few objectionable settlers is regarded in Japan as a national insult. To the Japanese our federal system is almost incomprehensi-

Japanese laborers rest on a California hillside, about 1910. These men were part of a road construction gang.

ble. In a nation where loyalty to the throne is an overmastering passion, the conception of a divided authority, permitting one section of a country to oppose or thwart the will of the rest, seems like governmental chaos, and the impression persists that somehow California might be overruled. A nagging policy is therefore the most irritating that could be devised. Exclusion would be more endurable to the Japanese than insinuation. If a proud and sensitive country should be goaded to retaliation, it would be because it had been treated superciliously, and because the government at Washington moves so slowly in reparation, if indeed it is moving at all. Here is the gravity of the case; and until the issue is dealt with, not as a tool of local politics, but as a case of in-

ternational comity, no satisfaction is likely to be felt in Japan. One state may do the nagging, but the whole country has to bear the blame. One state might involve us in a war which, as a San Francisco newspaper remarked, would make California "an object of derision from Bangor to New Orleans"; yet even then it would be difficult to follow the suggestion of an Oregon newspaper, and "let California do the fighting, while the other states look on." It is high time, then, to consider what are the elements in the problem which should be clearly recognized, if a policy of local nagging is to be supplanted by a policy of sane diplomacy.

The first of these conditions of settlement is an appreciation of the fact that we are dealing with an equal. It is often remarked with amusement by the Japanese that the Western nations did not think them worthy of respect until they had killed a great number of Russians. That achievement suddenly called to the attention of the West a people whose culture had its golden age before America was discovered, and whose arts, crafts, philosophies, passionate love of natural beauty, and not less passionate patriotism are quite without parallel in the world. . . .

A second step in adjusting this issue may be taken by a revision of our laws of immigration and naturalization. The practices now followed have become quite absurd and archaic. We recognize white and black; but when the Fifteenth Amendment was passed the yellow race had not risen above our horizon. We accept as citizens the offscourings of eastern Europe, and shut our door on the thrifty Japanese, whose color may be no darker, and whose descent may be from much the same original stock. What nags the Japanese in the matter is the indirect insinuation of bad blood, the intimation that a people whose education is compulsory and self-help is universal may not prove as serviceable elements in a commercial democracy as the average of Syrians or Copts; that, in short, the Far East is intrinsically inferior to the Near East. . . .

A third contribution to sanity and prudence in dealing with this issue may be suggested by considering the possible alternatives to the present friendly relations with Japan. If it be true that the world's trade is soon to seek the Pacific Ocean; that, as one hears in California, "the United States faces west"; if the Golden Gate is the gate of the future; then it certainly seems a questionable policy to irritate our nearest customer by nagging legislation. . . .

Japan is not a warlike nation. Her gifts and tastes are for the arts of peace, and all her capital—and much more—is needed for the industrial development which is one of the miracles of the modern world. Nonetheless, Japan has shown that she can fight for her life, and has given evidence of a patriotism which totally disregards defeat or death. If it were conceivable that she should be goaded beyond endurance, she could without serious effort take the Philippines, and perhaps get temporary possession of the Hawaiian Islands, she could then sit still and wait; and the United States would have on its hands a war of retaliation and recovery. And what a war! The vastness, dubiousness—not to say the wickedness—of such an enterprise make it not so much a political possibility as a rhetorical opportunity. . . .

We are brought by these considerations to a fourth, and the most important, means to a better understanding—namely, a better acquaintance. . . .

It may be true that the type of Japanese settler who has taken up land in California is apt to be pushing, suspicious, and even unscrupulous; but it would be strange indeed if any type except one not much desired at home could be tempted to settle where every possible means of force and law is employed to annoy and eject. The fact is, then, that we do not know the Japanese as they know us; and do not credit them, as they do us, with generous or even respectable motives. Their students run every risk of poverty and insult that they may have the chance to learn our sciences; but what do our students know of their subtle philosophies and tranquilizing religions? Their art has qualities which in their own sphere are unique and supreme, yet Japanese art still remains the precious possession of connoisseurs, and is purposely debased and vulgarized in order to meet American taste. They receive American travelers, physicians, and missionaries, not only with toleration, but with extreme teachableness, while the great majority of Americans either fancy the Japanese to be heathen, in their blindness, bowing down to wood and stone, or classify them roughly with Chinamen, whom they resemble in character and temperament about as much as a Frenchman does a Turk.

Letter of Protest to President Wilson
Francis J. Grimké

47

Woodrow Wilson was the first Southern-born majority-party candidate for the presidency since the Civil War, but in his campaign of 1912 he seemed more unequivocal in his advocacy of Negro rights than either Taft or Roosevelt. Many black citizens therefore voted for the Democratic ticket. A year had not passed before the blacks in America learned the value of campaign oratory. By the summer of 1913 segregation orders had been issued in most departments of the federal government—a reversal of a fifty-year policy. Wilson himself approved the segregation of facilities and jobs in the executive branch. The letter reprinted here protesting Wilson's segregationist policies was written September 5, 1913, by the Reverend Francis Grimké, pastor of the Fifteenth Street Presbyterian Church in Washington. Grimké was an influential voice in the black community, as pastor of the most prominent Negro congregation in America at the time. [Carter G. Woodson, ed., *The Works of Francis J. Grimké.* Washington, D.C., 1942. Vol. 4, pages 133–134.]

As an American citizen I desire to enter my earnest protest against the disposition, under your administration, to segregate colored people in the various departments of the government.

To do so is undemocratic, is un-American, is un-Christian, is needlessly to offend the self-respect of the loyal black citizens of the Republic. We constitute one-tenth of the population, and, under the Constitution, have the same rights and are entitled to the same consideration as other citizens. We had every reason to hope, from your high Christian character, and from your avowal of lofty principles prior to your election, that your accession to power would act as a check upon the brutal and insane spirit of race hatred that characterizes certain portions of the white people of the country. As American citizens we have a right to expect the President of the United States to stand between us and those who are bent on forcing us into a position of inferiority.

The lynching of Jesse Washington, a black 18-year-old boy, for an alleged rape at Waco, Texas, in 1916.

Library of Congress

Under the Constitution, resting upon the broad foundation of democratic principles as embodied in the Declaration of Independence, there are no superiors and inferiors. Before the law all citizens are equal, and are entitled to the same consideration. May we not expect, have we not the right to expect, that your personal influence, as well as the great influence which comes from your commanding official position, will be thrown against what is clearly, is distinctly, not in accordance with the spirit of free institutions? All class distinctions among citizens are un-American, and the sooner every vestige of it is stamped out the better it will be for the Republic.

Yours truly,
Francis J. Grimké

What I Am Trying to Do
Booker T. Washington

From the mid-1890s on, Booker T. Washington was the most highly regarded, if not always the most influential, voice among black Americans. An exponent of vocational, industrial education for Negroes, he won a good deal of support among whites as well as blacks; for white men often saw in his viewpoint a legitimization of their own disposition to "keep the Negro in his place." But Washington felt that only by taking an active part in the economy would the black man attain anything like parity with whites. The following article was published just two years before his death. [*World's Work*, November 1913.]

Soon after I settled down for my life's work near the little town of Tuskegee, Ala., I made up my mind to do as an individual that which I am striving to get my race to do throughout the United States. I resolved to make myself, so far as I was able, so useful to the community, the county, and the state that every man, woman, and child, white and black, would respect me and want me to live among them.

I foresaw, before I reached Tuskegee, that I should be classed as an "educated Negro," and I knew that this meant that people would expect me to be a kind of artificial being, living in the community but not a part of it in either my dress, talk, work, or in my general interests. My first duty, therefore, was to convince the people that I did not have "education," but only a head and heart to serve.

This personal illustration will, perhaps, suggest one thing that I am striving to do, that is, to get the Negro race as a whole to make itself so valuable and so necessary to the community in which it lives that it will not merely be tolerated, like a poor relation, but rather welcomed and sought after. To do this I learned years ago from my great teacher of Hampton Institute, Gen. S. C. Armstrong, that it would first be necessary to get out of the Negro's mind the idea that education unfitted a man for any kind of labor, whether with the hand or head. So from the first I have striven to get the educated Negro to feel that it was just as honorable and dignified for him to use his education in the field, the shop, the kitchen, or the laundry as to use it in teaching school or preaching the gospel.

The most difficult and delicate task that Tuskegee, in common with institutions like Hampton and others, had to perform has been to convince members of my race that in preparing them to use their knowledge of chemistry, mathematics, or any other form of knowledge, to improve the soil, develop the mineral resources, to construct a house, or prepare and serve a meal, it was not necessary to limit or circumscribe their mental growth or to assign them to any special or narrow sphere of life. I have constantly urged upon them that we must begin at the bottom instead of at the top; that there will be little permanent gain by "short cut" methods; that we must stick to that which is fundamental and enduring—and we must overcome evil with good.

But in all this I have not sought to confine the ambitions, nor to set limits to the progress of the race. I have never felt

that the Negro was bound to behave in any manner different from that of any other race in the same stage of development. I have merely insisted that we should do the first things first; that we should lay the foundation before we sought to erect the superstructure. . . .

At one time, while stopping for a day in one of the border states, I visited a colored family whose son had recently graduated and returned home from college. The mother of the young man was naturally very proud of her son and told me with great satisfaction how he had learned to speak Latin, but lamented the fact that there was no one in the neighborhood who was able to talk Latin with him. She had heard that I had some education and felt rather confident that I would be able to converse in the Latin language with him. When I was obliged to confess that I could not, her feathers

Booker T. Washington's ideas for the advancement of his race did not affect the majority of Negroes who were still poor Southerners looking for relief from the social and economic isolation of poverty. This tenant farmer and his family were photographed in front of their dilapidated cabin in the South in 1914.

Library of Congress

fell, and I do not believe she ever afterward had the same respect for me. However, I got acquainted with the son, and, as I knew more of the young man, learned to like him. He was an ambitious, high-strung young fellow, who had studied books, but he had not studied men. He had learned a great deal about the ancient world, but he knew very little of the world right about him. He had studied about things, through the medium of books, but had not studied things themselves. In a word, he had been infected with the college bacillus and displayed the usual symptoms. However, I had seen cases of this kind before and felt sure that he would in time recover.

This young man was exceedingly sensitive concerning the "rights" of his race, and propounded to me the very popular theory that the only reason the Negro did not have all the rights coming to him was that he did not protest whenever these rights were infringed upon. He determined to put this theory into practice and so wrote a very learned lecture which he delivered on every possible occasion. The subject of his lecture was "Manhood Rights." As he was really a rather brilliant speaker he was able to work up an audience with this lecture to a high pitch of enthusiasm and indignation in regard to the wrongs committed against the Negro race.

For a season this lecture was quite popular and the author was in some demand as a lecturer. During this time he was invariably present at every indignation meeting that was called to pass resolutions condemning some wrong meted out to members of the race. Here, again, his eloquence and burning words could excite an audience to the highest degree of indignation. . . .

In the course of time it gradually began to dawn upon my young friend and his mother that neither indignation meetings, the passing of resolutions, nor his lecture on "Manhood Rights" were providing him or the family with shelter, food, or clothes. For a while the old mother was quite puzzled to know why it was that neither eloquence nor Latin quotations would provide the family with the common necessities of everyday life. The young man himself grew morose, peevish, and miserable. He could neither eat nor sleep properly, because he was constantly thinking of the wrongs of his race. He was not only unhappy himself but he made everyone he came in contact with unhappy. Nevertheless, for a number of years, he went on the way that he had started. Finally he seemed to have struck bottom. He found himself face to face with, not a book world, but an actual world. Home, food, clothes, rent were now pressing so hard that something had to be done.

At this point I had an opportunity to renew my acquaintance with him. In fact, he called to see me. He had now become quite softened, mellowed, and even sweet, but I could discern that he was still troubled about the "rights" of his race, and he ventured to suggest a little vaguely once or twice that he would be willing to "die for his race." I noticed, however that he was not quite so emphatic in his desire to "die for his race" as he had been a year or two before, when I heard him pouring out his soul before a small but enthusiastic audience. In one of the first conversations I had with him after the mellowing process had set in, I ventured to suggest to him rather mildly that there were other methods by which he could help the Negro race to secure those rights and opportunities which both he and I were so anxious they should possess and enjoy.

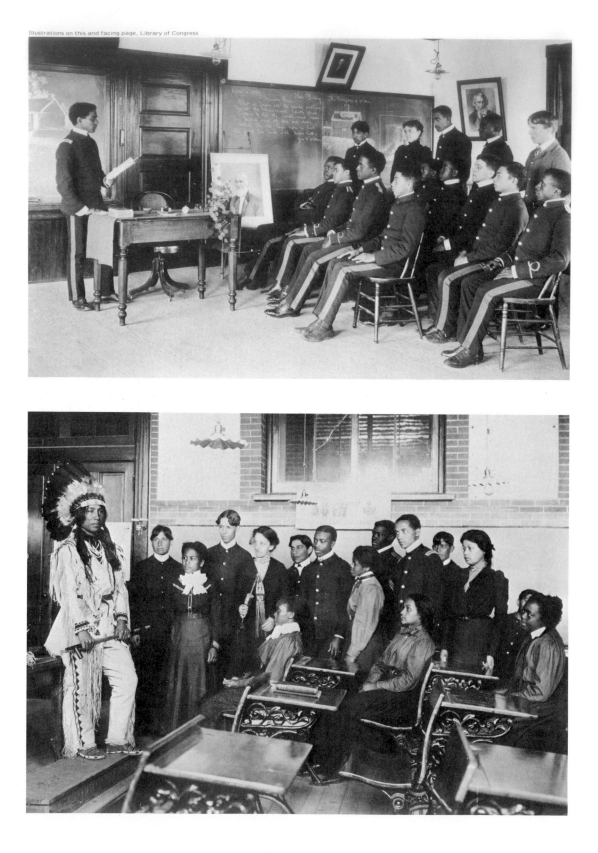

Hampton Institute, where Booker T. Washington received his schooling and many of his ideas about education, and where he later taught, was an agricultural, normal, and industrial school for Negroes. During the years Washington taught there, the school also began a program for American Indians. Tuskegee Institute, which Washington headed from its beginning in 1881 until his death in 1915, was the successful laboratory for his philosophies of education. (On facing page, top) A class at Hampton Institute in 1899 studies the work of John Greenleaf Whittier. (On facing page, bottom) An Indian poses before another Hampton class made up of Negroes and Indians. (Above) Women of the class of 1906 parade in ceremonies celebrating the 25th anniversary of Tuskegee. Among the onlookers is one of the school's greatest benefactors, Andrew Carnegie. (Right) A graduate of Hampton at home.

At first he was rather taken aback at the thought that I was just as much interested in the rights of the race as he was, and he was still further surprised when I told him that I felt just as indignant and outraged when my race was insulted and persecuted as he did. This opened the way for a heart to heart talk, which was followed by others, all which resulted in a changed life for my young friend, a change not in the end that he was seeking, but rather in the method of seeking that end. . . .

As the solution of the problems of the individual colored man consists very largely in turning his attention from abstract questions to the concrete problems of daily life—consists, in other words, in interesting and connecting himself with the local, practical, commonplace work and interests of the people among whom he lives—so, too, the solution of the Negro schools consists in connecting the studies in the classroom with the absorbing and inspiring problems of actual life.

Another thing that I am trying to do, therefore, is to get people to see that education in books and in the schoolroom can be articulated into the life and activities of the community surrounding the schoolroom in a way to make the local activities the basis for much of the mental training that is supposed to be furnished by the old traditional and abstract education. In using the local and practical activities as a means of education nothing is sacrificed in culture and discipline, and much is gained in interest and understanding and in earnestness. Children who hate the schoolroom and love the fishing pond, the berry patch, or the peach orchard frequently do so because one is artificial and the other real life. There is often a better opportunity to do this kind of work, I am convinced, with a

new race as mine is, whose ancestors for generations have not been educated in the old formal methods, than with a race that has much to unlearn. . . .

Another thing that I have tried to do has been to bring the white people in the Southern states and throughout the country into what seems to me a proper and practical attitude toward the Negro in his efforts to go forward and make progress. I am seeking to do this not only in the interest of my race, but also in the interest of the white race.

There are in the Southern states 9,000,000 Negroes. There are 3,000,000 Negro children of school age. Fifty-three percent, or more than half, never go to school. Many of these Negro children, particularly in the country districts, are in school only from three to four months in the year. I am trying to get the white people to see that, both from an economic point of view and as a matter of justice and fair play, these conditions must be changed. I am trying to get the white people to see that sending ignorant Negroes to jails and penitentiaries, putting them in the chain gang, hanging and lynching them does not civilize, but on the contrary, though it brutalizes the Negro, it at the same time blunts and dulls the conscience of the white man.

I want the white people to see that it is unfair to expect a black man who goes to school only three months in the year to produce as much on the farm as a white man who has been in school eight or nine months in the year; that it is unjust to let the Negro remain ignorant, with nothing between him and the temptation to fill his body with whiskey and cocaine, and then expect him, in his ignorance, to be able to know the law and be able to exercise that degree of self-control which shall enable him to keep it.

Still another thing that I am trying to get the people of the whole country to realize is that the education of the Negro should be considered not so much as a matter of charity, but as a matter of business, that, like any other business, should be thoroughly studied, organized, and systematized. The money that has already been spent by states, institutions, and individuals would have done vastly more good if there had been, years ago, more thorough organization and cooperation between the different isolated and detached members of the Negro school system in the Southern states.

I am trying to get the white people to realize that since no color line is drawn in the punishment for crime, no color line should be drawn in the preparation for life, in the kind of education, in other words, that makes for useful, clean living. I am trying to get the white people to see that in hundreds of counties in the South it is costing more to punish colored people for crime than it would cost to educate them. I am trying to get all to see that ignorance, poverty, and weakness invite and encourage the stronger race to act unjustly toward the weak, and that so long as this condition remains the young white men of the South will have a fearful handicap in the battle of life.

Education and Assimilation

1904–1913

The first twenty years of this century can appropriately be described as the "age of the immigrant." At no time before or since has the presence of a large number of foreign-born excited so much comment. Every magazine and newspaper carried articles—descriptive, sympathetic, or polemical—dealing with America's aliens. A basic concern of most Americans, whether nativist or not, was whether the new immigrants arriving in such great numbers from so many different countries could ever become good and useful citizens.

Gradually there grew up movements and organizations, local in origin at first, that worked to ensure the Americanization of the immigrants. The Americanization movement, though a continuous affair lasting until about 1921, had two phases: the earnest but more casual period from 1900 to 1914, and the frenetic era of militant nationalism from 1915 to 1921. It is the earlier period that is of concern in this chapter.

The main emphasis of the Americanization movement was education—the teaching of English and courses in citizenship. The main impetus did not come from educators, but instead from two sources that were not overly friendly to each other: the settlement houses and the patriotic societies. The settlement projects, of which Chicago's Hull House was the most famous, worked in local neighborhoods to ease the adjustments immigrants had to make from the Old to the New World. The settlement houses sympathized with the newcomers, and sought to mitigate their harsher social and economic problems.

The patriotic societies, such as the Daughters of the American Revolution, were nationalistic in outlook. Their primary concern was the welfare of the nation, not of the immigrant; in fact, they were frequently nativist oriented. They stressed assimilation as conformity, providing materials and classes to indoctrinate foreigners with loyalty to America through courses in civics and American history. The keynote of such education was, as the DAR stressed, "obedience to law, which is the groundwork of true citizenship." Much of the inspiration for the education of aliens came from the emotional reaction to the assassination in 1901 of President McKinley by self-proclaimed anarchist Leon Czolgosz (who was a native American). During the first phase of the Americanization movement, up to World War I, it was the settlement work that was the more successful.

The early efforts at promoting assimilation were sporadic and localized, whether based on settlement house or patriotic society activities. It was after 1910 that the movement became truly national in scope, thanks to the efforts of a single individual, Frances Kellor, who managed to combine a real sympathy for the alien with an ardent nationalism. She was director of New York's Bureau of Industries and Immigration, a state agency established to advise and protect immigrants. In 1914 she became vice-chairman of the Committee for Immigrants in America, which attempted to unify and direct the activities of all private and public agencies working with immigrants. The committee sought to define a national policy that would serve the cause of Americanization.

The stimulus for much of the assimilation program was the same conviction that inspired the reformers of the Progressive Era: a profound faith in democracy. The goal of the assimilators was to incorporate the masses of foreign-born into all cultural and social processes—recognizing that they were already part of the economy. As one sociological study of the foreign-born put it: "We must make the immigrants a working part in our system of life, ideal and political as well as economic, or lose the character of our culture. Self-preservation makes this necessary; the fact that they bring valuable additions to our culture makes it desirable. . . . They cannot be intelligent citizens unless they 'get the hang' of American ways of thinking as well as of doing."

(On facing page) Russian Jewish mother and child in the Ellis Island dining room, about 1905. Illustration Brown Brothers.

How It Feels to Be a Problem
Gino Speranza

49

American-born but of Italian descent, lawyer Gino Speranza frequently served in official capacities to aid immigrants and study their problems. He learned, as this selection indicates, that one of the chief hindrances to rapid assimilation of aliens was the attitude of the average native-born American toward foreigners. Speranza's article was subtitled "A Consideration of Certain Causes Which Prevent or Retard Assimilation." [*Charities,* May 7, 1904.]

The American nation seems to like to do some of its thinking aloud. Possibly this is true of other nations, but with this difference, that in the case of the American, the thinking aloud is not suppressed even when it deals with what may be termed the "country's guests." Older nations, perhaps because they lack the daring self-sufficiency of the young, prefer, in similar cases, to think in a whisper. All countries have problems to grapple with, economic, political, or social; but with America even the labor problem is popularly discussed as if its solution depended on that of the immigration problem.

Now, considering the large percentage of foreign-born in the population of the United States, it is a strange fact how few Americans ever consider how very unpleasant, to say the least, it must be to the foreigners living in their midst to be constantly looked upon either as a national problem or a national peril. And this trying situation is further strained by the tone in which the discussion is carried on, as if it applied to utter strangers miles and miles away, instead of to a large number of resident fellow citizens. Perhaps this attitude may be explained by the fact that to the vast majority of Americans "foreigner" is synonymous with the popular conception of the immigrant as a poor, ignorant, and uncouth stranger, seeking for better luck in a new land. But poverty and ignorance and uncouthness, even if they exist as general characteristics of our

immigrants, do not necessarily exclude intelligence and sensitiveness. Too often, let it be said, does the American of common schooling interpret differences from his own standards and habits of life, as necessarily signs of inferiority. Foreignness of features or of apparel is for him often the denial of brotherhood. Often, again, the fine brow and aquiline nose of the Latin will seem to the American to betoken a criminal type rather than the impress of a splendid racial struggle.

Then there is another large class of "plain Americans" who justify a trying discussion of the stranger within the gates by the self-satisfying plea that the foreigner should be so glad to be in the "land of the free" that he cannot mind hearing a few "unpleasant truths" about himself.

This is not an attempt to show that the tide of immigration does not carry with it an ebb of squalor and ignorance and undesirable elements. It is rather an endeavor to look at the problem, as it were, *from the inside.* For if America's salvation from this foreign invasion lies in her capacity to assimilate such foreign elements, the first step in the process must be a thorough knowledge of the element that should be absorbed.

Many imagine that the record and strength of the American democracy suffice of themselves to make the foreigner love the new land and engender in him a desire to serve it; that, in other words, assimilation is the natural tendency. Assimilation, however, is a dual process of forces interacting one upon the other. Economically, this country can act like a magnet in drawing the foreigner to these shores, but you cannot rely on its magnetic force to make the foreigner *an American*. To bring about assimilation the larger mass should not remain passive. It must attract, *actively attract,* the smaller foreign body.

It is with this in mind that I say that if my countrymen here keep apart, if they herd in great and menacing city colonies, if they do not learn your language, if they know little about your country, the fault is as much yours as theirs. And if you wish to reach us you will have to batter down some of the walls you have yourselves built up to keep us from you.

What I wish to examine, then, is how and what Americans are contributing to the process of the assimilation of my countrymen who have come here to live among them.

I have before me a pamphlet which a well-known American society prints for distribution among arriving immigrants. On the title page is the motto: *A Welcome to Immigrants and Some Good Advice.* The pamphlet starts out by telling the arriving stranger that this publication is presented to him "by an American patriotic society, whose duty is to teach American principles"—a statement which must somewhat bewilder foreigners. Then it proceeds to advise him. In America, it tells him, "you need not be rich to be happy and respected." "In other countries," it proceeds, "the people belong to the government. They are called subjects. They are under the power of some emperor, king, duke, or other ruler," which permits the belief that the patriotic author of this pamphlet is conversant mostly with medieval history. There are some surpris-

An Italian hod carrier, about 1910.

ing explanations of the Constitution, showing as wide a knowledge of American constitutional history as of that of modern Europe—but space forbids their quotation. "If the common people of other countries had faith in each other, there would be no czars, kaisers, and kings ruling them under the pretext of divine right." This is certainly a gem of historical exposition.

Then, in order to make the stranger feel comfortable, it tells him, "you must be honest and honorable, clean in your person, and decent in your talk." Which, of course, the benighted foreigner reads as a new decalogue. With characteristic modesty the author reserves for the last praise of his country: "Ours," he says, "is the strongest government in the world, because it is the people's government." Then he loses all self-restraint in a patriotic enthusiasm. "We have more good land in cultivation than in all Europe. We have more coal, and oil, and iron, and copper, than can be found in all the countries of Europe. We can raise enough foodstuffs to feed all the rest of the world. We have more railroads and navigable rivers than can be found in the rest of the civilized world. We have more free schools than the rest of the world. . . . So great is the extent (of our country), so varied its resources, that its people are not dependent on the rest of the world for what they absolutely need. Can there be any better proof that this is the best country in the world? Yes, there is one better proof. Our laws are better and more justly carried out."

Of course, criticism by the stranger within your gates seems ungracious; but whenever it is attempted it is suppressed by this common question: "If you don't like it, why don't you go back?" The answer is never given, but it exists. For the majority of us this is our home and we have worked very hard for everything we have earned or won. And if we find matter for criticism it is because nothing is perfect; and if we institute comparisons it is because, having lived in two lands, we have more of the wherewithal of comparisons than those who have lived in only one country.

Then there is the American press. How is it aiding our assimilation? It would not be difficult to name those few newspapers in the United States which give space either as news or editorially, to nonsensa-

tional events or problems with which Europe is grappling. As regards Italy, there is such a dearth of information of vital importance that little, if anything, is known by the average American, of the economic or political progress of that country. Columns on Musolino, half-page headlines on the Mafia, but never a word on the wonderful industrial development in northern Italy, never a notice of the financial policies that have brought Italian finances to a successful state!

What is the American press doing to help assimilate this "menacing" element in the Republic?

"Why is it," was asked of a prominent American journalist, "that you print news about Italians which you would not of other nationalities?"

"Well, it is this way," was the answer, "if we published them about the Irish or the Germans we should be buried with letters of protest; the Italians do not seem to object."

It would be nearer the truth to say that they have learned the uselessness of objecting unless they can back up the objection by a "solid Italian vote."

One result of the unfriendliness of the popular American press is that it drives Italians to support a rather unwholesome Italian colonial press. Why should they read American papers that chronicle only the misdeeds of their compatriots? Better support a local press which, however poor and ofttimes dishonest, keeps up the courage of these expatriates by telling them what young Italy is bravely doing at home and abroad. But this colonial press widens the cleavage between the nations, puts new obstacles in the way of assimilation and keeps up racial differences.

To feel that we are considered a problem is not calculated to make us sympathize with your efforts in our behalf, and those very efforts are, as a direct result, very likely to be misdirected. My countrymen in America, ignorant though many of them are, and little in touch with Americans, nevertheless feel keenly that they are looked upon by the masses as a problem. It is, in part, because of that feeling that they fail to take an interest in American life or to easily mix with the natives. And though it may seem farfetched, I believe that the feeling that they are unwelcome begets in them a distrust of those defenses to life, liberty, and property which the new country is presumed to put at their disposal. They have no excess of confidence in your courts and it is not surprising, however lamentable, that the more hotheaded sometimes take the law into their own hands. You cannot expect the foreigner of the humbler class to judge beyond his experience—and his experience of American

Italian construction workers, about 1910.

justice may be comprised in what he learns in some of the minor tribunals controlled by politicians, and in what he has heard of the unpunished lynchings of his countrymen in some parts of the new land. What appeal can the doctrine of state supremacy and federal noninterference make to him? Imagine what you would think of Italian justice if the American sailors in Venice, in resisting arrest by the constituted authorities, had been strung up to a telegraph pole by an infuriated Venetian mob, and the government at Rome had said, with the utmost courtesy: "We are very sorry and greatly deplore it, but we can't interfere with the autonomy of the province of Venetia!"

I am aware that the question is often asked: If these people are sensitive about being discussed as a problem and a menace, why do they come here? It is a question asked every day in the guise of an argument, a final and crushing argument. But is it really an argument? Is it not

Brown Brothers

203

rather a question susceptible of a very clear and responsive answer? They come because this is a new country and there is a great deal of room here, and because you invite them. If you really did not want them you could keep them out, as you have done with the Chinese. . . .

It is true that, as a nationality, Italians have not forced recognition; though numerically strong there is no such "Italian vote" as to interest politicians. They have founded no important institutions; they have no strong and well-administered societies as have the Germans and the Irish. They have no representative press, and well-organized movements among them for their own good are rare. Those who believe in assimilation may be thankful for all these things; for it could be held that it is harder to assimilate bodies or colonies well organized as foreign elements, than individuals held together in imperfect cohesion.

Yet the Italian in America as an individual is making good progress. In New York City, the individual holdings of Italians in savings banks is over $15 million; they have some 4,000 real estate holdings of the clear value of $20 million. About 10,000 stores in the city are owned by Italians at an estimated value of $7 million, and to this must be added about $7.5 million invested in wholesale business. The estimated material value of the property of the Italian colony in New York is over $60 million, a value much below that of the Italian colonies of St. Louis, San Francisco, Boston, and Chicago, but, a fair showing for the great "dumping ground" of America.

But the sympathetic observer will find the most remarkable progress on what may be called the spiritual side of the Italians among us. It is estimated that there are more than 50,000 Italian children in the public schools of New York City and adjacent cities where Italians are settled. Many an Italian laborer sends his son to Italy to "finish his education" and when he cannot afford this luxury of doubtful value, he gets him one of the *maestri* of Little Italy to perfect him in his native language. In the higher education you will find Italians winning honors in several of our colleges, universities, and professional schools. I know of one Italian who saves money barbering during the summer and on Sundays, to pay his way through Columbia University. I know of another who went through one of our best universities on money voluntarily advanced by a generous and farseeing professor. The money was repaid with interest and the boy is making a mark in the field of mathematics. I know of a third, the winner of a university scholarship, who paid his way by assisting in editing an Italian paper during spare hours; a fourth, who won the fellowship for the American School at Rome, and thus an American institution sent an Italian to perfect his special scholarship in Italy.

New York City now counts 115 Italian registered physicians, 63 pharmacists, 4 dentists, 21 lawyers, 15 public school teachers, 9 architects, 4 manufacturers of technical instruments, and 7 mechanical engineers. There are two Italian steamship lines with biweekly sailings, sixteen daily and weekly papers, and several private schools. Italians support several churches, one modest but very efficient hospital, one well-organized savings bank, and a chamber of commerce. They have presented three monuments to the municipality, one, the statue of Columbus, a valuable work of art. They are raising funds to build a school in Verdi's honor, under the auspices of the Children's

Dock workers, mostly Italian, unloading banana boats in New York City, about 1905.

Aid Society, and are planning to organize a trust company.

I have given the statistics for New York City because the Italian colony on Manhattan is less flourishing than those in other large American cities. So that what is hopeful for New York is even more promising in Philadelphia, St. Louis, and Boston. . . .

There is one more question that an Italian, speaking for his countrymen here, may urge upon Americans who are interested in the problem of assimilation. It is this: that you should make my countrymen love your country by making them see what is truly good and noble in it. Too

many of them, far too many, know of America only what they learn from the corrupt politician, the boss, the *banchiere,* and the ofttimes rough policeman. I have been in certain labor camps in the South where my countrymen were forced to work under the surveillance of armed guards. I have spoken to some who had been bound to a mule and whipped back to work like slaves. I have met others who bore the marks of brutal abuses committed by cruel bosses with the consent of their superiors. What conception of American liberty can these foreigners have?

This, then, is the duty upon those who represent what is good and enduring in Americanism—to teach these foreigners the truth about America. Remember these foreigners are essentially men and women like yourselves whatever the superficial differences may be. This is the simple fact far too often forgotten—if not actually denied. And this must be the excuse if you discuss these people as a menace, pitching your discussion as if we were beyond hearing, and beneath feeling, and sometimes even as if beyond redemption.

Make us feel that America has good friends, intelligent, clear-sighted friends; friends that will not exploit us; friends that will not be interested merely because of what Italy did in the past for all civilization, but friends that will extend to us the sympathy which is due from one man to another. You will thereby make us not merely fellow voters, but will prepare us for the supreme test of real assimilation— the wish to consider the adopted country as a new and dear fatherland.

Public Versus Parochial Schools

50

Majorities among all immigrant nationalities favored the public school system over church-controlled elementary education. This sentiment did not always bespeak an anticlerical bias; as often as not it was based on the conviction that sending children to American public schools would hasten the day of Americanization for the whole family. And Americanization meant both social acceptance and the prospect of a higher standard of living. This article from the Greek-language Chicago newspaper *Star* of October 21, 1904, was undoubtedly a little more vehement than the overall sentiments of the Greek community. [Chicago Foreign Language Press Survey, WPA Project, 1942.]

With our Greek schools in America springing up like mushrooms beside Greek churches, the Greeks in Chicago and elsewhere are warned to bear in mind the futile efforts of the church in the past to dominate public instruction. History tells us that the church for many centuries took to itself the role of guardian of the entire education of youth. In Spain, Italy, Austria, Greece, and the other countries where the church exercised such influence, and its superstitions flourished unchecked, the result was an increase in those dubious theories which are the precursors of sciolism [superficial learning]. This happened simply because the complete education of youth was left in the hands of the church, or rather the church succeeded in dominating the education of youth.

Under so superstitious an education, ignorance, antagonism to science, and intolerable nonsense reached such heights that history records no other characteristic products of this theocratic education than religious dogmas, letters of blood, and the resigned submission of the populace.

The real educational system, under which the human mind expands cosmologically, and by which false theories and superstitions are routed, is to be found here in America. And we Greeks of America, for our own interest, the interest of coming generations, the interest of our adopted country, and the interest of the church itself must accept this great American educational system, which is free from any ecclesiastical domination. Church is an imperative necessity for a nation, but school is the nation's whole life, and public schools, which are free from theocracy, are the real bulwarks of the country. Let us profit by the pitfalls into which others have fallen and maintain freedom of education if we wish to produce good, useful, broad-minded citizens whose knowledge and enlightenment will promote and protect the welfare of the church.

Americans of Irish Origin
Theodore Roosevelt

51

This selection is a portion of a speech given by President Roosevelt on March 17, 1905, to the Society of Friendly Sons of St. Patrick in New York. By this date the Irish had become a real force in American politics, especially in city government. Roosevelt could genuinely expand on their contributions to American society in a way that minimized ethnic background and emphasized the new common nationality of all immigrants. [*American Problems.* New York, 1926.]

The people who have come to this country from Ireland have contributed to the stock of our common citizenship qualities which are essential to the welfare of every great nation. They are a masterful race of rugged character, a race the qualities of whose womanhood have become proverbial, while its men have the elemental, the indispensable virtues of working hard in time of peace and fighting hard in time of war.

And I want to say here, as I have said and shall say again elsewhere, as I shall say again and again, that we must never forget that no amount of material wealth, no amount of intellect, no artistic or scientific growth can avail anything to the nation which loses the elemental virtues. If the average man cannot work and fight, the race is in a poor way; and it will not have, because it will not deserve, the respect of anyone.

Let us avoid always, either as individuals or as a nation, brawling, speaking discourteously, or acting offensively toward others, but let us make it evident that we wish peace, not because we are weak, but because we think it right; and that while we do not intend to wrong anyone, we are perfectly competent to hold our own if anyone wrongs us. There has never been a time in this country when it has not been true of the average American of Irish birth or parent, that he came up to this standard, able to work and able to fight at need.

But the men of Irish birth or of Irish descent have been far more than soldiers—I will not say more than, but much in addition to, soldiers. In every walk in life in this country men of this blood have stood and now stand preeminent, not only as soldiers but as statesmen, on the bench, at the bar, and in business. They are doing their full share toward the artistic and literary development of the country.

And right here let me make a special plea to you, to this society and kindred societies. We Americans take a just pride in the development of our great universities, and more and more we are seeking to provide for creative and original work in these universities. I hope that an earnest effort will be made to endow chairs in American universities for the study of Celtic literature and for research in Celtic antiquities. It is only of recent years that the extraordinary wealth and beauty of the old Celtic sagas have been fully appreciated, and we of America, who have so large a Celtic strain in our blood, cannot

(Above) Irish immigrant mothers and children, 1902.
(Right) Charles Murphy and Tom Foley, Irish leaders
of New York City's Tammany Hall, march in the
funeral of "Big Tim" Sullivan. By the turn of the
century Irish political power had become so strong that
even Republicans of long standing like Theodore
Roosevelt were forced to seek Irish favor.

afford to be behindhand in the work of
adding to modern scholarship by bringing
within its ken the great Celtic literature of
the past.

My fellow countrymen, I have spoken
tonight especially of what has been done
for this nation of ours by men of Irish
blood. But, after all, in speaking to you,
or, to any other body of my fellow citizens, no matter from what Old World
country they themselves or their forefathers may have come, the great thing is to
remember that we are all of us Americans. Let us keep our pride in the stocks
from which we have sprung, but let us
show that pride, not by holding aloof
from one another, least of all by preserv-
ing the Old World jealousies and bitter-

nesses, but by joining in a spirit of generous rivalry to see which can do most for our great common country.

Americanism is not a matter of creed or birthplace or descent. That man is the best American who has in him the American spirit, the American soul. Such a man fears not the strong and harms not the weak. He scorns what is base or cruel or dishonest. He looks beyond the accidents of occupation or social condition and hails each of his fellow citizens as his brother, asking nothing save that each shall treat the other on his worth as a man, and that they shall all join together to do what in them lies for the uplifting of this mighty and vigorous people. In our veins runs the blood of many an Old World nation. We are kin to each of these nations and yet identical with none.

Our policy should be one of cordial friendship for them all, and yet we should keep ever before our eyes the fact that we are ourselves a separate people with our own ideals and standards, and destined, whether for better or for worse, to work out a wholly new national type. The fate of the 20th century will in no small degree—I ask you to think of this from the standpoint of the world—the fate of the 20th century as it bears on the world will in no small degree depend upon the type of citizenship developed on this continent. Surely such a thought must thrill us with the resolute purpose so to bear ourselves that the name American shall stand as the symbol of just, generous, and fearless treatment of all men and all nations. Let us be true to ourselves, for we cannot then be false to any man.

Federal Report on the Japanese in San Francisco

52

On October 11, 1906, the San Francisco school board passed a resolution barring Japanese children from the regular public schools and forcing them to attend a school in Chinatown. Such a resolution was not novel, for the Chinese were already segregated in public education. But the reaction of the Japanese government was so vehement that President Theodore Roosevelt intervened to have the order withdrawn. The following selection is part of a report made by Secretary of Commerce Victor H. Metcalf on the general situation of the Japanese in San Francisco, including business boycotts and public assaults on individual immigrants. [59 Congress, 2 Session, *Senate Document No. 147.*]

I have the honor to submit the following:

In my previous report I said nothing as to the causes leading up to the action of the school board in passing the resolution of October 11, and the effect of such action upon Japanese children, residents of the city of San Francisco, desiring to attend the public schools of that city. A report on this matter will now be made, therefore; and after describing the local public sentiment concerning the recent disturbances with regard to the Japanese, an account will be given, first, of the boycott maintained by the Cooks and Wait-

ers Union of San Francisco against Japanese restaurants doing business in that city, and, second, of the several cases of assault or injury inflicted upon the persons or property of Japanese residents.

It seems that for several years the board of education of San Francisco had been considering the advisability of establishing separate schools for Chinese, Japanese, and Korean children, and on May 6, 1905, passed the following resolution:

Resolved, That the board of education is determined in its efforts to effect the establishment of separate schools for Chinese and Japanese pupils, not only for the purpose of relieving the congestion at present prevailing in our schools, but also for the higher end that our children should not be placed in any position where their youthful impressions may be affected by association with pupils of the Mongolian race.

And on October 11 the board passed the following resolution:

Resolved, That in accordance with Article X, Section 1662, of the school law of California, principals are hereby directed to send all Chinese, Japanese, or Korean children to the Oriental Public School, situated on the south side of Clay Street, between Powell and Mason Streets, on and after Monday, October 15, 1906.

The action of the board in the passage of the resolutions of May 6, 1905, and October 11, 1906, was undoubtedly largely influenced by the activity of the Japanese and Korean Exclusion League, an organization formed for the purpose of securing the enactment by the Congress of the United States of a law extending the provisions of the existing Chinese Exclusion Act so as to exclude Japanese and Koreans. The league claims a membership in the state of California of 78,500, three-fourths of which membership is said to be in the city of San Francisco. The membership is composed almost entirely of members of labor organizations. Section 2, Article 2, of the constitution of the league is as follows:

The league as such shall not adopt any measures of discrimination against any Chinese, Japanese, or Koreans now or hereafter lawfully resident in the United States.

Yet, on October 22, 1905, at a meeting of the league held in San Francisco, as reported in the San Francisco *Chronicle* of October 23, 1905, a resolution was adopted by the league instructing its executive committee to appear before the board of education and petition for separate schools for the Mongolian children of San Francisco.

Prior to the action of the league, the board of education, as I am informed, received many protests from citizens of San Francisco, whose children were attending the public schools, against Japanese being permitted to attend those schools. These protests were mainly against Japanese boys and men ranging from sixteen to twenty-two, twenty-three, and twenty-four years of age attending the primary grades and sitting beside little girls and boys of seven and eight years of age. When these complaints became known to Japanese residents, I am informed that some of the older pupils left the primary grades.

On the day when the order of October 11 went into effect, viz., October 15, there were attending the public schools of the city of San Francisco ninety-three Japanese pupils. These pupils were distributed among twenty-three schools of the primary grades. There are eight grades in the public schools of San Francisco, the first grade being the lowest and the eighth the highest—graduates of the eighth grade going into the high school. Of this total of ninety-three pupils, sixty-eight were born in Japan and twenty-five in the United States. Those born in the United States would, of course, under Section I of Article XIV of the Constitution of the United States, be citizens of the United States and of the state wherein they reside, and as such subject to the laws of the nation as well as of the state. . . .

I found the sentiment in the state very strong against Japanese young men attending the primary grades. Many of the people were outspoken in their condemnation of this course, saying that they would take exactly the same stand against American young men of similar ages attending the primary grades. I am frank to say that this objection seems to me a most reasonable one. All of the political parties in the state have inserted in their platforms planks in favor of Japanese and Korean exclusion, and on March 7, 1905, the state legislature passed a joint resolution urging that action be taken by treaty or otherwise to limit and diminish the further immigration of Japanese laborers into the United States.

The press of San Francisco pretty generally upholds the action of the board of education. Of the attitude of the more violent and radical newspapers it is unnecessary to speak further than to say that their tone is the usual tone of hostility to "Mongol hordes," and the burden of their claim is that Japanese are no better than Chinese, and that the same reasons which dictated the exclusion of the Chinese call for the exclusion of the Japanese as well.

The temper and tone of the more conservative newspapers may better be illustrated by an epitome of their argument upon the public school question. That argument practically is as follows: The public schools of California are a state and not a federal institution. The state has the power to abolish those schools entirely, and the federal government would have no right to lift its voice in protest. Upon the other hand, the state may extend the privileges of its schools to aliens upon such terms as it, the state, may elect, and the federal government has no right to question its action in this regard. Primarily and essentially the public schools are designed for the education of the citizens of the state. The state is interested in the education of its own citizens alone. It would not for a moment maintain this expensive institution to educate foreigners and aliens who would carry to their countries the fruits of such education. Therefore, if it should be held that there was a discrimination operating in violation of the treaty with Japan in the state's treatment of Japanese children, or even if a new treaty with Japan should be framed which would contain on behalf of Japanese subjects the "most-favored-nation" clause, this could and would be met by the state, which would then exclude from the use of its public schools all alien children of every nationality and limit the rights of free education to children of its own citizens, for whom the system is primarily designed and maintained, and if the state should do this the federal government could not complain, since no treaty right could be violated when the children of Japanese were treated precisely as the children of all foreign nations.

The feeling in the state is further intensified, especially in labor circles, by the report on the conditions in the Hawaiian Islands as contained in Bulletin 66 of the Bureau of Labor, Department of Commerce and Labor. The claim is made that white labor has been almost entirely driven from the Hawaiian Islands, and that the Japanese are gradually forcing even the small white traders out of business.

Many of the foremost educators in the state, on the other hand, are strongly opposed to the action of the San Francisco Board of Education. Japanese are admitted to the University of California, an institution maintained and supported by the state. They are also admitted to, and gladly welcomed at, Stanford University. San Francisco, so far as known, is the only city which has discriminated against Japanese children. I talked with a number of prominent labor men and they all said that they had no objection to Japanese children attending the primary grades;

that they wanted Japanese children now in the United States to have the same school privileges as children of other nations, but that they were unalterably opposed to Japanese young men attending the primary grades.

The objection to Japanese men attending the primary grades could very readily be met by a simple rule limiting the ages of all children attending those grades. All of the teachers with whom I talked while in San Francisco spoke in the highest terms of the Japanese children, saying that they were among the very best of their pupils, cleanly in their persons, well behaved, studious, and remarkably bright.

The board of education of San Francisco declined to rescind its resolution of October 11, claiming that, having established a separate school for Chinese, Japanese, and Korean children, the provisions of Section 1662 of the political code became mandatory. . . .

Assaults have from time to time been made upon Japanese subjects resident in the city of San Francisco. I was informed by the chief of police that upon receipt of a communication from the Japanese consul he at once instructed captains of police to make every effort to stop these assaults, and, if necessary, to assign men in citizens' clothes to accomplish the purpose. . . .

These attacks, so I am informed, with but one exception were made when no policeman was in the immediate neighborhood. Most of them were made by boys and young men; many of them were vicious in character, and only one appears to have been made with a view of robbing the person attacked. All these assaults appear to have been made subsequent to the fire and earthquake in San Francisco, and my attention was not called to any assaults made prior to the 18th day of April, 1906.

Dr. F. Omori, of the Imperial University of Tokyo, one of the world's most distinguished scientists, and, as stated by Prof. George Davidson, of the University of California, one of the greatest living authorities in seismography, sent to San Francisco by the Japanese government to study the causes and effects of the earthquake, was stoned by hoodlums in the streets of San Francisco. Prof. T. Nakamura, professor of architecture in the Imperial University of Tokyo, was also stoned in the streets of San Francisco by young toughs and hoodlums. Doctor Omori was also assaulted when visiting Eureka, Cal. Neither of these eminent gentlemen made formal complaint of these assaults, and wished that no official recognition be taken of them. I attach hereto copy of letter of Professor Davidson, calling the attention of the press of San Francisco to these assaults, as also copies of letters of the postmaster of San Francisco, the mayor of San Francisco, the governor of the state, and the mayor of Eureka, expressing their great regret for these assaults and apologizing that they should have been made.

I know that these assaults upon the Japanese are universally condemned by all good citizens of California. For months the citizens of San Francisco and Oakland have been terrorized by numerous murders, assaults, and robberies, both at day and night. The police have been powerless. The assaults upon the Japanese, however, were not made, in my judgment, with a view of robbery, but rather from a feeling of racial hostility, stirred up possibly by newspaper accounts of meetings that have been held at different times relative to the exclusion of Japanese from the United States.

Japanese children on their way to school, California, about 1900.

The police records of San Francisco show that between May 6, 1906, and November 5, 1906, 290 cases of assault, ranging from simple assaults to assaults with deadly weapons and assaults with murderous intent, were reported to the police of San Francisco. Of the number so reported, seven were for assaults committed by Japanese, and two complaints were made against Japanese for disturbing the peace. The Japanese population in San Francisco is about 6,000. The total population of San Francisco today is estimated to be between 325,000 and 350,000.

While the sentiment of the state of California, as manifested by the public utterances of the Japanese and Korean Exclusion League, by articles in many of the leading newspapers in the state, by declarations of the political parties in their platforms, and by the passage of a joint resolution by the state legislature on March 7, 1905, is in favor of the exclusion of Japanese coolies, yet the overwhelming sentiment in the state is for law and order and for the protection of Japanese in their persons and their property.

The chief of police of the city of San Francisco, as also the acting mayor of the city, assured me that everything possible would be done to protect the Japanese subjects in San Francisco, and they urgently requested that all cases of assault and all violations of law affecting the Japanese be at once reported to the chief of police.

I impressed very strongly upon the acting mayor of the city, as also upon the chief of police, the gravity of the situation, and told them that, as officers charged with the enforcement of the law and the protection of property and person, you looked to them to see that all Japanese subjects resident in San Francisco were afforded the full protection guaranteed to them by our treaty with Japan. I also informed them that if the local authorities were not able to cope with the situation, or if they were negligent or der-

elict in the performance of their duty, then the entire power of the federal government within the limits of the Constitution would be used, and used promptly and vigorously, to enforce observance of treaties, which, under the Constitution, are the supreme law of the land, and to secure fit and proper treatment for the people of a great and friendly power while within the territory of the United States.

If, therefore, the police power of San Francisco is not sufficient to meet the situation and guard and protect Japanese residents in San Francisco, to whom under our treaty with Japan we guarantee "full and perfect protection for their persons and property," then, it seems to me, it is clearly the duty of the federal government to afford such protection. All considerations which may move a nation, every consideration of duty in the preservation of our treaty obligations, every consideration prompted by fifty years or more of close friendship with the empire of Japan, would unite in demanding, it seems to me, of the United States government and all its people, the fullest protection and the highest consideration for the subjects of Japan.

The Sons of Old Scotland in America

53

Between 1820 and 1950 nearly three-quarters of a million immigrants from Scotland came to America. The number of Scots who came in the century prior to 1820 is impossible to ascertain; records were not kept, and in any case, it would be virtually impossible to distinguish between Irish and Scotch-Irish in the early period. Like his fellow immigrants from the British Isles, the Scot assimilated easily; for the barrier of language and customs that continental immigrants faced hardly existed for him. Also, like his fellows from Britain, the Scot was normally an artisan, merchant, skilled farmer, or professional man, and could therefore take his place more easily in America than the newcomer who had to hire out as unskilled labor. This article by Herbert Casson sums up the contributions of the Scottish immigrant and his descendants. [*Munsey's Magazine,* February 1906.]

There are not so many men and women of Scottish birth in the United States—

not more than 300,000. But every Scot counts. Probably no other nation has sent us so many men of mark and so few dead-heads, in proportion to the number of its immigrants. . . . There has never been any other body of citizens of equal number that has stamped its record and its traditions so indelibly upon our national life and character as have the sons of Scotland. . . .

Taking up the directory of New York, I find thirty-three pages of "Macs." Probably not one in fifty of the owners of these names was born in Scotland, but the Scottish strain is undeniably there. Mayor George B. McClellan, for instance, was born in Germany, and his father in Philadelphia; but if you dig down to the roots of his family tree, you will find the Clan McClellan, of Galloway. Besides the five Scottish-Irish Presidents, three more—Monroe, Grant, and Hayes—were of Scottish ancestry; and so is President Roosevelt on his mother's side.

Within the limits of this article it would be impossible to call the roll of the host of Scots who have figured in American public life. To name some of the living men, Governor McLane, of New Hampshire, is a Scot; and New York has a Bruce as lieutenant-governor. When Massachusetts astonished the whole country, two years ago, by the election of a Democratic governor, it was found to be a Douglas that had worked the miracle in the old Bay State. The new mayor of Buffalo is a Peebles man who bears the oldest of Scotch names—J. N. Adam. In New York, a Glasgow man, John Kennedy Tod, holds the purse for the Citizens' Union, and carries worthily the honor of being one of the most vigilant foes of municipal corruption in the metropolis.

Among our statesmen of national prominence, the leading Scot is James Wilson, secretary of agriculture, who was seventeen years old before he had seen

any other place than Ayrshire, the home of Burns. The Scots have always been unusually skillful farmers and gardeners, and they have good reason to pride themselves on the fact that a Scottish farmer is now presiding over the vast agricultural interests of the United States—the most responsible position of the kind in the world. Ex-Speaker David B. Henderson, too, was six years old before he left the land of the heather; and Congressman James McLachlan, of California, is a native of Scotia who has climbed to prominence upon the ladder of self-help. . . .

The solid handiwork of the Scot is especially conspicuous when we turn to our system of education. No race, not even the Jews, has a greater reverence for learning. If John Knox could have had his way, there would have been a grammar school in every Scottish parish, a high school in every town, and a university in every city. The second American college—preceded only by Harvard—was founded by a Scot, James Blair. In fact, this historic college of William and Mary, as it is still called, is several years older than Harvard, if we reckon from the date upon which it received its grant of land.

The Presbyterian Church, which, with its 2,000,000 members in the United States, is mainly a product of Scotland and Scottish influences, has established not only Princeton University, but forty-eight colleges as well. Looking down the long list of its eminent ministers, we might select George A. Gordon, of the famous Old South Church, Boston, as the one who best represents both Scottish birth and American self-help. Arriving from Aberdeen thirty-five years ago, a penniless boy, Dr. Gordon has risen to the most historic pulpit in New England.

Lindley Murray, a Scottish-American, gave us our first English grammar, and

Henry Ivison our first American series of school readers. Thomas Hutchins was our pioneer geographer. Samuel Mitchell founded the earliest scientific magazine. William McLuce has been called the "father of American geology." Fanny Wright, of Dundee, was our first woman lecturer. Ormsby McKnight Mitchel, a Scottish-American of the most varied accomplishments and amazing energy, was the first to popularize astronomy. Two of our most eminent naturalists have been Alexander Wilson and Spencer F. Baird. An Ayrshire man, James McCosh, was for a quarter of a century one of our most famous philosophers and educators. Under his presidency, Princeton rose to a first-rate place among the universities of the world. Dr. McCosh was one of the few of his generation who foresaw the scientific discoveries of today, and labored like a Titan to prepare the way for them.

Among the Scottish-born educators of the present day, there is none, perhaps, so widely known as Dr. McCosh. But there is John Muir, of California, whose name will be perpetuated in the great Muir Glacier, which he discovered, in Alaska. He might fitly be called the American Livingstone because of his explorations, and for the work he has done to preserve our forests and establish national parks. Other Scottish-Americans well known in the educational world are Dr. William Keiller, of the University of Texas; Duncan Black Macdonald, of Hartford Theological Seminary; Robert Edgar Allardice, of Stanford University; James K. Patterson, president of the Kentucky State College; John S. Reid, of Cornell; Alexander Smith, of the University of Chicago; and James Cameron Mackenzie, formerly headmaster of Lawrenceville.

Arriving at the field of literature, the first Scottish-American name is that of Washington Irving, whose father was born and bred in Orkney. When European writers remarked upon the fact that the young American republic had continued for more than forty years without producing an eminent man of letters, it was Irving who removed the stigma. Edgar Allan Poe was also of Scottish ancestry.

The founder of modern American journalism—the man who broke away from European traditions and originated the system of giving as much of the news as possible to as many people as possible—was a thorough Scot, James Gordon Bennett. Seventy years ago he printed his first issue of the *Herald* in a Wall Street cellar. It was an insignificant little penny sheet, which the great editors of the day contemptuously ignored. It made enemies of the few and friends of the many. It was written like a conversation, not like a book of philosophy. And—here was an absolutely new idea in the newspaper world—it was published, not to gratify the literary vanity of its editor, but to please the people by obeying their wishes and expressing their opinions.

The late John Swinton, friend and associate of Charles A. Dana on the New York *Sun,* was nineteen before he set sail from Scotia. Among other journalists of Scottish ancestry but American birth, the best known are the redoubtable Watterson, of the Louisville *Courier-Journal;* Whitelaw Reid, now ambassador to Great Britain; the learned Patterson, of the Chicago *Tribune;* the masterful McLean, of the Cincinnati *Enquirer;* and the brilliant Arthur Brisbane, of the New York *Journal.* Four weekly papers are published for the sole benefit of Americanized Scots, one of them, the *Scottish American,* having had Dr. A. M. Stewart as its editor for nearly half a century.

Of Scottish-American doctors there have always been several at the top, from Dr. James Craik, the family doctor of George Washington, to Charles McBurney, who is today a leader of his profession in New York, and S. Weir Mitchell, the eminent author and nerve specialist, of Philadelphia. Among the actors, the veteran of the American stage is James H. Stoddart, who was born in England of Scottish parents when John Quincy Adams was the President of the United States. And a well-known younger player is Robert Bruce Mantell. Our first great portrait painter belonged to the noble family of Stuarts—Gilbert Charles Stuart, who painted Washington, Jefferson, Madison, and scores of their famous contemporaries. He was born in Rhode Island, but both his art and his ancestry were Scottish. Another Scottish-American is the sculptor, Frederick MacMonnies, whose work was described in an article published in this magazine last month.

But it is when we come to the realm of commerce that we find the Caledonian names scattered most thickly. Business, after all, is the Scot's delight. It may be fairly said that in the activities of legitimate business, he has never had a superior. He is a born trafficker. He can buy low and sell high. He wants "gear and siller." The joys of poverty and the simple life he may appreciate, but not until the day's work is over and the cash is in the bank. Yet he does not want money for money's sake. Very seldom is he a gambler or a schemer of the get-rich-quick species. To him, the main charm of business is the business itself, though his eye is ever fixed keenly upon the profits. John D. Rockefeller, for example, is a man of the true Scots type. He does not claim Caledonian descent, but there must surely be a strong infusion of Scottish blood in his veins.

It is this rare blending of sentiment and shrewdness which gives so much interest to the Scottish national character. It is hard to tell which has done the most to mold it, the Shorter Catechism or the multiplication table. From his ledger and his Burns, the Scot takes equal pleasure. From the stubborn soil of Caledonia he has learned to be thrifty. Every bawbee has meant a spadeful of earth—perhaps a dozen spadefuls. To waste anything, however trifling, is a crime. And yet, on the other hand, his nature has been indelibly influenced by the picturesque beauty of his native land. The heathery hills, embroidered by foaming rivulets; the tranquil lakes that reflect the rugged crags above them; the little gray cottages that nestle sociably in groups beside the winding road; and the long, hazy twilight that follows the busy day—these are the things that make the Scot romantic and sentimental.

Ever since our earliest fur-trading days, the success of the Scots in business has been phenomenal. Among the cities they have founded are Paterson, Pittsburgh, and Chicago. Henry Chisholm might appropriately be called the Father of Cleveland, for the reason that it was he who established its steel manufactures. Until recently, Charles Lockhart, Robert Pitcairn, and Andrew Carnegie were the "big three" of Pittsburgh, representing the three chief industries of oil, railroading, and steel.

The Pennsylvania Railroad, from Colonel Thomas A. Scott to Alexander Johnston Cassatt, has been mainly built up by men who were either Scots or of Scottish descent. Among the shoemaking towns of New England, no name is better known than that of Gordon McKay, the Scot who invented the sole-stitching machine and revolutionized the shoe trade. In Chicago the first banker, George Scott, was a highly respected Scot who piled up a $50 million fortune. And one of the leading Western bankers at the present time is James Berwick Forgan, a thorough Scot by both birth and training, who succeeded Lyman J. Gage as president of the First National Bank of Chicago when Mr. Gage became secretary of the United States treasury.

Besides James Wilson, the city of Washington has at least two other well-known Scots—Alexander Graham Bell, of telephone fame, and James Duncan, first vice-president of the American Federation of Labor. In New York there has always been an influential Scottish element since the days of Philip Livingstone. Robert Lenox, founder of the Presbyterian Hospital and the Lenox Library, was one of the five wealthiest New Yorkers for years before his death in 1840. Henry Burden, inventor of the horseshoe machine, and founder of the Burden fortunes, was born in Dunblane. Robert L. Stuart and Archibald Russell have had high rank among philanthropists, as John Stewart Kennedy has today. The handsome United Charities Building was a gift from Mr. Kennedy to the various societies which it houses.

And what shall be said of Andrew Carnegie, the richest and most freehanded Scot who ever lived? Never in the whole length of her heroic history has "Auld Scotia" produced a son who has wielded so wide an influence, or worked so mightily to shape the destiny of the human race. Sixty years ago he was a wee barefooted laddie in the streets of Allegheny, the son of a poor weaver, who had been driven from his home in Scotland by lack of work. Five years ago he retired from

business the second richest man in the world. To climb from the cobblestones of poverty to the throne of dominion over a vast industry—to abdicate this throne at the height of his power and become a sort of human Providence—such, in a sentence, has been the story of Andrew Carnegie.

But the "star-spangled Scot," as the British call Carnegie, did more than make $300 million for himself. In addition to this, he made about $200 million for his friends and partners, and a large proportion of these fortunate men are of Scottish birth or descent. George Lauder, Carnegie's cousin and a typical Scot, is now living in quiet retirement in Pittsburgh, with at least a score of millions at his disposal. Thomas Morrison, also a distant relation, and Alexander R. Peacock, another son of Dunfermline, are two of the Carnegian lieutenants who awoke one morning to find themselves wealthy beyond their dreams. Other partners of Carnegie with names that are undeniably Scottish are Blackburn, McLeod, Kerr, Lindsay, Gayley, Ramsay, and James Scott. And among his earlier associates were David McCandless and David A. Stewart.

Such are the Scots—a few of them—who have wrought well both for themselves and for the United States. They are said to be clannish, and the charge is true. A Scot will always help a Scot. Centuries of struggle and hardship have taught the Scottish people to be "in all changes of fortune, and down to the gates of death, loyal and loving one to another," to use the beautiful phrase of Robert Louis Stevenson. No amount of world wandering can make them forget their national traditions. Even if their little homeland were to be rolled out flat, it would be smaller than Indiana; yet to Scottish eyes there is no land like it.

"Of course, Heaven maun be verra like the Hielands," said a Highlander of whose patriotism Carnegie loves to tell.

But however much the Scot may sing of his native heath and its heroes, the non-Scots notice that when once he is established in America he seldom goes back. Of all the Scots who have won fame in the United States, only four have returned to Scotland with their laurels. "Few of us really care to go home again," said W. Butler Duncan, president of the New York St. Andrew's Society, himself born in Scotland of Scottish-American parents.

The Scot is here to stay. May his record in the future be as honorable and meritorious as it has been in the past!

The Future of Lithuanians in America

54

The following rather gloomy view of Lithuanian immigrant life in America was written during the early years of their arrival, while they were still, along with many other groups, at the bottom of the economic ladder. Thousands of Lithuanians had located in Chicago, where many of them worked in the large meat-packing plants. The portrayal of immigrant existence in Upton Sinclair's novel *The Jungle* (published in 1906) probably seemed an unfavorable reflection on his particular nationality to the immigrant who wrote this article, J. Hertmanavicia. [Chicago Foreign Language Press Survey, WPA Project, 1942. *Lietuva,* November 22, 1907.]

United States statistics show that there are over 80,000,000 inhabitants here. How many Lithuanians [there are] nobody knows. Some say 300,000, others that there are 500,000. I will take the middle figure, 400,000 Lithuanians.

Now then if there are 80,000,000 inhabitants, for every 200 people there is one Lithuanian.

It is very easy to compare the standard of Lithuanians with Americans. The Lithuanians are far behind.

The three most essential factors in the life of the nation, those on which the nation stands, are morality, enlightenment, and wealth.

Morality. To compare the morality of Lithuanians with Americans, we must look into the court records, where we can make a comparison as to whether the Lithuanians stand higher or lower in morality. The American writer, Upton Sinclair, in his book *The Jungle*, about the

Immigrant children pose as "Citizens of Tomorrow" in a parade in Chicago, 1921. The children were from the University of Chicago Settlement House.

Courtesy Chicago Historical Society

stockyards, describes the Lithuanians on a low plane of morality.

From the point of view of enlightenment, on this question we do not need to make a search; the enlightenment of Lithuanians is far behind that of the Americans. I have previously stated that for every Lithuanian there are 200 Americans. Then for every 200 American students there must be one Lithuanian; to every 200 American professionals there ought to be one Lithuanian, etc. The country of America is free; we Lithuanians are great lovers of liberty; therefore, let us make an effort to fill this above-mentioned gap. Then we can prove to the American public that we are just as good and know how to use opportunity like the Americans do.

From the material point of view. This also we can compare with the proportion above stated. If the Lithuanians were more advanced, business and industry among Lithuanians would be the same as the professional proportion.

There are more problems which we need to discuss, but I will omit them. The other problem is very important, let us say the fourth one, is politics. We Lithuanians are very honest people, so we look on politics as a dirty occupation. We must not neglect politics. In a free country, we must mingle in political affairs, we must participate in political activity, take the leadership, and then we can be elected to some minor or higher office—by being some kind of official we can do something for the benefit not only of the Lithuanians but of the general public as well.

The above-mentioned problems the Lithuanians ought to take under consideration. If we want to have a brighter future, let us take action to do away with our bad habits, let us begin reading scientific literature, books, and newspapers; they will show us the road to progress, civilization, and fortune.

Finns as American Citizens

55

Emigrants from Finland have made up a very small segment of America's foreign-born—slightly more than 1 percent. But their role in the economy has outweighed their numbers in those areas where they have concentrated. They have been especially active in the labor movement and in the formation of consumer cooperatives. The following laudatory article was written by William Frank McClure, Midwestern advertising executive. [*Chautauquan,* January 1908.]

The most important feature of the coming of the Finns to the United States is that they are desirable citizens. Physically they are strong. Thousands of them own their own homes. One-half the American population are church members and among few nationalities is the cause of temperance growing more rapidly.

Industrially the Finns in America are filling a most important niche. Some 20,000 of them in the Mesabi iron range alone are digging out the ore that is giving America her prestige in the production of iron and steel. Thousands more are rehandling this heavy product at the harbors of Lake Erie where it is transferred from 10,000-ton ships to fifty-ton railroad cars, en route to the furnaces of the Mahoning Valley and Pittsburgh. In so doing they are performing a kind of hard labor for which it is very difficult to engage our English-speaking workmen.

Out in Wyoming again the Finnish laborers are digging coal. In Colorado they are helping to uncover the nation's gold. At Astoria, Oregon, we find them extensively engaged in the industry of salmon fishing. Altogether there are more than 4,000 Finnish people in Astoria. There are also good-sized Finnish settlements in California, Washington, Utah, Montana, South Dakota, and Nebraska. Not all the Finns in the United States, however, are at the lake ports and in the West. In Massachusetts there are thousands more, 3,000 of whom are at Fitchburg.

Not only are these people an important factor in our American industrial life but in very many places their influence is felt in the civic and political life of the community in which they live, and this influence is usually for good. Substantial illustrations of this fact have been afforded at Ashtabula, Ohio, harbor, the world's greatest iron ore receiving port. Here are located several thousand Finns, three Finnish churches, and two large temperance halls. In the city are 100 saloons. With a view to driving out these grog-shops not long ago a local option election was held. The result was close and the issue was defeated but, to the everlasting credit of the Finns, a survey of the situation disclosed the fact that the proposition was lost in the best residential section while the Finnish territory carried overwhelmingly "dry."

A few years ago it was not an uncommon thing for laborers on the lower lake docks to carry liquor with them to their work. The first nationality among these handlers to make a move in the direction of total abstinence was the Finns. Twenty-two years ago a temperance society was established among the Finnish people of Ashtabula harbor. Year after year the sentiment grew. Finally it crystallized among those who were employed upon the docks belonging to the late Senator

Finnish farm woman in Minnesota in the early 1900s.

Marcus A. Hanna. The Finns and the Swedes united in the movement and it was not long until the fact was widely heralded along the lakes with an immediate and decided influence for good. At that time the Finns at this port possessed no temperance hall. Mr. Hanna therefore erected for them a plain frame building for a reading room, gymnasium, and meeting place on an eminence overlooking the docks.

Incidentally, Ashtabula harbor holds a unique place among Finnish settlements. It is the doorway through which many thousands of Finns have passed to the Northwest. Large numbers of these people on their arrival at New York proceed at once to Ashtabula and are met by relatives or friends who have preceded them by perhaps several years. Here they remain a year or two until they become accustomed to American ways and learn to speak some English. They are then ready either to select some other part of the country as their home or to begin in earnest the pursuit for homes of their own and a livelihood in the immediate vicinity.

Once naturalized and full-fledged residents of a city or town, it is not uncommon for them to be selected for offices of public trust. At both Ashtabula and Conneaut in recent years, Finns have been elected to the city council. In the state legislature of Minnesota there is a Finn who is serving his second term. Another is a member of the legislature of Wyoming. At Longville, Idaho, the postmaster is a Finn. At New York Mills, Minnesota, another occupies the office of justice of the peace. In Houghton County, Michigan, Finns have held both the offices of county prosecutor and treasurer.

As already inferred, the Finns are a decidedly religious people. The church of the Motherland is the Lutheran Church and the majority of the Finns in this country are still its adherents. Most of the ministers in the United States who are serving Finnish pastorates were ordained in Finland. It is difficult to find a Finnish settlement, no matter how small, without a meetinghouse of some kind and many of them are quite large. The first of these

churches was built in 1873 at Calumet, Michigan, which is one of the oldest settlements in the United States.

About five years ago, a new church movement was inaugurated among the Finns in this country looking toward the abolishment of many of the forms and ceremonies of the church as conducted in Finland. This church was known as 'The Finnish Independent Evangelical Lutheran Church of America of the Kansan Synod." The first meeting was held at Ashtabula harbor and was attended by delegates from settlements in Minnesota, Pennsylvania, and Ohio. Since then the church has been growing in many sections of the country. At a subsequent national meeting, plans were laid for the establishment of a theological seminary in connection therewith.

Some important features of the new church may be summed up as follows: The length of the ceremonies is greatly shortened and more time given to the sermon. The mass required in the Motherland is not obligatory but at the same time is not abolished, the matter being left to the option of the different churches of the synod. In Finland those who do not partake of the communion in ten years are in a sense ostracized, while under the regime of the new church this distinction is largely obliterated.

There is also a comparatively small portion of our Finnish population connected with the long-established evangelical churches of this country. There are twenty Finnish Congregational churches in the United States. Most of these are in Massachusetts, New Hampshire, and Maine. The first one, however, was established at Ashtabula harbor some fifteen years ago and this was the only one for some five years.

The temperance societies of the Finns

Finnish Temperance Society in Ely, Minnesota, about 1905.

at their inception carried out simply the literal or liberal meaning of the word "temperance," making moderation the chief requirement. Today temperance with the Finns means total abstinence. The temperance halls, some of which cost as high as $10,000, are used for temperance meetings sabbath afternoons but weekdays often are utilized for the presentation of Finnish dramas or for social events. Not a few of them are fitted up with a large stage and scenery. At the sabbath afternoon meetings it is not uncommon for one of the members to be called publicly to account when he is known to have broken his temperance pledge. . . .

Very few Finns who come for admission to this country are sent back. They are splendidly developed. This is said to be due in part to the coarse bread and other plain food which they eat and to their steam baths. Even the farms in Finland are equipped with bathhouses. The one disease which sometimes bars these people from coming into the United States is trachoma, a disease of the eye.

Since the bettering of conditions in Finland, a few Finns from this country are returning to the Motherland. Quite a goodly number went back during the strike of the ore handlers at Duluth last spring. The number, however, in no way compares with those who are coming into the United States and not a few of those who went to Finland in the spring or early summer are now coming back to America.

The Ordeal of Naturalization
John Spargo

56

Cornishman John Spargo was not a typical immigrant; he was a well-educated political activist before arriving in America in 1901. He soon became prominent in Socialist circles and was for some time an influential figure in the American Socialist Party, until strong differences of opinion about World War I led him to dissociate himself. His most famous work was the 1906 book *The Bitter Cry of the Children,* a product of research into the sweatshop conditions of New York City. The article reprinted here chronicles Spargo's long struggle with the red tape of American naturalization procedures. As a sophisticated Englishman he was far less tolerant of petty officialdom than immigrants from the Continent, who were not given to open criticism of the workings of democracy. [*Independent,* October 29, 1908: "On Becoming an American Citizen."]

Eight years ago I came to America from England, my native country. For centuries ancestors of mine had shared in its political and ecclesiastical government, leaving their names respectably enshrined in its history. In turn, I prepared to follow the family trail to respectable glory—either the trail leading to some quiet bishopric or archdeaconry, or that leading to the solemn shades of the House of Commons. But fate led me away from these to seek literary fame and fortune, first in company with the shades of Fleet Street—Dr. Johnson's and the rest—and then in New York City.

At first New York was cold, neglectful, and heartless. No cheer came during the first year or two. Then suddenly her great heart seemed to warm with a kindly glow, and I was no longer a stranger, friendless and homesick in a strange land. New York had become a foster mother to me. So I would have the adoption made formal and decided to take out my "first papers."

I went, early in 1904, to the Supreme Court in New York City, and made my application. I stood at the end of a long line of human beings such as one sees nowhere else, a cosmopolitan line in which every nation on earth seemed to be represented. I heard men renounce allegiance to all the governments, princes, and potentates of the world, I think. They made their renunciations upon oath, glibly enough, though I had a suspicion that there were many who answered in the affirmative without knowing in the least what the cud-chewing Irishman with the finely developed Galloway brogue was asking. But they knew in a general way that they must say "Ya" if they would become foster sons of New York.

To get "first papers" was easy enough. There was a long wait, to be sure, but it was mildly interesting, and, since smoking was not forbidden, I could endure it with philosophic calm. I guessed rather than understood what the Irishman with the Galloway brogue asked, and answered each question promptly. At first he was brusque and rude, evidently regarding me as one of "thim dagoes," his name for all the timid applicants for citizenship. But I won his homage and respect by volunteering to fill out the official blank for him; not even the centuries'-old hatred of Ireland for my England could survive that shock of admiration. Most of his "dagoes" could barely write their names, much less fill out a blank. We shook hands, and there was an Irish-English alliance immediately effected. I paid a dollar for the first paper, officially styled "a declaration of intention to become a citizen of the United

States," and went out. I was now on probation for at least three years. After that time I might hope for my "second papers."

I let the year 1907 pass without finishing the process of becoming a citizen. Not living in New York City any longer, it was necessary to appear at the supreme court of the county in which I reside, and that involved a good deal of trouble. Then, too, there was no election of very great importance that year, and naturally, I wished my first vote to be historic. So when 1908 came there began to stir political ambitions. I wanted to become one of the sovereign electors, to cast a vote in the great quadrennial presidential contest. To find out what step I should take next, I consulted a legal friend and discovered that I would have to attend a hearing at the county clerk's office, taking with me two witnesses who could testify to having known me for at least five years.

Accordingly, one morning in March of this year, I attended such a hearing with my two witnesses. These were men whose time was valuable, one being an employer of labor, with a considerable business. I, too, am an unusually busy man, and my time is rather more valuable than that of most men who appear in the naturalization court. We hoped, therefore, to get through in good time and to avoid a long wait by being at the court office a little while before the opening hour, which was, I had learned, nine o'clock. Others had reasoned in a similar manner, evidently, for even at that time there were ten applicants standing in line before me, their witnesses being seated around the room. I took my position as the eleventh in line, consoling myself with the thought that in an hour at most my turn would come.

Being an Englishman by birth and training, I have always been accustomed to regard government offices of all kinds as examples of punctuality. If an English court or government office is scheduled to begin business at nine o'clock, it begins at nine o'clock, and not five minutes past nine. But in America this is not the case, as I have found to my sorrow upon more than one occasion. It was five minutes past ten when a young insolent clerk came, and ten minutes later when he got to work, having first to rid himself of a thrilling story of a riotous spree the night before by recounting its incidents to a fellow clerk. Evidently a naturalized Italian, this young man of a class closely related to the yahoo and the hoodlum was most offensive in his attitude toward the applicants for citizenship before him, regarding us all as his inferiors, to be mocked by him at will. I felt angry—all the more because I knew that an indictment for participation in election frauds loomed before him. And I could not help thinking that in the land whose citizenship I was relinquishing there would have been no possibility of such disgraceful conduct toward applicants for anything. . . .

It was twelve minutes to four in the afternoon when my turn came. I had waited for seven hours and my witnesses had done the same! To say that each of us valued that time and the extra time spent in travel at $20, making a total of $60, would be a very conservative statement. Of course, we were all three enraged, but nevertheless we were fortunate as compared with half a score who stood behind me, some of whom had waited just as long. For when I got through, at eleven minutes past four, the clerk announced, "No more today!" closed his books with a bang, and hurried out. Here were half a score of men, all of the laboring class.

Ellis Island is located in New York's Upper Bay. In its peak year of operation, 1907, it was the major immigrant-processing station in the U.S. Accommodations for newcomers included dining and dormitory space for 1,000 people, social welfare rooms, a general hospital, a kindergarten, library, and recreation room.

Library of Congress

Brown Brothers

Ellis Island is a U-shaped piece of land, the center of which is a narrow basin used as a ferry slip. The ferry brought passengers to the island's main processing center. (On facing page, top) Immigrants wait for the ferry after disembarking from their ship, 1911. (On facing page, bottom) Swedish immigrants board the ferry boat that will take them to the main port of the island, early 1900s. (Above) Immigrants eat in the Ellis Island dining hall while awaiting admission to America, 1907. The hall and dormitory accommodated 1,000 people, but the arrival of 5,000 aliens in a given day was not uncommon, resulting in deplorably crowded conditions. World War I began to check the influx in 1915.

Illustrations on this and facing page, Brown Brothers

One similarity of all American immigrants was their desire for a better life in a new land. Aside from this common goal, they varied widely in costume and custom, as is evidenced by these photographs. (Above) Three women from Guadeloupe upon their arrival in America. (Above, right) A Dutch immigrant woman in traditional headdress. (Right) An Albanian soldier at Ellis Island. (On facing page) A Serbian gypsy family waits to be processed.

Immigrants at Ellis Island had to pass physical and mental
fitness tests before being granted admission to America.
(Above) A U.S. inspector examines the eyes of newcomers.
(On facing page, top) A woman gets a physical
examination. (On facing page, bottom) Due to language
barriers and differences in educational background,
intelligence tests like the one being given in this picture had
to use universally understood symbols.

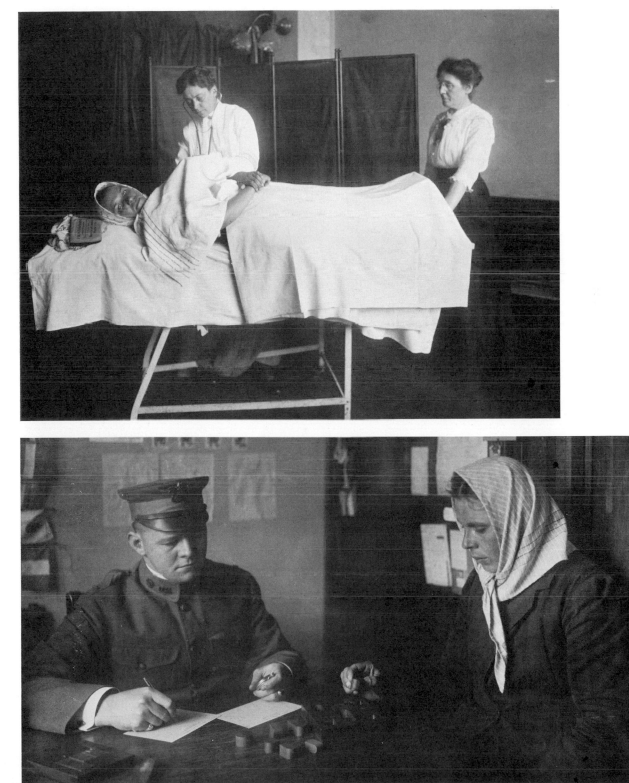

Illustrations Brown Brothers

Illustrations George Eastman House Collection

Brown Brothers

When an immigrant had gone through the many steps involved in gaining admission to the U.S., he was ready to leave for his destination. (On facing page, top) A uniformed interpreter helps a man purchase a railroad ticket. (On facing page, bottom) Each person was given a tag, written in English, indicating his railroad and destination. (Above) Those who did not pass inspection tests were ordered to return home. Rejected immigrants like this mother and child were allowed to appeal to the "Board of Final Resort" for reconsideration. (Below) Baggage that the immigrants could not carry was loaded on carts and sent to the railroad stations.

Culver Pictures

Each man had brought two witnesses and each of these had lost a day's wages in all probability, which the applicants in most cases would pay. Figuring their wages at $2.00 per day, each of the half-score of disappointed ones had been taxed $6.00 that day for nothing at all, and would have to come again and make the same sacrifice. And all merely to *make application* for citizenship!

When I had handed over $4.00 to the clerk, that being the fee prescribed by law, my petition was filed and I was free to go. I had no receipt for my money, and even my precious "first paper" had been taken away. Yet I was proudly conscious that I was advanced a long way toward citizenship. But my pride was dulled a bit by the things I had seen; by my consciousness of great shortcomings in our manner of conducting public business. Why should it be possible for a young ignoramus to insult and browbeat honest workingmen when they come knocking at the door seeking citizenship? Why should it be possible for a whisper in the ear from a politician to get the last man in line attended to before the first man? Why should I have been treated so deferentially when my turn came and the clerk, who had been so insolent a moment before, glanced at my application? I had answered the question concerning my occupation by writing "author and journalist." That was all. Ordinarily I write something much less boastful, but the insufferable conduct of the clerk led me to so describe myself. I wanted to see whether he would dare treat me as an ignorant and helpless creature to be made sport of and the result disquieted me.

After ninety days, I was told, my two witnesses and myself would be required to attend the supreme court and appear before the judge for examination. Then, if

nothing prevented, I should get my certificate of naturalization, enabling me to vote in the coming election. Meantime, my name would be posted at various places throughout the county, so that any person interested in the matter would be able to protest against my admission to citizenship. There can be no objection to such posting of the names of applicants, of course, but it seemed to me that unless some person entered objection to my application I ought not to be compelled to bring two witnesses to the court again when they had already sworn to all that the law requires. It seems to me now that after filling out that formidable petition and having it duly witnessed, then having my petition on file for ninety days, during which any person could enter any objection he might have to my admission, I should have been admitted at once, as a matter of course, upon satisfying the court or some responsible body that I understood enough of the political government of the country to be an intelligent voter. Only in the event of a protest, it seems to me, ought it to be necessary for one to appear in court with witnesses whose testimony is already recorded.

Before the ninety days expired I received a notice that I must appear with my two witnesses for a "preliminary examination" at the city hall in my own town on a given day. Grumbling, we went and spent another couple of hours each. I was asked all the questions I had answered in my petition and many supplementary questions, which were for the most part ridiculous. For example, I was pressed to fix the date and manner of my first meeting with each of my witnesses: What was the exact date when you first met Mr. B——? Where did you meet him? Who introduced you to him? What was the nature of the public gathering at which you first met Mr. C——? In what year and on what date in the year did you move from the house you formerly lived in on Myrtle Street into your present house on Ivy Terrace? Such were the questions with which one was plied by a very harmless little assistant from the office of the attorney general at Washington, a fussy little fellow, overwhelmed with consciousness of his dignity, but courteous to everybody.

He read the main questions from printed sheets; they were not of his invention. He had hardly originality enough to change a syllable in the questions to make their meaning clearer. And such questions! Some of them absolutely horrified me. I had been in lands where one had to have passports to travel, and where life is spent under very strict government surveillance, but never where the lines were more tightly drawn round one's personal liberty. I thought of Russia and then of the England I had already renounced. Did I really want to give up English freedom for citizenship in a land where I could not be free to read what books I liked, or to attend public meetings of all kinds? "Are you an anarchist?" I was asked, and, as upon the former occasion, I answered that I was not. "Do you ever read any anarchist books or papers?" I was then asked, and I stood for a moment dumfounded. I ought to have said: "I decline to answer that question here," but I did not. I parried it by saying: "I *do* not read anarchist papers," laying some slight emphasis upon the present tense. It was perhaps a cowardly answer. I despised myself for making it. For of course I *have* read anarchist books. I have read my Thoreau on the "Duty of Civil Disobedience"; I have read much in Herbert Spencer's pages which the anarchists claim to be good gospel. I have read Tolstoi and Kropotkin. But that pompous little representative of the United States government would never have been able to get into his head that a man could read such books and be other than an "undesirable citizen."

Then I was asked whether I ever attended anarchist meetings. To this I could truthfully enough give a negative answer. Still, the answer shamed me somewhat. Why should I not attend an anarchist lecture if I should feel disposed to do so? What right has the government of the United States to ask what kind of meetings I like any more than to ask what kind of pudding I like?

The anarchist bogey has evidently frightened the authorities at Washington. Their representative looked very solemn and spoke with a comical attempt at impressiveness: "What do you think of anarchy?" It never entered the poor fellow's stupid brain that if a man never read anything about it, nor listened to expositions of it, his opinion of anarchism could not be of any value to himself or anybody else. He was a man without a sense of humor, representing authority at Washington likewise without a sense of humor.

I smiled at the question. "How much space have you for that answer, Mr. Attorney?" I asked. He showed me just one short line. My opinion of anarchism must be compressed into a single line therefore. So I said: "Mr. Attorney, you will please record my opinion that anarchism is 'a very foolish proposition.'"

I doubt whether the attorney has yet wondered that one who never read any anarchist literature could have such opinions as my "unofficial" opinion of anarchism above quoted! Quickly he passed to the next question. "Explain why you desire to become an American citizen," he commanded. I replied to the effect that I believed it to be my duty to the country in which I reside to assume my fair share of civic responsibilities. In the mind of the attorney this answer was translated in the following words, which he wrote in his report: "Because I want to vote." But I let it go at that.

Why on earth that examination should have been held no one has been able to inform me. It did not save any applicant or witness from attending the supreme court, for each person was told that it would still be necessary to appear in court. It did not save a single moment in court so far as I have been able to learn, for every bit of the performance had to be gone over again.

About a week later, in company with my two witnesses, I attended the court as directed. The courtroom was almost full of applicants for citizenship and their witnesses. Arriving promptly at nine o'clock we were among the first present and hoped that we might get away in reasonable time. Fifty minutes we waited for the judge to appear, and then when he came in at ten minutes to ten we were shocked to see the jury seats begin to fill up. A moment later our fears were realized: the judge announced that there would be no naturalization hearings until one o'clock, an officer of the court repeated the announcement and came to where we were packed together and practically ordered us to leave the courtroom. I was desperate. One of my witnesses had an important engagement at one o'clock twenty miles away and to miss it would mean a loss of hundreds of dollars perhaps. Striding up to the judge I explained the situation, and he was good enough to agree to "swear in" that witness and take his testimony, so that he could leave. My other witness and myself must return at one o'clock.

That was a small mercy, but we were grateful enough. My second witness and myself, with three hours to kill, took a drive into the country and luncheon at a well-known roadhouse, returning to the courtroom five minutes before one o'clock. The court was still in session, but we were informed that there would be no naturalization after all; that a few minutes after all the applicants and witnesses had been sent out of the courtroom another judge had appeared, and, having nothing else to do, decided to take the naturalization cases! Nearly thirty applicants had gone away as ordered and would return at one o'clock, but there were two or three belated arrivals in court. These applicants were disposed of, and no others being present at the time the hearing of naturalization cases were declared finished for the day, the judge going home. There we sat, thirty applicants with witnesses, about ninety persons in all, stunned and enraged.

Again I went up to the judge who had been so obliging in the morning and asked if he could not dispose of my case under the circumstances. He was very cordial and polite, apologizing profusely for the manner in which I had been hounded from pillar to post. "You have a right to kick," he said. "It is not a fair deal. I would like to help you out and hear your case if I could. But I am helpless. The representative of the federal government (the same who had examined us in our city hall) must be present to do the examining, and he has gone away. Moreover, there are no books and no records of your previous examination. It's too bad, but I cannot help you." Then, over the protest of the clerk of the court, he agreed to "swear in" and examine my second witness, in the hope that the United States representative would accept that in lieu of further appearance at court.

The examination was conducted by the clerk amid much confusion. Perhaps because the irritating turn events had taken had irritated him, my witness became confused, and in reply to the question "How long were you in this country before you got your certificate of naturalization?" answered "About two years." Immediately the clerk turned to the judge, who had been attending to other matters, and asked that my petition be dismissed, on the ground that the witness himself had, by his own showing, no legal right to his citizenship, having obtained his papers before he was in the country five years. Here was a pretty kettle o' fish! At first the judge agreed to the request for a dismissal of my application, but changed it to an adjournment in response to my plea.

What had happened was that my witness in his excitement had misunderstood the drift of the question and supposed that it referred to his "first papers," his declaration of intention. As a matter of fact, he had been in the country almost ten years before getting his final papers, as he was able later to prove by various deeds to property in his possession. But I had had a very narrow escape!

Acting on the advice of the judge, we hastened back to our home town and sought out the United States attorney, explaining the situation to him. He was in no good humor, apparently resenting the action of the judge in taking it upon himself to examine my witnesses in his absence. He promised to see that I received notice to appear at the next session of the court at which naturalization cases would be taken up, intimating that the previous examination of my witnesses would not be taken into account at all, and that they must both reappear. Progress to citizen-

ship was exceedingly slow!

No notice came of that next hearing. Luckily, however, my witnesses and myself had decided to be present. I was determined, if possible, to force a hearing this time. Again we were present at nine o'clock, the scheduled opening time, and again the judge was late, appearing a few minutes after ten o'clock. I saw with relief that the judge was an old friend, and knew that if I could only get my case called, success was assured. But to get called was not easy. Not having been notified, my name was not on the list. Further, there were many applicants, and most of them were brought by machine politicians. Men holding political offices, party leaders, swarmed within the enclosure reserved for counsel. They went up to the clerk and dictated the order in which names were to be called, and themselves acted as witnesses in all these cases. I observed that in these cases the examination was almost a farce, practically all the questions relating to the applicant's knowledge of our form of government being omitted.

Evidences of "pull" were abundant. To say that I was disgusted is to describe my feelings mildly. Again I was asking myself whether citizenship was, under the circumstances, worth striving for. I appreciated the feelings of the old Scotchman who, the week before, appeared in the office of the representative of the United States and threw down his certificate of citizenship in disgust, saying: "Take this paper. I do not want it, for I am sick of the corruption and favoritism shown everywhere. I don't want to be a citizen in a land where there is no justice."

The attitude of my friend, the judge, interested me. The unimaginative attorney asked an Italian laborer if he believed in polygamy, and the poor fellow sat helpless and puzzled, wondering what he should say. Finally, when the question was repeated, he answered, "Ya." Just then the judge was listening and he broke in sharply: "What's the use of asking him if he believes in polygamy, when he does not understand the word?" Then, turning to the applicant, he said: "Do you think one wife at a time is enough for a man?" and the applicant understood. He fairly shook with laughter as he replied: "Ya. One wife trouble enough for any man." Another man was asked if he believed in anarchy, and likewise failed to comprehend. "Ask him whether he believes in burning down a man's house," directed the judge, and again the reply was a very certain negative. It was rather a queer definition of anarchy, but I am sure the judge got far nearer to the real man in the witness chair than did the hidebound representative of the United States.

At last, after nearly four hours' waiting, I reached the witness chair. The judge was chatting with a group of lawyers and quite unconscious of my presence, otherwise I should have had an easier time. As it was, the examination was by no means a severe ordeal. All the questions I had twice before answered were repeated, and I replied to them as patiently as possible, once more swearing that I did not believe in polygamy or anarchism, once more testifying about myself and my family. A few questions about the government of the United States and I was passed, subject to a satisfactory examination of my witnesses. I stepped up to sign my name in a big book at the judge's desk and was at once warmly greeted by my friend and engaged in a chat. I am inclined to think that I thus unconsciously enjoyed the benefits of a "pull," for my witnesses were both rushed through, and

instead of being treated roughly and rudely by every minor court functionary, I was at once the object of marked courtesy and deference.

Officially, I was now a citizen of the United States, but there were still some formalities to go through. Before I could get my certificate I must wait for all the other applicants to get through with their hearings. Then I must stand in line and wait for my turn to get such particulars as the color of my hair and eyes, the shape of my nose, my height and weight, entered in my certificate. I say I had to "wait my turn," but that is not quite correct. One does not object to taking one's turn in line upon the principle of "first come first served," but rebels against having the last man come first because of a whisper from some politician. First the fortunate possessors of "pull" were attended to by the little clerk with an indictment for fraud menacing his future. How long I should have had to wait I cannot say, but quite early a prominent member of the legal profession came along, and, after a word of greeting, upon his own initiative, spoke my name in the ear of the little clerk. The effect was magical! I was attended to, even before the favored protégés of the political bosses, and left at once, followed by the envious and angry glances of the wronged crowd. Thus, by a strange fate, my first experience of citizenship in a republic was the enjoyment of undue privilege obtained by "pull."

That the present naturalization law is unconstitutional I have been assured by eminent jurists. There is good reason to believe that the states themselves have a right to determine the terms upon which they will grant citizenship to the alien, and grave doubt of the right of the federal government to assume sole jurisdiction in the matter. However that may be—and I am not a constitutional lawyer—I believe that this simple record of personal experience will show that the present method of naturalization involves a great deal of quite useless red tape. The whole procedure is unnecessarily tedious, irksome, and costly to the applicant for citizenship, and well calculated to deter the most intelligent and self-respecting from becoming citizens.

I do not hesitate to say that the present method is a grave scandal and should be changed as speedily as possible. Like all Englishmen, I have ever enjoyed the right to grumble. In England I should have written a letter to *The Times* about such abuses, or insisted that the member for my division "ask a question about it" in Parliament. I have abandoned my English allegiance, but cannot so readily abandon my English instinct to protest against what seems to me a crying evil. As an American citizen with the English instinct for justice and fair play, therefore, I protest against the present ridiculous and unjust methods of naturalizing aliens.

The Dangers of Neglecting the Younger Generation

57

Every ethnic group that arrived in the United States during the age of industrialization experienced many of the same difficulties, especially if they selected one of the large cities to settle in. They were all socially disadvantaged and poor. Their goal was a higher standard of living and a degree of acceptance by the community at large. The insecurity bred by their weak economic position frequently led them, whether Pole, Italian, Czech, or Russian, to feel that the process of assimilation was too slow. The pessimism of the following article from the newspaper *Dziennik Zwiazkowy,* on June 21, 1909, exaggerated the situation of the Poles in relation to the other nationalities. [Chicago Foreign Language Press Survey, WPA Project, 1942.]

In several articles we have pointed out the needs of our younger generation, but without any appreciable success, for the reason that the upbringing of children is done on the lowest level where it suffers shame, damage, loss, and despair. Polish quarters in American cities, outside the Italian, breed the greatest number of delinquents. The average American hesitates to pass, in the late hours of the evening, through streets that are inhabited by Polish people, for even during the day some misfortune is liable to occur to him. We all see this, are very hurt, and yet do nothing to right the wrongs.

In a recent article, under the title "Parents, Wake Up," we made a formal appeal to Polish parents, an appeal to help their children, as much as possible, obtain an education or training in some particular field. Their conduct was pointed out, along with the losses suffered by them, which are tremendously high among Polish-American youth, due to the negligence of the parents who permit them to loaf about the streets, which is the cause of their degradation and vagrancy. We have brought out the importance of training children in their early years, especially at school, where they come in contact with American customs. This is typical of metropolitan centers and has an important bearing upon the child's later years.

Within a short time the vacation period will be here. Tens of thousands of Polish children will leave the confines of the schoolroom to rest for two months and absorb enough energy for further study. Among those that take interest in the younger generation, various activities are sponsored to aid them physically and morally. As an example we have the American people who look after the best interest of their children. They organize, during the vacation period, many kinds of activities conducive to the children's well-being. This is one of the reasons why we see so many of them attending summer school. Here they receive valuable training. After school they are found at many clubs organized for them. These social and athletic clubrooms assist them to better sportsmanship, give them training in executive position, and help them to come in contact with prominent people through their social activities. These youths find no time to mingle with the loafers and the hoodlums of the streets. Their chosen activity builds strong character, domineering personalities, which in later years become priceless gifts.

Poland in recent years has done a great deal for her younger generation. During the vacation periods manual training courses have been set up, many activities in various parks have been created where youth can obtain healthful physical training. Many lodges offer disciplinary courses for those who are about to enter the army. For the younger and physically unfit, colonies are offered where thousands are sent to be built up, to gather strength and knowledge, to keep physically fit. In this respect they not only become good citizens but become healthful specimens for posterity.

It is only the Polish people in America that do not do anything to improve the conditions of their youth. Up to now not a thing has been done. If only they would organize some sort of classes that would give this youth a chance to be better fitted morally and physically! Never has this generation needed such guidance as at the present time in America. The Polish youth in reality is facing a rather precarious position, and is awaiting a worse fate. Their degeneracy is not only affecting us but also American youth, American traditions. The American press daily publishes news about the wrongdoing of our youth, which is on the increase. These articles have damaging effects and tend to put the entire Polish population before the public eye. This kind of publicity does not help the position of the Polish people. We cannot protest, for the facts tell the story.

We ought to get together and organize forces to hold in check the fatalities and crimes perpetrated by our youth. This should be done on a great scale. It would benefit both the parents and the children. This project can get a foothold through the churches, schools, and lodges. The priests and sister teachers can promote and sponsor many kinds of classes and activities that would be beneficial to our children. To check crime and foster good citizenship, we should follow the examples set by American and European countries.

Generation Conflicts Among the Immigrants
Jane Addams

58

In an age of reform, Jane Addams stood out for her social work and advocacy of unpopular causes. She founded Hull House in September 1889 on the near Southwest Side of Chicago; it eventually became the most famous of all settlement houses. Located in an immigrant neighborhood, Hull House was a catalyst in the difficult transition from alien to citizen for thousands of newcomers. In this selection from her semiautobiographical story of the settlement house, Miss Addams described the problems that arose between the generations as the children of immigrants proceeded to Americanize much more rapidly than their parents. [*Twenty Years at Hull House* (1910). New York, 1960. Chapter 11, "Immigrants and Their Children."]

An overmastering desire to reveal the humbler immigrant parents to their own children lay at the base of what has come to be called the Hull House Labor Museum. This was first suggested to my mind one early spring day when I saw an old Italian woman, her distaff against her homesick face, patiently spinning a thread by the simple stick spindle so reminiscent of all southern Europe. I was walking down Polk Street, perturbed in spirit, because it seemed so difficult to come into genuine relations with the Italian women and because they themselves so often lost their hold upon their Americanized children. It seemed to me that Hull House ought to be able to devise some educational enterprise, which should build a bridge between European and American experiences in such wise as to give them both more meaning and a sense of relation. I meditated that perhaps the power to see life as a whole is more needed in the immigrant quarter of a large city than anywhere else, and that the lack of this power is the most fruitful source of misunderstanding between European immigrants and their children, as it is between them and their American neighbors; and why should that chasm between fathers and sons, yawning at the feet of each generation, be made so unnecessarily cruel and impassable to these bewildered immigrants? Suddenly I looked up and saw the old woman with her distaff, sitting in the sun on the steps of a tenement house. She might have served as a model for one of Michaelangelo's Fates, but her face brightened as I passed and, holding up her spindle for me to see, she called out that when she had spun a little more yarn, she would knit a pair of stockings for her goddaughter. The occupation of the old woman gave me the clue that was needed. Could we not interest the young people working in the neighboring factories in these older forms of industry, so that, through their own parents and grandparents, they would find a dramatic representation of the inherited resources of their daily occupation? If these young people could actually see that the complicated machinery of the factory had been evolved from simple tools, they might at least make a beginning towards that education which Dr. Dewey defines as "a continuing reconstruction of experience." They might also lay a foundation for reverence of the past which Goethe declares to be the basis of all sound progress. . . .

There are many examples of touching fidelity to immigrant parents on the part of their grown children; a young man who day after day attends ceremonies which no longer express his religious convictions and who makes his vain effort to interest his Russian Jewish father in social problems; a daughter who might earn much more money as a stenographer could she work from Monday morning till Saturday night, but who quietly and docilely makes neckties for low wages because she can thus abstain from work Saturdays to please her father; these young people, like poor Maggie Tulliver, through many painful experiences have reached the conclusion that pity, memory, and faithfulness are natural ties with paramount claims.

This faithfulness, however, is sometimes ruthlessly imposed upon by immigrant parents who, eager for money and accustomed to the patriarchal authority of peasant households, hold their children in a stern bondage which requires a surrender of all their wages and concedes no time or money for pleasures.

There are many convincing illustrations that this parental harshness often results in juvenile delinquency. A Polish boy of seventeen came to Hull House one day to ask a contribution of fifty cents "towards a flower piece for the funeral of an old Hull House club boy." A few questions made it clear that the object was fictitious, whereupon the boy broke down and half-defiantly stated that he wanted to buy two twenty-five cent tickets, one for his girl and one for himself, to a dance of the Benevolent Social Twos; that he hadn't a penny of his own although he had worked in a brass foundry for three years and had been advanced twice, because he always had to give his pay envelope unopened to his father; "just look at the clothes he buys me," was his concluding remark.

Perhaps the girls are held even more rigidly. In a recent investigation of 200 working girls it was found that only 5 percent had the use of their own money and that 62 percent turned in all they earned, literally every penny, to their mothers. It was through this little investigation that we first knew Marcella, a pretty young German girl who helped her widowed mother year after year to care for a large family of younger children. She was content for the most part although her mother's Old Country notions of dress gave her but an infinitesimal amount of her own wages to spend on her clothes, and she was quite sophisticated as to proper dressing because she sold silk in a neighborhood department store. Her mother approved of the young man who was showing her various attentions and agreed that Marcella should accept his invitation to a ball, but would allow her not a penny towards a new gown to replace one impossibly plain and shabby. Marcella spent a sleepless night and wept bitterly, although she well knew that the doctor's bill for the children's scarlet fever was not yet paid. The next day as she was cutting off three yards of shining pink silk, the thought came to her that it would make her a fine new waist to wear to the ball. She wistfully saw it wrapped in paper and carelessly stuffed into the muff of the purchaser, when suddenly the parcel fell upon the floor. No one was looking and quick as a flash the girl picked it up and pushed it into her blouse. The theft was discovered by the relentless department store detective who, for "the sake of the example," insisted upon taking the case into court. The poor mother wept bitter tears over this downfall of her *frommes Mädchen* [innocent young girl] and no one had the heart to tell her of her own blindness.

I know a Polish boy whose earnings were all given to his father who gruffly refused all requests for pocket money. One

Christmas his little sisters, having been told by their mother that they were too poor to have any Christmas presents, appealed to the big brother as to one who was earning money of his own. Flattered by the implication, but at the same time quite impecunious, the night before Christmas he nonchalantly walked through a neighboring department store and stole a manicure set for one little sister and a string of beads for the other. He was caught at the door by the house detective as one of those children whom each local department store arrests in the weeks before Christmas at the daily rate of eight to twenty. The youngest of these offenders are seldom taken into court but are either sent home with a warning or turned over to the officers of the Juvenile Protective Association. Most of these premature lawbreakers are in search of Americanized clothing and others are only looking for playthings. They are all distracted by the profusion and variety of the display, and their moral sense is confused by the general air of openhandedness.

These disastrous efforts are not unlike those of many younger children who are constantly arrested for petty thieving because they are too eager to take home food or fuel which will relieve the distress and need they so constantly hear discussed. The coal on the wagons, the vegetables displayed in front of the grocery shops, the very wooden blocks in the loosened street paving are a challenge to their powers to help out at home. A Bohemian boy who was out on parole from the old detention home of the juvenile court itself, brought back five stolen chickens to the matron for Sunday dinner, saying that he knew the committee were "having a hard time to fill up so many kids and perhaps these fowl would

Family of the stockyard district in Chicago, 1904.

help out." The honest immigrant parents, totally ignorant of American laws and municipal regulations, often send a child to pick up coal on the railroad tracks or to stand at three o'clock in the morning before the side door of a restaurant which gives away broken food, or to collect grain for the chickens at the base of elevators and standing cars. The latter custom accounts for the large number of boys arrested for breaking the seals on grain freight cars. It is easy for a child thus trained to accept the proposition of a junk dealer to bring him bars of iron stored in freight yards. Four boys quite recently had thus carried away and sold to one man, two tons of iron.

Four-fifths of the children brought into the juvenile court in Chicago are the children of foreigners. The Germans are the greatest offenders, Polish next. Do their children suffer from the excess of virtue in those parents so eager to own a house and lot? One often sees a grasping parent in the court, utterly broken down when the Americanized youth who has been brought to grief clings as piteously to his peasant father as if he were still a frightened little boy in the steerage.

Many of these children have come to grief through their premature fling into city life, having thrown off parental control as they have impatiently discarded foreign ways. Boys of ten and twelve will refuse to sleep at home, preferring the freedom of an old brewery vault or an empty warehouse to the obedience required by their parents, and for days these boys will live on the milk and bread which they steal from the back porches after the early morning delivery. Such children complain that there is "no fun" at home. One little chap who was given a vacant lot to cultivate by the City Garden Association, insisted upon raising only popcorn and tried to present the entire crop to Hull House "to be used for the parties," with the stipulation that he

would have "to be invited every single time." Then there are little groups of dissipated young men who pride themselves upon their ability to live without working, and who despise all the honest and sober ways of their immigrant parents. They are at once a menace and a center of demoralization. Certainly the bewildered parents, unable to speak English and ignorant of the city, whose children have disappeared for days or weeks, have often come to Hull House, evincing that agony which fairly separates the marrow from the bone, as if they had discovered a new type of suffering, devoid of the healing in familiar sorrows. It is as if they did not know how to search for the children without the assistance of the children themselves. Perhaps the most pathetic aspect of such cases is their revelation of the premature dependence of the older and wiser upon the young and foolish, which is in itself often responsible for the situation because it has given the children an undue sense of their own importance and a false security that they can take care of themselves.

Americanizing the Poles of Buffalo

59

Americanization has normally been a complex social process for the immigrants, but gradually it was recognized that there was one basic ingredient on which all other factors depended: a higher standard of living. Learning English, getting an education, and understanding American mores were important. But the immigrants found out soon enough that the ability to earn a living successfully was the one thing more than anything else that would gain them acceptance by native-born Americans and guarantee their status as first-class citizens. In this selection, John Daniels, director of the Buffalo Social Survey, analyzed the problems of the large Polish colony in his city as they established themselves in their new homeland. [*Survey,* June 4, 1910: "Americanizing Eighty Thousand Poles."]

Buffalo has the largest Polish colony of any city in America except Chicago. It numbers about 80,000 people. The Poles form a sixth of the entire population. . . . And so a little Poland has grown up in

Buffalo, only it is not so very little. It covers an entire section of East Buffalo, extending a mile and a half east from St. Stanislaus Church, and a mile north and south at its mean width. This section is now almost solidly Polish. There are two small outlying colonies, one to the southeast near the city line and the other at Buffalo's northwest corner. Outside these three localities Poles are extremely scarce; inside of them, extremely numerous. Geographically the Poles are cut off from the rest of the city. They are separated also by difference of language, for they still cling to Polish as the language of common use. They are in the Buffalo community, but they are not of it. They have their own churches, their own stores and business places, their own newspapers. They are content to live alone and be let alone, and the rest of the population generally knows little about them and cares less.

But at last Buffalo is undertaking to deal with the problem of how to make its Poles an active and vital part of the community. . . .

As has been said, few of these immigrants on their arrival in Buffalo have actually been penniless, but few of them have had more than enough to maintain them a few months.

In three of the four savings banks of Buffalo, according to figures furnished by these banks after a thorough inspection of their books, the Poles have today approximately $1.5 million. In the other savings bank, the largest of the four, they have probably about $1 million, making the total $2.5 million.

To get at the facts as to Polish ownership of property, three of the clerks in the assessor's department were employed to go through the last tax books. This task, as well as many other parts of the inquiry, was facilitated by the fact that nearly all the Poles live by themselves in certain districts of the city, and also by the fact that most Polish names are easily recognizable as such. It was found that the Poles own

taxable property of an assessed value of $5,505,890, and nontaxable property, consisting almost entirely of ten church holdings, of an assessed value of $1,533,145, making a total of $7,039,035. The market value of this property may be estimated at close to $12 million. Of course, mortgage indebtedness must be allowed for. Most of the churches have large mortgages. Of the taxable property, about 30 percent is clear of mortgage, and the rest is mortgaged to the extent, on an average, of 50 percent of its market value.

Of this taxable property, the number of vacant lots is only 512, as compared with 4,304 built up. Over 90 percent of the property built up consists of homes. In the case of the great majority of shops and business places, the proprietors live on the premises. These figures surely bear witness to the fact that the Poles are thrifty. As soon as they come here and get work, they try to save, and if they succeed, at the earliest possible moment they make a first payment on a little home. "I find that the Polish citizen," one real estate dealer has written me, "first desires to own a home, and that he and the entire family will bend their entire energies toward the payment for that home, and that it is very, very seldom they lose their property through foreclosure proceedings."

Of shops and various business places, the Poles have about 1,000 in the city, of which nearly 800 are in the one big Polish district in East Buffalo. Most of these places are small, but a few have grown to proportions which would qualify them to compete with other establishments of the same sort in the city at large. The largest business in the city managed by a Pole is the brewery of the Schreiber Brewing Company. Anthony Schreiber, president of the company, is the highest officer of the Polish National Alliance. A. and M. Nowak's grain and feed store and mill, M. A. Cwiklinski's wholesale and retail lumberyard and contracting plant, Stanislaus Lipowicz's wholesale grocery, and M. J. Nowak's plating works stand out prominently. Frank Ruszkiewicz is an enterprising real estate operator, who in the last three years has bought 150 lots, most of which he has already built up and sold. B. Dorasewicz, F. Gorski, and S. S. Nowicki are conspicuously successful dealers in insurance and mortgages. The progress which the Poles have made in a business way should be considered in connection with the fact that most of the immigrants were peasants in the Old Country, with no business experience or aptitude.

The Poles are industrious, thrifty, pertinacious, home-building, family-founding. So they possess many of the qualities fundamental to the best citizenship. With their homes and business places they have built up a large area of the city. These are the things which make them an asset to Buffalo.

But though there are about 5,000 Polish deposits in the savings banks, there are, say, 35,000 heads of families and self-supporting adults who might have deposits. Though there are about 4,000 homes owned, there are over 15,000 families who might be homeowners. It will appear, moreover, that ownership of a home does not necessarily mean that the owner is relieved from a struggle for existence. Though the Poles form a sixth part of the city's population, the value of their taxable property holdings is only 1.8 percent of the value of the taxable property holdings in the city. Though there are 1,000 Polish shops and business places the profits accruing from the great majority of these fall far short of putting their proprietors in the plutocrat class.

The conditions of the great mass of the Poles are sufficiently in need of amelioration.

A very thorough investigation was made concerning Polish laborers and their wages. Letters were sent to 580 of the largest industrial establishments of the city. Seventy percent of the entire number, and 90 percent of the largest, have been heard from. The number of establishments which employ Poles is 221, and the number of Poles employed 14,103, of whom 2,429 are women, and 11,609 are men. Of the women, 84 percent are in factories, and the others in hotels, laundries, junk and rag shops. Of the men, 87 percent are in manufacturing, and 12 percent are employed by railroads, lumberyards, and contractors. It is close to the facts to estimate that the Poles contribute a fifth of the entire labor supply of the city, a fourth of the labor outside of mercantile and clerical lines, and fully a third of the rough labor in manufacturing. They are in Buffalo's elemental industries, and as they are dependent upon these industries for their livelihood, so these industries are vitally dependent upon them for their operation.

The information received by means of the letters mentioned shows that of the men, the great majority of whom are at present or will soon be heads and natural supports of families, 60 percent are common laborers, 30 percent semiskilled, and .3 percent highly skilled; and that 64 percent receive in wages not over $1.75 a day, 32 percent from $1.75 to $2.50, 3.7 percent from $2.50 to $3.50, and .4 percent more than $3.50. The average weekly earnings of those who receive not more than $1.75 a day are $9.60, and of those who receive from $1.75 to $2.50, $13.50. Even if these laborers were to work every weekday in the year on full time, their annual earnings would be but $499 and $702. But there is a great deal of unemployment, and it is if anything below the facts to estimate that, on an average, these laborers are unemployed a quarter of the time. This reduces their yearly earnings to $375 and $525.

In 1908, under the auspices of the Russell Sage Foundation, an investigation was made in Buffalo into the question of what is a living income for a typical laboring family, consisting of wife, husband, and three children. One hundred families, of whom twenty-five were Polish, were studied. The conclusion arrived at was that an income of from $635 to $735 is necessary for such a family to subsist without falling upon charity.

The fact emerges, therefore, that 64 percent of Polish laborers are receiving less by $260, and another 32 percent less by $110 than the minimum yearly wage required for family subsistence. These figures are startling—but they are true.

It does not follow that the families of these laborers are, in consequence, starving to death. But there are certain results which do follow. It does follow that the children are taken out of school at the earliest possible moment and sent to work, and this means the cutting short of their education and the probable impairment of their physical constitution, especially in the case of the girls, who when they marry are often unable, on account of sapped vitality, to nurse their babies. It does follow that wives and mothers, except when family duties and housework absolutely prevent, are compelled to go out to work, to the neglect of home and children. It does follow that there is an excessive falling upon charity—Poles forming over a third of all those assisted by the overseers of the Poor and Charity Organization Society. It does follow that

the temptation to crime, particularly theft, is increased, as is proved by the court records, which show that in 1908, during the hard times, the convictions for stealing were three times as numerous as in the following year when good times returned. And it does follow that the families of these laborers have to huddle together in the smallest possible living space, and in a large proportion of cases have to take boarders. . . .

The measures urged as necessary to ameliorate these conditions and to bring the Poles into the life of the community and raise them up to its level—in brief, to Americanize them—are the following.

To reduce unemployment, which at present works much havoc, an active city employment bureau should be established, whose function should be to receive and register all applications for work and, by keeping in daily touch with employers, to supply work to a maximum number of applicants. As the surest means of raising wages, in the long run, and thus of effecting material betterment, industrial schools should be started. This need has been brought to the attention of the Department of Public Instruction, and Superintendent Emerson has undertaken to establish two such schools in the principal Polish district next fall, as well as another, previously arranged for, in one of the outlying Polish settlements. An efficient system of vocational training, made as practicable as possible, should be worked out, not, of course, to be confined to the Poles, but to cover the entire city, for it is needed badly enough in all quarters. To improve housing conditions, the first step to be taken is more adequate tenement inspection. At this point, too, the city has moved. It has authorized the appointment of six additional inspectors, making the total number nine. As it happens, the health commissioner, Dr. Francis E. Fronczak, is himself a Pole, or rather, a Polish-American of the best type, and he now has the opportunity to render great service both to his racial kinsmen and to his city. A sufficient number of inspectors, constantly going about through the Polish district, will not only enforce the wise provisions of the law, but more important still, will surely educate the Poles to a higher standard of living. But to supplement the good which will thus be accomplished, a general campaign of education in hygienic living should be undertaken by the city, through the Departments of Health and Public Instruction, by means of illustrated lectures, demonstrations, and related methods; by all private societies which are in a position to help; and by the Poles themselves, through their churches, schools, organizations, and newspapers.

These measures will also prove most effective in lessening lawbreaking and criminality. For this purpose, however, there should be combined with them an effort to restrict the number of saloons and, by determined enforcement of the laws, to root out some of the most vicious. Such a movement also would have to and indeed ought to apply to the entire city. Finally, with respect to educational

conditions: first of all, compulsory school attendance should be enforced, both as to children not in school at all and to those who are playing truant; second, the standard of instruction in the parochial schools must be raised, especially in the matter of instruction in English; third, all practicable pressure should be brought to bear upon Polish parents to encourage their children to speak English and keep their children in the public schools as long as they can, and public school facilities, particularly in the form of evening and vacation schools, should be extended. The new School Census Board, to the secretary of which, Charles H. Brown, Jr., the writer is indebted for much assistance, is doing effective work in putting children into school, and 50 percent of all the children put into school up to date have been Polish. Four additional truant officers, one of them a Pole, have recently been appointed, but yet there are by no means a sufficient number. It is to be hoped that steps will be taken to meet the grave needs in the educational situation.

It is a simple question in social economy which is before Buffalo and the Poles in Buffalo today. Will Buffalo make the most of the Poles, and will the Poles make the most of themselves?

A Mixing Bowl for Nations
Ernest Poole

60

The early novels of Chicago-born Ernest Poole had as their theme urban, industrial America. He helped Upton Sinclair gather material for *The Jungle,* the famous 1906 novel of immigrant workers in the meat-packing industry. Poole's best-known work, *The Harbor,* dealt with New York City dock workers. For this selection, Poole visited the ethnic haunts of his native city, especially the coffee shops, for the coffee shop was an Old World institution transplanted to the New. [*Everybody's Magazine,* October 1910.]

Chicago, the greatest industrial city on earth. So say most observers, watching

the stockyards, the steel mills, and Pullman, the sweatshops and factories,

An outdoor market on Maxwell Street, a primarily Jewish area of Chicago, 1906.

foundries, tanneries, harvester works. And they miss the most vital process of all. For if, when the roar of the day's work has subsided, you watch the men, women, and children that pour out of factories, shops, and mills; the Germans and Irish and Scotch, the Swedes, Norwegians, Poles, and Jews, Bohemians, Slovaks, Italians, Greeks; if you follow the human tides to the great foreign quarters of the city, you may be amazed at the scenes you will suddenly enter; opening scenes in a slow but irresistible process, which has for its raw material all the old peoples of Europe, and for a finished product, when at last these shall be fused—a new race of men upon the earth. The Tower of Babel's drama reversed. Chicago a mixing bowl for the nations.

In the Café Acropolis the night had just begun. It was six o'clock. Outside the open doors, on Halsted Street, the crowds were coming home; there was a ceaseless

251

At the turn of the 20th century, the streets of every large city rang with the cries of street peddlers from many countries. The pictures on these two pages were all made on New York City's Lower East Side about 1905. (On facing page, top) A Jewish man selling coat hangers. (On facing page, bottom) An Italian immigrant selling cold drinking water. (Above) Two Italian merchants sell regular and roasted walnuts from their outdoor stall. (Left) A Chinese vendor selling litchi nuts and tea.

An orange vendor on New York's Lower East Side, about 1900.

shuffling tread of feet, and laughing, shouting, talking in a curious babel of tongues. But in here was only Greece. Not a word of English, but a hum of deep, harsh voices from a dozen groups of men, some playing pool in the rear, but most at little round tables, sipping Turkish coffee in small, thick, white cups; reading the *Chronos* (*Times*), an American newspaper printed in Greek; and smoking cigarettes or long Turkish water pipes. Above in festoons hung gay paper ropes of all colors. On one wall, from a gilded picture frame, the Athenian Acropolis looked down; on another, a print of a classic old Parthenon statue, stately and severe, completely ignored its gay neighbor—a gorgeous chromo of Anna Held displaying a new five-cent cigar.

At four of the tables all eyes were intent on the cards.

"Poker?" I suggested, looking for chips.

"No," said the tall, swarthy waiter disdainfully. "Not like it at all. It is a Greek game. You begin. You never want to go. Some time maybe you play all the night."

Here many come to seek news from home. On the wall at one spot were pinned some score of letters, the addresses in strange Greek scrawl. When the postman came in with the evening mail, a half dozen rose and crowded around him, but came back disgusted; except for one chubby-faced man who took a blue letter—also chubby—back to his corner table, and sat complacently smiling down, lighting a fresh cigarette before beginning to read. Stories cluster thick round this rough, simple post office, but of these you can get only hints. There was a boy of eighteen who walked in every night for over six months, never asking for letters, but simply glancing up at the place on the wall—for the missive which never came. On the wall are some envelopes dingy with months of waiting for readers, the stories still hidden inside. And here one night an anxious group of big workmen sat breathing hard over a letter to be sent to a mother in Greece, to say that her son had lost his leg in a tunnel explosion, that by passing the hat in the café for the past five evenings they had collected enough for his passage, and that he would soon start for home.

At some tables faces drew close together scowling, or were thrown far back laughing—over first adventures in America. For this café is a meeting place for Greeks from all over the land. Here stories are told of faraway camps, of the railroads, the mills, and the mines; but more often of South Water Street, near by, the fruit mart of America. For fruit is the Greek's main business field. Thousands peddle it along the city streets, and a few already own big South Water Street stores. . . .

The city is full of contrasts. On any winter's afternoon about five o'clock, in a snug little place far out in the northwest quarter, you may find the Swedish at coffee.

An oasis of comfort is here. Outside, the street is already dark, poorly lighted, cheerless and dirty and gray; the sweatshops lie close around, from the small three-room affairs to the big, whirring factory lofts. In here is a long low room, bare but spotlessly clean, brightly lighted and warm from the stout, crackling stove near the door. Nearby is a counter piled with a tempting assortment of Swedish sweet bread and cakes, just baked, and a tall, bright urn steaming with the fragrance of coffee. Beyond are a score of small tables, each with its prim paper napkins and thick white china cups and plates.

Since half past four the people have been arriving. A few are doctors and lawyers and small shopkeepers; but most are straight from the sweatshops, the more skilled workers—cutters and operators—in their working clothes, some of the men without hats, many of the women with shawls thrown over their heads. For the time is brief; only half an hour here, and then back to the day's last stretch of swift, buzzing labor. Each group, as they enter, choose their sweet bread or cakes at the counter, and then go on to a table. By five the room is full. . . .

Many of the men are reading newspapers. On the wall hang papers just arrived from Stockholm, and Chicago papers in Swedish. One is of a radical tone. About a score of the young unmarried men come regularly for their meals, and here they have long evening discussions.

The proprietor and his wife are strictly religious and will do no business whatever on Sunday; but every Sunday afternoon this room and the one behind it are thrown open to meetings, where all kinds of topics—religious, industrial, political—are seriously discussed.

These people are in the end to be fused with the Greek mountaineers!

For Italian haunts I had a long search. Rich Italian cafés run for American trade—these were easy to find; but the real "Guinney hangouts" seemed lacking; from all quarters came the opinion that "Guinneys love to stay home." But, knowing that great numbers of them have homes only faraway in Italy, and that over a hundred thousand are young, industrial hoboes, moving with railroad and mining and tunnel gangs over the country, I went to the railroad terminal district that lies just south of the business center. And here I found three barrooms for "Guinneys," with real cafés behind.

The Café Torino is run by Tony Carbonato. As I came in, Mr. Carbonato sat in his shirt-sleeves, with some ten jovial, noisy young peasants who were playing cards at two square tables near the bar. He took me into the back room, where a dozen tables were already set for supper, with comfortable old tablecloths and a general air of "Auld Lang Syne." Supper was served for twenty-five cents, including a flask of Chianti. Among the dishes were soup with noodles, a meat stew highly spiced, potatoes and garlic, spaghetti with cheese, and pudding with brandy sauce. . . .

So in Chicago immense Italian quarters have already appeared. It is here that they "love to stay home."

In one such quarter I found a café that had a most hopeless, dismantled, dejected appearance. But a new life was beginning.

The bar, where glasses had so seldom clinked, was now crowded with bottles. The stout bartender, his two boys, his wife, and his little girl sat in a group on the floor, all busily filling more bottles with red and white wine.

"No use," he grunted. "We wait long enough. Nobody come. All stay home. So now we put it in bottles, sell in homes, get rich soon!"

They stay home. But there are many social gatherings; feast day processions and dances and holiday meetings; and sometimes opera, concert, or drama.

Romance and singing, a deep-bred love of beauty, childlike simplicity, hot blood of the south—to be fused at last into the main stock of Chicago's future people!

Late one afternoon, in the course of my ramblings, I had a delightful surprise. There are but a few thousand French in Chicago, and though there are many French cafés where *some of the waiters* are French, I had never hoped that my story might include a real haunt of the café makers.

The street was sooty and noisy and full of business faces. And my eyes were growing weary, when suddenly I spied rising from the dingy sidewalk two jaunty green palms, beneath them one vivid red bench and in front of the bench a tiny red table. I went in.

It was only a common barroom in shape. But the bar held many little French bottles; at the table by the wall sat a Frenchman writing a letter, with cool green absinthe before him; on the wall were many letters from France, and scenes from the old Paris life, and a few grotesque cartoons.

From the French bartender I learned how a shrewd, industrious saloonkeeper had become a *café propriétaire,* and how homesick Frenchmen had come eagerly flocking in. The back of the place was filled with tables; and so was an inner room, where three tables pulled close together told of last night's convivial crowd. This little inner room was gay with cartoons and rough pencil sketches. A piano stood in one corner, with music piled on top. Here some twenty-five boon companions gather regularly for *déjeuner* at noon, again for dinner in the evening. And here are songs and memories of old Paris—and fervent hopes that "Bohemian" Americans will not crowd in to spoil it.

The real Bohemian café, when at last I found it on a dirty tenement street far out in the southwest part of the city, was a large, square room that seemed double its size, so low was the ceiling. I came in to supper at seven o'clock, when the evening had just begun. A few spruce youngsters, probably clerks, were playing billiards in shirt-sleeves at two tables in the rear. Around the walls, at small tables, sat men of all ages, from young Czechs in their teens to three white-headed old chums who sat together peacefully smoking their pipes, with looks on their faces that were a disgrace to tense, hardheaded, rushing Chicago. All degrees of prosperity were here. Men with good clothes and assured demeanor sat close to men who, from the looks of their clothes and hands, might have come from the neighboring stockyards, where thousands of Czechs are employed. The general air was of prosperity; for the Czechs, working hard in factories, shops, and big stores, and even in office buildings, get ahead faster than all the more recent immigrant races—only excepting the Jews.

But they are slow to forget Bohemia. Around me I heard not a word of English, but only the low, deep, guttural hum of the Czechish tongue, which they proudly claim is the richest language on earth: in its beauty, its fine shades of meaning, its power and rhythm. And truly it has a strange fascination—this speech that for hundreds of years, outlawed by the Teutons, has had to fight for its very life, and has only lately won back its freedom. As you listen, it is easy to imagine wild gorges, old castles, and desperate struggles for liberty. The castles were there, in dusky pictures on the walls: old, gray, ruined, turreted affairs perched high on rocky cliffs; and there were romantic scenes of patriots round bivouac fires in mountain glens. And close beside these dusky old scenes was a brand new, flaring American poster, entitled "Hurdle Automobiles in the White City at Night." . . .

And when I left, four hours later, a big man with heavy black beard and blue eyes still sat at the piano. He had no sheets of music before him. But the tables were still crowded with listeners. He would go on, I was told, until one or two in the morning. His music was full of Bohemian dreams and longings, disappointments, despair, the old feeling of struggling upward in the dark. And as he played men kept turning round from the cards; laughing groups grew suddenly silent, eyes following smoke wreaths or staring into the memories far away. Because he felt the Old Country—this big man who was playing.

It was here that Kubelik came one night, fresh from his downtown triumphs. Downtown he won thousands of dollars and much hearty applause. But it was here, in the little Czech theater close overhead, the Chicago home of Bohemian music and drama, that Kubelik played his best. And late at night, when at last the audience, even standing and kneeling in the aisles, would consent that he put up

Children in front of a Polish saloon in Chicago, 1903.

his fiddle, he came down here. And then this place was packed tight with men and boys standing and sitting on tables and chairs—until three o'clock, when they carried him on their shoulders out to his automobile.

The Czechs are to be our kindred!

Even more prosperous than the Czechs, and by far the most intellectual of all the latest comers are the Russian Jews.

When they come, they are deeply, intensely religious. Late one autumn night, over in the ghetto, I found a little café transformed for the week into a synagogue, packed with men and women,

258

close and stifling. It was the eve of the last day of Atonement Week. These people believed that in the great Book of Doom, before the judgment seat of Jehovah, their sins and good deeds for the year had all been entered; and now, before the Book should be sealed on the morrow, there was still the chance for redemption by deep contrition, fasting, and prayer. In the dimly lighted room they stood in rows: the men in front, wearing their prayer shawls; the women behind. And all faced the holy ark, before which a man in priestly garb bowed continually as he chanted. This constant, monotonous bowing you could see all through the room, and from every corner the low, repentant chanting was heard. Now and then you heard sobs from the women's quarter.

I watched one tall, bony elder with great, snowy beard; the light shone full on his face; and, as he prayed, the tears welled in his deep, sunken eyes, trickling slowly down his broad cheeks.

All at once the prayer rose to a wail—high, loud, beseeching. And now all the dark faces, tense and haggard from fasting and excitement, seemed in a very ecstasy of remorse and supplication. Almost fanaticism: the same that in Russia for hundreds of years has survived the countless legal persecutions, the massacres secretly planned by the high police of the czars.

Most of the men here were old. Among the young in Chicago the ancient religion is changing into more liberal form, or passing away. . . .

Just as the Germans and the Irish, coming in huge waves decades ago, have toiled slowly up into the skilled work of our industries and have united by thousands with the American-born, so the Poles, coming now into the vast fields of unskilled labor, are slowly pushing up, leaving Italians behind them; and already the uppermost stratum is beginning to fuse with the native stock. In the stockyards for some two months I watched the lowermost strata, the beginners in the slow climbing process.

One Saturday night on Whisky Row, from a hall up over a Polish saloon café, came such shouts and laughter and squeaking of fiddles that I went up the steep stairs and entered.

"Just a weddin'," said the stout Irish policeman, who stood in one corner complacently taking it in. Around the walls stood and sat some 200 of all ages, from the white-headed old woman across the room to the wee, chubby grandchild that stolidly slept in her lap. On the floor were a dozen couples whirling and stamping, some laughing, others as though their very lives depended on the power of each stamp. From the platform the little orchestra was playing fast and hard, repeating the same short, rhythmic squeak over and over.

The week's long grind in the stockyards, the worries, the anxious planning to save up for a cottage home—all were forgotten. Each time the fiddles resumed their frenzy, the whirling and stamping and laughing began as though it were eight o'clock instead of twelve. Only the babies were silent and dignified—sound asleep.

It is true that at one end of the room, at the little bar, the barkeeper was kept hard at work. Couples were continually crowding up before him. But the drink was only light beer.

"Only two drunks," said the cop, "and we fired 'em both downstairs. These people ain't here for that kind of a time."

Over in one corner stood the bride, a husky young girl of perhaps eighteen, dressed in traditional white with a meager veil cheerfully doing its best to flutter and flow in the breeze from the window. She sat by her mother. Her broad, rather dull face was rosy now and glowing. She breathed deep, smiling to herself, now glancing at the coarse white roses in her lap, now at the dancers, now at her brand new husband, a tall, thin Pole who stood stiff and awkward, but grinning with delight. When a man came over and seized her hand, she bounced up with a quick laugh. And then came new excitement.

For every male guest is expected to ask the bride to dance; and, to defray wedding expenses, the price of each dance is $1.00. On the floor is a thick white plate, upon which the guest may throw his coin with all his force, and if he breaks it his money is returned. But whether from the generous caution of the guests or the thickness of the plate provided by the bride's discreet mamma, this accident rarely happens. And often, if the bride be a belle and the groom a good fellow, the sum amounts to $200 or even $300—with enough left over to furnish the new American home which is to begin on the morrow.

New homes, new music and dancing, new energy, new vital hopes are here. For it is the lustiest youth, the very bone and sinew of Poland, that is now crowding in, to help make the new race of the future.

And so it is with the Lithuanians, Hungarians, and Slovaks—huge, healthy peasants, the best of raw material. Scattered over the city far and wide, there are little cafés and back rooms of saloons, there are churches and schools and society rooms, where you may catch glimpses of all these peoples. Bewildering glimpses they are, and you wonder how all are ever to be fused in the common stock. Until you think of the Germans and Irish. Into

what corners of industry, business, professions, and politics have these two races not reached! The intermarriages how common, and how wholesome the result!

Off under the trees, in a big, cool, quiet beer garden, the band is playing just now something dreamy and low. And here it is good to smoke and dream of a future race—or indeed a future anything. All around you in family groups are Teutons young and old. And half-Teutons, too, for in many groups the son-in-law or the daughter-in-law is plainly "pure Chicagoan" (if such a phrase be possible); and the wee grandchildren, who speak both English and German, make one more step in the slow growth from the old Yankee stock.

"But all this was done before," the reader may object. "The thirteen colonies long ago went through the whole mixing business. That's how we were made."

So we were; but the same mixing business is now to be repeated on a scale tenfold more tremendous. And not only this: the races to be mixed are infinitely farther apart in climatic and racial differences. And not only this: for as all things under heaven move faster now than at any other age since the flood, so this mixing is to be done not slowly as before, in quiet, scattered farming communities, but in vast human hives called cities and factory towns, at a speed which even in our lifetime seems certain to produce changes dramatic and deep in the city life of the nation.

Now it is just beginning. The greatest of all immigration waves has come only in the past twenty years; and its ten millions of immigrants—the Italians, Bohemians, Jews, and Poles, the Swedes, Norwegians, and Greeks—are only beginning to form first blood ties with the peoples who have come here before them.

The Case for Trade Schools

61

The following article is from the Chicago Polish-language newspaper *Narod Polski,* of October 5, 1910. It was written at a time when trade schools and various institutions for vocational training were coming into prominence. A number of leading educators had advocated the combining of mechanical training with the high school curriculum, because most high school students, especially from poorer and immigrant families, went to work in factories or shops as soon as it was practicable. Many children, of course, never saw the inside of a high school at all, because their earnings were needed at home, or because what was taught at school seemed irrelevant to what they would be doing in adult life. Immigrants often found themselves in a dilemma: they could use the money their children earned; but they also knew that education was the sure road to Americanization and prosperity, for their children if not for themselves. [Chicago Foreign Language Press Survey, WPA Project, 1942.]

The school is an institution about which we can write and discuss continually. It constitutes a never exhausted subject for pedagogues, psychologists, medics, historians, and critics, because it is the main source and foundation of our national life.

As is the school, so is the nation; or the nation is just like its school, that is, the eyes of all of us are turned toward it and it constitutes a subject of general interest.

It is not our intention to make a long description of our parochial or public schools, but we wish to call your attention to a certain school problem about which we also should start to think.

In our numerous settlements we have magnificent school buildings in which,

Immigrant children in a New York industrial school, about 1900.

Museum of the City of New York; Jacob A. Riis Collection

besides the elementary education, trades can also be taught, as it is in France, Germany, Switzerland, Sweden, and America. Those schools are considered a very important factor in the physical and mental development, and constitute a means to livelihood.

Trade schools develop energy in the highest degree; they educate the aesthetic sense, teach systematic work, the value of time, and inspire ambition.

Our youth leave school too soon and start working too early in factories, doing the lowest kind of work and receiving very little for their work, with no chance for advancement.

If our schools in large cities would teach trade, our young men would be able to secure positions as foremen, which is very important today in America. The foremen hire and discharge men in factories; they keep those whom they like and make it easier for them. Many of them, as you know, discriminate against Polish workers. They tease and annoy our workers.

A young man who has experience in any trade has a better chance and is not obliged to be a slave of any foreman. As a proof, we submit the following case.

A certain Polish mechanic, well acquainted with American mechanical technique, applied for a position to the owner of the factory, from whom he secured an order for a position. The foreman of the shop gave him a suspicious look, took the slip of paper from him, and sent him to the corner. The young man, very much humiliated, rolled up his sleeves and started to work, disregarding the humiliation. After a few days, a foreman, seeing that the young man did not pay much attention to him, told him to go home. A little while later the owner of the shop happened to be in the shop and asked the foreman about the young man. The foreman, without even thinking, replied that the young man was no good and that he had let him go. The owner did not believe the story told him by the foreman. Returning to the office, he was surprised to see the young man who had been discharged by the foreman.

After a short conference, the owner took the young man back to the factory and instructed the foreman not to discharge that young man any more. You can imagine how the young man felt. However, this condition did not last very long. Today the young man, who was discharged for being no good, is a foreman in that factory and a first hand of the owner. Right now that firm employs many workers of Polish nationality.

The foregoing story is related here for the purpose of showing that the owners themselves do not discriminate against Polish employees if they distinguish themselves by possessing some ability. At present there is plenty of so-called manpower or common laborers, but there is a shortage of so-called skilled labor.

If our schools would teach all kinds of trades and supply factories with skilled workers, we would undoubtedly profit materially and morally.

While it is true that such a school is a very expensive proposition, it is also true that in the end it would pay for itself for the parents, and later on pupils themselves would pay for it.

Graduates of such schools are not obliged to look for employment, for the manufacturers themselves will look for them and offer them positions. Perhaps, instead of building more colleges, it would be advisable to build more trade schools, especially in large cities. Also those parochial schools which have plenty of space and funds should teach trades.

The Importance of Citizenship

62

In spite of the pessimistic tone of the editorial reprinted below, Poles in America were becoming citizens and they were certainly intent on staying in the United States. The process of naturalization was always slower for the first generation of those who came speaking a different language. Many of them did envision the day when they would return to the Old Country and live among old friends and family. But it was only a vision; as their children grew up and became Americanized, the first generation came to realize that it did have roots in America. Even so, it was no easy matter for men and women in their mature years to go through all the procedures required for naturalization. This editorial is from the Polish-language paper *Dziennik Zwiazkowy,* November 17, 1911. [Chicago Foreign Language Press Survey, WPA Project, 1942.]

The negligence of the Poles about accepting American citizenship is absolutely incredible. These people are obviously afraid to renounce allegiance to the governments of the czar, the Prussians, or the Austrians, as though they liked these governments better than the government of the free American republic. Our country, Poland, certainly will not condemn any of her sons because they have renounced allegiance to the brutal governments of our oppressors in order to accept citizenship under the Star-Spangled Banner, the symbol of freedom and human rights. Being a citizen of the United States does not in the least prevent us from loving our mother country or from working for her interests, and by becoming citizens of the United States we can accomplish a great deal for Poland through the influence we can exert on this nation's policies.

There is much shouting that the Poles are discriminated against, because they cannot get their people into higher political offices. But why is this so? Few people ever discuss the real reason. We make an impression in some cities because of our large numbers, but if we were to determine how many Poles in these large groups are citizens, we would have to blush to our very ears with shame.

Naturally, if this large group of Poles was composed of citizens of this country—or even if a majority of the Poles were citizens—then surely our people would attain higher offices; they would be shown greater respect by other nationalities, and would not expose themselves to scorn and sneers. Often we gather in great crowds at political meetings, but in these crowds one could count on one's fingers the Poles who are citizens.

In Chicago, for instance, it is said that there are about 300,000 Poles. Out of this number we should have about 100,000 citizens, whereas, actually, who knows whether there are even 40,000? The same situation, if not a worse one, holds true in other cities; therefore, it is not surprising that we stand so low on the political ladder, since we do not look after our own interests.

To complain about our alleged lack of solidarity, and to inveigh against the manner in which we are misrepresented and ignored by other nationalities, will not help in the least as long as we do not try to obtain citizenship and do not take an active part in the political life of this country. If there were only twice as many citizens among us as there are now, we would be found occupying our deserved position in politics; we would then achieve solidarity, because we would have the strength of numbers on our side. At present, since we lack this strength, many Poles who are citizens must ask favors of other nationalities, because they cannot expect much aid from their own people.

But we must be concerned with more than political recognition; we must not run the risk, by remaining aliens, of giving the citizens here a valid reason for scorning us and treating us like parasites. Furthermore, if we are aliens, the United States government cannot assure us its protection when we travel beyond the borders of this country, and upon our return it is not obliged to readmit us.

An alien is looked upon here as unnecessary ballast, to be thrown overboard at the first opportunity. Therefore, he who considers his own welfare, and looks into the future, should become a citizen of the United States.

The Promise of Free Education
Mary Antin

63

Mary Antin was one of the most eloquent supporters of the new immigration. Her memorable book *They Who Knock at Our Gates,* published in 1914, attempted to eradicate the artificial line drawn between native Americans and immigrants. She saw all Americans as immigrants of one generation or another, whether they had landed at Plymouth Rock or Castle Garden. She herself was brought to the United States from Russian Poland as a teenager in 1894. In the portion of her autobiography reprinted here, she tells of her first encounter with the public school system. [*The Promised Land.* Boston, 1912. Chapter 9.]

Our initiation into American ways began with the first step on the new soil. My father found occasion to instruct or correct us even on the way from the pier to Wall Street, which journey we made crowded together in a rickety cab. He told us not to lean out of the windows, not to point, and explained the word "greenhorn." We did not want to be "greenhorns," and gave the strictest attention to my father's instructions. . . .

The first meal was an object lesson of much variety. My father produced several kinds of food, ready to eat, without any cooking, from little tin cans that had printing all over them. He attempted to introduce us to a queer, slippery kind of fruit, which he called "banana," but had to give it up for the time being. After the meal, he had better luck with a curious piece of furniture on runners, which he called "rocking chair." There were five of us newcomers, and we found five different ways of getting into the American machine of perpetual motion, and as many ways of getting out of it. One born and bred to the use of a rocking chair cannot imagine how ludicrous people can make themselves when attempting to use it for the first time. We laughed immoderately over our various experiments with the novelty, which was a wholesome way of letting off steam after the unusual excitement of the day.

In our flat we did not think of such a thing as storing the coal in the bathtub. There was no bathtub. So in the evening of the first day my father conducted us to the public baths. As we moved along in a little procession, I was delighted with the illumination of the streets. So many lamps, and they burned until morning, my father said, and so people did not need to carry lanterns. In America, then, everything was free, as we had heard in Russia. Light was free; the streets were as bright as a synagogue on a holy day. Music was free; we had been serenaded, to our gaping delight, by a brass band of many pieces, soon after our installation on Union Place.

Education was free. That subject my father had written about repeatedly, as comprising his chief hope for us children, the essence of American opportunity, the treasure that no thief could touch, not even misfortune or poverty. It was the one thing that he was able to promise us when he sent for us; surer, safer than bread or shelter. On our second day I was thrilled with the realization of what this freedom of education meant. A little girl from across the alley came and offered to conduct us to school. My father was out, but we five between us had a few words of English by this time.

We knew the word "school." We understood. This child, who had never seen us till yesterday, who could not pronounce our names, who was not much better dressed than we, was able to offer us the freedom of the schools of Boston! No application made, no questions asked, no examinations, rulings, exclusions; no machinations, no fees. The doors stood open for every one of us. The smallest child could show us the way.

This incident impressed me more than anything I had heard in advance of the freedom of education in America. It was a concrete proof—almost the thing itself. One had to experience it to understand it.

It was a great disappointment to be told by my father that we were not to enter upon our school career at once. It was too near the end of the term, he said, and we were going to move to Crescent Beach in a week or so. We had to wait until the opening of the schools in September. What a loss of precious time—from May till September! . . .

The apex of my civic pride and personal contentment was reached on the bright September morning when I entered the public school. That day I must always remember, even if I live to be so old that I cannot tell my name. To most people their first day at school is a memorable occasion. In my case the importance of the day was a hundred times magnified, on account of the years I had waited, the road I had come, and the conscious ambitions I entertained.

I am wearily aware that I am speaking in extreme figures, in superlatives. I wish I knew some other way to render the mental life of the immigrant child of reasoning age. I may have been ever so much an exception in acuteness of observation, powers of comparison, and abnormal self-consciousness; nonetheless were my thoughts and conduct typical of the attitude of the intelligent immigrant child toward American institutions. And what the child thinks and feels is a reflection of the hopes, desires, and purposes of the parents who brought him overseas, no matter how precocious and independent the child may be. Your immigrant inspectors will tell you what poverty the foreigner brings in his baggage, what want in his pockets. Let the overgrown boy of twelve, reverently drawing his letters in the baby class, testify to the noble dreams and high ideals that may be hidden beneath the greasy caftan of the immigrant. Speaking for the Jews, at least, I know I am safe in inviting such an investigation. . . .

And when the momentous day arrived and the little sister and I stood up to be arrayed, it was Frieda herself who patted and smoothed my stiff calico; who made me turn round and round to see that I was perfect; who stooped to pull out a disfiguring basting thread. If there was

Jewish boy wearing his prayer shawl during Jewish New Year in New York City, 1911.

anything in her heart besides sisterly love and pride and goodwill, as we parted that morning, it was a sense of loss and a woman's acquiescence in her fate; for we had been close friends, and now our ways would lie apart. Longing she felt, but no envy. She did not grudge me what she was denied. . . .

The two of us stood a moment in the

doorway of the tenement house on Arlington Street, that wonderful September morning when I first went to school. It was I that ran away, on winged feet of joy and expectation; it was she whose feet were bound in the treadmill of daily toil. And I was so blind that I did not see that the glory lay on her, and not on me.

Father himself conducted us to school. He would not have delegated that mission to the President of the United States. He had awaited the day with impatience equal to mine, and the visions he saw as he hurried us over the sun-flecked pavements transcended all my dreams. Almost his first act on landing on American soil, three years before, had been his application for naturalization. He had taken the remaining steps in the process with eager promptness, and at the earliest moment allowed by the law, he became a citizen of the United States. It is true that he had left home in search of bread for his hungry family, but he went blessing the necessity that drove him to America. The boasted freedom of the New World meant to him far more than the right to reside, travel, and work wherever he pleased; it meant the freedom to speak his thoughts, to throw off the shackles of superstition, to test his own fate, unhindered by political or religious tyranny. He was only a young man when he landed—thirty-two; and most of his life he had been held in leading strings. He was hungry for his untasted manhood.

Three years passed in sordid struggle and disappointment. He was not prepared to make a living even in America, where the day laborer eats wheat instead of rye. Apparently the American flag could not protect him against the pursuing nemesis of his limitations; he must expiate the sins of his fathers who slept across the seas. He had been endowed at birth with a poor constitution, a nervous, restless temperament, and an abundance of hindering prejudices. In his boyhood his body was starved, that his mind might be stuffed with useless learning. In his youth this dearly gotten learning was sold, and the price was the bread and salt which he had not been trained to earn for himself. Under the wedding canopy he was bound for life to a girl whose features were still strange to him; and he was bidden to multiply himself, that sacred learning might be perpetuated in his sons, to the glory of the God of his fathers. All this while he had been led about as a creature without a will, a chattel, an instrument.

In his maturity he awoke, and found himself poor in health, poor in purse, poor in useful knowledge, and hampered on all sides. At the first nod of opportunity he broke away from his prison and strove to atone for his wasted youth by a life of useful labor; while at the same time he sought to lighten the gloom of his narrow scholarship by freely partaking of modern ideas. But his utmost endeavor still left him far from his goal. In business, nothing prospered with him. Some fault of hand or mind or temperament led him to failure where other men found success. Wherever the blame for his disabilities be placed, he reaped their bitter fruit. "Give me bread!" he cried to America. "What will you do to earn it?" the challenge came back. And he found that he was master of no art, of no trade; that even his precious learning was of no avail, because he had only the most antiquated methods of communicating it.

So in his primary quest he had failed. There was left him the compensation of intellectual freedom. That he sought to realize in every possible way. He had very little opportunity to prosecute his education, which, in truth, had never been begun. His struggle for a bare living left him no time to take advantage of the public evening school; but he lost nothing of what was to be learned through reading, through attendance at public meetings, through exercising the rights of citizenship. Even here he was hindered by a natural inability to acquire the English language. In time, indeed, he learned to read, to follow a conversation or lecture; but he never learned to write correctly, and his pronunciation remains extremely foreign to this day.

If education, culture, the higher life were shining things to be worshiped from afar, he had still a means left whereby he could draw one step nearer to them. He could send his children to school, to learn all those things that he knew by fame to be desirable. The common school, at least, perhaps high school; for one or two, perhaps even college! His children should be students, should fill his house with books and intellectual company, and thus he would walk by proxy in the Elysian Fields of liberal learning. As for the children themselves, he knew no surer way to their advancement and happiness.

So it was with a heart full of longing and hope that my father led us to school on that first day. He took long strides in his eagerness, the rest of us running and hopping to keep up.

At last the four of us stood around the teacher's desk; and my father, in his impossible English, gave us over in her charge, with some broken word of his hopes for us that his swelling heart could no longer contain.

Instructions on Naturalization

64

Naturalization and Americanization are not the same thing. It is quite possible to participate in one and not the other. The distinction was frequently blurred, however, during the early years of the drive to assimilate the immigrants. In the minds of some native Americans and immigrants alike, to follow the formal procedural steps toward citizenship was tantamount to becoming an American in every sense. But in reality, many newcomers were fully Americanized long before they got their second papers; while the spirit of others remained in the Old World, even after the certificate of citizenship was in hand. This selection describes the procedures of naturalization. It is taken from an instruction book for aliens written by two San Jose, California, attorneys, R. K. O'Neil and G. K. Estes. [*Naturalization Made Easy,* 4th edition. San Francisco, 1913. Pages 9–16.]

FIRST PAPER

If you wish to become a citizen of the United States, and you now belong to a nationality or race entitled to citizenship in this country, and have not taken out your first paper, called Declaration of Intention, you must go before the clerk of the superior court, or other court having jurisdiction where you reside, and tell him that you wish to take out your first paper. He will then fill out for you a blank form, according to the answers which you will give to questions which he will ask you, and when it is completed you will have to sign your name to the paper and two copies of it, and swear to it, if the contents of the paper are correct. He will then give you a copy of the paper, charging you $1.00, and will send the other copy to the department at Washington. This paper is your Declaration of Intention, and in it you declare your intention to become a citizen of the United States, and to renounce forever all allegiance and fidelity to any foreign prince, potentate, state, or sovereignty, and particularly by name to the prince, potentate, state, or sovereignty of which you happen to be at the time a citizen or subject; and you also set forth your name, age, occupation, personal description, that is, your color, whether white or otherwise, the color of

your eyes and hair, your complexion and your height, and any visible distinguishing marks, the place of your birth, your last foreign residence and allegiance, the date of your arrival in the United States, and the name of the vessel, if any, in which you came, and your present place of residence. It is particularly important that you know the name of the vessel, if any, in which you came and the date of its arrival.

In order that you may take out these citizenship papers, you must belong to the white race, or be of African nativity or of African descent, as no aliens of other races are permitted to become citizens of the United States, and you must be eighteen years of age or over. You may take out this first paper immediately upon your arrival in the United States, and you are not required to sign it in your own handwriting, if you are not able to do so.

Not less than two years nor more than seven years after taking out this first paper, provided you have reached the age of twenty-one years, you may take out your second, or final paper, called Certificate of Naturalization, entitling you to all the rights of a citizen of this country. In order to do this, you must have been five years in the United States, continuously, and at least one year immediately preceding the date of the filing of your petition in the state, territory, or district in which your application is made, and have taken out your first paper at least two years before. If your first paper was taken out on or after June 29, 1906, you must make and file your application for your final paper within seven years after the date of your first paper, or you will have to begin over and take out your first paper again. If your first paper was taken out before June 29, 1906, you should make your application for your final paper before June 29, 1913, as the government seems inclined to construe the second paragraph of Section 4 of the present law to mean that those who took out their first papers before June 29, 1906, must make their final application within seven years after that date.

Under Section 4 of the Naturalization Act, as amended June 25, 1910, certain persons are permitted to become naturalized without proof of former declaration of intention on their part to become a citizen of the United States.

SECOND PAPER

When you wish to get your final paper, you must apply to the clerk of the court, as before—it need not be in the same city or the same state, so long as it is in the United States, and you can produce your witnesses—and make your Petition for Naturalization, bringing with you your first paper and at least two witnesses who are citizens of the United States and who have known you for at least one year in the state or territory where you make application, and as much longer in the United States as possible; it will be necessary by these witnesses, or by these witnesses and the depositions of other witnesses taken in the manner hereinafter indicated, to prove your residence in the United States for a period of at least five years continuously, and of the state, territory, or district in which you make your petition for a period of at least one year immediately preceding the date of the filing of your petition, and that they each have personal knowledge that you are a person of good moral character and qualified in their opinion to be admitted a citizen of the United States.

It is not necessary, however, that you should prove your residence in the United States for the entire period of five years by any two certain witnesses. So long as there are at least two credible witnesses testifying as to each fraction of the period, so as to cover the whole, the statutory requirement is satisfied.

It is important in selecting your witnesses that you choose persons who are permanent residents of your locality, and who are thus likely to be on hand when you need them at the hearing of your petition as hereinafter indicated, as you will be required to produce these same witnesses at the hearing or give some good reason why you have not done so, and if you should have to produce new witnesses it may cause delay. The law provides that in case your original witnesses "cannot be produced" upon the hearing other witnesses may be summoned, but it is not intended by this provision that witnesses may be changed for light or trivial cause, but only where the original witnesses cannot be produced by the ordinary process of subpoena, as in case of death, or sickness, or removal from the county. The burden is upon you to satisfy the court that your original witnesses, or either of them, cannot be produced, and, if any suspicion arises, the court may postpone the hearing, and give the government time in which to investigate the matter. It was formerly held that substitute witnesses should be permitted only after the names of such witnesses had been posted for ninety days in the same manner as the names of original witnesses, but these decisions have been overruled by later ones and the present rulings seem to be as above stated.

It is also important that you should choose witnesses who are qualified, as if either of your original witnesses should prove at the hearing not to be a citizen, or not to have known you for the full time stated in his affidavit to your petition continuously, your petition will be dismissed.

The clerk will first collect from you the customary fee of $4.00, and will then take and file your first paper, and will ask you a number of questions, and will put your answers upon the blank form which he will furnish, and when this is completed you will sign your name to the paper and one copy, and swear to the contents of the paper before the clerk; and your two witnesses must swear that they have known you for a certain length of time in the United States and for at least one year in the state, territory, or district, and that you have a good character and will make a good citizen, as above indicated.

If you have arrived in the United States on or after June 29, 1906, it will be necessary for you to file with the clerk, in addition to your first paper, a certificate from the Department of Commerce and Labor. This certificate is not being furnished to immigrants as they land, but will be furnished to such as subsequently seek naturalization upon application therefor. You should send for this certificate at least a month before making your application to the clerk in order that the department at Washington may have time to send it. You can probably obtain a form for this application and full instructions in regard to it from the clerk of the court where you intend to file your petition.

The clerk will then instruct you to come back into court with your two witnesses and be examined by the judge on a day which he will then set, and which must be at least ninety days from the day when you make and file your petition, but must not be within thirty days preceding the holding of any general election within the territorial jurisdiction of the court.

Should you wish to subpoena your witnesses in order to be sure of having them in court at the proper time, the clerk will issue a subpoena for this purpose upon receiving from you a sum of money sufficient to cover the expenses of subpoenaing and paying the legal fees of the witnesses; but usually it will not be necessary to have your witnesses subpoenaed. If it is going to be necessary for you to have depositions taken to supplement the testimony of your resident witnesses, this should be attended to at once, and the department at Washington notified immediately of the fact, so that you will have the depositions ready to produce at the hearing. Blank forms for the taking of these depositions are furnished by the government and can be procured from the clerk at the time of filing your petition.

Upon the day thus appointed for the hearing of your petition, you must come into court and bring your witnesses with you. You will take the witness stand and be sworn, and the judge or the United States attorney will ask you a number of questions to see whether you know enough about the country and its institutions, etc., and whether you are a good enough person, and have been long enough in the country, to become a citizen. He will also examine your witnesses about you, as to what kind of a person you are, and how long they have known you, and how long you have been in the

United States, and he will also examine any depositions which you may produce, and if the judge is satisfied that you have been long enough in this country, and that your character is good, and that you know enough about the country, etc., he will admit you as a citizen; otherwise he will deny your application.

Before admitting you to citizenship, the judge will require you to declare on oath in open court that you will support the Constitution of the United States, and that you absolutely and entirely renounce and adjure all allegiance and fidelity to any foreign prince, potentate, state, or sovereignty, and particularly by name the prince, potentate, state, or sovereignty of which you have been a citizen or subject, and that you will support and defend the Constitution and the laws of the United States against all enemies, foreign and domestic, and bear true faith and allegiance to the same.

He will then sign the order admitting you as a citizen, and the clerk will make out your Certificate of Naturalization and hand it to you, and will send a duplicate of it to the department at Washington.

When you receive this certificate, you will then be an American citizen, and be entitled to all the rights and privileges of a citizen.

The Bookworms of New York

65

All immigrants desired an education, but few pursued it with the avidity of the Russian Jews of New York City. The public schools and colleges, the settlement houses, and the libraries were crammed with eager students who rightly gauged advancement in terms of education. Other nationalities, too, strongly favored learning, but for some the necessity of work stood in the way: the whole family would work to make it possible for one member to get through high school and into college. Many Jewish families varied the pattern; work became a stepping-stone for all members of a family to get through school if they wanted to. This article by Carl W. Ackerman portrays the eagerness with which New York City's immigrants used the public libraries. [*Independent*, January 23, 1913.]

Abe Martin, the quaint Hoosier philosopher, says, "Cheer up! What if you wuz a worm an' had t' live in a wild crab apple?" The immigrants who land in New York have found the answer to this conundrum; eat the fruit and crawl out.

For the first year or two they live huddled together in tenements on Manhattan. During that time they learn English, read thousands of books on science, philosophy, and economics, as well as classical literature, and save enough money to move to the suburbs.

Some weeks ago the librarian of the Seward Park branch of the New York Public Library, which stands on the business thoroughfare of the Russian ghetto, investigated the addresses of fifty readers of three years' standing. The names were picked at random from the card index and only one still lived in that community.

Once on New York soil the most persistent work of the foreigner is self-education. His appetite for knowledge is more insatiate than that of the seminary student in the university. This is shown by the records of eight of the forty branches of the public library. During 1912 approximately 53 percent of all books circulated from these centers were nonfiction, and of the 47 percent of fiction more than

Peddlers in front of a movie theater, New York, 1915.

half were the works of Dickens, Thackeray, Scott, Dumas, Shaw, and Tolstoi. Modern fiction—the "best sellers"—remain dusty on the shelves. And these eight libraries are tucked between fire-escape facades of the tenements in Poverty's Pocket of the metropolis.

The Bowery, at one time famous as the society street of the city, is now the toboggan down which the derelicts coast from the Tenderloin. Chatham Square is the end or "jumping-off" place. Yet last October the library in this community circulated 12,281 books; of these 5,860 were fiction. A record of 493 books read daily—and only 196 of them fiction. Of course, it is not the castaways who do the reading, but their neighbors, the aggressive, eager Russians, Rumanians, Greeks, Italians, and Hungarians.

A stout, deep-eyed, dark-complexioned Russian came to the librarian of the Seward Park branch several years ago and asked for books on advanced chemistry. He had read all those available through the library, but lacked enough money to buy the more expensive and technical volumes. His request was similar to those she had frequently heard and she as often had been compelled to refuse. She knew the young man, however, and in a few days interested a chemist from one of the large manufacturing concerns of the city.

In the spirit of adventure this man climbed the stairs of a narrow Canal Street tenement and knocked at the door of an attic room. When the Russian admitted him the visitor stood at the threshold dumbfounded. He thought he was calling at the "bunk" of an immigrant. Instead he walked into a shabby but fully equipped chemical laboratory, hidden under the rafters of a five-story building.

Here was a young man who had been banished from Odessa because he was a Jew. He had sought political and religious freedom in the United States and did his first work in a sweatshop. From there he went to a clothing store, and in the evening tutored himself with public books. The few dollars he could save he spent for instruments.

Not many days after this meeting he was supplied with the latest books. He then passed the Regents' examinations and now is professor of chemistry in a Brooklyn institute.

Preceding the recent presidential campaign the demand for books on political economy, trusts, finance, and the tariff could not be supplied by these eight libraries. During the Dickens celebration

500 volumes of the author's works were inadequate in one branch alone. There are times when 100 copies of *David Copperfield*, in another library, do not meet the needs. Woodrow Wilson's *The State* is in constant demand. So are the books of William James, Henri Bergson, and Professor Tausig.

By far the larger percent of books read by these foreigners are printed in English. At the Hamilton Fish branch, of 25,000 volumes only 1,800 are printed in other languages. The 22,740 volumes in the Chatham Square library are divided into 19,541 of English; 1,211, Yiddish; 680, Russian; 444, Italian; 434, German; 199,

Jewish boy at work in New York's garment district, about 1916.

Brown Brothers

Chinese; 144, modern Greek, and 87, French. The proportions vary in other libraries, the number of each depending upon the percent of population in that locality which reads. The average is about one book in a foreign tongue out of every ten in English.

Formerly the boundaries between the different nationalities in Manhattan were as distinct as those dividing European countries. Today these lines are gradually being erased. The Russians are invading all sections. The Italians are moving among the Greeks, the Germans, and Irish. "Little Italy" is still a separate community, but not so exclusive as it was. Chinatown is really the only survival of bygone days.

Each nationality, however, still has its main business street. Houston Street, for instance, is packed every day by pushcart merchants selling their wares among Rumanians and Hungarians. New York has no Halsted Street like Chicago, where one can walk for twenty miles and at every sixth or seventh intersection enter a community of different people, but there are still many streets where only Italian, Yiddish, or modern Greek is spoken.

In each of these communities there is a public library—so placed, not by design, but by accident. Their readers once were mostly of one nationality. Now various peoples read in all of them. In the evening the men who work in the stores, the factories, on the docks, or streets, come to the library for the books. Those who have families carry home the volumes as paternally as they lug food or clothing—perhaps more so if they happen to be very poor. . . .

A good many of the readers are studying for the Regents' examinations of the College of the City of New York—a university maintained by the city. During the day they follow the occupations of their fathers, but most of them are spurred by a desire for leadership and they are picking education as a path to the goal. This is strikingly shown by the large number of clubs, debating societies, and other organizations among the immigrants.

In this phase of the foreigner's life these libraries are also indispensable. All of them have large assembly rooms, where these organizations hold their meetings. Only one restriction is made— that religion be taboo. In this way these public libraries are performing the function of community centers which reformers in Wisconsin and other Western states are making of schoolhouses. Any group of people may meet here. At various times lectures on hygiene, civics, and other topics are given by leaders in these subjects, and all of them are well attended.

The success of the immigrant in New York may be measured by the distance he moves from lower Manhattan after he has been here a few years. If he stays in the tenements it is invariably an indication that he is unable to keep pace with the progress of his neighbors. This is not altogether at the basis of the extreme poverty there, for many of those who are skimping are saving a few hundred dollars and awaiting the time when they can move to a suburb. Many of them cannot withstand privation. Disease handicaps them. This is especially true among the Russians. They have sold their homes in the far north to come to America—their libation for freedom. When they are forced to change from a life out-of-doors to one cooped in a tenement they suffer.

The librarians who meet these immigrants all day long study their characteristics. From their observations they say the United States simply gives an outlet for a further expression of the national aspirations of these people. The Russian who has been persecuted studies our government, and as a rule becomes a radical Socialist. It is said that but for the corruption in one of the congressional districts in New York a Russian Socialist would have been elected to Congress at the last election. The Italian who likes to do tasks with his hands reads the more practical books. The Hungarian loves poetry and good literature. While the Russians show a preference for their own authors, such as Tolstoi and Gorki, they as a rule have read most of these books before they emigrated. They, however, reread many of them in English. . . .

Although these people are reading mostly English books, they are doing their own thinking and bringing into this country different ideals and standards. In a measure they all become Americanized, but they are also making the United States, and especially New York, a fusion of the Russian's radicalism, the Italian's practicality, the Hungarian's pleasure, the Greek's industry, with the frugality of the German, the loyalty of the Irish, and the ambition of the Scotch. They are being educated in American public libraries, but their national traits are being felt—a very little as yet, but perceptible just the same.

The Future of Bohemian-American Literature 66

There have been many writers of ethnic nationality fiction in America: Willa Cather, Abraham Cahan, Ole Rölvaag, James T. Farrell, William Saroyan, and Elia Kazan, to name a few. But the total amount of good work by, and about, any single nationality group is not very large. Journalism was the preeminent literary form for the immigrants, but once the foreign-language press began to diminish in numbers, it was never superseded by a more permanent literature. As Czech historian Thomas Čapek has well noted: "The output in prose and verse as a rule does not get beyond the newspapers." The expectations aroused by this article from the Bohemian-language *Denni Hlasatel* on April 11, 1913, were never to be fulfilled. [Chicago Foreign Language Press Survey, WPA Project, 1942.]

A few days ago a certain Chicago daily newspaper brought the news that a well-known banker has donated a $100 prize for the best dramatic or other literary work by a Bohemian-American author. A contest will be conducted to determine the winner of this prize. A committee of judges will be selected especially for this purpose. The Bohemian-American public will no doubt welcome this news and show deserved appreciation to the donor for his noble act, because literature, too, is one of the component elements of Bohemian national life in America—indeed, an element of considerable importance.

Certainly all of us hope and trust that the American branch of the Bohemian nation—our branch—will prosper and grow stronger; that it will not wither; and that the Bohemian element will not disappear like a drop in the immense sea of other nations. This is also the only ultimate aim and purpose of our Bohemian-American national groups. What else would they be striving for but that we do not perish, that we do not lose the strategic positions gained so far, that these positions be enlarged and strengthened? This is also the reason why all of our associations, lodges, and societies contribute so generously to our Bohemian schools; and there is nobody who would dare to maintain that money spent on schools is money wasted. We do not want to see our youth lose its nationality entirely, forget its origin, its native tongue. The old statement of Vaclav Hanka (a Bohemian patriot of the first decades of the 19th century) that a nation does not die as long as its language lives, has not lost any of its validity. By saving our language we shall save our nationality.

What then is the first and foremost means of keeping our language from drowning in the torrent of foreign streams? Without a doubt, it is literature. It is the Bohemian book which keeps us thinking and feeling Bohemian, and which will guide the vessel of our national existence through the rocky waters and keep it from foundering in America.

To try to prove this is unnecessary. All we need is to look into the history of the Bohemian nation at the beginning of the 19th century when it began to awaken to a new life from a sleep of almost 200 years; when, as if by a miracle, it accomplished its resurrection; and to the astonishment of all Europe, it stood up at the side of other nations who had never believed that it would revive. Then it was the Bohemian book that performed this miracle and awakened in us the desire for a new respectable life. It was not the sword that accomplished this resurrection and brought about the renaissance of ancient Bohemia—it was the writer's pen. For this reason our countrymen in Bohemia hold their authors in high esteem and honor them as resurrectors.

However, the developments in our American branch have been quite different. We did not need to be awakened from an agelong sleep. It was not necessary to prove that we are a living nation—all that we need here is to maintain, promote, and strengthen our national consciousness. And that is the duty of literature. So far, the Bohemian-American literature has been pitifully poor. This can easily be explained by the proverbial American haste and hustling, the maddening chase after material and financial success which makes it difficult even for the most fine-feeling and idealistic people to devote their efforts to something seemingly as petty and inconsequential as literature. In this, however, we Bohemians are not alone. It is characteristic of all America, which, with all its greatness, its stirring history, can point to only a very small number of really important writers. Just a few names will cover this field.

It is a great pity that Bohemian literature in America has not had opportunity to develop and prosper. The life of Bohemians in this land of freedom differs so greatly from the life in the Old Country. It is so interesting and so distinctive in character that an able treatment of American life would enrich our literature to a surprisingly large degree. The life of a Bohemian in America—what a fascinating and promising theme for an author!

It behooves us, therefore, to welcome gratefully and with satisfaction the news that some of our prominent men have started to show an interest in this phase of our national life—an interest which is not only academic, but, as it should be in America, practical. Our benefactor's offer of a literary prize is a noble, cultural deed. It is the first experiment of this kind. For the first time our Bohemian-American writers have an opportunity to enter into competition and show their mettle, their literary skill. Every competition is a very valuable encouragement for new efforts, which no doubt will also prove to be true in this case.

The Difficulties of Becoming American

67

The following letter was sent to the Massachusetts Immigration Commission in 1913 by an anonymous Polish immigrant. It illustrates the difficulties faced by many aliens as they sought to become Americanized. [*Report of the Commission on Immigration on the Problem of Immigration in Massachusetts.* Boston, 1914. Page 134.]

I'm in this country four months (from 14 Mai 1913—Noniton—Antverpen).

I am polish man. I want be american citizen—and took here first paper in 12 June N 625. But my friends are polish people—I must live with them—I work in the shoes-shop with polish people—I stay all the time with them—at home—in the shop—anywhere.

I want live with american people, but I do not know anybody of american. I go 4 times to teacher, and must pay $2 weekly. I wanted take board in english house, but I could not, for I earn only $5 or 6 in a week, and when I pay teacher $2, I have only $4—$3—and now english board house is too dear for me. Better job to get is very hard for me, because I do not speak well english and I cannot understand what they say to me. The teacher teach me—but when I come home—I must speak polish and in the shop also. In this way I can live in your country many years—like my friends—and never speak—write well english—and never be good american citizen. I know here many persons, they live here 10 or moore years, and they are not citizens, they don't speak well english, they don't know geography and history of this contry, they don't know constitution of America—nothing. I don't like be like them I wanted they help me in english—they could not—because they knew nothing. I want go from them away. But where? Not in the country, because I want go in the city, free evening schools and lern. I'm looking for help. If somebody could give me another job between american people, help me live with them and lern english—and could tell me the best way how I can fast lern—it would be very, very good for me. Perhaps you have somebody, here he could help me?

If you can help me, I please you.

I wrote this letter by myself and I know no good—but I hope you will understand whate I mean.

Excuse me,
F. N.

An Armenian Jew at Ellis Island, 1905.

George Eastman House Collection

The German Language in the Public Schools

68

The public school systems of the United States reflected the social ferment of the Progressive Era. Most pedagogues were divided among themselves over the goals and means of education. One of the focal points of conflict was the issue of vocational training versus the traditional curriculum. This battle had been raging in educational circles with varying degrees of intensity since the 1880s, and by the end of World War I, the emphasis on practical training would give birth to the progressive education movement. Critics of vocational and manual training inveighed against the stress on the practical, claiming it would compromise the quality of education needed to make good and useful citizens. One such opponent was the author of this selection, Marion D. Learned, a specialist in German history, language, and literature and a student of German emigration to America. [*German American Annals,* January–April 1913: "German in the Public Schools."]

In the recent reports of the Bureau of Education in Washington, treating the subject of the teaching of modern languages in American schools, colleges, and universities, there is ample evidence of the necessity of directing the attention of our school boards and college administrations to the perilous conditions of the educational method, now running riot in American education. There is imminent danger that the ill-informed demands of the public for vocational training, at the expense of a fundamental education for all, may rob the next generation of even the essentials of efficient training. This vocationalism would reduce all education to the simple problem of acquiring a breadwinning occupation and ignore the fundamentals of national culture.

In the darkness of this confusion of educational aims and purposes it is highly necessary to examine into the subjects which make for true national culture and constitute the first duty of the state or municipality to the rising generation, and at the same time to sound a warning to our educators against removing the foundations upon which our culture must always rest.

The experience of 2,500 years teaches us that language and literature are the cornerstones of any efficient system of education. Even the most radical reformers of the last quarter of the 19th century recognized the necessity of retaining a mastery of modern cultural languages as subjects of instruction in the practical and technical schools (*Realschulen und Technische Hochschulen*). But our American schoolmasters, in their misguided enthusiasm, threaten even the essentials of the national idiom as a means to cultural efficiency.

The first and fundamental discipline of all education is the mastery of that language which is the means of daily intercourse. In the Middle Ages this language was Latin among the educated classes. In later times it was the native language of the people. In the case of Americans it has been English. In all recent times, however, there have been two mediums of communication for all civilized nations—one the native tongue, the other that language which serves as the key to the highest culture of the world at large. This foreign language for centuries to the several nations of Western civilization was French, traces of which are still found in our diplomatic intercourse with foreign nations.

In the 19th century the language of international culture has shifted from French to German, because the German people have risen to the foremost place in modern intellectual life in all the fields of science and letters.

The efficiency of our American culture as of the culture of every other nation is measured by the mastery of the national language, the medium of national intercourse and of our science and literature. The study of this language should be the first aim of our national education. While the necessity of the study of English is theoretically recognized, English is one of the most poorly taught subjects in our American schools from the kindergarten to the university. The cause of this is that in spite of our educational progress, we are still under the bane of the tradition of incompetent teaching and confused notions of the real purpose of public education. Any trained scholar must blush when he goes into the elementary schools and observes the lack of knowledge and method displayed in the teaching of English. The writer can remember the time when the great aim in the study of English was to commit to memory the thirty-two rules of Smith's *English Grammar,* while it seemed not to occur even to the teacher that these rules were intended to be put into practice in speaking and writing the language. The result was that the pupils left the English class with the same slipshod habit of incorrect speaking with which they entered.

At present the demands upon the educated man are far more complex. The old grammars have been replaced by more up-to-date books, but the teaching is still far from satisfactory and fails to awaken a *sense* for language and to cultivate a *habit* of accurate thought and expression in daily life. To one accustomed to correct English the use of the language heard in our schools is simply abhorrent. It is the common experience of teachers in the colleges that the first principles of the mother tongue have to be taught in the college classes. The knowledge of grammar, derivation and distinction of words, the essentials of syntax and style are but a hazy mass of ideas to the average freshman entering college. One wonders how the schools could have spent so many years in such fruitless preparation. There is a class of students who form a notable exception to this helplessness in the use of English and in general discipline, viz., those who have been trained in Latin and Greek. Students with the training in strongly inflected languages exhibit a far better grasp of the mother tongue as well as of other kindred subjects.

The conclusion is self-evident that the discipline of studying a highly developed ancient or modern speech cultivates the habit of analytic logical thought and precise expression in the native tongue. If there were no other argument for the study of Latin and Greek in American schools, this one should be sufficient to keep the classical languages in the school curriculum.

What is true of the disciplinary value of the study of Latin and Greek applies also with equal force to German, which has a highly inflected structure. A further advantage for the English-speaking pupil in the study of German is that it is a cognate language having a common basic vocabulary with English and therefore enriching the speech content of the pupil's knowledge.

But there is a more cogent argument for the teaching of German in the public schools of America, even at the exclusion of some of the subjects now taught. This reason is that German is the key which unlocks the best sources of literary and scientific knowledge of our age.

A national system of education should

equip the pupil with those branches of knowledge which are essential to the most efficient service in any trade, occupation, or profession in life. These essential elements of a fundamental general education are languages, geography, history, elementary mathematics, hygiene, and government. The subjects to be most emphasized are the native speech and the great culture-bearing foreign languages, geography and history.

Much confusion has come into our courses of study during recent years by the reckless tampering of incompetent educators with well-established ideals of education and by the clamor of the patronizing and temporizing public in demanding of the state public vocational training from the beginning of school work. It is not the first business of the state or municipality to provide vocational or trade education for the pupil any more than to provide free public schools of law or medicine. The first duty of the state is to give the pupil—every boy and girl—the fundamental training necessary to all vocations. If the state then wishes to furnish special vocational training, in which pupils may prepare for the trades, let it offer such training in special trade schools, after the fundamental education is obtained.

In this essential training foreign languages should be included in order to secure to every pupil in the plastic years a command of some speech outside of his native tongue, so that in later years he may be able to enter with ease any calling in life. That language or those languages should be selected which every well-educated man or woman will need in order to come into touch with the best culture of his time. The cultural value of foreign languages does not depend upon the number of persons speaking that language in this or that country or even in America, but that language which is the medium of the most important culture of the age. If it depended upon the numbers of persons speaking the foreign language, Germans, French, Italians, Scandinavians, Russians, Poles, Jews, Hungarians, Greeks, and many others would all be insisting that their respective tongues be taught in American schools, thus turning our public schools into a confusion of tongues worse than that of Babel. . . .

In the proper teaching of foreign languages, much depends upon the phonetic process of producing the sounds of these languages, but phonetics in general, even as applied to English, is a terra incognita, a Bohemian forest, to most American educators.

Let the public schools, then, introduce the study of German into the grade schools, and have it taught by teachers able to speak and write both English and German, and let it be taught with the avowed purpose of enabling the pupils to read and write German. This will be a paying investment, even if some of the numerous nonessential vocational studies have to be removed from the course to make way for the foreign language which will be a permanent factor of efficiency in any vocation, be it a trade or a learned profession. In such a study of the foreign tongues the pupil will acquire a true feeling or sense for language, and will enormously facilitate his study of English, and will at the same time have the key to the best works in the several fields of science, literature, and art. Young America will thus acquire a new appreciation of language, a new sense of liberty, by emancipating himself from the thralldom of a single speech.